We're into the double digits!

Somehow, that's deeply moving.

For once, there were a lot of stories in this volume that focus on Shu, and they were a real pleasure to draw. Enjoy!

Naoshi Komi

NAOSHI KOMI was born in Kochi Prefecture, Japan, on March 28, 1986. His first serialized work in *Weekly Shonen Jump* was the series *Double Arts*. His current series, *Nisekoi*, is serialized in *Weekly Shonen Jump*.

NISEKOI:
False Love
VOLUME 10
SHONEN JUMP Manga Edition

Story and Art by
NAOSHI KOMI

Translation ✐ Camellia Nieh
Touch-Up Art & Lettering ✐ Stephen Dutro
Design ✐ Fawn Lau
Shonen Jump Series Editor ✐ John Bae
Graphic Novel Editor ✐ Amy Yu

NISEKOI © 2011 by Naoshi Komi
All rights reserved.
First published in Japan in 2011
by SHUEISHA Inc., Tokyo.
English translation rights arranged
by SHUEISHA Inc.

The stories, characters and incidents mentioned
in this publication are entirely fictional.

Printed in the U.S.A.

Published by VIZ Media, LLC
P.O. Box 77010
San Francisco, CA 94107

10 9 8 7 6 5 4 3 2 1
First printing, July 2015

www.shonenjump.com   www.viz.com

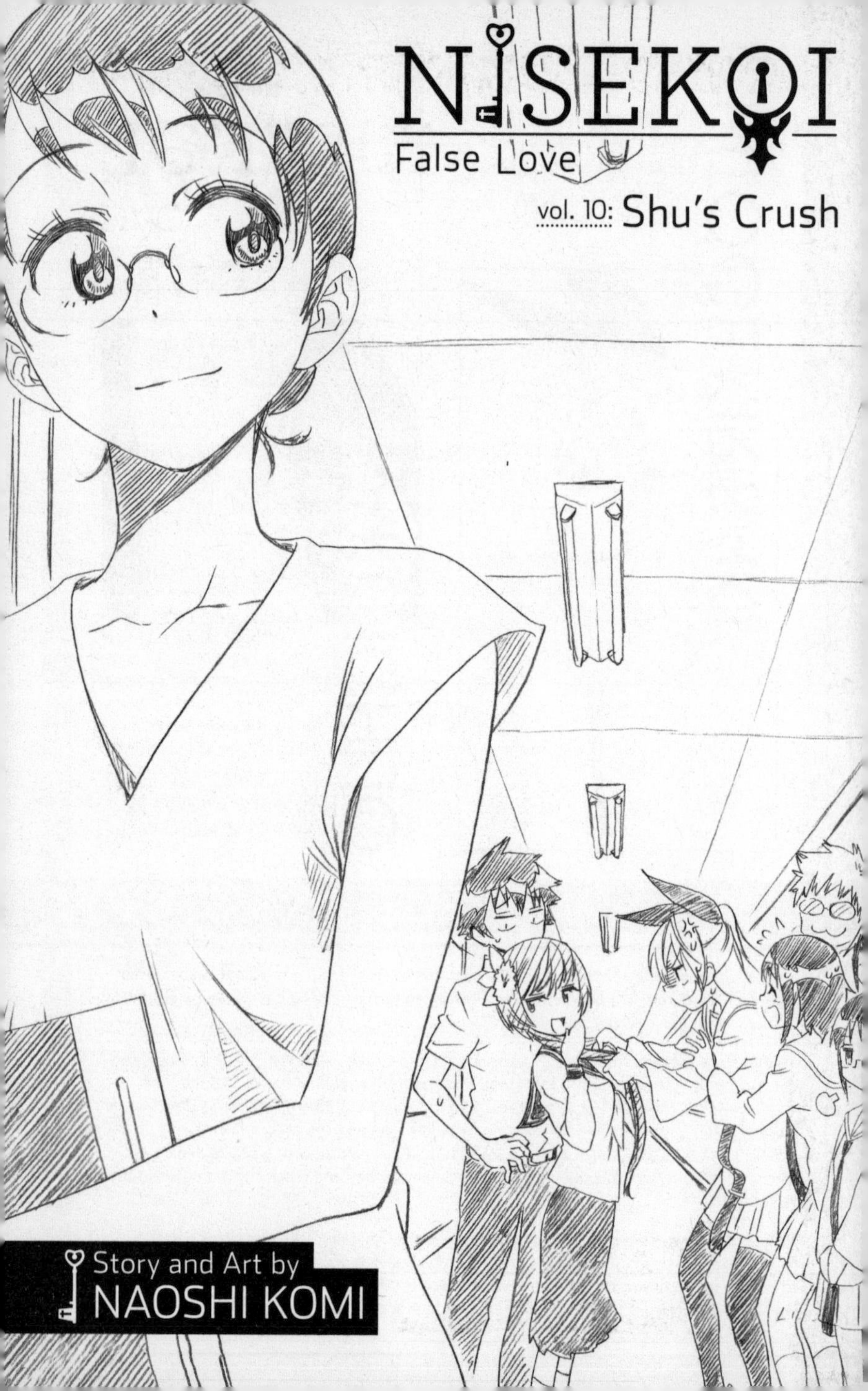

NISEKOI
False Love

vol. 10: Shu's Crush

Story and Art by
NAOSHI KOMI

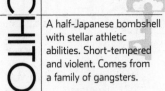

CHITOGE KIRISAKI

A half-Japanese bombshell with stellar athletic abilities. Short-tempered and violent. Comes from a family of gangsters.

RAKU ICHIJO

A normal teen whose family happens to be yakuza. Cherishes a pendant given to him by a girl he met ten years ago. Has a crush on Kosaki.

CHARACTERS & STORY

Raku Ichijo is an ordinary teen...who just happens to come from a family of yakuza! His most treasured item is a pendant he was given ten years ago by a girl whom he promised to meet again one day and marry.

Thanks to family circumstances, Raku is forced into a false relationship with Chitoge, the daughter of a rival gangster, to keep their families from shedding blood. Despite their constant spats, Raku and Chitoge manage to fool everyone. One day, Chitoge discovers an old key, jogging memories of her own first love ten years earlier. Meanwhile, Raku's crush, Kosaki, confesses that she also has a key and made a promise with a boy ten years ago. To complicate matters, Marika Tachibana has a key as well and remembers a promise ten years ago.

Raku and his friends are now second-year students. One day, Raku rescues a young girl from a group of delinquents. She turns out to be Kosaki's younger sister, Haru! Haru's extremely protective of Kosaki and immediately sees Raku as an enemy. The situation worsens when Haru finds Raku's missing pendant and refuses to give it back...

KOSAKI ONODERA

A girl Raku has a crush on. Beautiful and sweet, Kosaki has no shortage of admirers. She's a terrible cook but makes food that *looks* amazing.

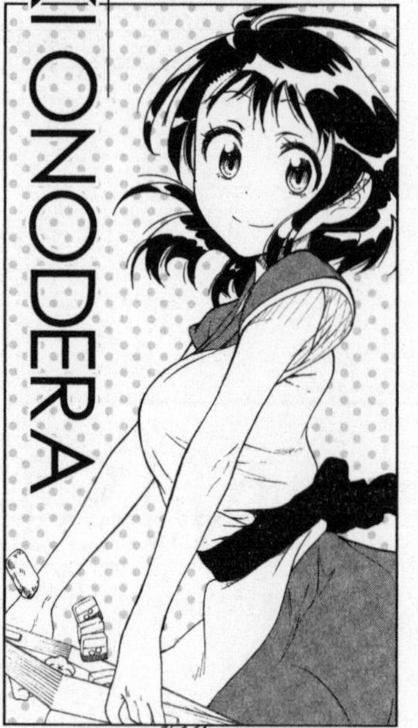

MARIKA TACHIBANA

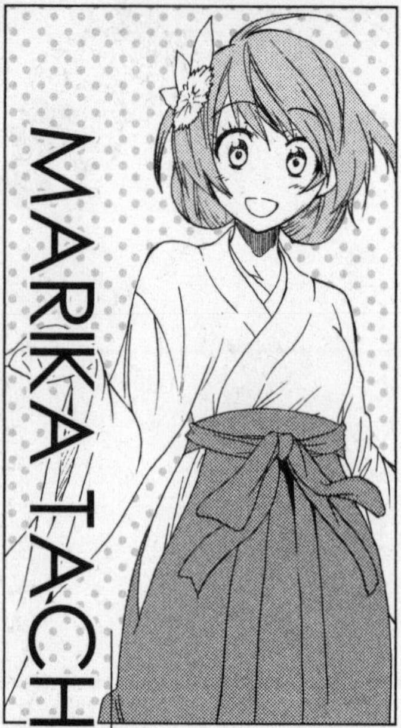

Daughter of the chief of police, Marika is Raku's fiancée, according to an agreement made by their fathers—an agreement Marika takes very seriously! Also has a key and remembers making a promise with Raku ten years ago.

SHU MAIKO

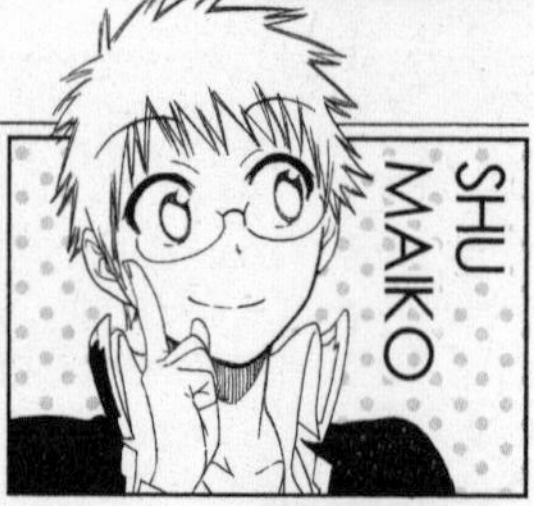

Raku's best friend. Outgoing and girl-crazy. Always tuned in to the latest gossip at school.

SEISHIRO TSUGUMI

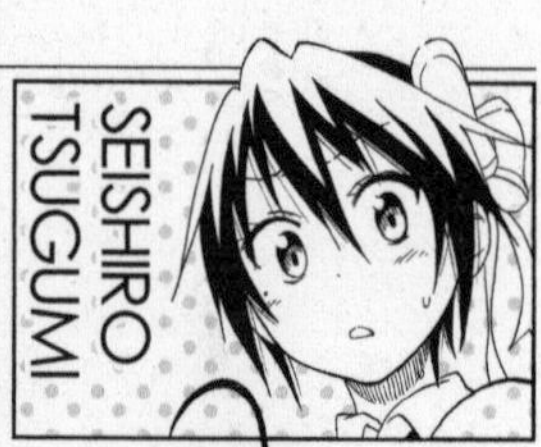

Adopted by Claude as a young child and raised as a top-notch assassin, Seishiro is 100% devoted to Chitoge. Often mistaken for a boy, Tsugumi's really a girl.

RURI MIYAMOTO

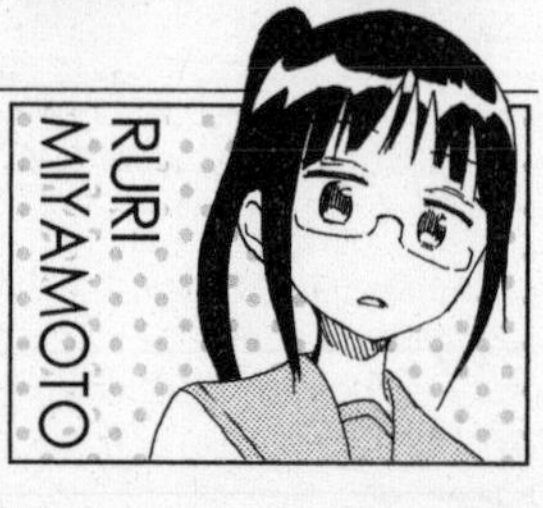

Kosaki's best gal pal. Comes off as aloof, but is actually a devoted and highly intuitive friend.

HARU ONODERA

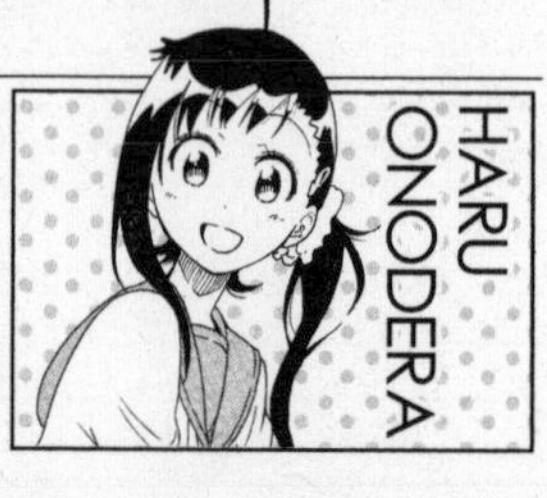

Kosaki's younger sister who's emotionally attached to her. Has a low opinion of Raku.

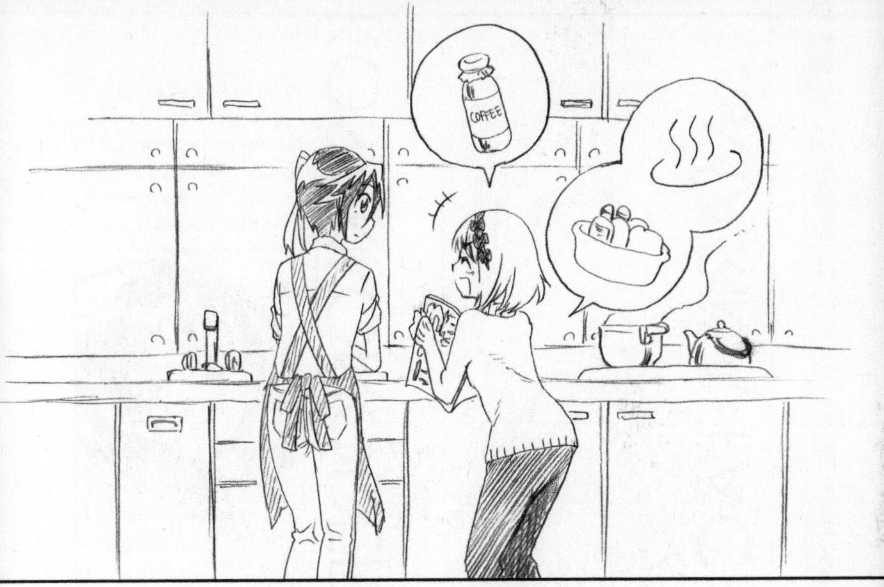
COFFEE

NISEKOI
False Love
vol. 10: Shu's Crush

TABLE OF CONTENTS

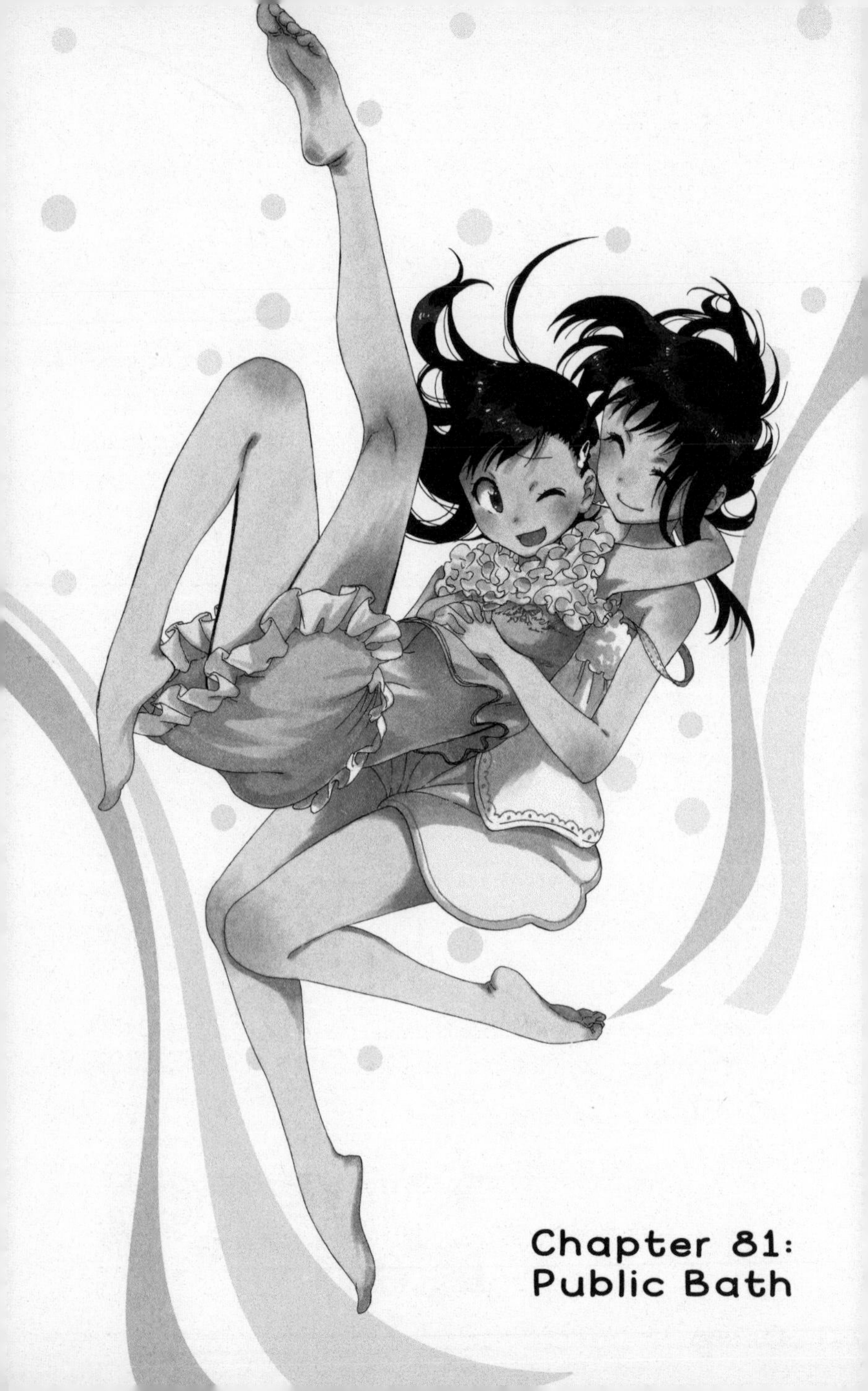

Chapter 81: Public Bath

NISEKOI

False Love

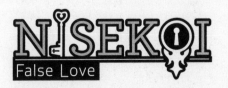

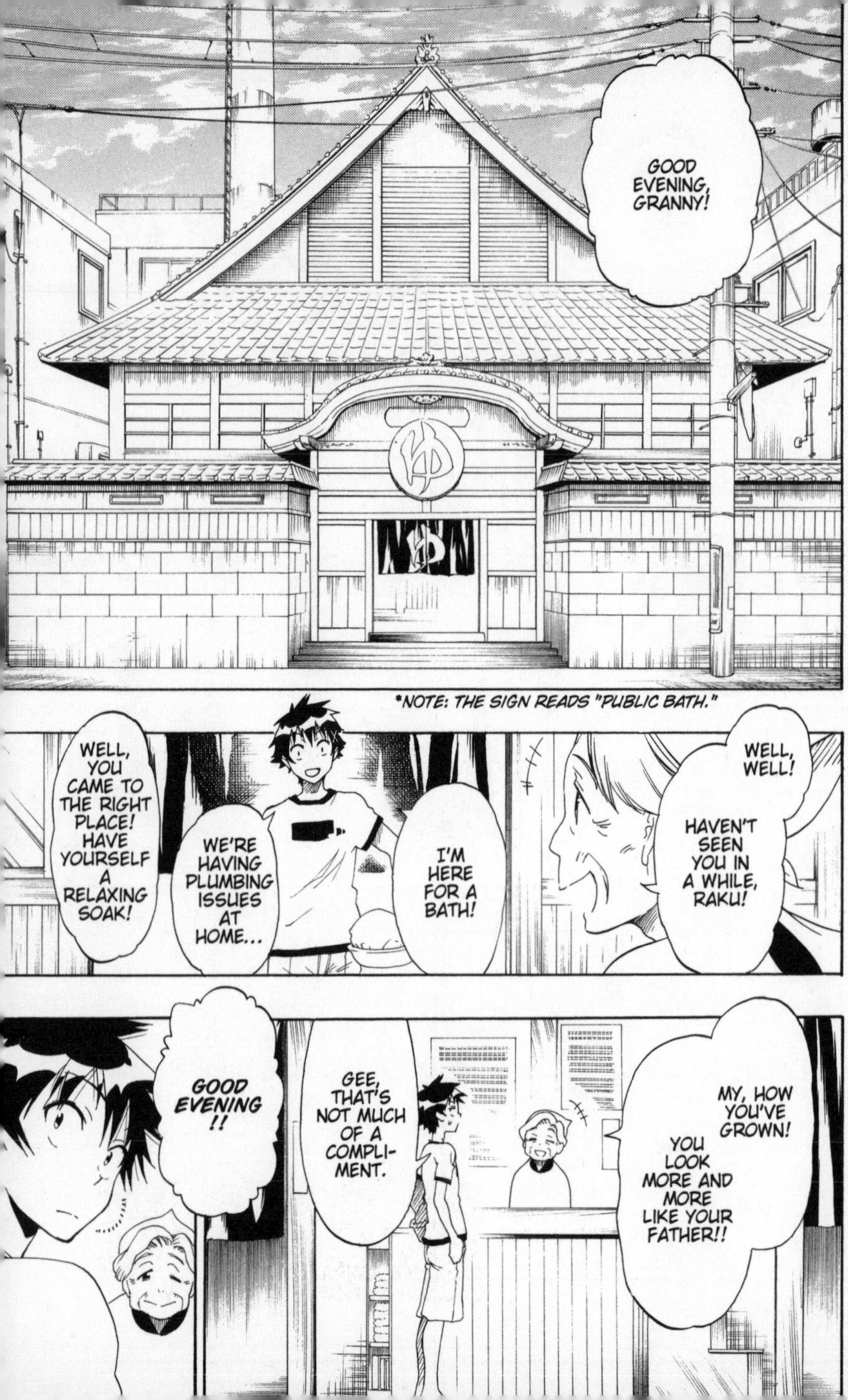
GOOD EVENING, GRANNY!
*NOTE: THE SIGN READS "PUBLIC BATH."
WELL, WELL!
HAVEN'T SEEN YOU IN A WHILE, RAKU!
I'M HERE FOR A BATH!
WE'RE HAVING PLUMBING ISSUES AT HOME...
WELL, YOU CAME TO THE RIGHT PLACE! HAVE YOURSELF A RELAXING SOAK!
MY, HOW YOU'VE GROWN!
YOU LOOK MORE AND MORE LIKE YOUR FATHER!!
GEE, THAT'S NOT MUCH OF A COMPLIMENT.
GOOD EVENING!!

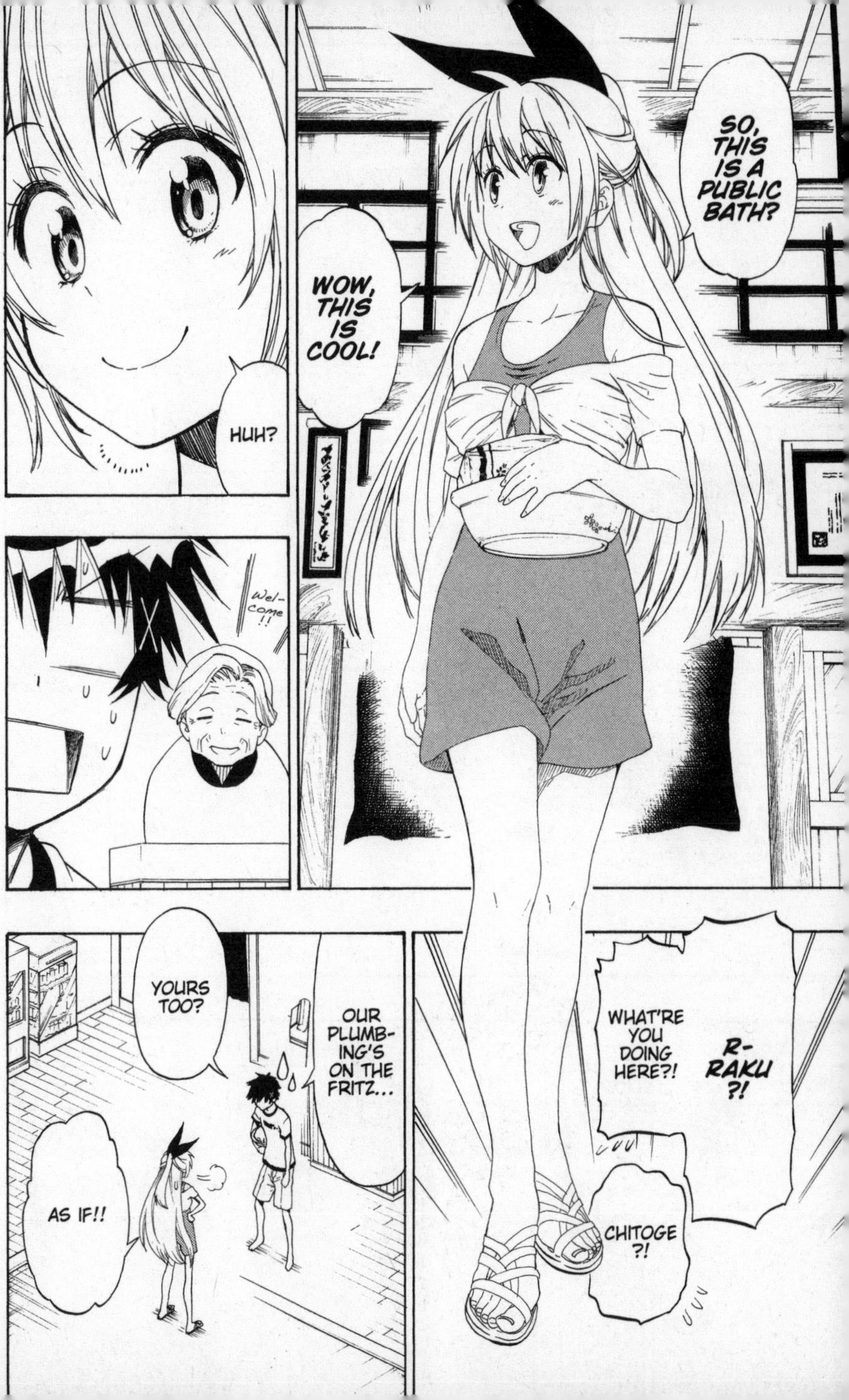
SO, THIS IS A PUBLIC BATH?
WOW, THIS IS COOL!
HUH?
Wel-come!!
R-RAKU?!
WHAT'RE YOU DOING HERE?!
CHITOGE?!
OUR PLUMB-ING'S ON THE FRITZ...
YOURS TOO?
AS IF!!

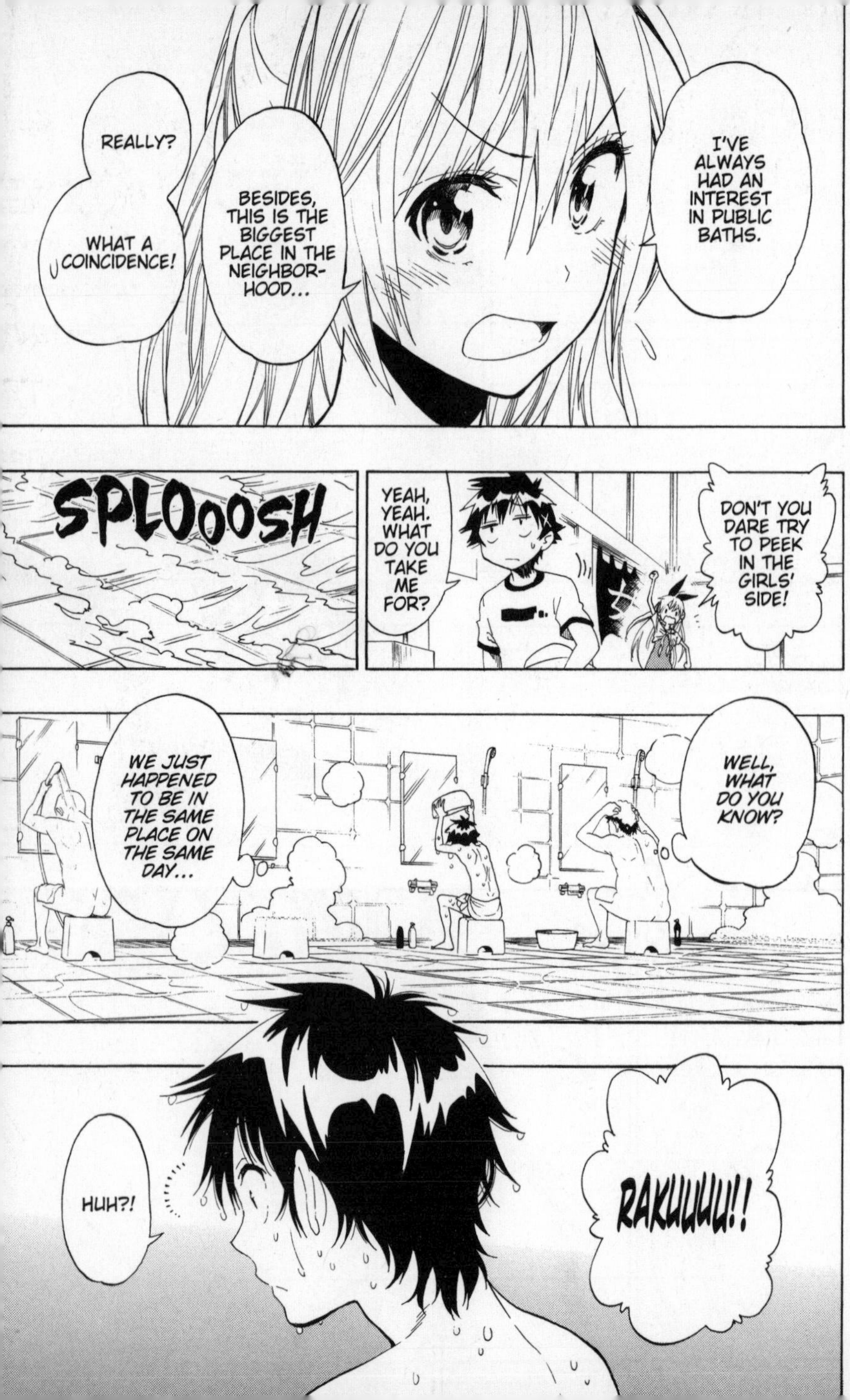
I'VE ALWAYS HAD AN INTEREST IN PUBLIC BATHS.
BESIDES, THIS IS THE BIGGEST PLACE IN THE NEIGHBOR-HOOD...
REALLY?
WHAT A COINCIDENCE!
DON'T YOU DARE TRY TO PEEK IN THE GIRLS' SIDE!
YEAH, YEAH. WHAT DO YOU TAKE ME FOR?
SPLOOOSH
WELL, WHAT DO YOU KNOW?
WE JUST HAPPENED TO BE IN THE SAME PLACE ON THE SAME DAY...
RAKUUUU!!
HUH?!

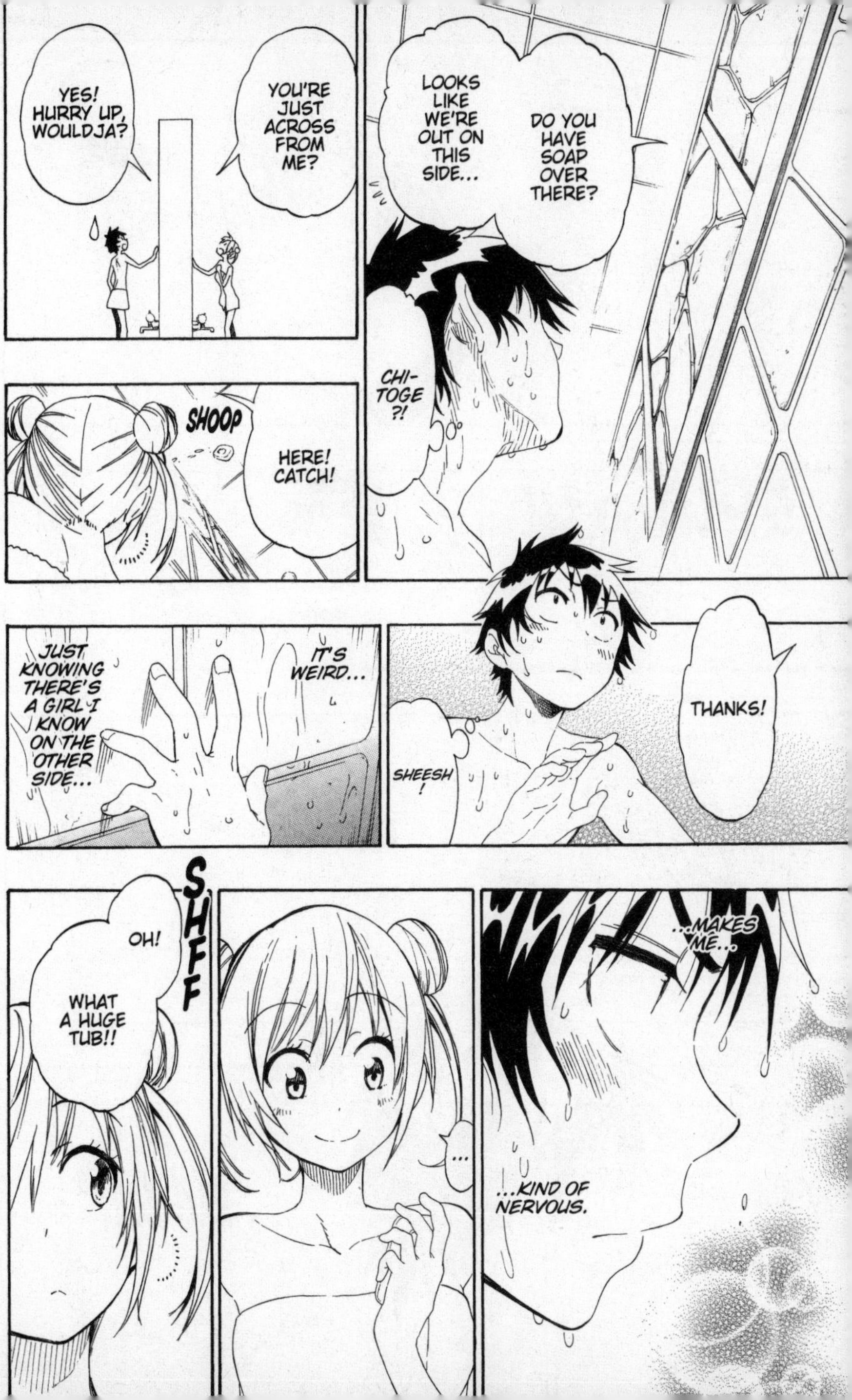

LOOKS LIKE WE'RE OUT ON THIS SIDE...
DO YOU HAVE SOAP OVER THERE?
CHI-TOGE?!
YOU'RE JUST ACROSS FROM ME?
YES! HURRY UP, WOULDJA?
HERE! CATCH!
SHOOP
THANKS!
SHEESH!
IT'S WEIRD...
JUST KNOWING THERE'S A GIRL I KNOW ON THE OTHER SIDE...
...MAKES ME...
...KIND OF NERVOUS.
...
SHFF
OH!
WHAT A HUGE TUB!!

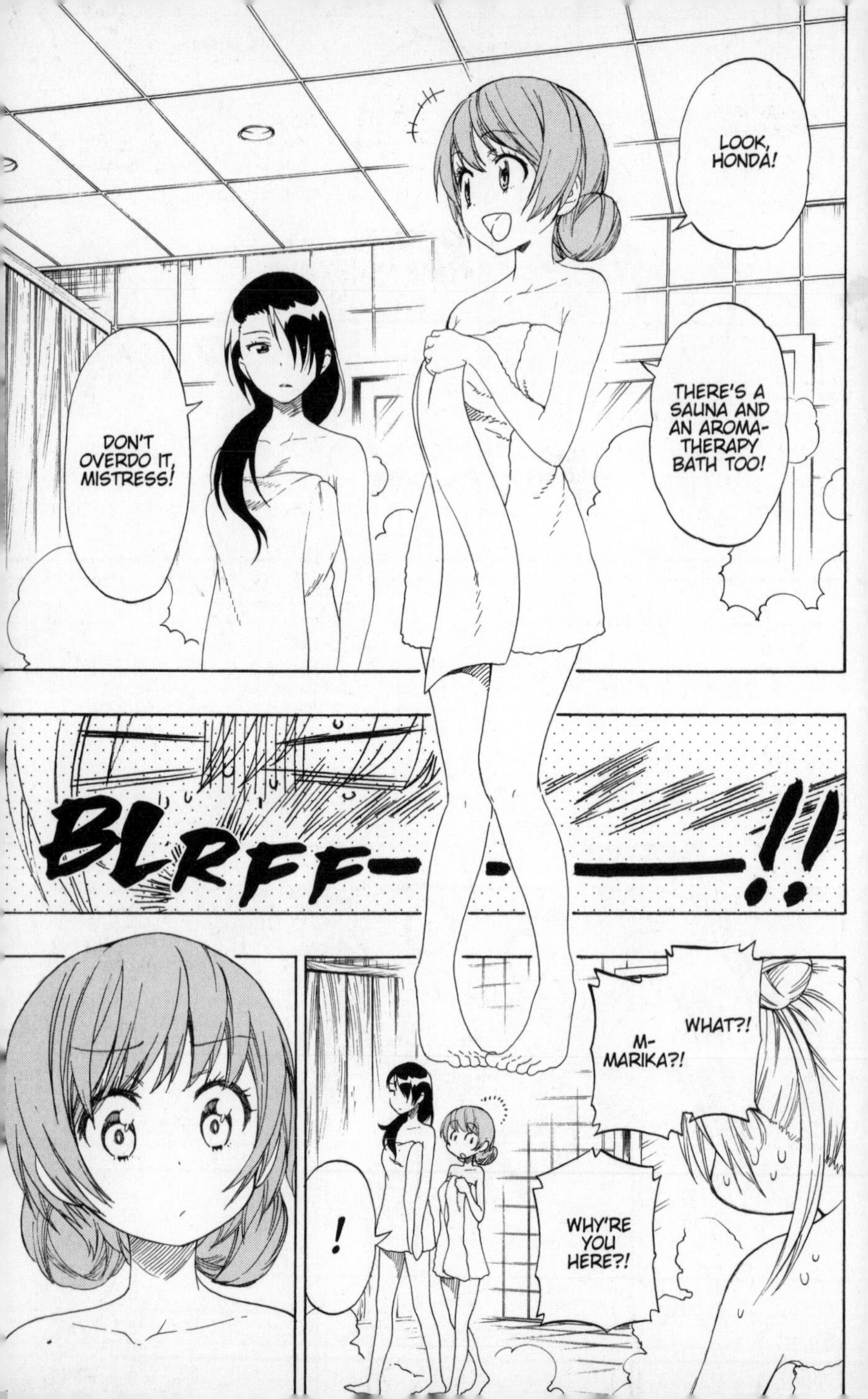
LOOK, HONDA!
THERE'S A SAUNA AND AN AROMA-THERAPY BATH TOO!
DON'T OVERDO IT, MISTRESS!
BLRFF———!!
WHAT?!
M-MARIKA?!
WHY'RE YOU HERE?!
!

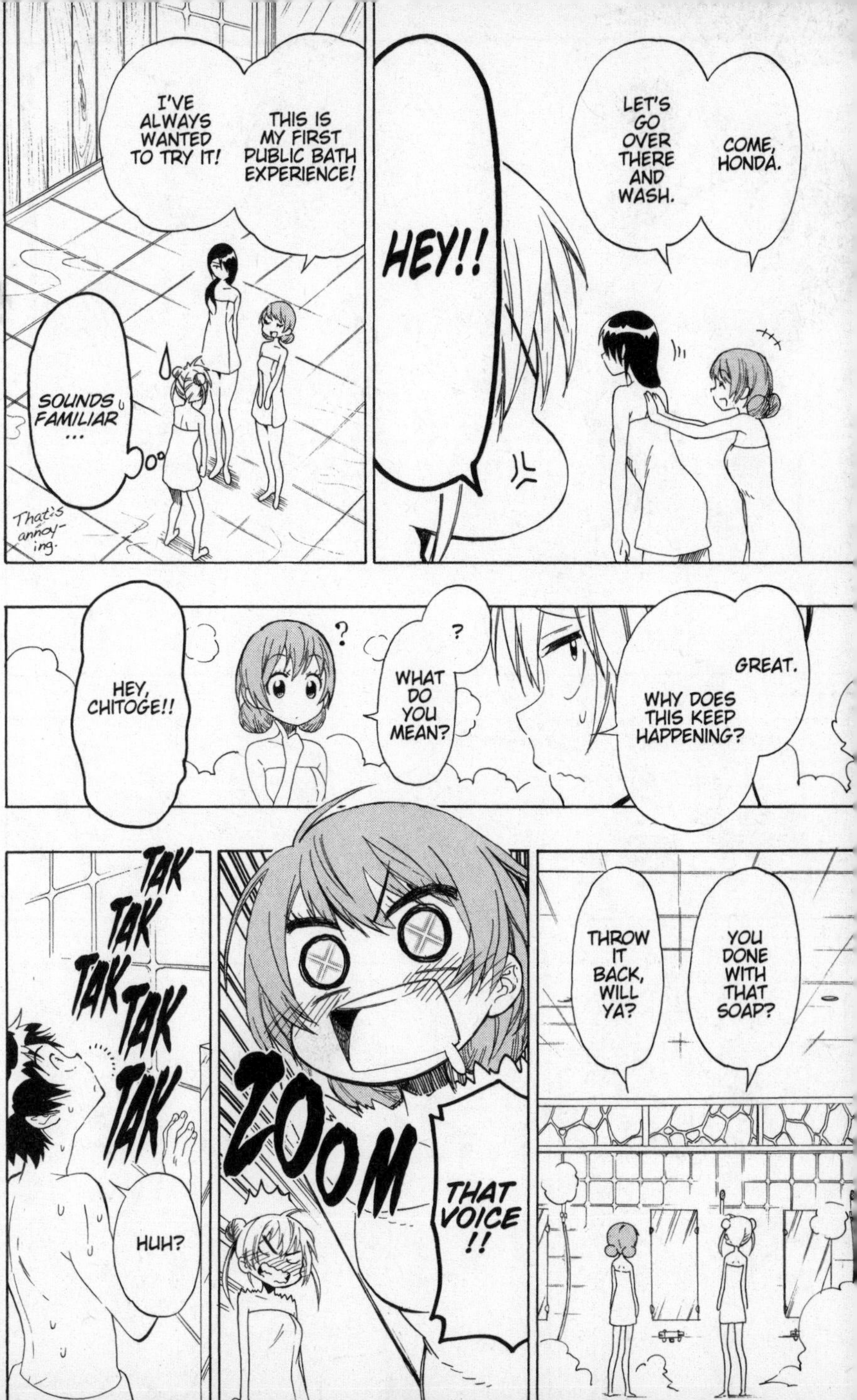
COME, HONDA.
LET'S GO OVER THERE AND WASH.
HEY!!
THIS IS MY FIRST PUBLIC BATH EXPERIENCE!
I'VE ALWAYS WANTED TO TRY IT!
SOUNDS FAMILIAR...
That's annoying.
GREAT.
WHY DOES THIS KEEP HAPPENING?
WHAT DO YOU MEAN?
HEY, CHITOGE!!
YOU DONE WITH THAT SOAP?
THROW IT BACK, WILL YA?
ZOOM
THAT VOICE!!
TAK TAK TAK TAK TAK
HUH?

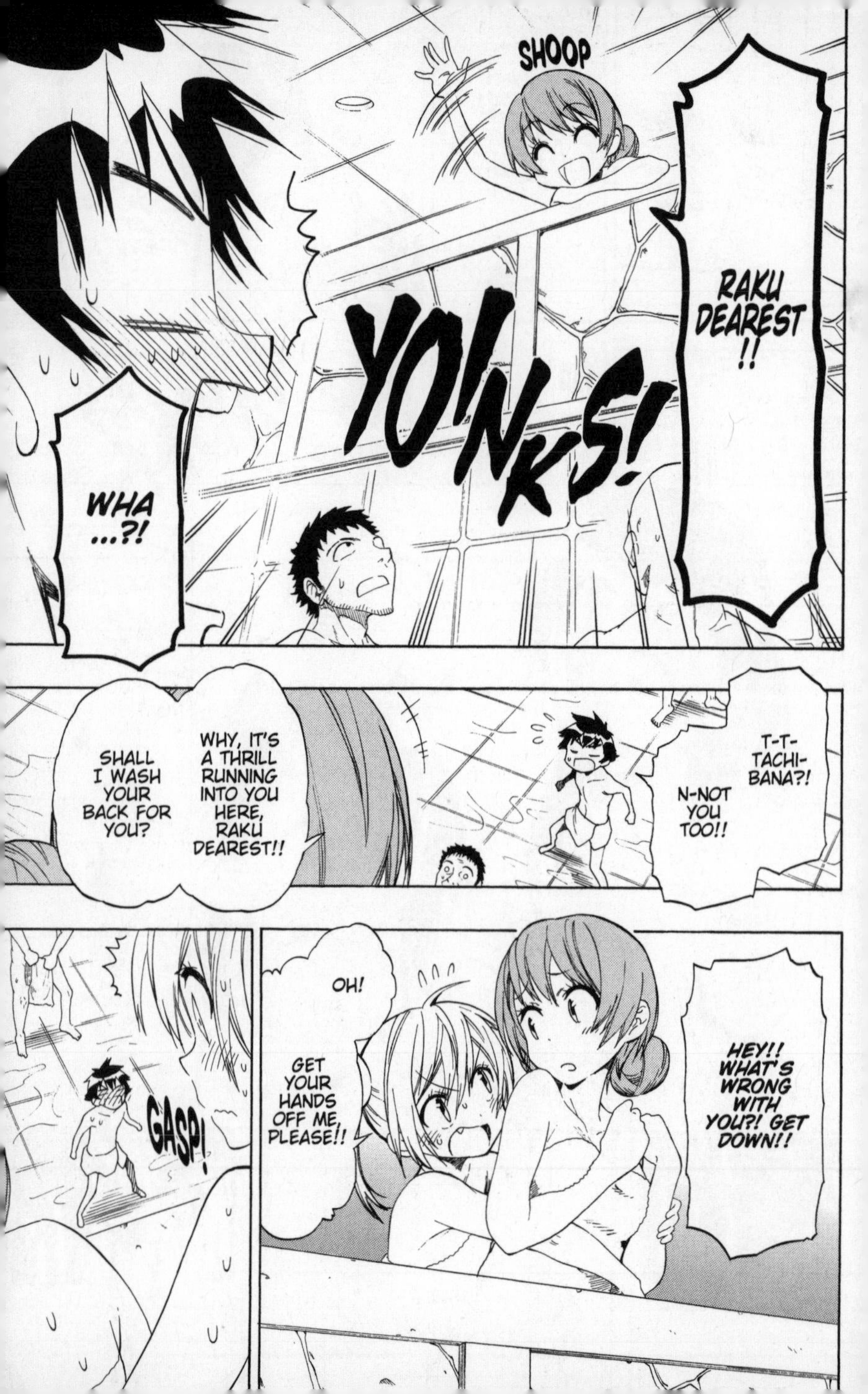
SHOOP
RAKU DEAREST!!
YOINKS!
WHA...?!
T-T-TACHIBANA?!
N-NOT YOU TOO!!
WHY, IT'S A THRILL RUNNING INTO YOU HERE, RAKU DEAREST!!
SHALL I WASH YOUR BACK FOR YOU?
HEY!! WHAT'S WRONG WITH YOU?! GET DOWN!!
OH!
GET YOUR HANDS OFF ME, PLEASE!!
GASP!

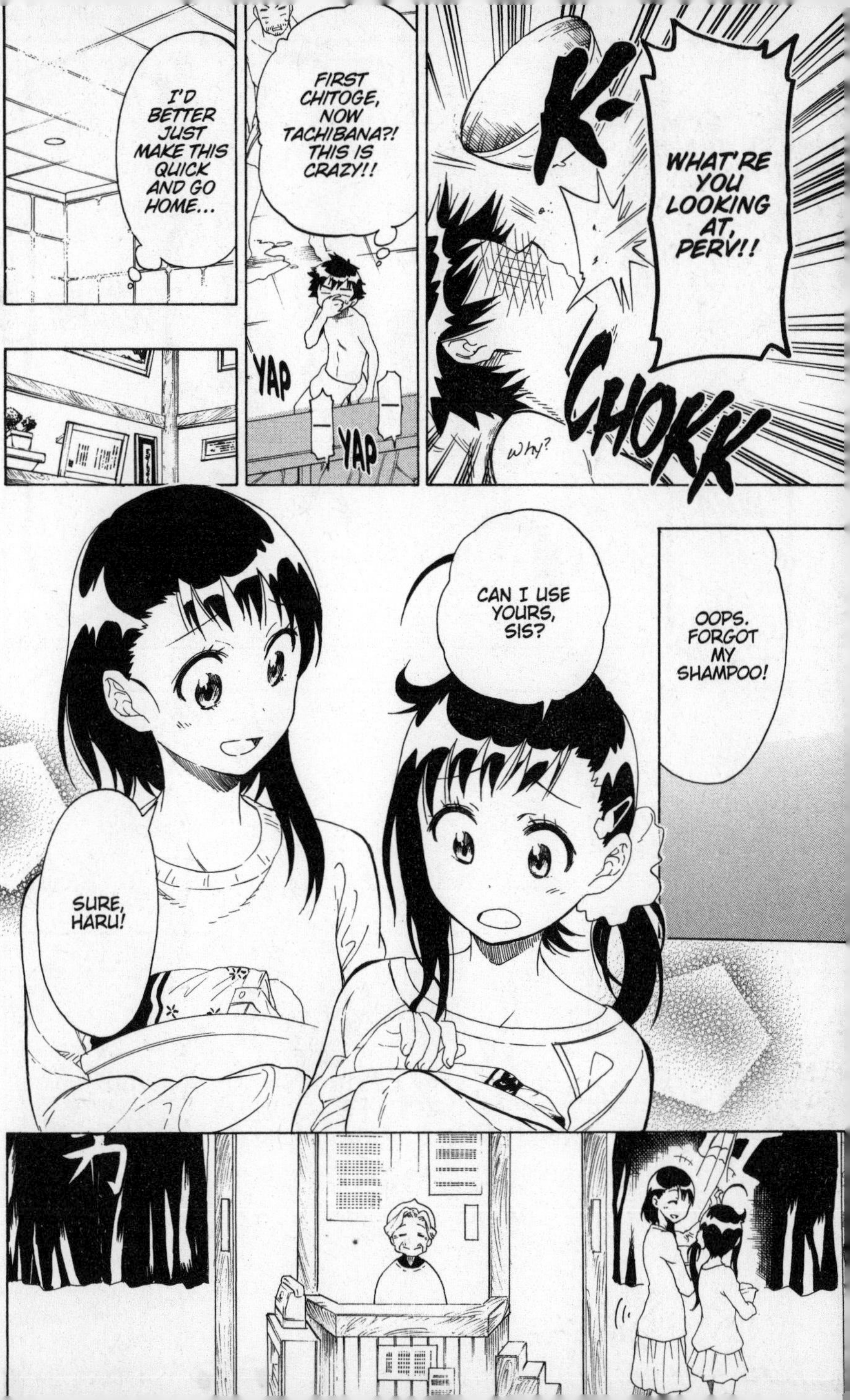
WHAT'RE YOU LOOKING AT, PERV!!
K-
CHOKK
why?
FIRST CHITOGE, NOW TACHIBANA?! THIS IS CRAZY!!
YAP
YAP
I'D BETTER JUST MAKE THIS QUICK AND GO HOME...
OOPS. FORGOT MY SHAMPOO!
CAN I USE YOURS, SIS?
SURE, HARU!

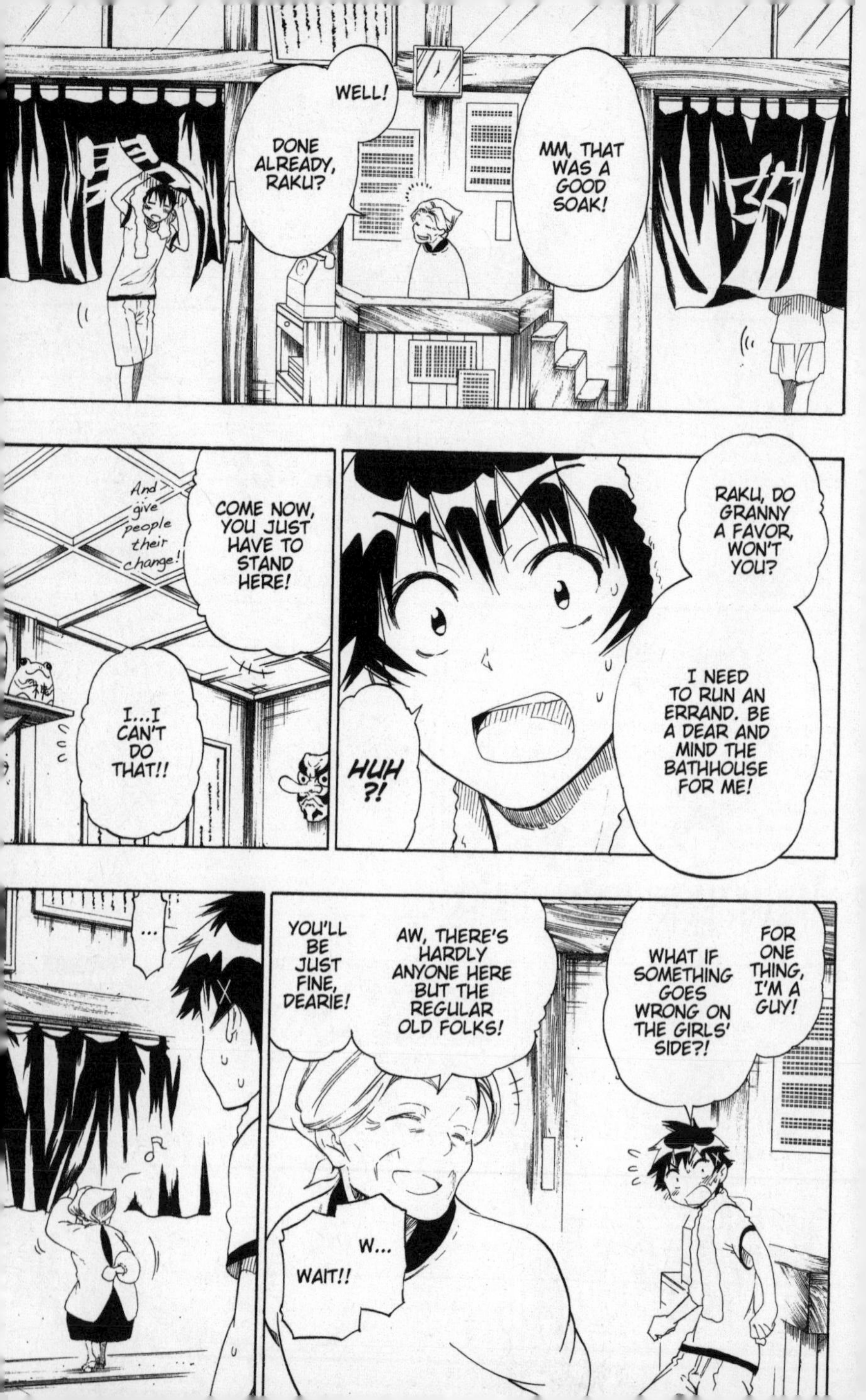
MM, THAT WAS A GOOD SOAK!
WELL!
DONE ALREADY, RAKU?
RAKU, DO GRANNY A FAVOR, WON'T YOU?
I NEED TO RUN AN ERRAND. BE A DEAR AND MIND THE BATHHOUSE FOR ME!
HUH?!
COME NOW, YOU JUST HAVE TO STAND HERE!
And give people their change!
I...I CAN'T DO THAT!!
FOR ONE THING, I'M A GUY!
WHAT IF SOMETHING GOES WRONG ON THE GIRLS' SIDE?!
AW, THERE'S HARDLY ANYONE HERE BUT THE REGULAR OLD FOLKS!
YOU'LL BE JUST FINE, DEARIE!
...
W...
WAIT!!

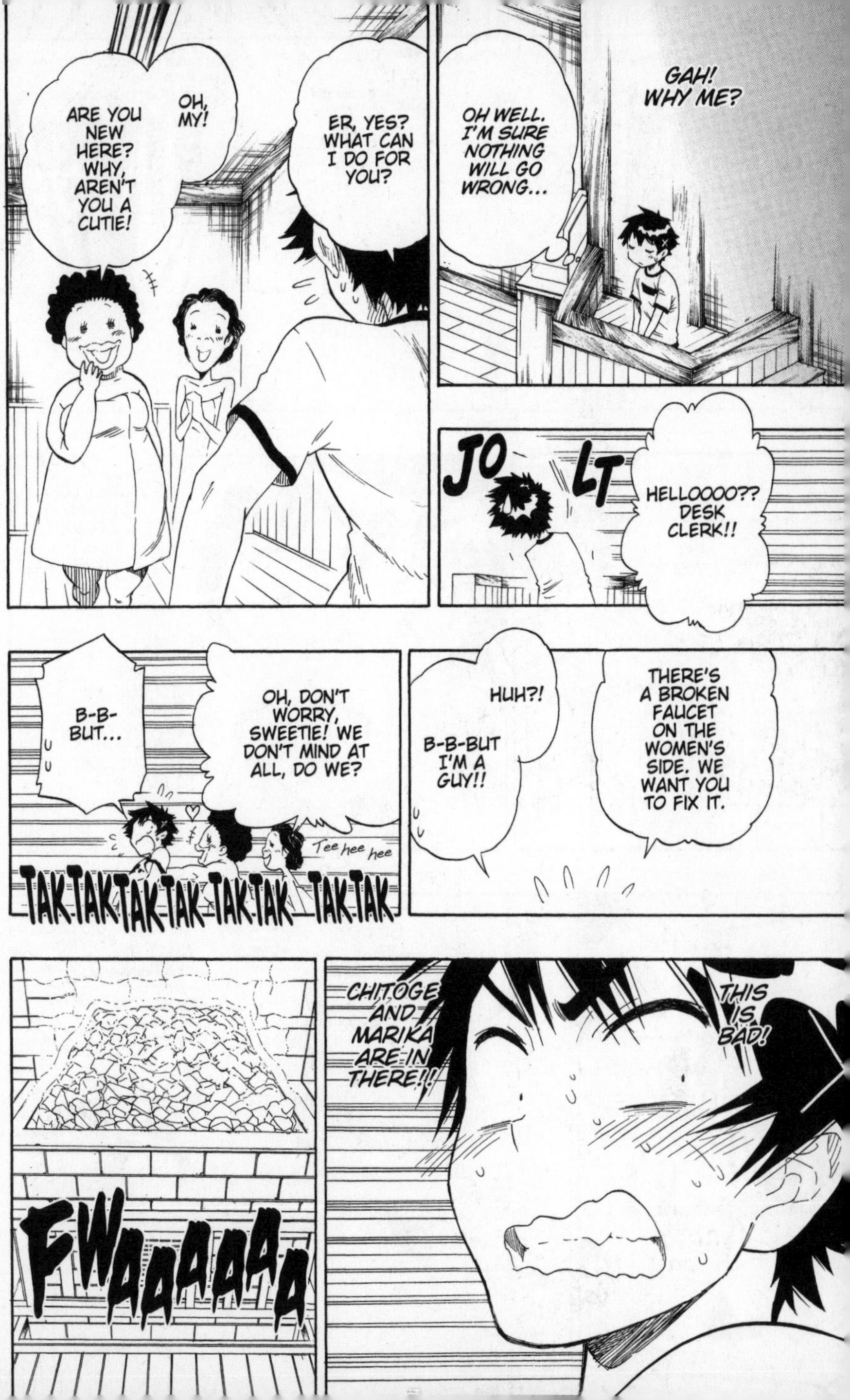
GAH! WHY ME?
OH WELL. I'M SURE NOTHING WILL GO WRONG...
HELLOOOO?? DESK CLERK!!
JOLT
ER, YES? WHAT CAN I DO FOR YOU?
OH, MY!
ARE YOU NEW HERE? WHY, AREN'T YOU A CUTIE!
THERE'S A BROKEN FAUCET ON THE WOMEN'S SIDE. WE WANT YOU TO FIX IT.
HUH?!
B-B-BUT I'M A GUY!!
OH, DON'T WORRY, SWEETIE! WE DON'T MIND AT ALL, DO WE?
B-B-BUT...
Tee hee hee
TAK TAK TAK TAK TAK TAK TAK TAK
THIS IS BAD!
CHITOGE AND MARIKA ARE IN THERE!!
FWAAAAAA

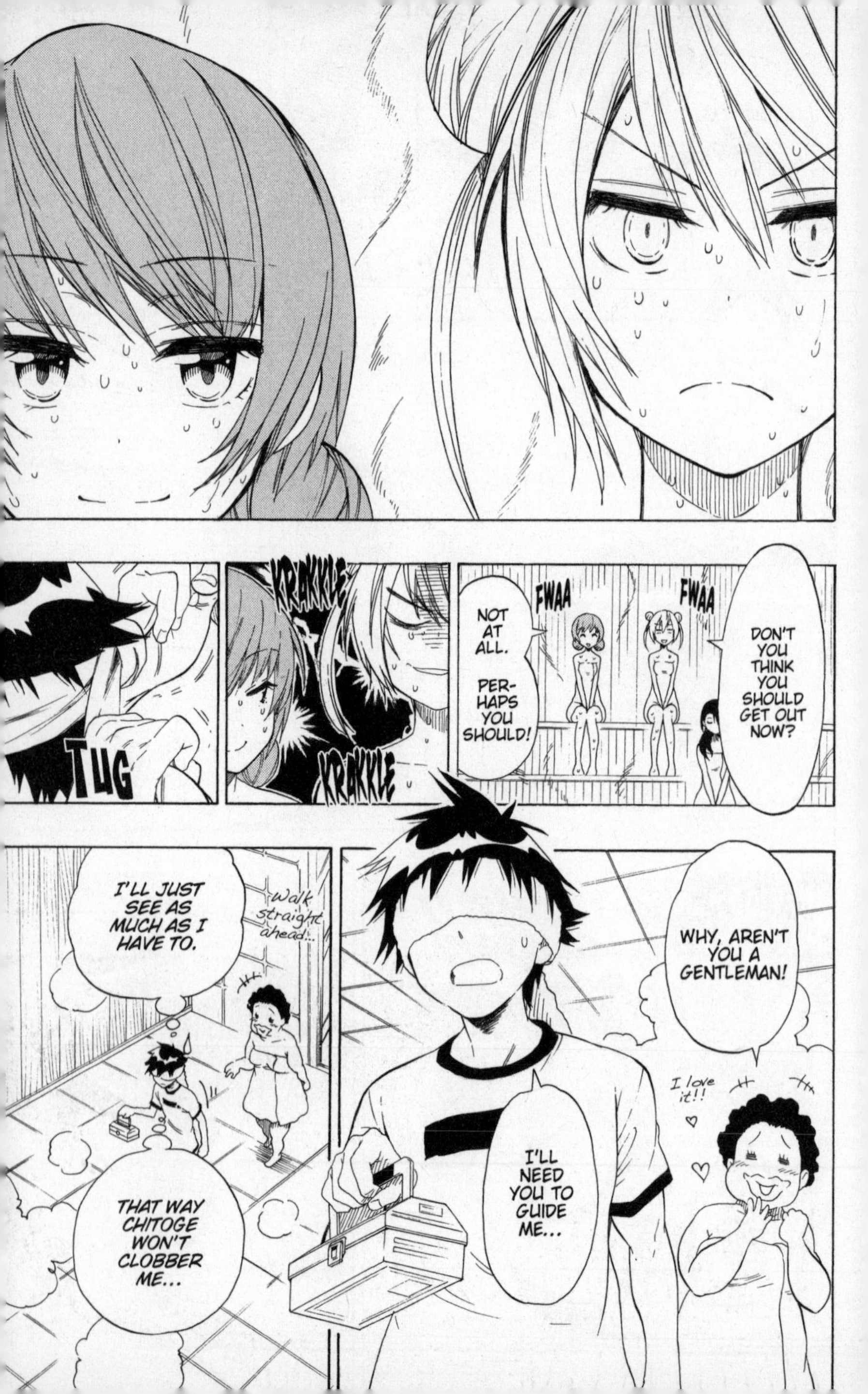
FWAA
DON'T YOU THINK YOU SHOULD GET OUT NOW?
FWAA
NOT AT ALL.
PER-HAPS YOU SHOULD!
KRAKKLE
KRAKKLE
TUG
WHY, AREN'T YOU A GENTLEMAN!
I love it!!
I'LL NEED YOU TO GUIDE ME...
I'LL JUST SEE AS MUCH AS I HAVE TO.
Walk straight ahead...
THAT WAY CHITOGE WON'T CLOBBER ME...

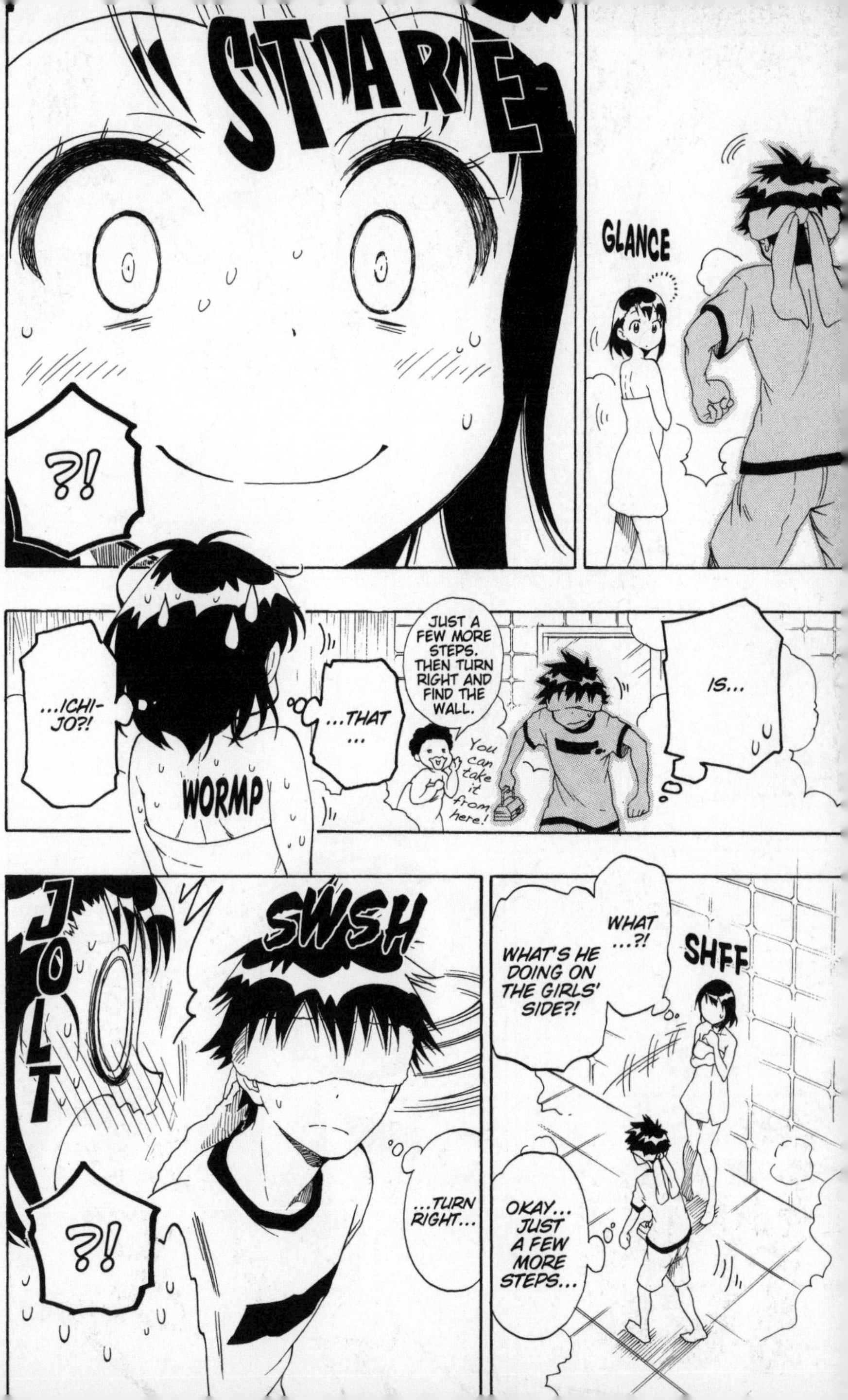
GLANCE
STARE
?!
IS...
JUST A FEW MORE STEPS. THEN TURN RIGHT AND FIND THE WALL.
You can take it from here!
...THAT ...
...ICHI-JO?!
WORMP
WHAT ...?!
WHAT'S HE DOING ON THE GIRLS' SIDE?!
SHFF
OKAY... JUST A FEW MORE STEPS...
SWSH
...TURN RIGHT...
JOLT
?!

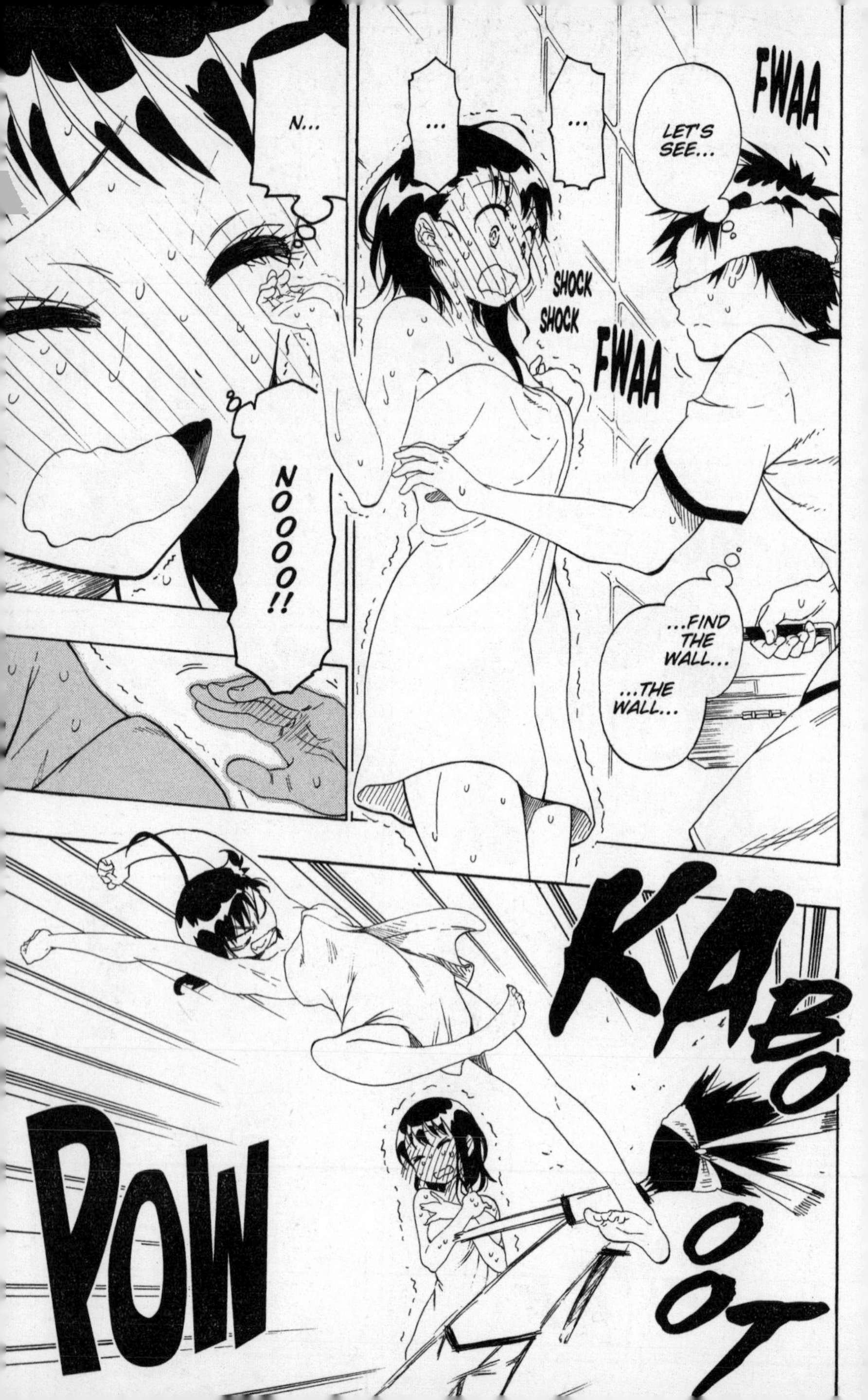
LET'S SEE...
FWAA
...
...
SHOCK SHOCK
FWAA
...FIND THE WALL...
...THE WALL...
N...
NOOOOO!!
KABOOOT
POW

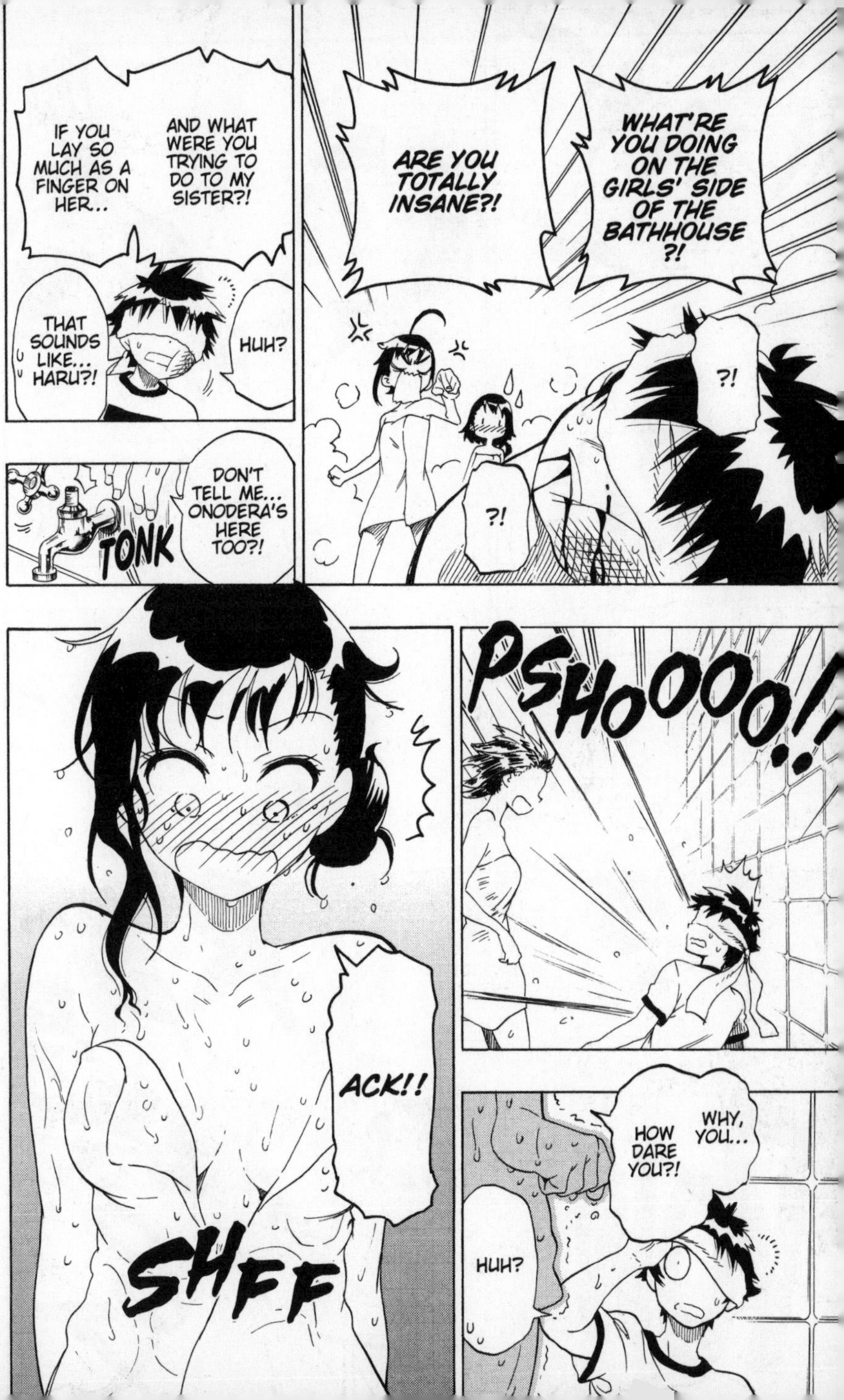
WHAT'RE YOU DOING ON THE GIRLS' SIDE OF THE BATHHOUSE?!
ARE YOU TOTALLY INSANE?!
?!
?!
AND WHAT WERE YOU TRYING TO DO TO MY SISTER?!
IF YOU LAY SO MUCH AS A FINGER ON HER...
HUH?
THAT SOUNDS LIKE... HARU?!
DON'T TELL ME... ONODERA'S HERE TOO?!
TONK
PSHOOOO!!
WHY, YOU...
HOW DARE YOU?!
HUH?
ACK!!
SHFF

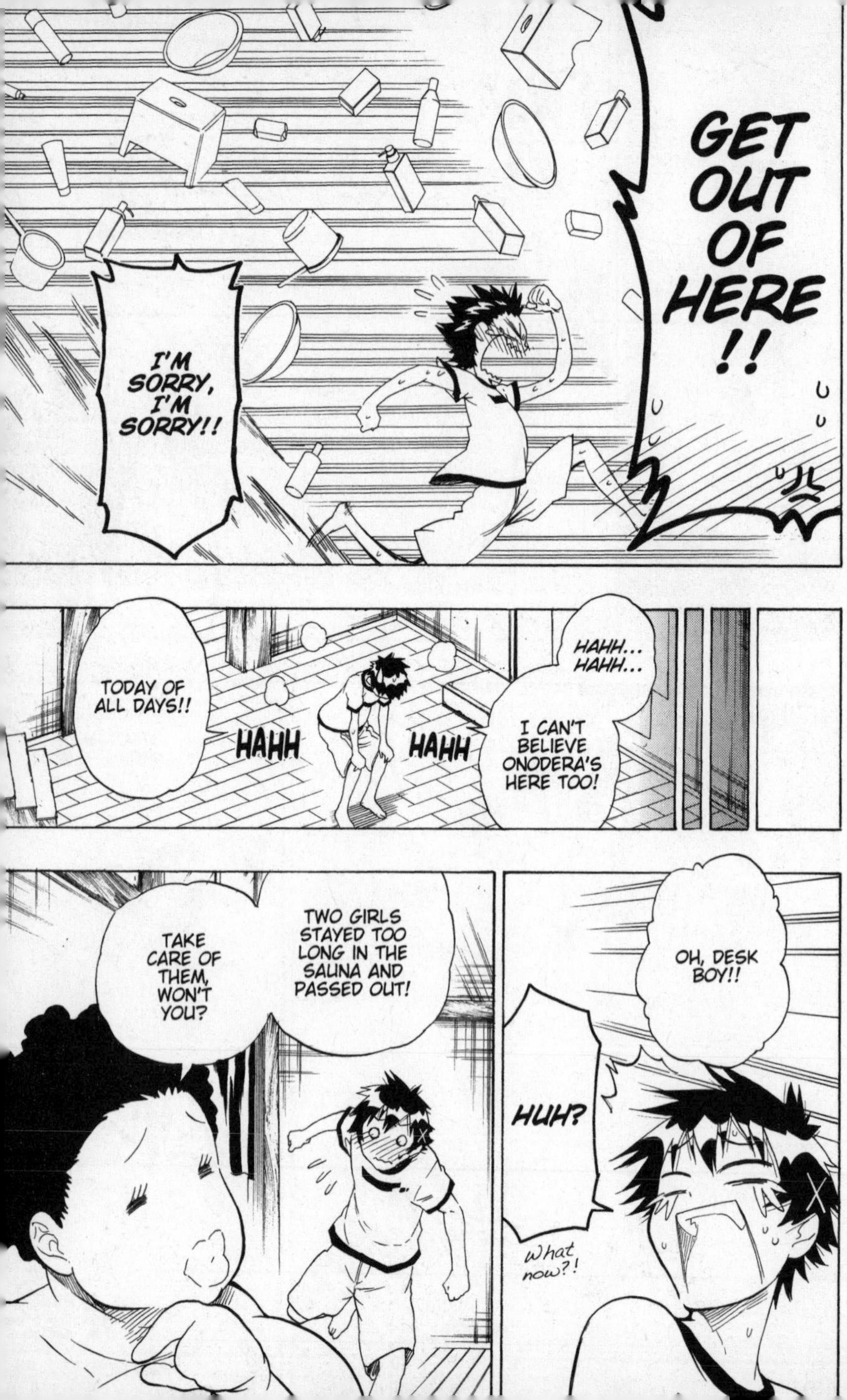
GET OUT OF HERE!!
I'M SORRY, I'M SORRY!!
HAHH... HAHH...
I CAN'T BELIEVE ONODERA'S HERE TOO!
HAHH
HAHH
TODAY OF ALL DAYS!!
OH, DESK BOY!!
HUH?
What now?!
TWO GIRLS STAYED TOO LONG IN THE SAUNA AND PASSED OUT!
TAKE CARE OF THEM, WON'T YOU?

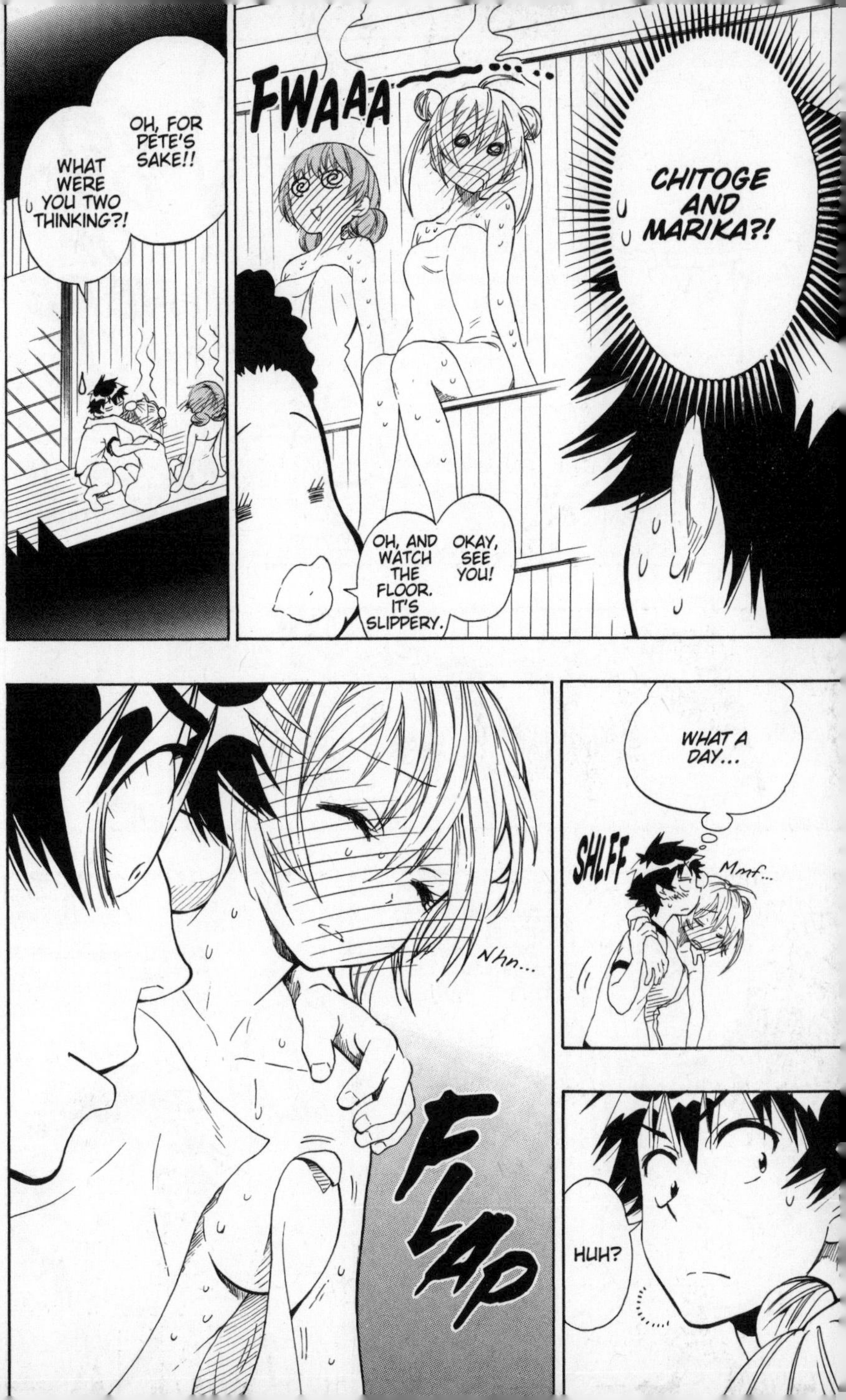
CHITOGE AND MARIKA?!
FWAAA
OKAY, SEE YOU!
OH, AND WATCH THE FLOOR. IT'S SLIPPERY.
OH, FOR PETE'S SAKE!! WHAT WERE YOU TWO THINKING?!
WHAT A DAY...
SHLFF
Mmf...
HUH?
Nhn...
FLAP

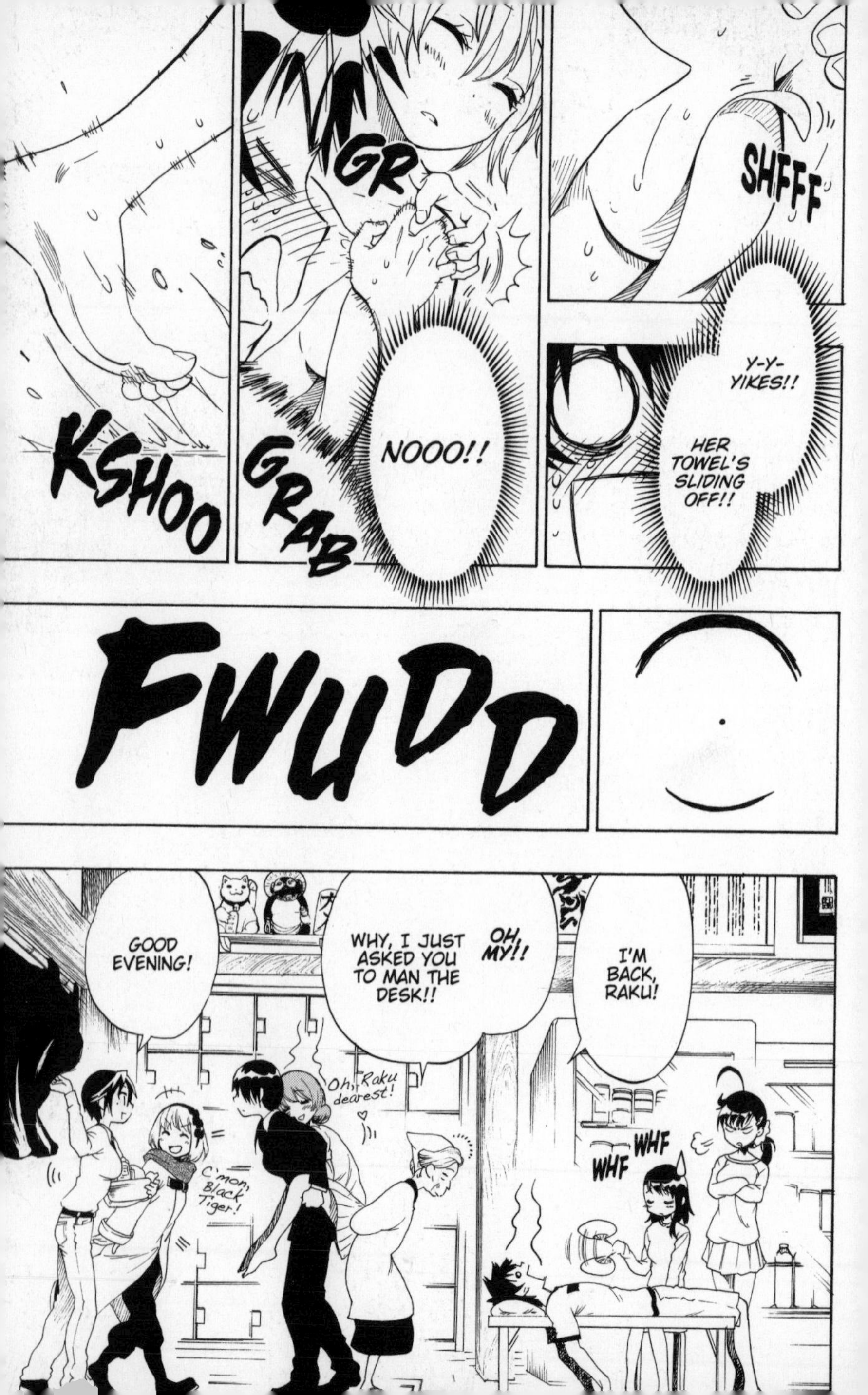
SHFFF
Y-Y-YIKES!!
HER TOWEL'S SLIDING OFF!!
GR
NOOO!!
GRAB
KSHOO
FWUDD
I'M BACK, RAKU!
WHF
WHF
OH, MY!!
WHY, I JUST ASKED YOU TO MAN THE DESK!!
Oh, Raku dearest!
GOOD EVENING!
C'mon, Black Tiger!

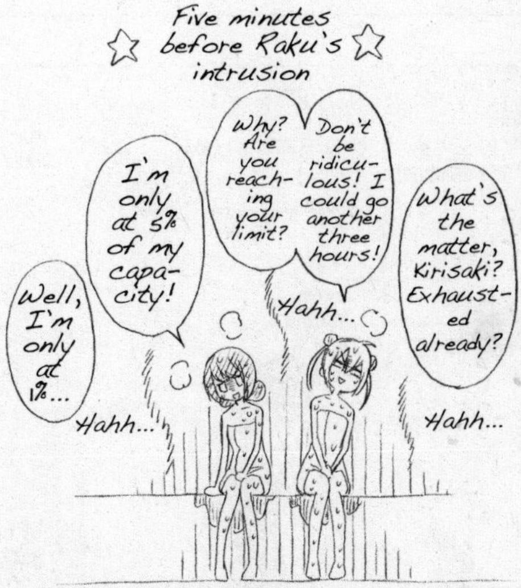
Five minutes before Raku's intrusion
What's the matter, Kirisaki? Exhausted already?
Hahh...
Don't be ridiculous! I could go another three hours!
Why? Are you reaching your limit?
Hahh...
I'm only at 5% of my capacity!
Well, I'm only at 1%...
Hahh...

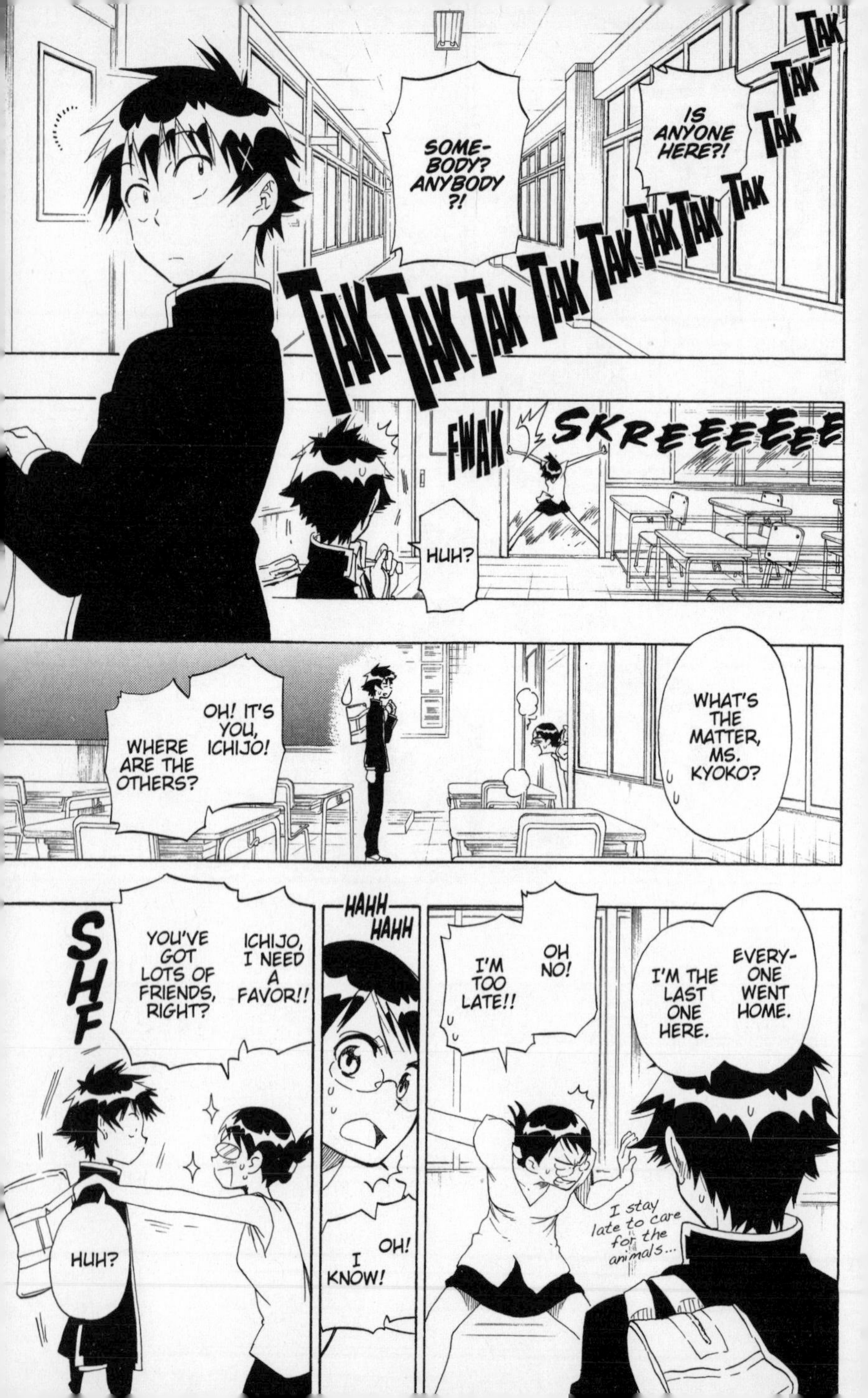
TAK TAK TAK TAK
IS ANYONE HERE?!
SOME-BODY? ANYBODY?!
TAK TAK TAK TAK TAK TAK TAK TAK
FWAK
SKREEEEEEE
HUH?
WHAT'S THE MATTER, MS. KYOKO?
OH! IT'S YOU, ICHIJO!
WHERE ARE THE OTHERS?
EVERY-ONE WENT HOME.
I'M THE LAST ONE HERE.
I stay late to care for the animals...
OH NO!
I'M TOO LATE!!
HAHH HAHH
OH!
I KNOW!
ICHIJO, I NEED A FAVOR!!
YOU'VE GOT LOTS OF FRIENDS, RIGHT?
SHF
HUH?

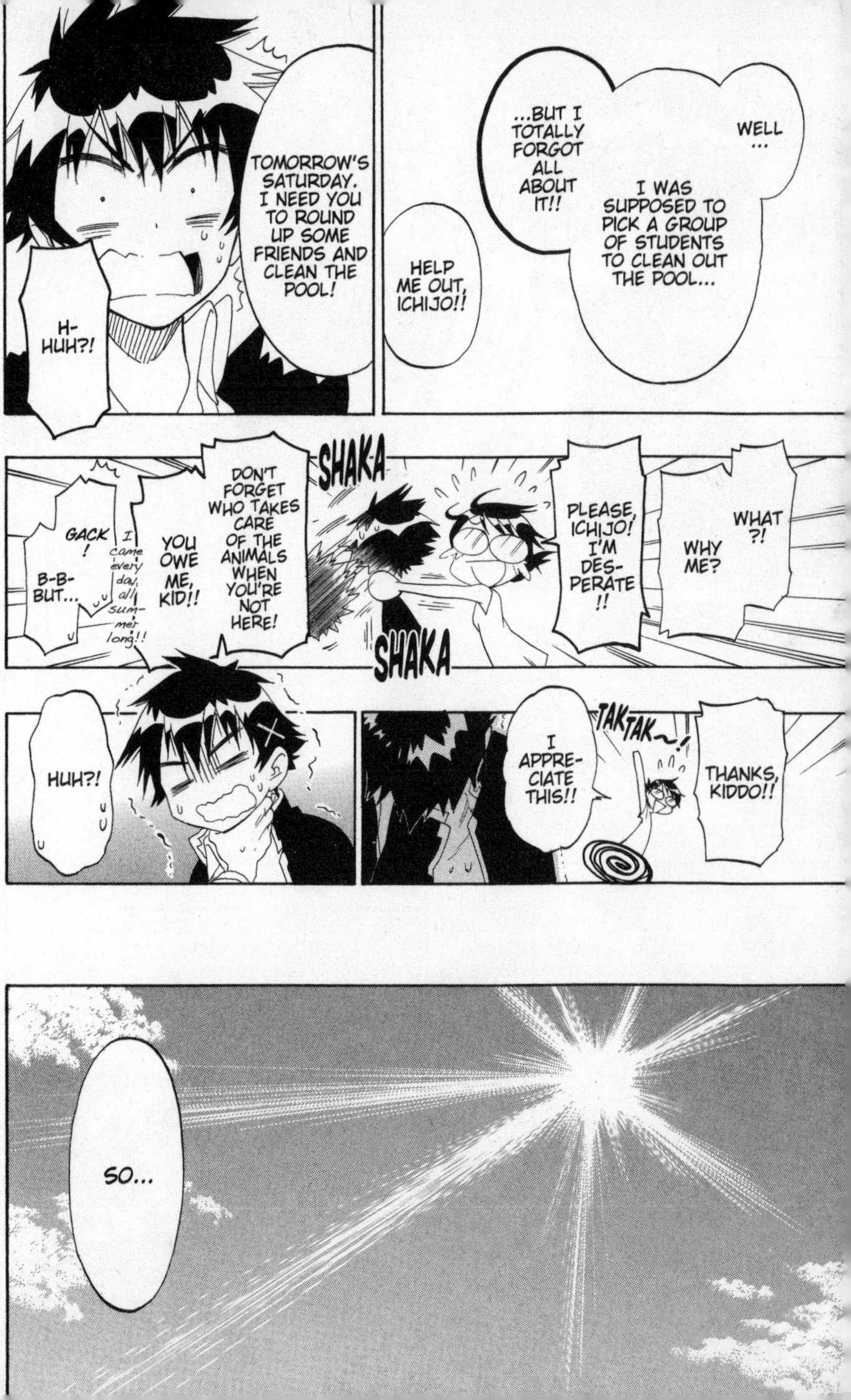
WELL...
I WAS SUPPOSED TO PICK A GROUP OF STUDENTS TO CLEAN OUT THE POOL...
...BUT I TOTALLY FORGOT ALL ABOUT IT!!
HELP ME OUT, ICHIJO!!
TOMORROW'S SATURDAY. I NEED YOU TO ROUND UP SOME FRIENDS AND CLEAN THE POOL!
H-HUH?!
WHAT?!
WHY ME?
PLEASE, ICHIJO! I'M DES-PERATE!!
SHAKA
SHAKA
DON'T FORGET WHO TAKES CARE OF THE ANIMALS WHEN YOU'RE NOT HERE!
YOU OWE ME, KID!!
I came every day all sum-mer long!!
GACK!
B-B-BUT...
THANKS, KIDDO!!
TAKTAK~!
I APPRE-CIATE THIS!!
HUH?!
SO...

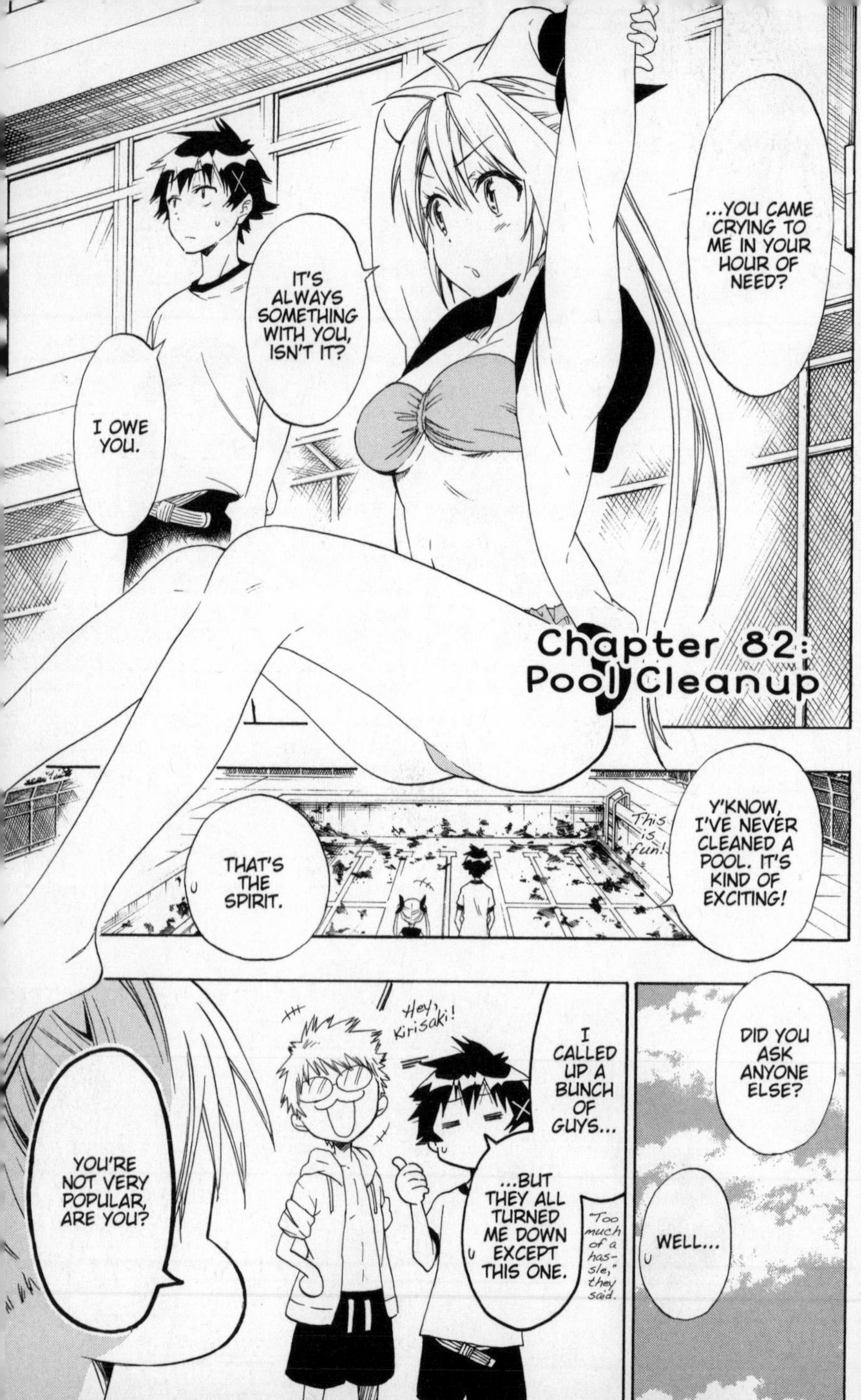
...YOU CAME CRYING TO ME IN YOUR HOUR OF NEED?
IT'S ALWAYS SOMETHING WITH YOU, ISN'T IT?
I OWE YOU.
Chapter 82: Pool Cleanup
Y'KNOW, I'VE NEVER CLEANED A POOL. IT'S KIND OF EXCITING!
This is fun!
THAT'S THE SPIRIT.
DID YOU ASK ANYONE ELSE?
WELL...
I CALLED UP A BUNCH OF GUYS...
...BUT THEY ALL TURNED ME DOWN EXCEPT THIS ONE.
"Too much of a hassle," they said.
Hey, Kirisaki!
YOU'RE NOT VERY POPULAR, ARE YOU?

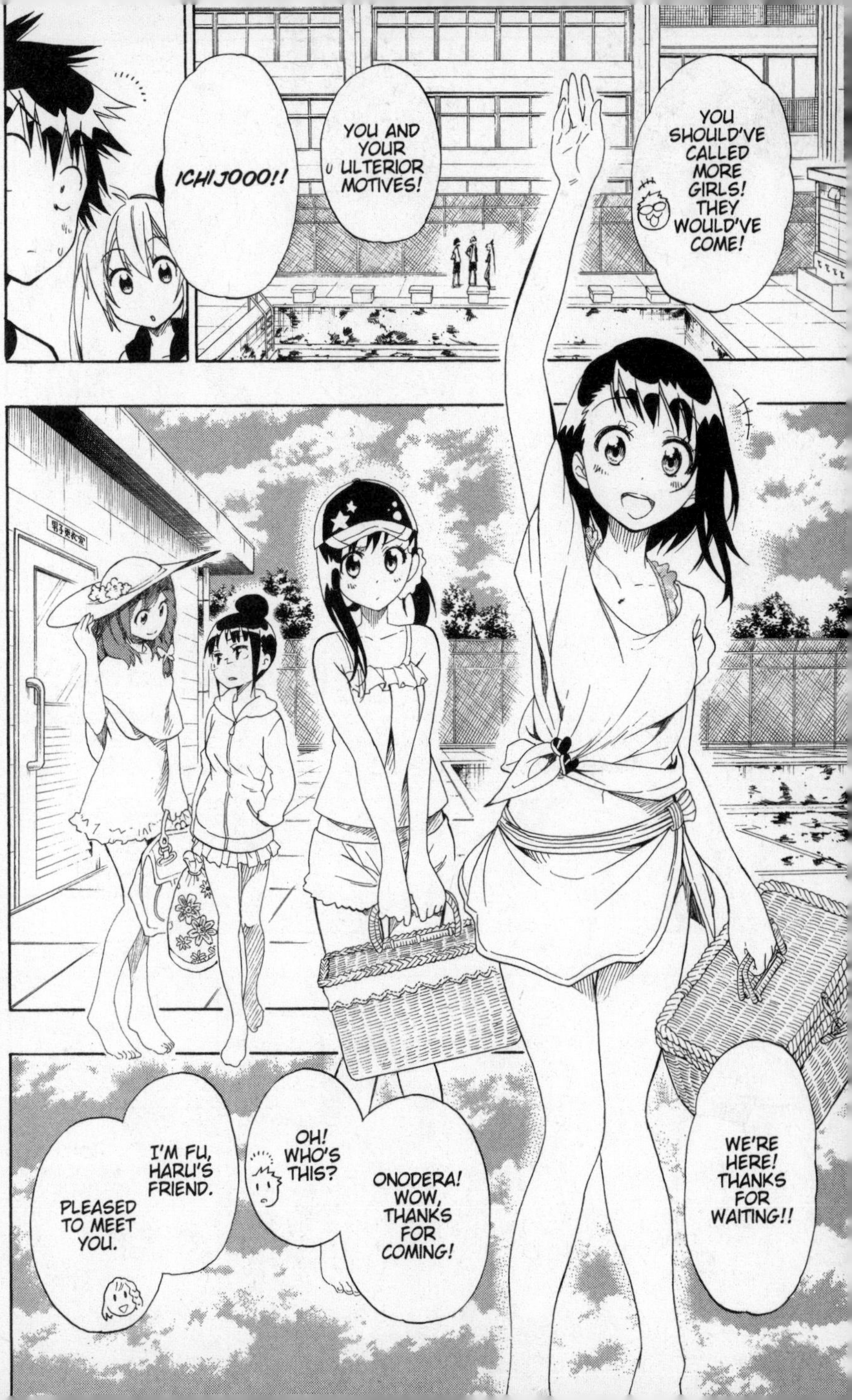
YOU SHOULD'VE CALLED MORE GIRLS! THEY WOULD'VE COME!
YOU AND YOUR ULTERIOR MOTIVES!
ICHIJOOO!!
WE'RE HERE! THANKS FOR WAITING!!
ONODERA! WOW, THANKS FOR COMING!
OH! WHO'S THIS?
I'M FU, HARU'S FRIEND.
PLEASED TO MEET YOU.

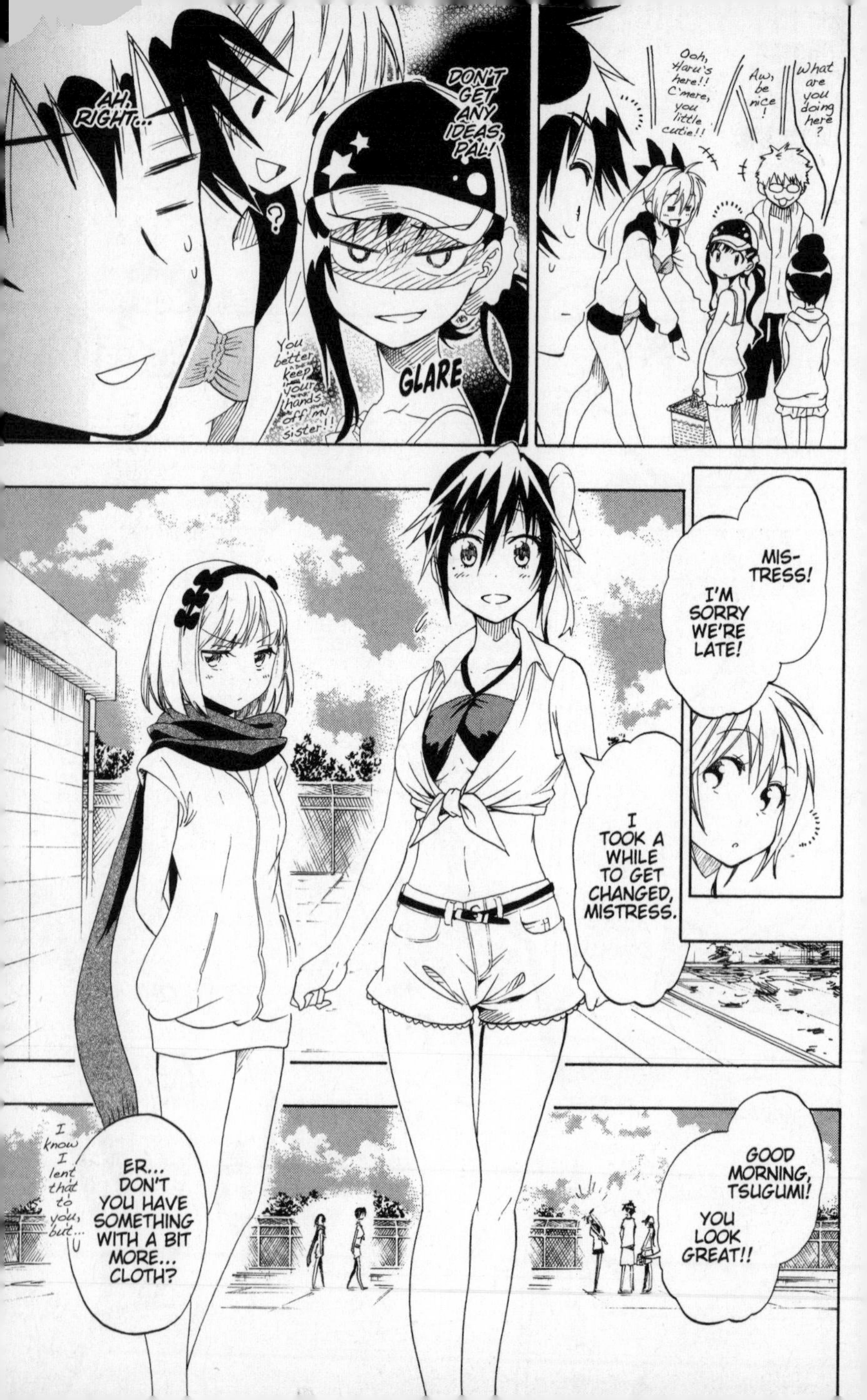
What are you doing here?
Aw, be nice!
Ooh, Haru's here!! C'mere, you little cutie!!
DON'T GET ANY IDEAS, PAL!
AH, RIGHT...
GLARE
You better keep your hands off my sister!!
MIS-TRESS!
I'M SORRY WE'RE LATE!
I TOOK A WHILE TO GET CHANGED, MISTRESS.
GOOD MORNING, TSUGUMI!
YOU LOOK GREAT!!
ER... DON'T YOU HAVE SOMETHING WITH A BIT MORE... CLOTH?
I know I lent that to you, but...

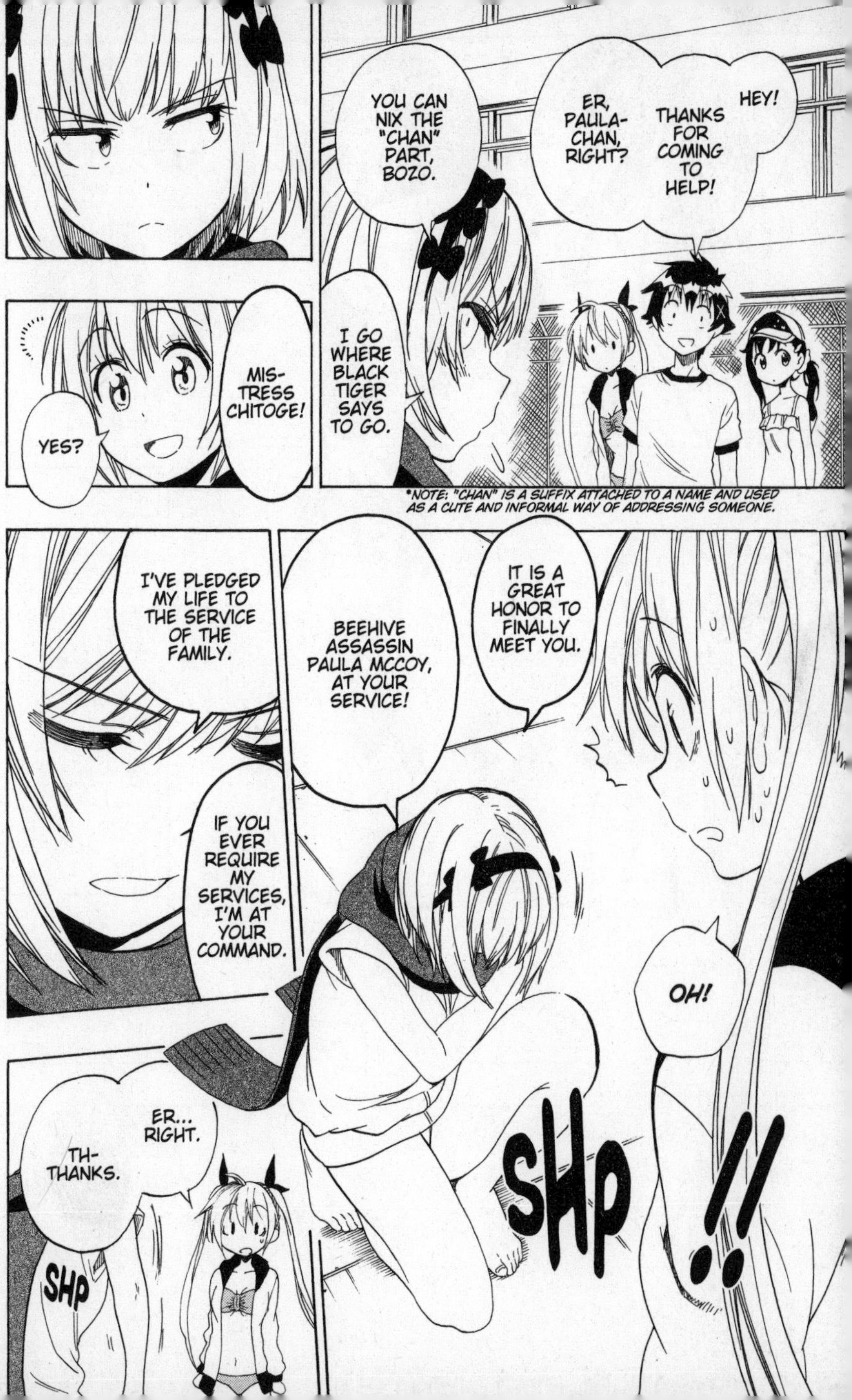
HEY!
THANKS FOR COMING TO HELP!
ER, PAULA-CHAN, RIGHT?
YOU CAN NIX THE "CHAN" PART, BOZO.
I GO WHERE BLACK TIGER SAYS TO GO.
MIS-TRESS CHITOGE!
YES?
*NOTE: "CHAN" IS A SUFFIX ATTACHED TO A NAME AND USED AS A CUTE AND INFORMAL WAY OF ADDRESSING SOMEONE.
IT IS A GREAT HONOR TO FINALLY MEET YOU.
BEEHIVE ASSASSIN PAULA MCCOY, AT YOUR SERVICE!
I'VE PLEDGED MY LIFE TO THE SERVICE OF THE FAMILY.
IF YOU EVER REQUIRE MY SERVICES, I'M AT YOUR COMMAND.
OH!
SHP!!
ER... RIGHT.
TH-THANKS.
SHP

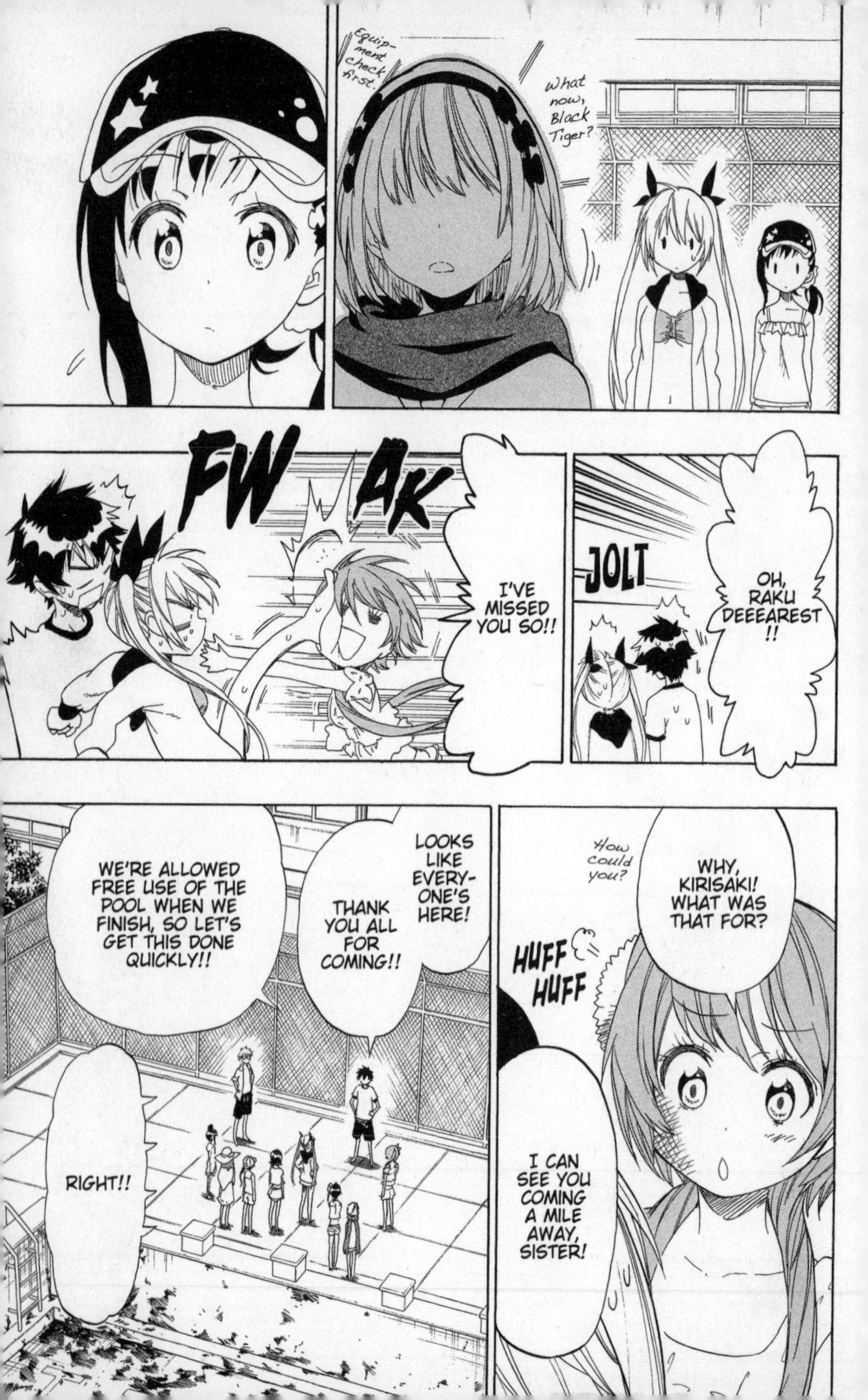
What now, Black Tiger?
Equipment check first.
OH, RAKU DEEEAREST!!
JOLT
I'VE MISSED YOU SO!!
FWAK
How could you?
WHY, KIRISAKI! WHAT WAS THAT FOR?
HUFF HUFF
I CAN SEE YOU COMING A MILE AWAY, SISTER!
LOOKS LIKE EVERYONE'S HERE!
THANK YOU ALL FOR COMING!!
WE'RE ALLOWED FREE USE OF THE POOL WHEN WE FINISH, SO LET'S GET THIS DONE QUICKLY!!
RIGHT!!

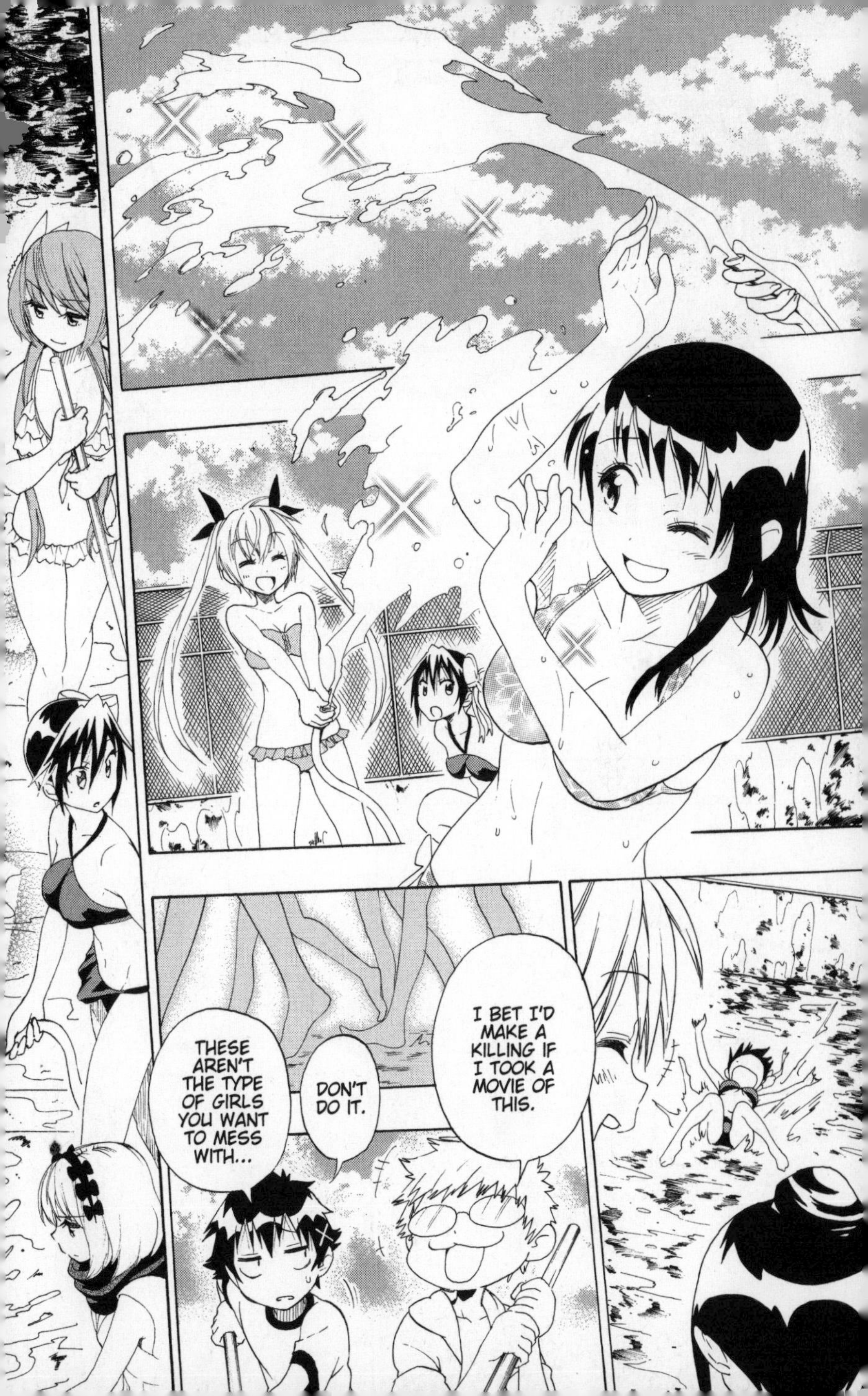
I BET I'D MAKE A KILLING IF I TOOK A MOVIE OF THIS.
DON'T DO IT.
THESE AREN'T THE TYPE OF GIRLS YOU WANT TO MESS WITH...

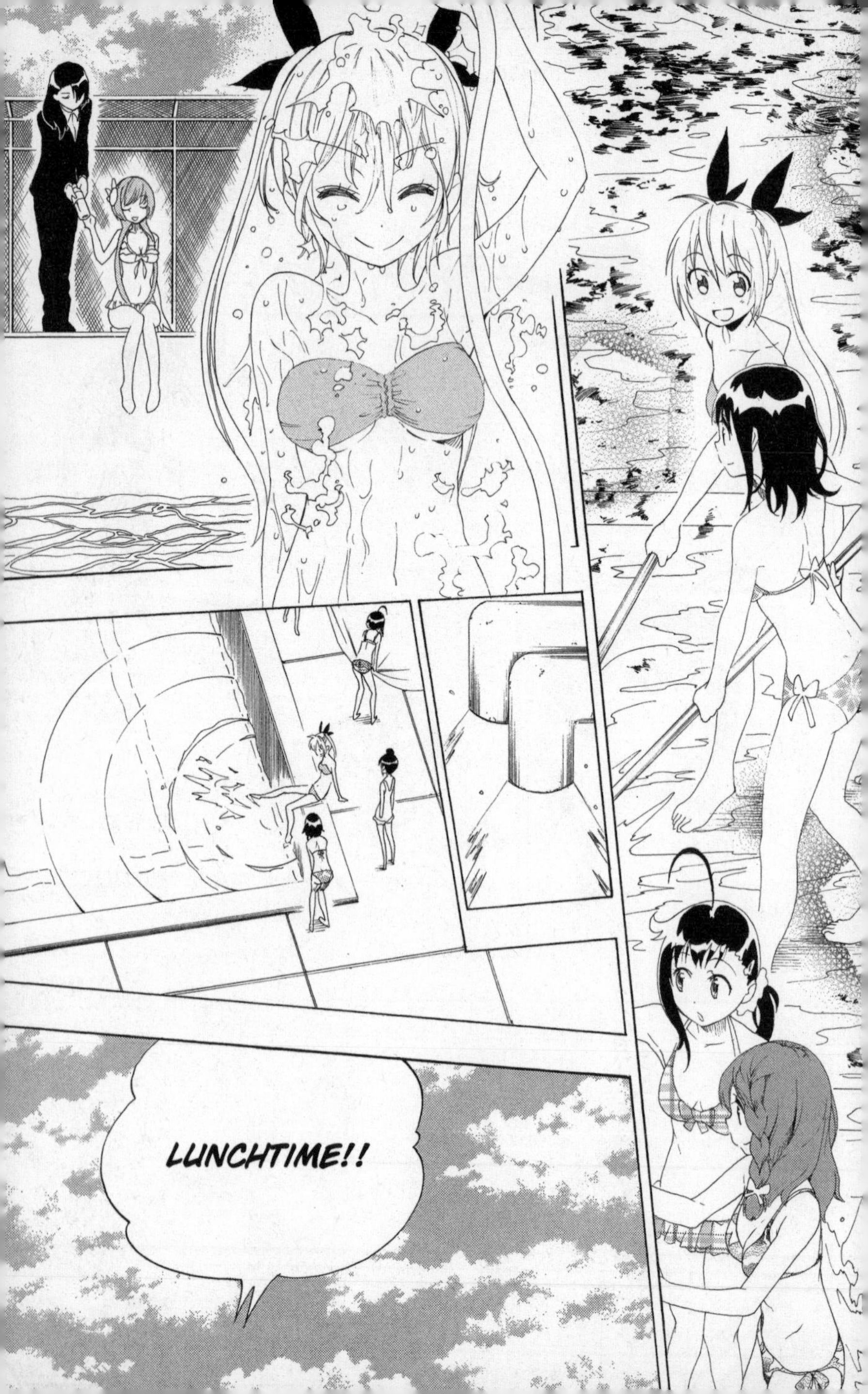
LUNCHTIME!!

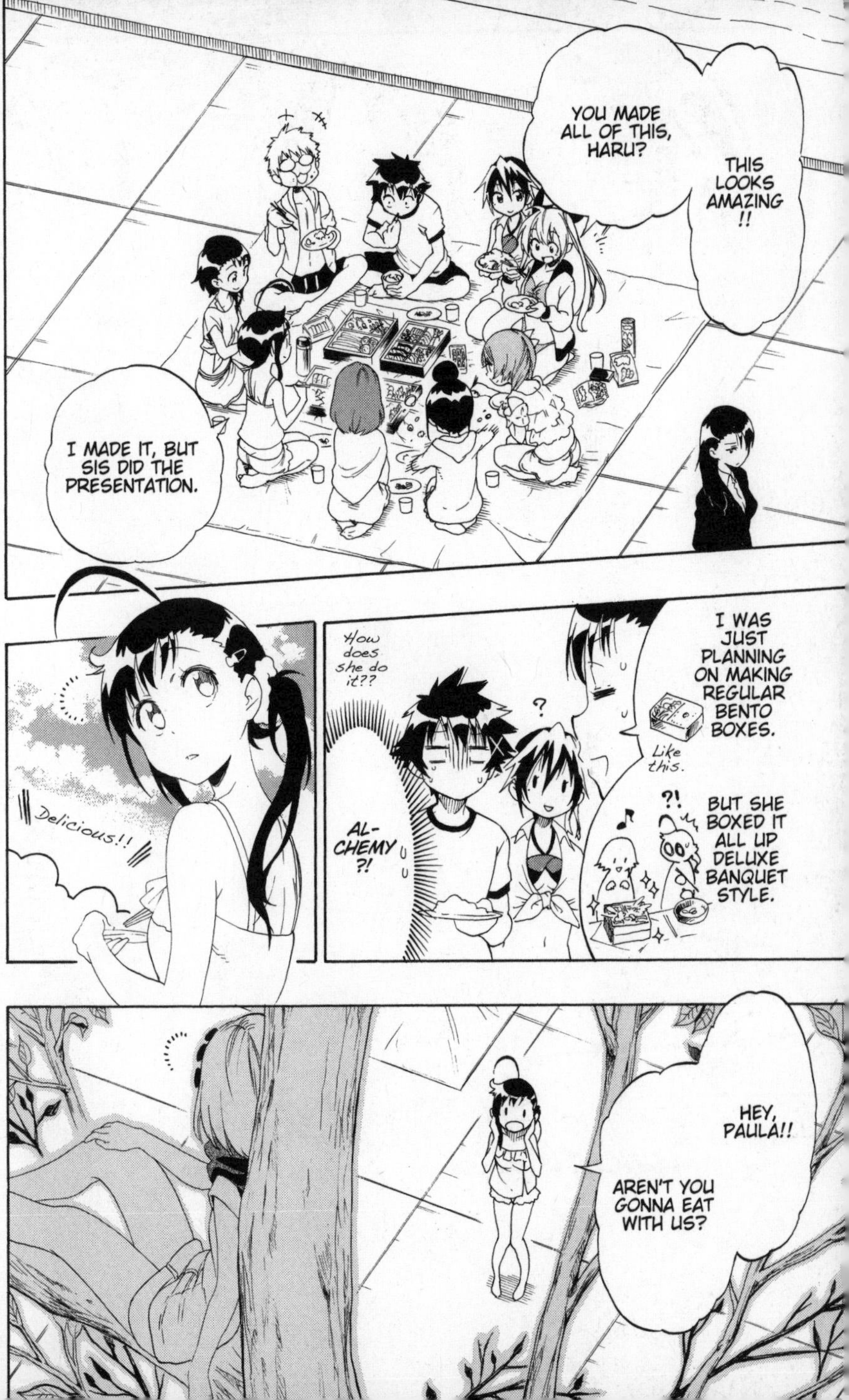
YOU MADE ALL OF THIS, HARU?
THIS LOOKS AMAZING!!
I MADE IT, BUT SIS DID THE PRESENTATION.
I WAS JUST PLANNING ON MAKING REGULAR BENTO BOXES.
Like this.
BUT SHE BOXED IT ALL UP DELUXE BANQUET STYLE.
?!
How does she do it??
AL-CHEMY?!
Delicious!!
HEY, PAULA!!
AREN'T YOU GONNA EAT WITH US?

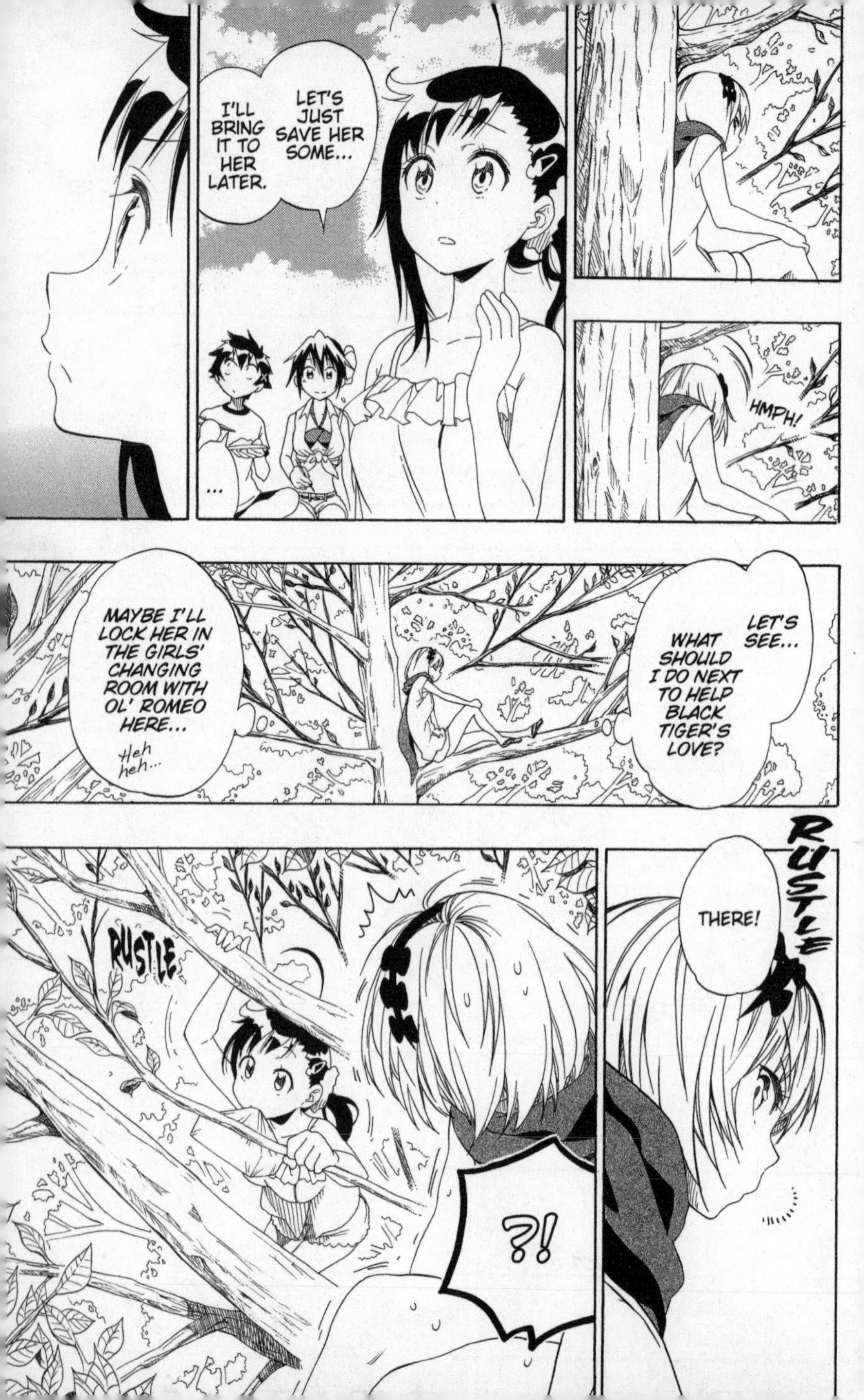
HMPH!
LET'S JUST SAVE HER SOME...
I'LL BRING IT TO HER LATER.
...
LET'S SEE... WHAT SHOULD I DO NEXT TO HELP BLACK TIGER'S LOVE?
MAYBE I'LL LOCK HER IN THE GIRLS' CHANGING ROOM WITH OL' ROMEO HERE...
Heh heh...
RUSTLE
THERE!
RUSTLE
?!

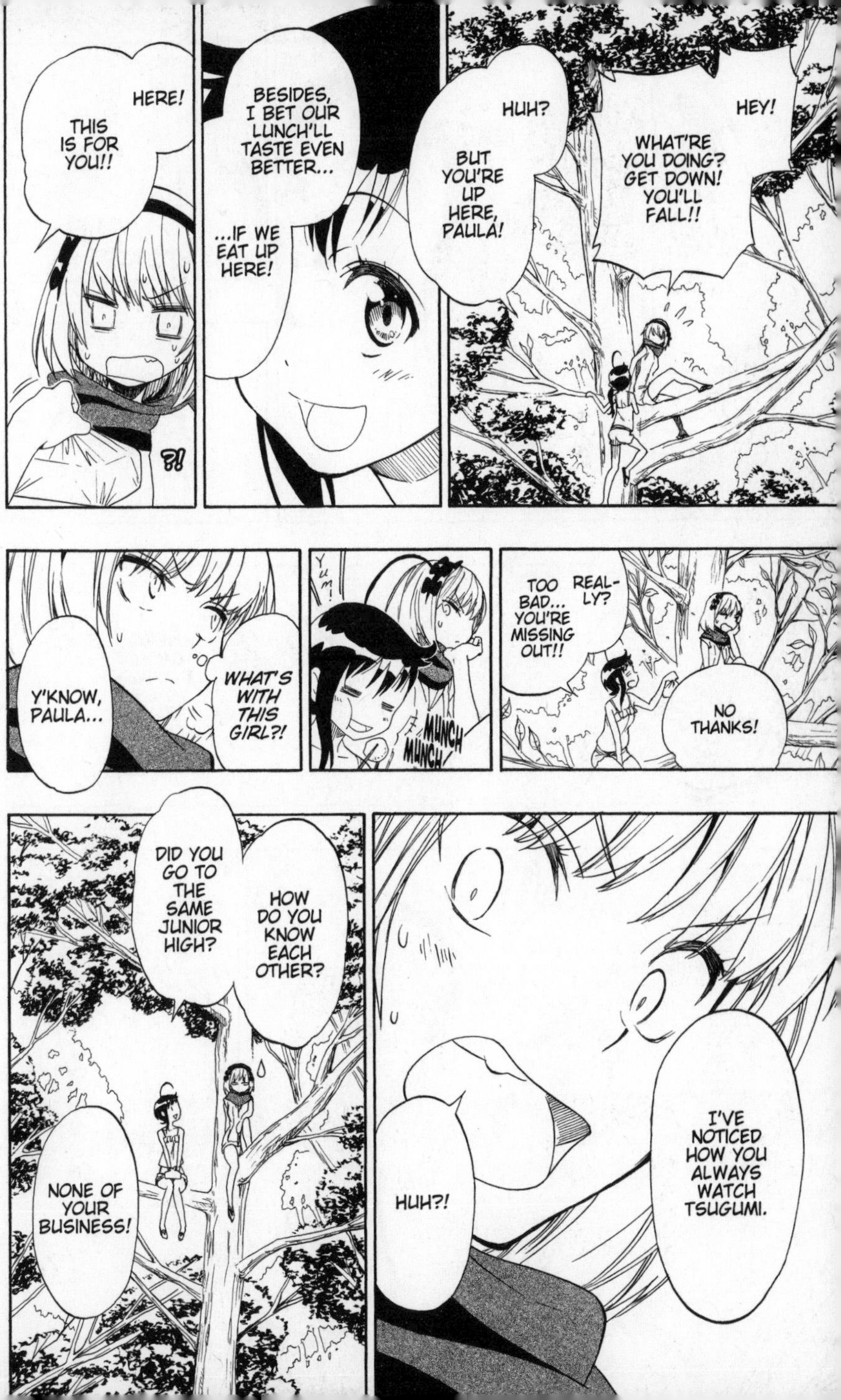
HEY!
WHAT'RE YOU DOING? GET DOWN! YOU'LL FALL!!
HUH?
BUT YOU'RE UP HERE, PAULA!
BESIDES, I BET OUR LUNCH'LL TASTE EVEN BETTER...
...IF WE EAT UP HERE!
HERE!
THIS IS FOR YOU!!
?!
REALLY?
TOO BAD... YOU'RE MISSING OUT!!
NO THANKS!
YUM!
MUNCH MUNCH
WHAT'S WITH THIS GIRL?!
Y'KNOW, PAULA...
I'VE NOTICED HOW YOU ALWAYS WATCH TSUGUMI.
HUH?!
HOW DO YOU KNOW EACH OTHER?
DID YOU GO TO THE SAME JUNIOR HIGH?
NONE OF YOUR BUSINESS!

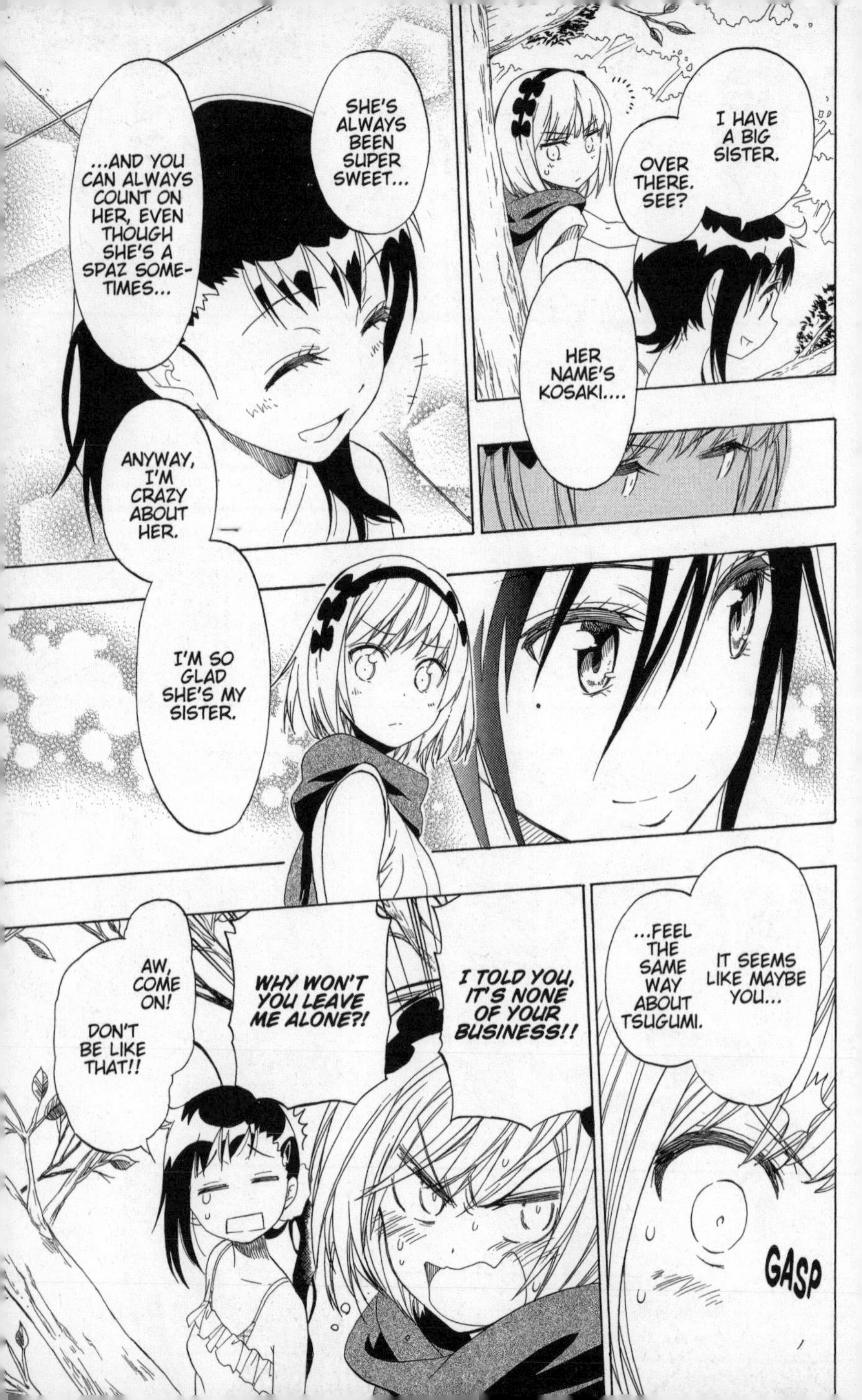
I HAVE A BIG SISTER.
OVER THERE. SEE?
HER NAME'S KOSAKI....
SHE'S ALWAYS BEEN SUPER SWEET...
...AND YOU CAN ALWAYS COUNT ON HER, EVEN THOUGH SHE'S A SPAZ SOME-TIMES...
ANYWAY, I'M CRAZY ABOUT HER.
I'M SO GLAD SHE'S MY SISTER.
IT SEEMS LIKE MAYBE YOU...
...FEEL THE SAME WAY ABOUT TSUGUMI.
GASP
I TOLD YOU, IT'S NONE OF YOUR BUSINESS!!
WHY WON'T YOU LEAVE ME ALONE?!
AW, COME ON!
DON'T BE LIKE THAT!!

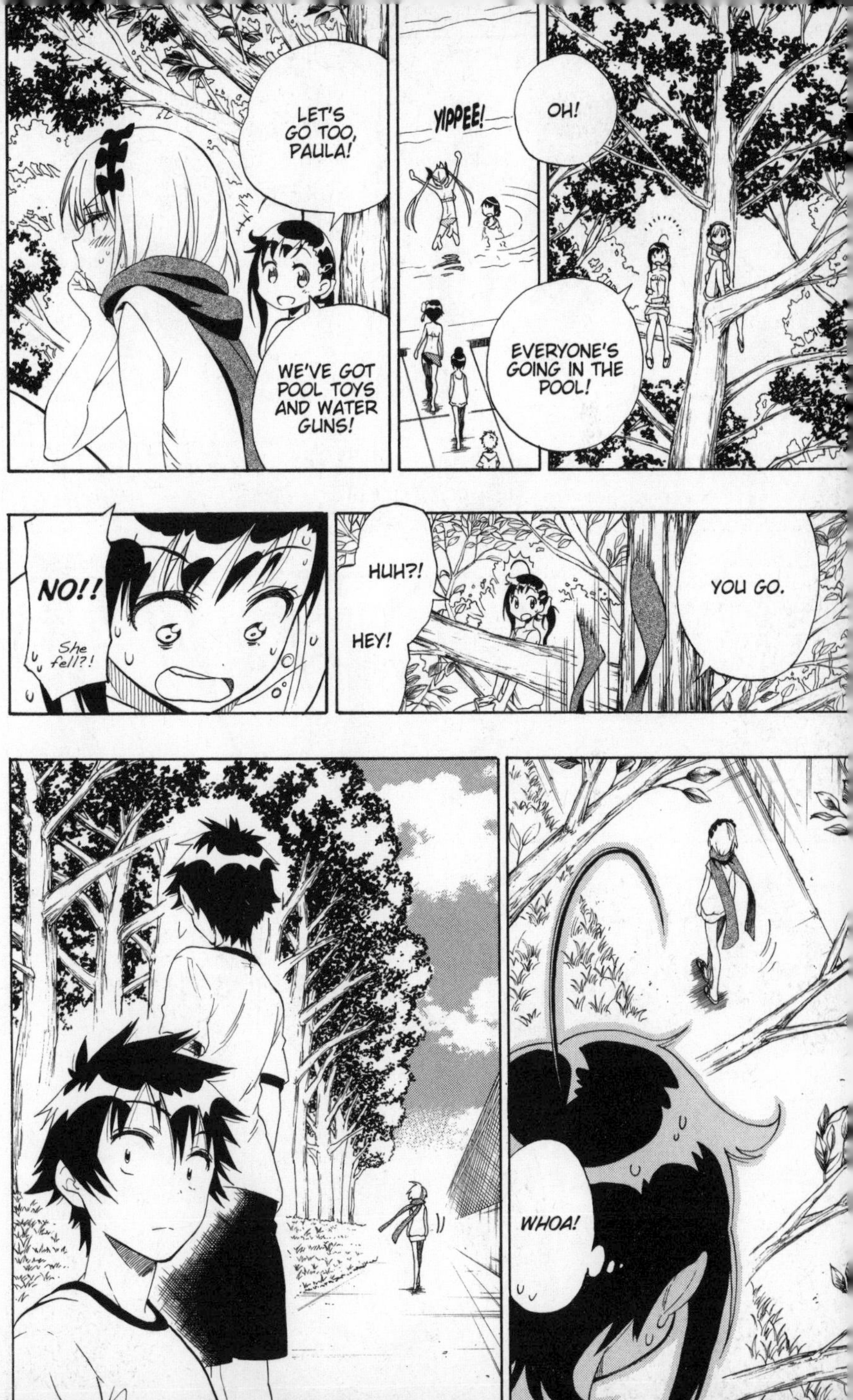
OH!
EVERYONE'S GOING IN THE POOL!
YIPPEE!
LET'S GO TOO, PAULA!
WE'VE GOT POOL TOYS AND WATER GUNS!
YOU GO.
HUH?!
HEY!
NO!!
She fell?!
WHOA!

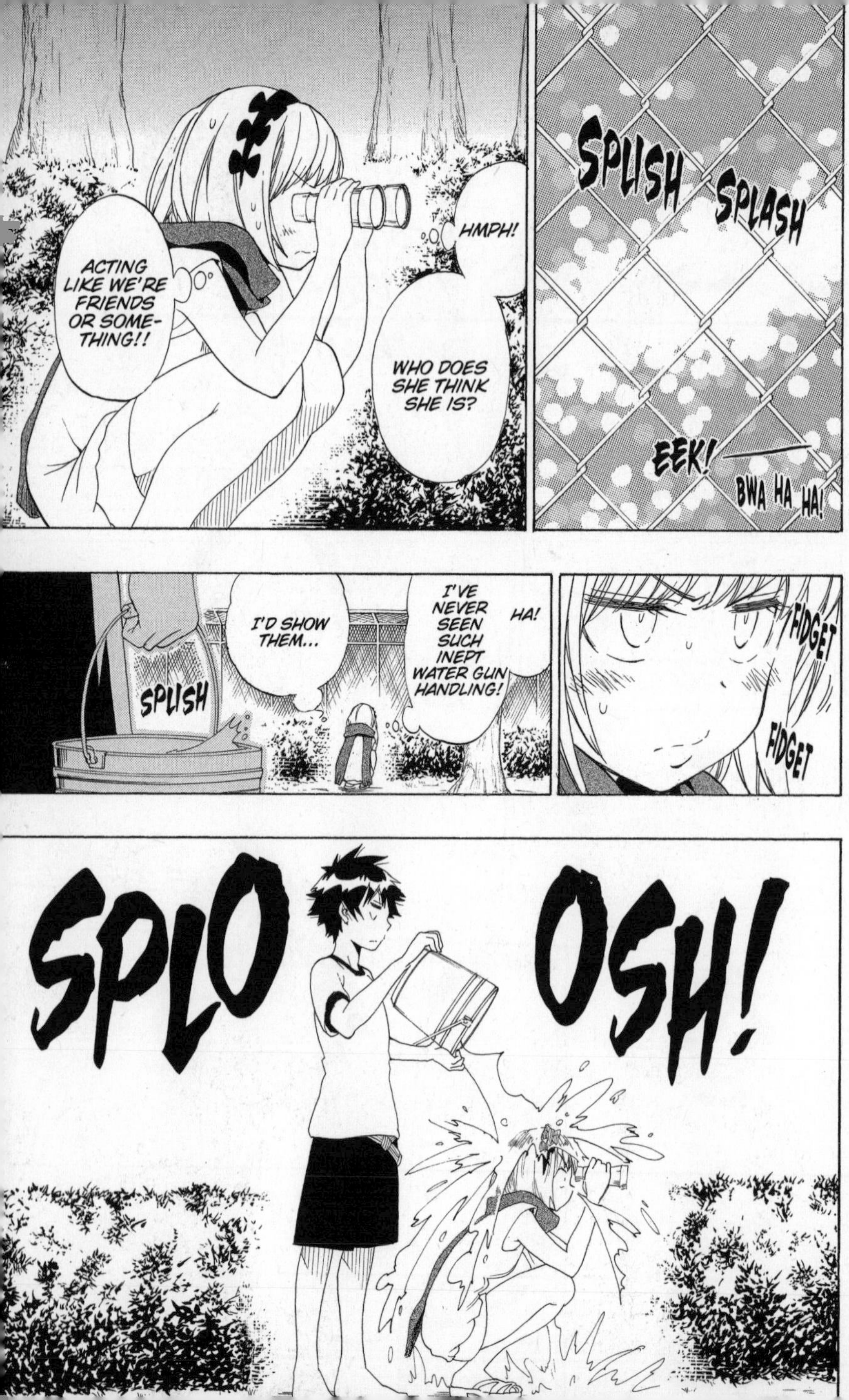
SPLISH
SPLASH
EEK!
BWA HA HA!
HMPH!
WHO DOES SHE THINK SHE IS?
ACTING LIKE WE'RE FRIENDS OR SOME-THING!!
FIDGET
FIDGET
HA!
I'VE NEVER SEEN SUCH INEPT WATER GUN HANDLING!
I'D SHOW THEM...
SPLISH
SPLO OSH!

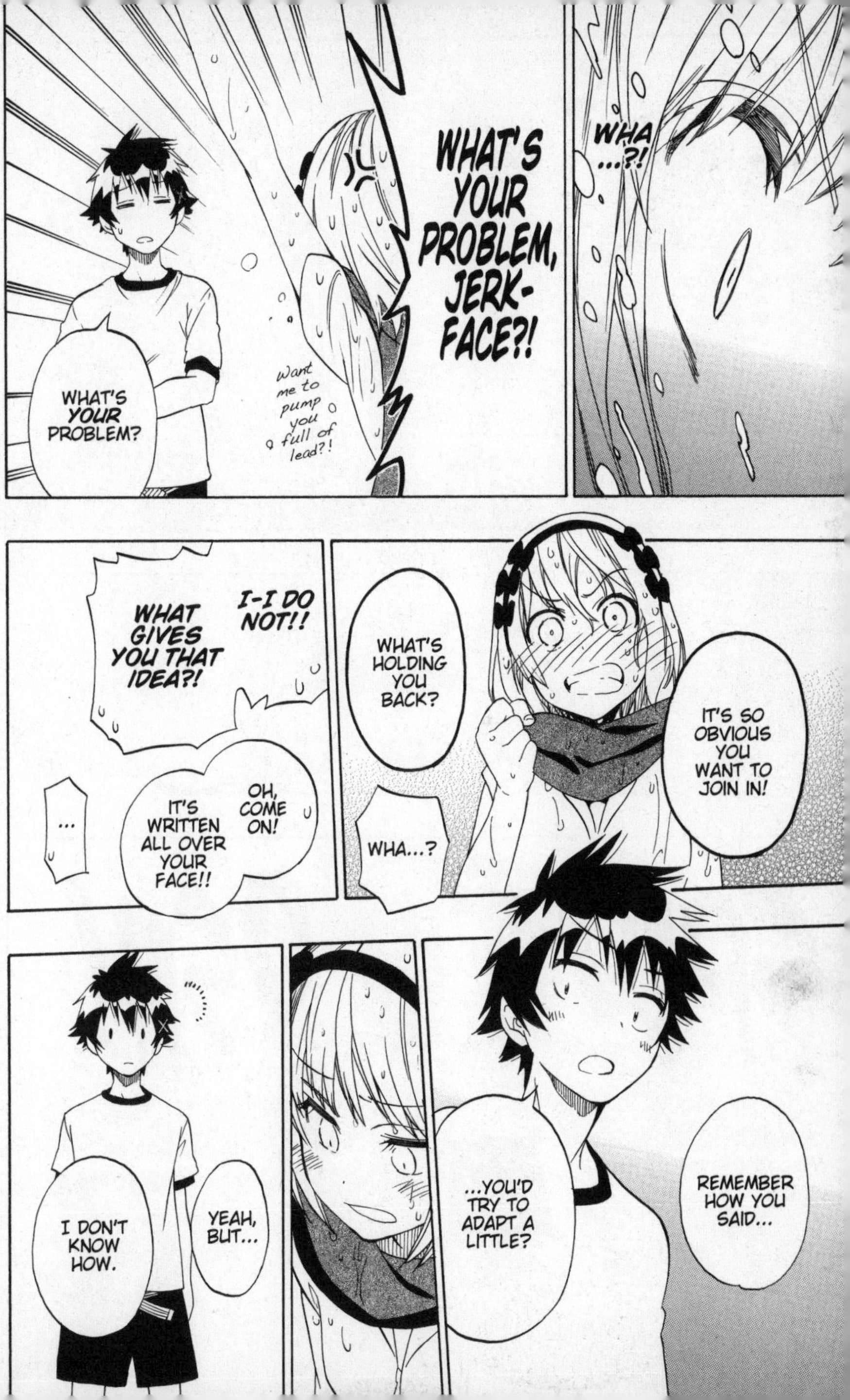
WHA ...?!
WHAT'S YOUR PROBLEM, JERK-FACE?!
Want me to pump you full of lead?!
WHAT'S YOUR PROBLEM?
IT'S SO OBVIOUS YOU WANT TO JOIN IN!
WHAT'S HOLDING YOU BACK?
WHA...?
I-I DO NOT!!
WHAT GIVES YOU THAT IDEA?!
OH, COME ON!
IT'S WRITTEN ALL OVER YOUR FACE!!
...
REMEMBER HOW YOU SAID...
...YOU'D TRY TO ADAPT A LITTLE?
YEAH, BUT...
I DON'T KNOW HOW.

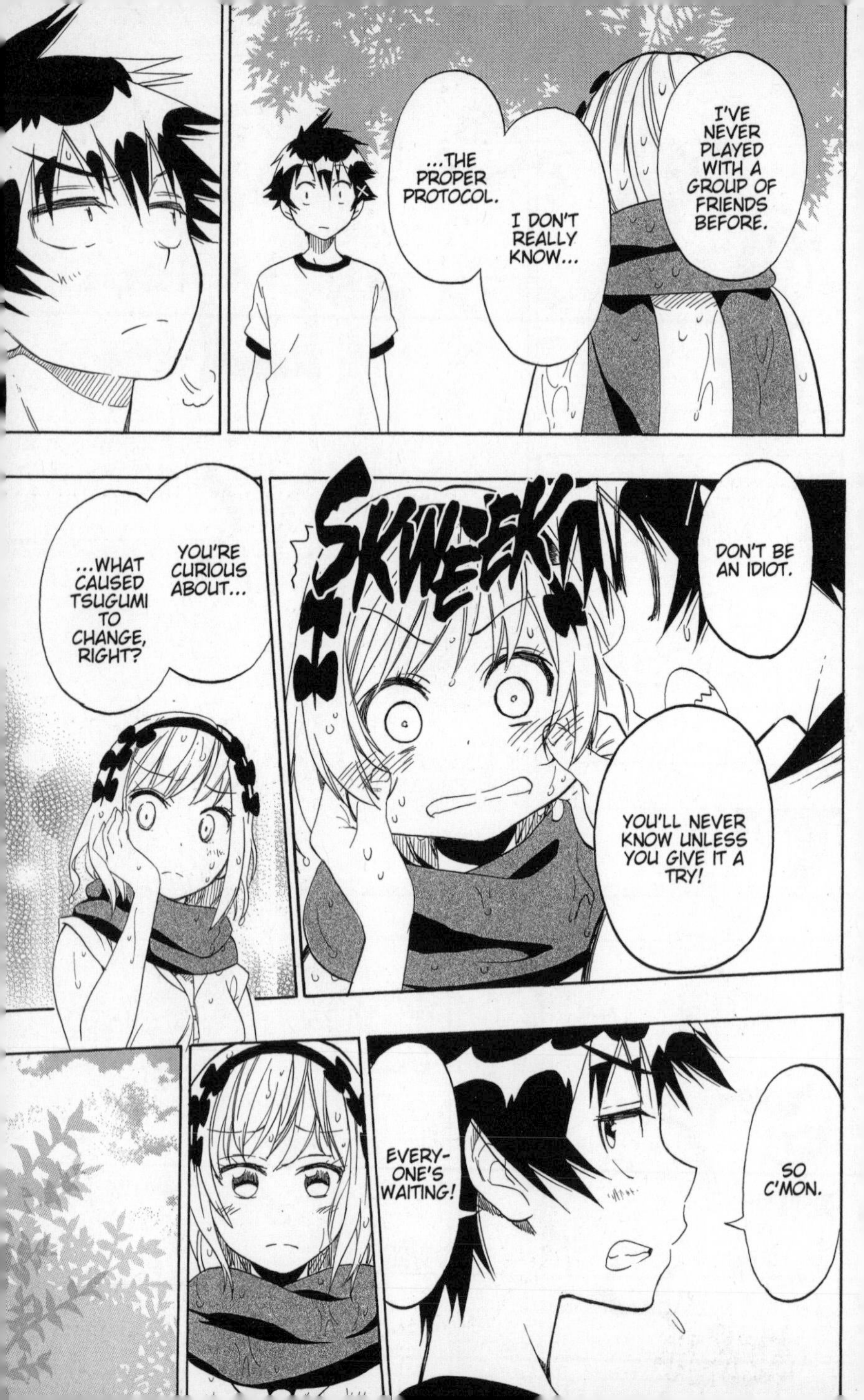
I'VE NEVER PLAYED WITH A GROUP OF FRIENDS BEFORE.
I DON'T REALLY KNOW...
...THE PROPER PROTOCOL.
DON'T BE AN IDIOT.
SKWEEK
YOU'LL NEVER KNOW UNLESS YOU GIVE IT A TRY!
YOU'RE CURIOUS ABOUT...
...WHAT CAUSED TSUGUMI TO CHANGE, RIGHT?
SO C'MON.
EVERY-ONE'S WAITING!

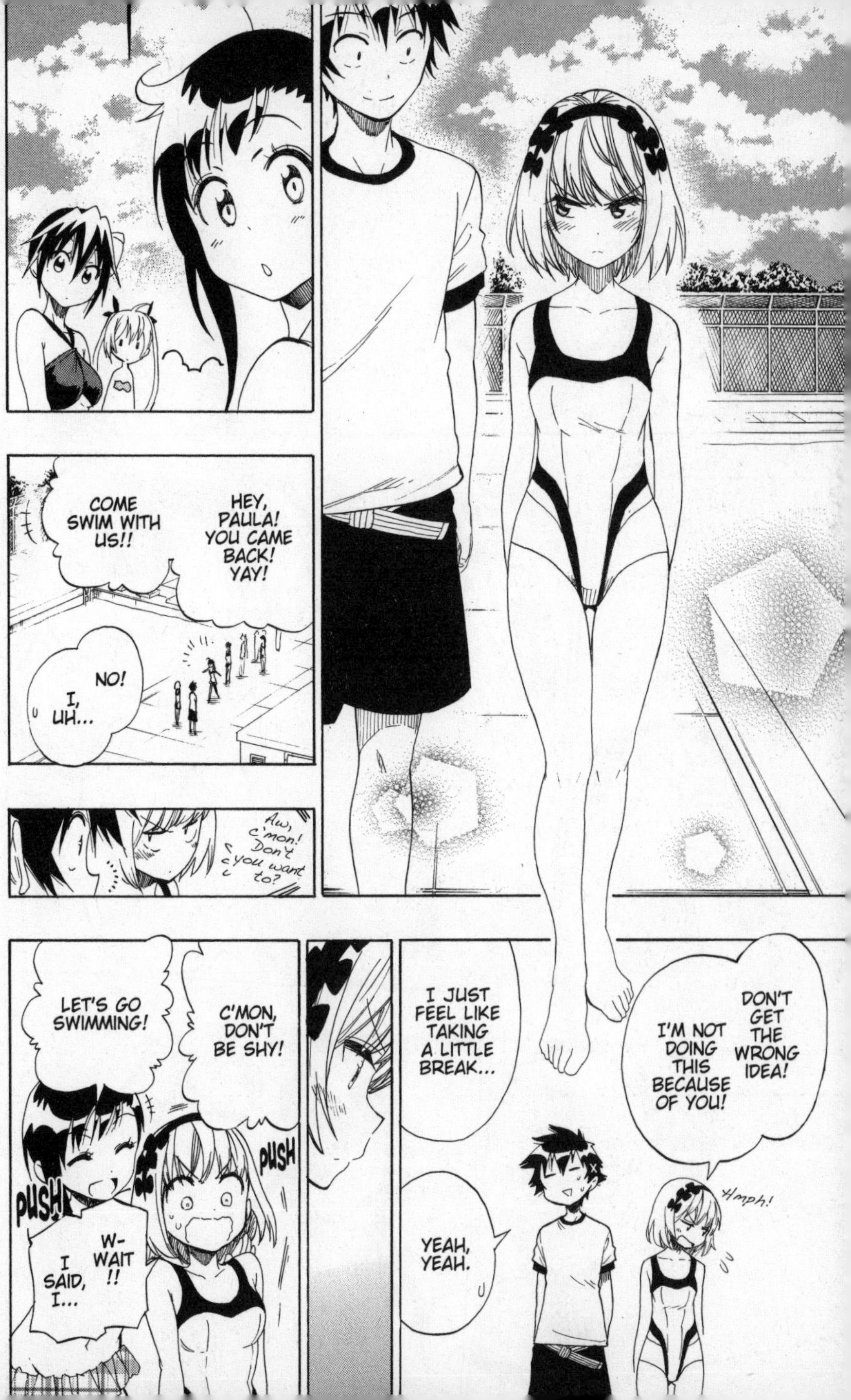
HEY, PAULA! YOU CAME BACK! YAY!
COME SWIM WITH US!!
NO! I, UH...
Aw, c'mon! Don't you want to?
DON'T GET THE WRONG IDEA!
I'M NOT DOING THIS BECAUSE OF YOU!
Hmph!
I JUST FEEL LIKE TAKING A LITTLE BREAK...
YEAH, YEAH.
C'MON, DON'T BE SHY!
LET'S GO SWIMMING!
PUSH
PUSH
W-WAIT!!
I SAID, I...

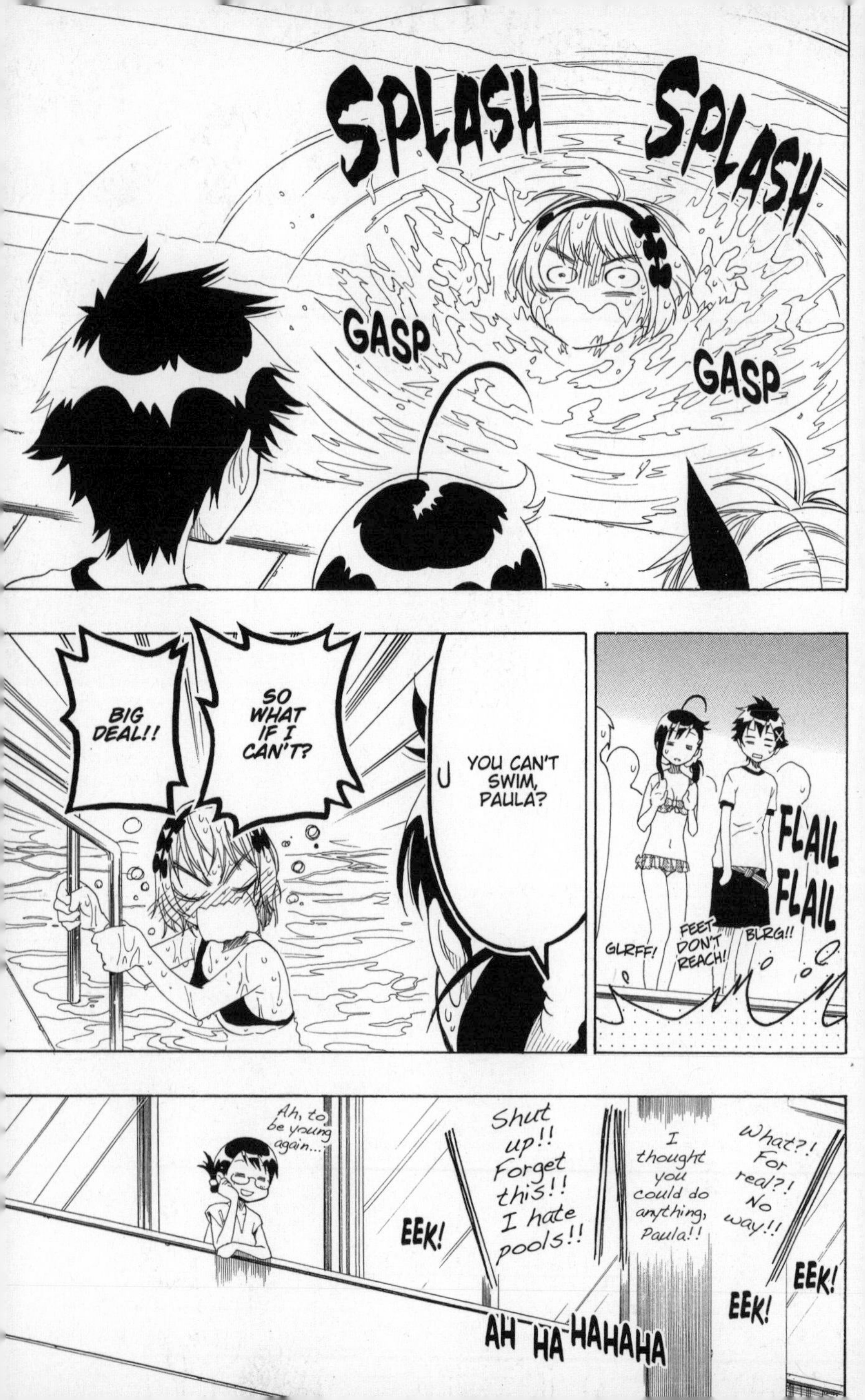
SPLASH
SPLASH
GASP
GASP
FLAIL
FLAIL
BLRG!!
FEET DON'T REACH!
GLRFF!
U
YOU CAN'T SWIM, PAULA?
SO WHAT IF I CAN'T?
BIG DEAL!!
EEK!
What?! For real?! No way!!
EEK!
I thought you could do anything, Paula!!
Shut up!! Forget this!! I hate pools!!
EEK!
AH HA HAHAHA
Ah, to be young again...

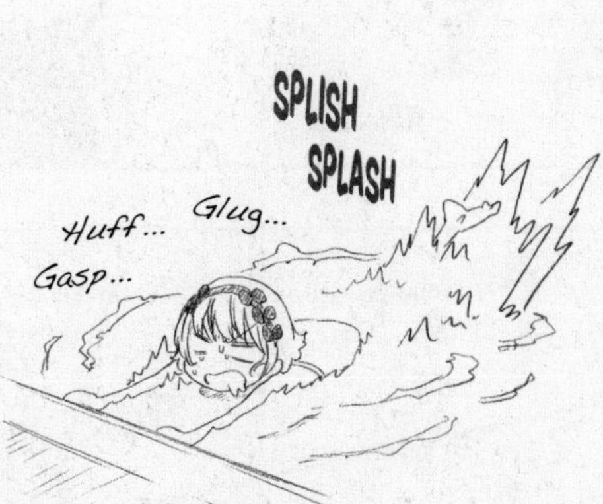
SPLISH
SPLASH
Glug...
Huff...
Gasp...

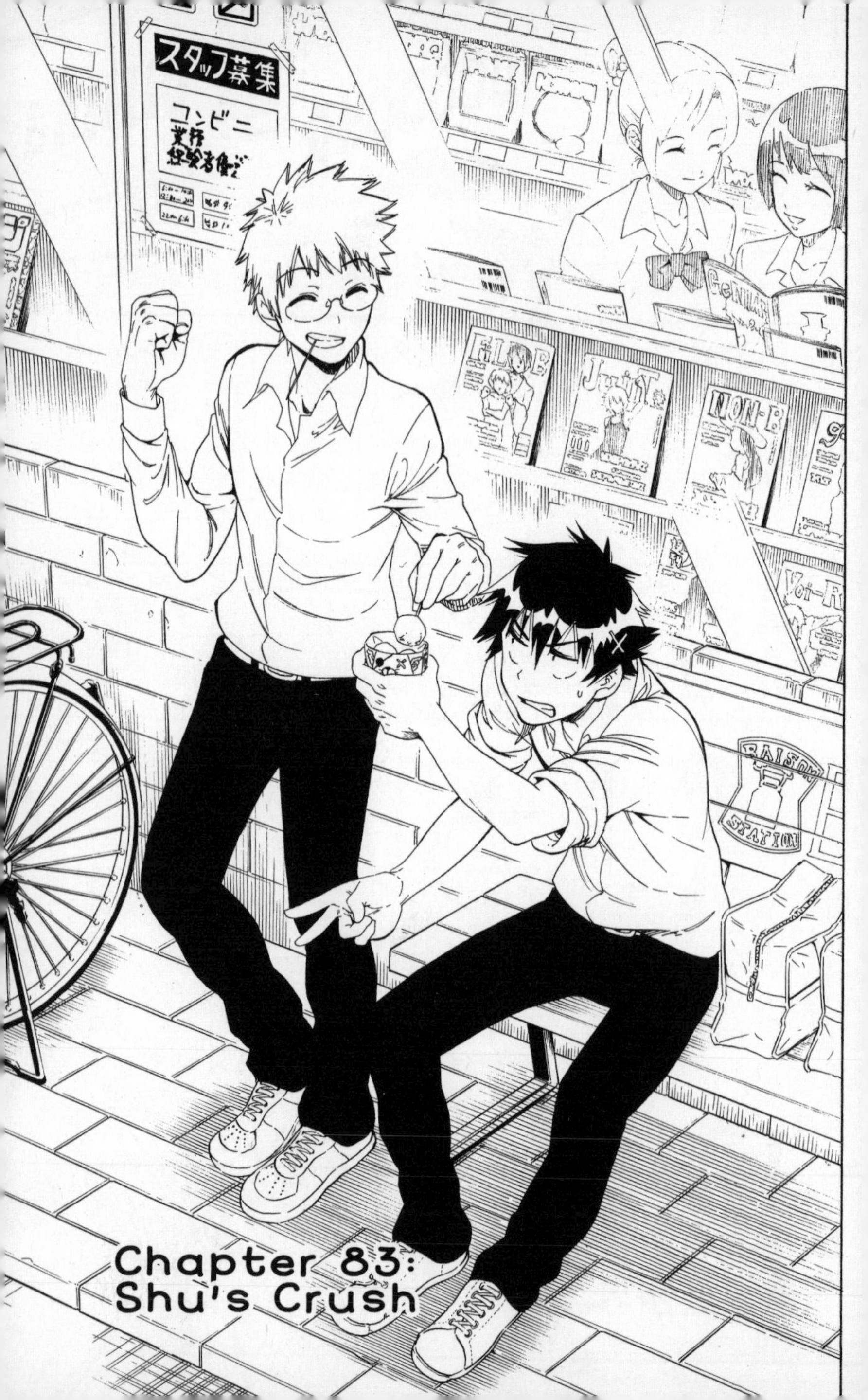
スタッフ募集
コンビニ
NON-B

Chapter 83: Shu's Crush

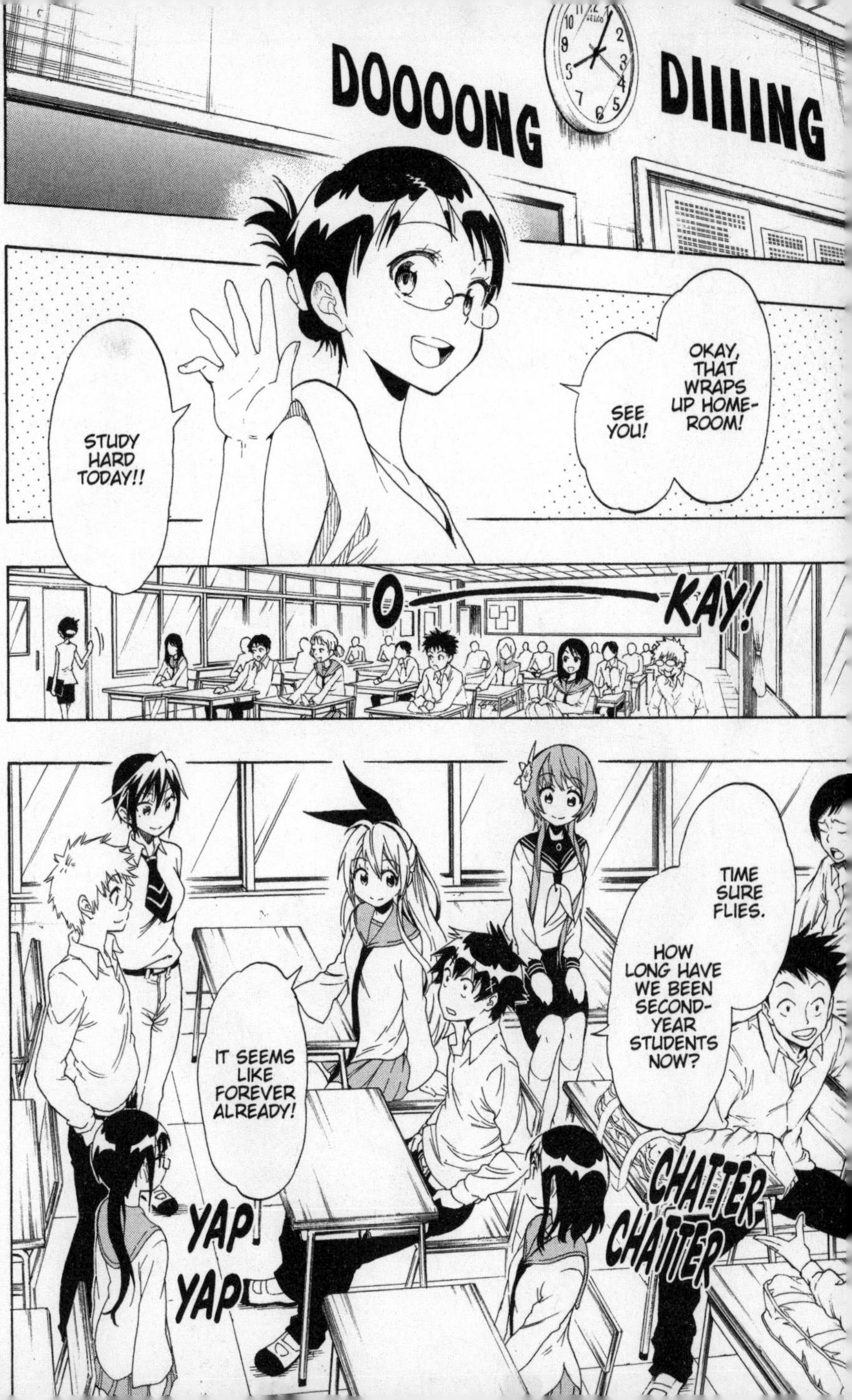
DIIIING
DOOOONG
OKAY, THAT WRAPS UP HOME-ROOM!
SEE YOU!
STUDY HARD TODAY!!
O——KAY!
TIME SURE FLIES.
HOW LONG HAVE WE BEEN SECOND-YEAR STUDENTS NOW?
CHATTER CHATTER
IT SEEMS LIKE FOREVER ALREADY!
YAP YAP

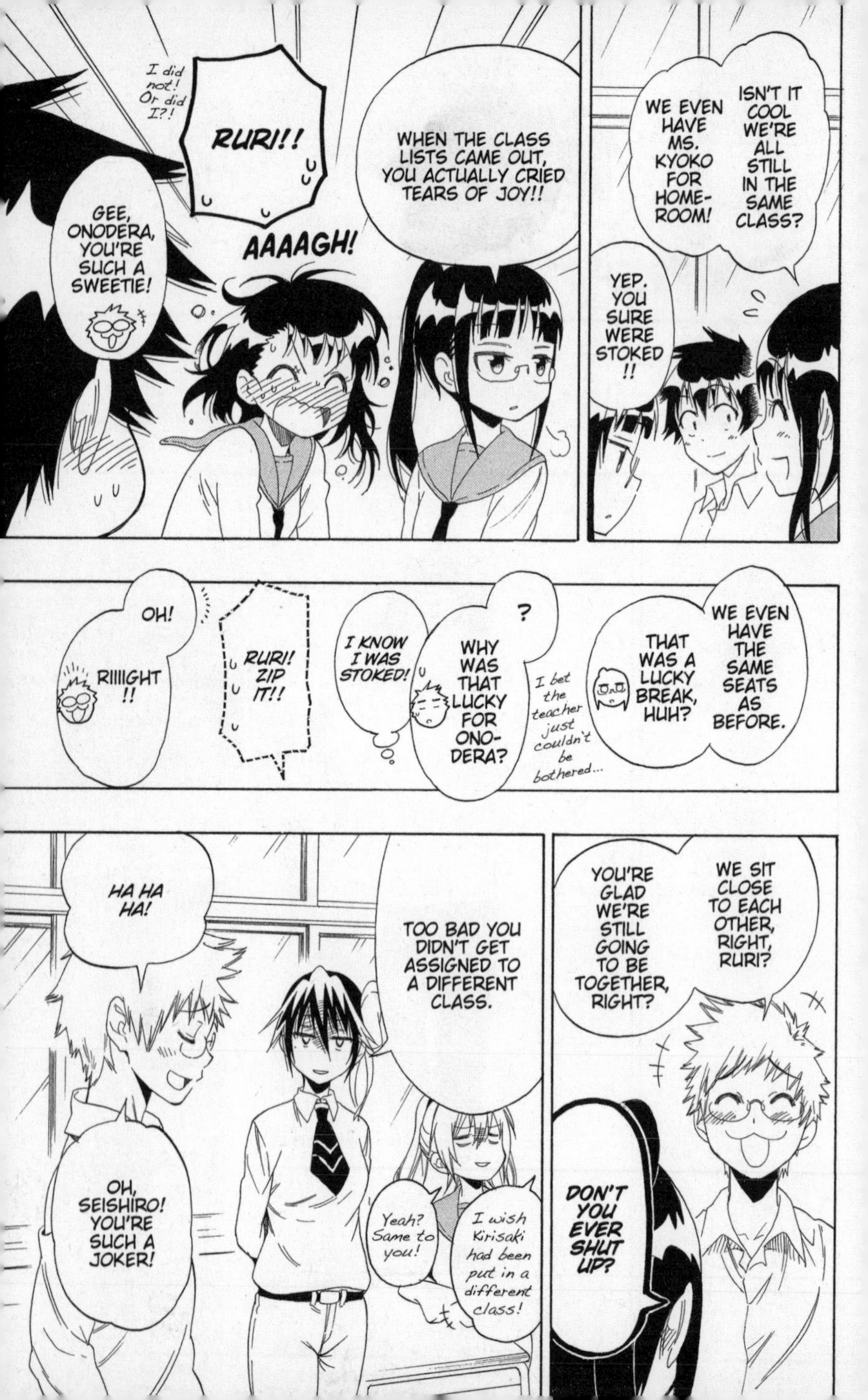
ISN'T IT COOL WE'RE ALL STILL IN THE SAME CLASS?
WE EVEN HAVE MS. KYOKO FOR HOME-ROOM!
YEP. YOU SURE WERE STOKED!!
WHEN THE CLASS LISTS CAME OUT, YOU ACTUALLY CRIED TEARS OF JOY!!
RURI!!
I did not! Or did I?!
AAAAGH!
GEE, ONODERA, YOU'RE SUCH A SWEETIE!
WE EVEN HAVE THE SAME SEATS AS BEFORE.
THAT WAS A LUCKY BREAK, HUH?
I bet the teacher just couldn't be bothered...
?
WHY WAS THAT LUCKY FOR ONO-DERA?
I KNOW I WAS STOKED!
RURI! ZIP IT!!
OH!
RIIIGHT!!
WE SIT CLOSE TO EACH OTHER, RIGHT, RURI?
YOU'RE GLAD WE'RE STILL GOING TO BE TOGETHER, RIGHT?
DON'T YOU EVER SHUT UP?
TOO BAD YOU DIDN'T GET ASSIGNED TO A DIFFERENT CLASS.
I wish Kirisaki had been put in a different class!
Yeah? Same to you!
HA HA HA!
OH, SEISHIRO! YOU'RE SUCH A JOKER!

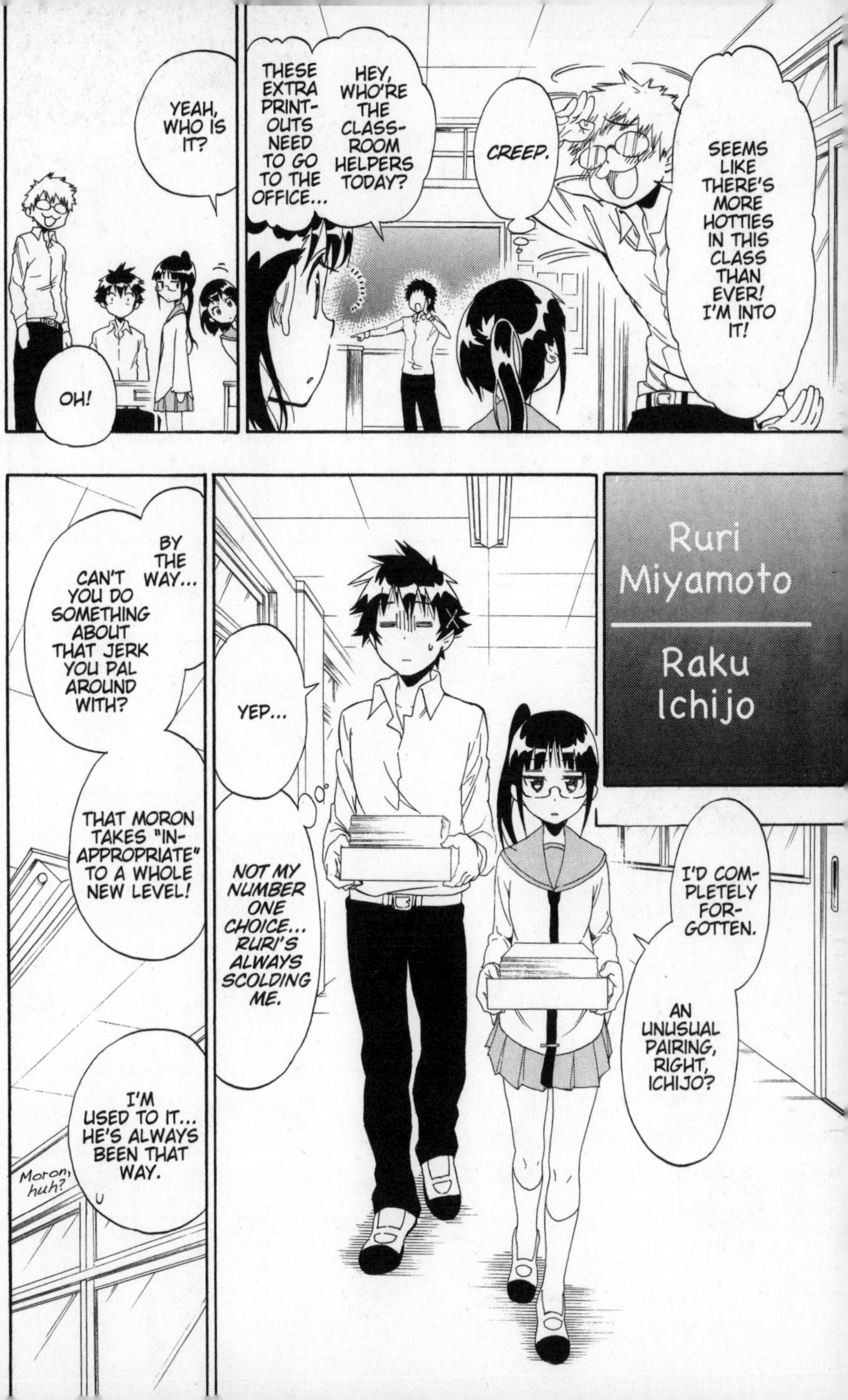
SEEMS LIKE THERE'S MORE HOTTIES IN THIS CLASS THAN EVER! I'M INTO IT!
CREEP.
HEY, WHO'RE THE CLASSROOM HELPERS TODAY?
THESE EXTRA PRINTOUTS NEED TO GO TO THE OFFICE...
YEAH, WHO IS IT?
OH!
Ruri Miyamoto
Raku Ichijo
I'D COMPLETELY FORGOTTEN.
AN UNUSUAL PAIRING, RIGHT, ICHIJO?
YEP...
NOT MY NUMBER ONE CHOICE... RURI'S ALWAYS SCOLDING ME.
BY THE WAY...
CAN'T YOU DO SOMETHING ABOUT THAT JERK YOU PAL AROUND WITH?
THAT MORON TAKES "INAPPROPRIATE" TO A WHOLE NEW LEVEL!
I'M USED TO IT... HE'S ALWAYS BEEN THAT WAY.
Moron, huh?

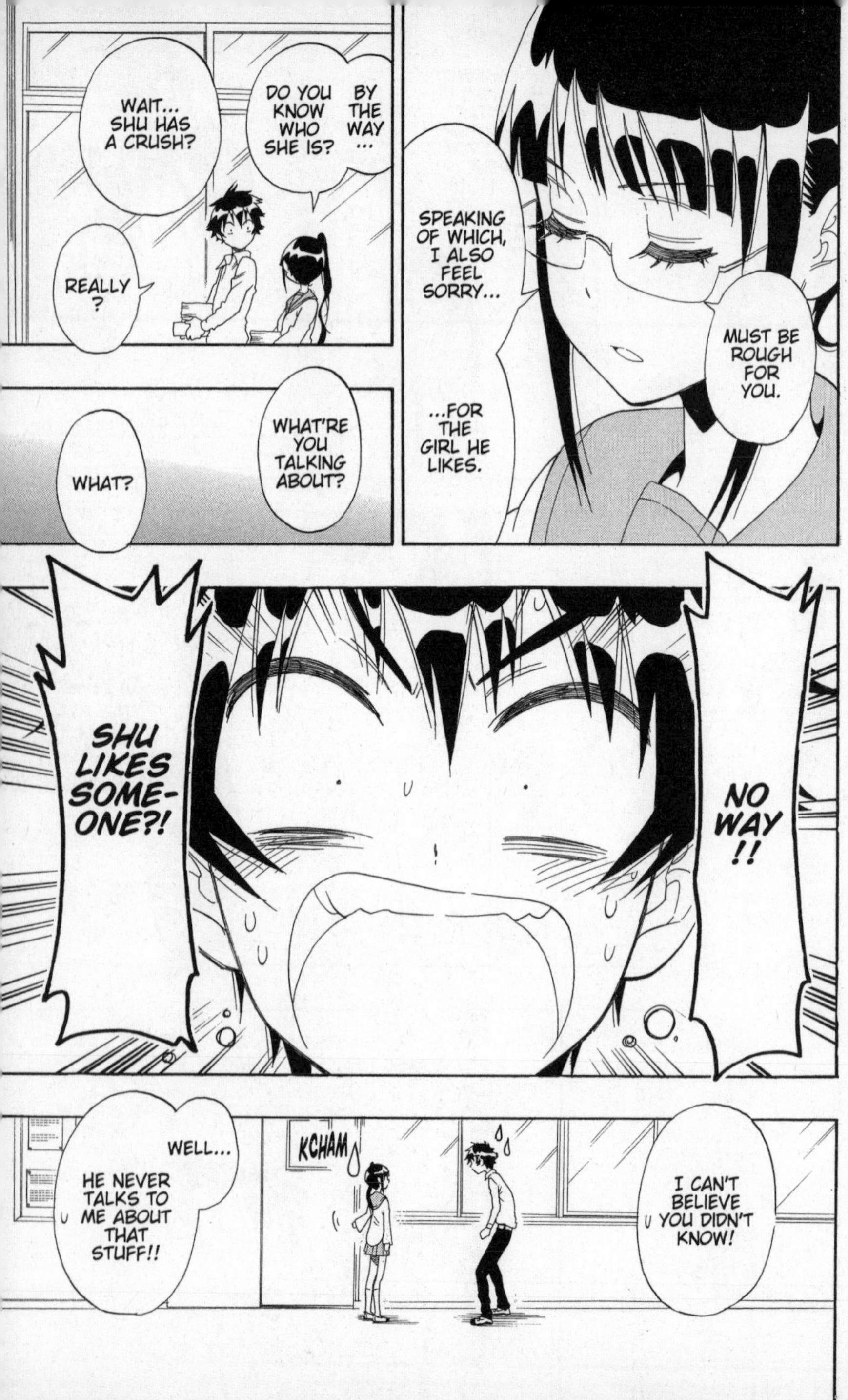
MUST BE ROUGH FOR YOU.
SPEAKING OF WHICH, I ALSO FEEL SORRY...
...FOR THE GIRL HE LIKES.
BY THE WAY...
DO YOU KNOW WHO SHE IS?
WAIT... SHU HAS A CRUSH?
REALLY?
WHAT'RE YOU TALKING ABOUT?
WHAT?
NO WAY!!
SHU LIKES SOME-ONE?!
I CAN'T BELIEVE YOU DIDN'T KNOW!
KCHAM
WELL...
HE NEVER TALKS TO ME ABOUT THAT STUFF!!

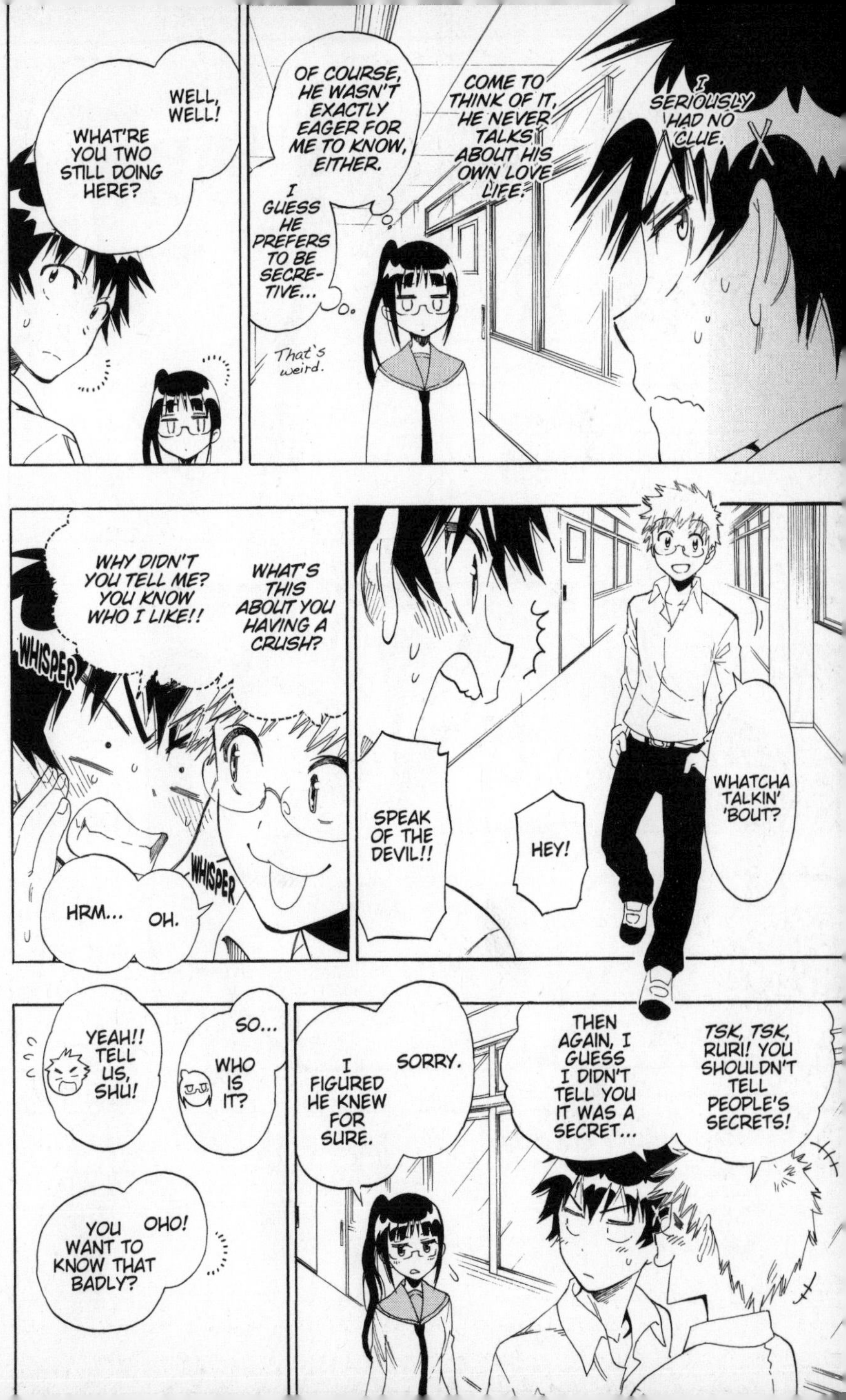

I SERIOUSLY HAD NO CLUE.
COME TO THINK OF IT, HE NEVER TALKS ABOUT HIS OWN LOVE LIFE.
OF COURSE, HE WASN'T EXACTLY EAGER FOR ME TO KNOW, EITHER.
I GUESS HE PREFERS TO BE SECRE-TIVE...
That's weird.
WELL, WELL!
WHAT'RE YOU TWO STILL DOING HERE?
WHATCHA TALKIN' 'BOUT?
HEY!
SPEAK OF THE DEVIL!!
WHAT'S THIS ABOUT YOU HAVING A CRUSH?
WHY DIDN'T YOU TELL ME? YOU KNOW WHO I LIKE!!
WHISPER
WHISPER
OH.
HRM...
TSK, TSK, RURI! YOU SHOULDN'T TELL PEOPLE'S SECRETS!
THEN AGAIN, I GUESS I DIDN'T TELL YOU IT WAS A SECRET...
SORRY.
I FIGURED HE KNEW FOR SURE.
SO...
WHO IS IT?
YEAH!! TELL US, SHU!
OHO!
YOU WANT TO KNOW THAT BADLY?

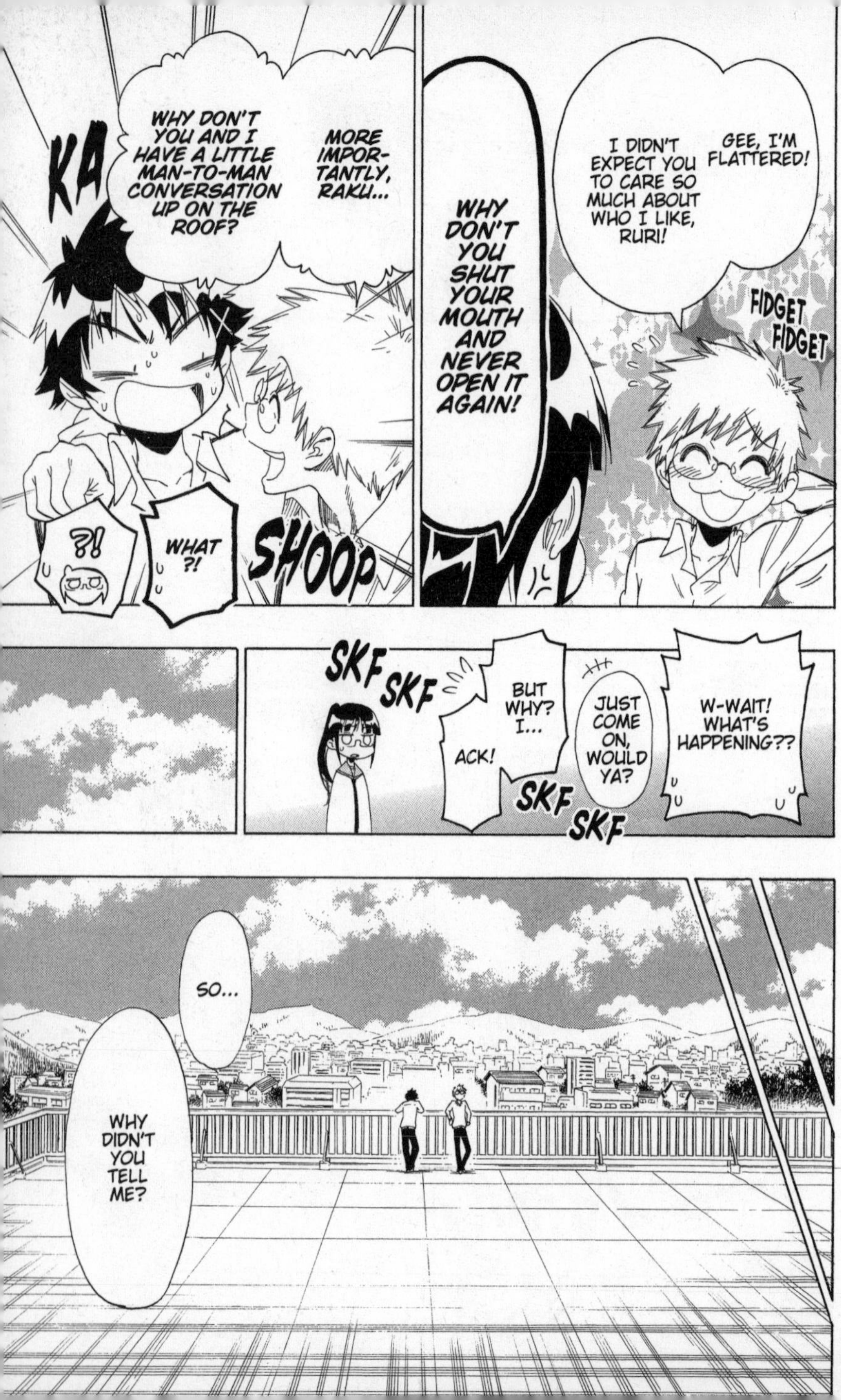
GEE, I'M FLATTERED!
I DIDN'T EXPECT YOU TO CARE SO MUCH ABOUT WHO I LIKE, RURI!
FIDGET FIDGET
WHY DON'T YOU SHUT YOUR MOUTH AND NEVER OPEN IT AGAIN!
MORE IMPORTANTLY, RAKU...
WHY DON'T YOU AND I HAVE A LITTLE MAN-TO-MAN CONVERSATION UP ON THE ROOF?
KA
SHOOP
WHAT?!
?!
W-WAIT! WHAT'S HAPPENING??
JUST COME ON, WOULD YA?
BUT WHY? I...
ACK!
SKF SKF
SKF SKF
SO...
WHY DIDN'T YOU TELL ME?

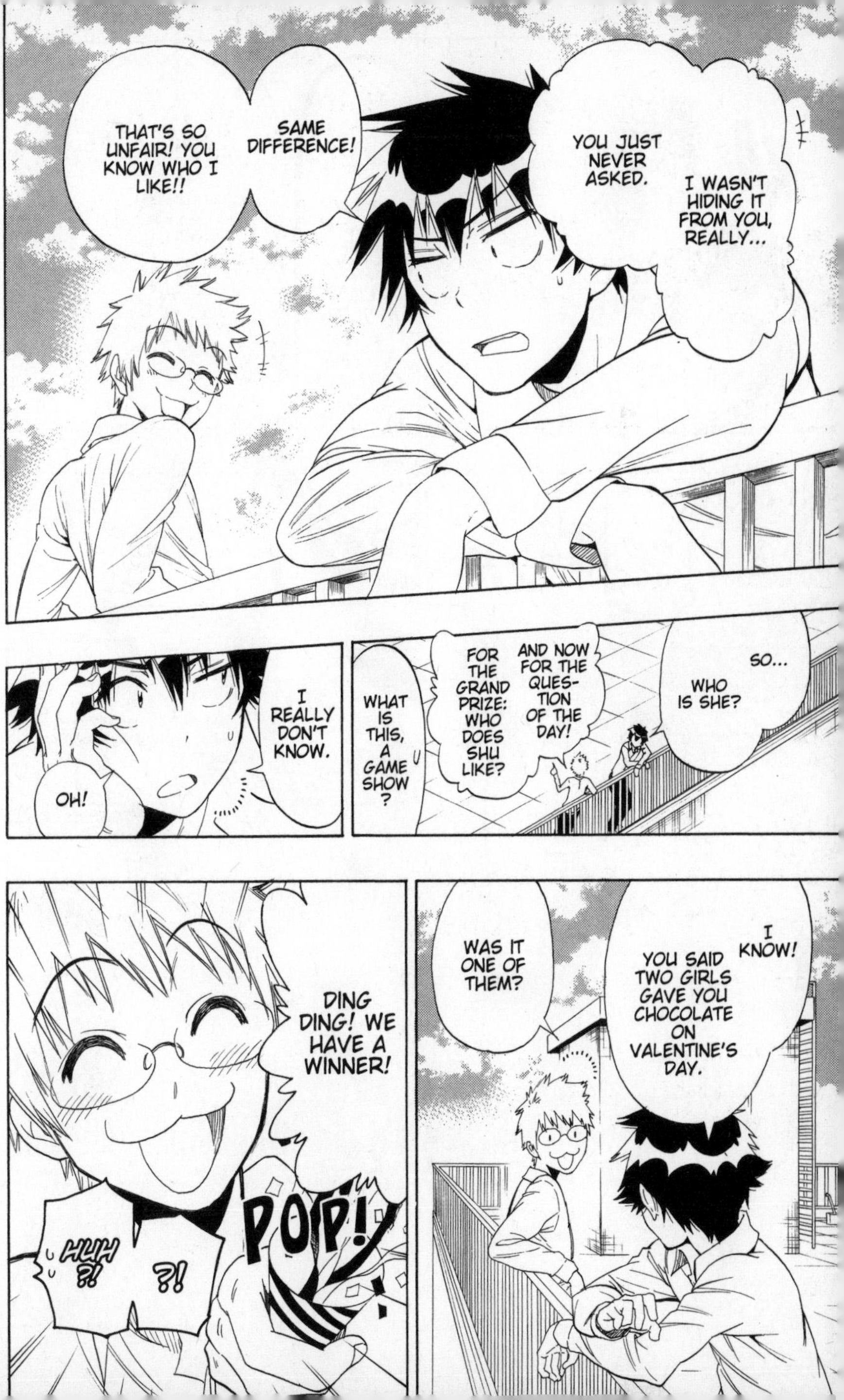
I WASN'T HIDING IT FROM YOU, REALLY...
YOU JUST NEVER ASKED.
SAME DIFFERENCE!
THAT'S SO UNFAIR! YOU KNOW WHO I LIKE!!
SO... WHO IS SHE?
AND NOW FOR THE QUES-TION OF THE DAY!
FOR THE GRAND PRIZE: WHO DOES SHU LIKE?
WHAT IS THIS, A GAME SHOW?
I REALLY DON'T KNOW.
OH!
I KNOW!
YOU SAID TWO GIRLS GAVE YOU CHOCOLATE ON VALENTINE'S DAY.
WAS IT ONE OF THEM?
DING DING! WE HAVE A WINNER!
POP!
?!
HUH?!

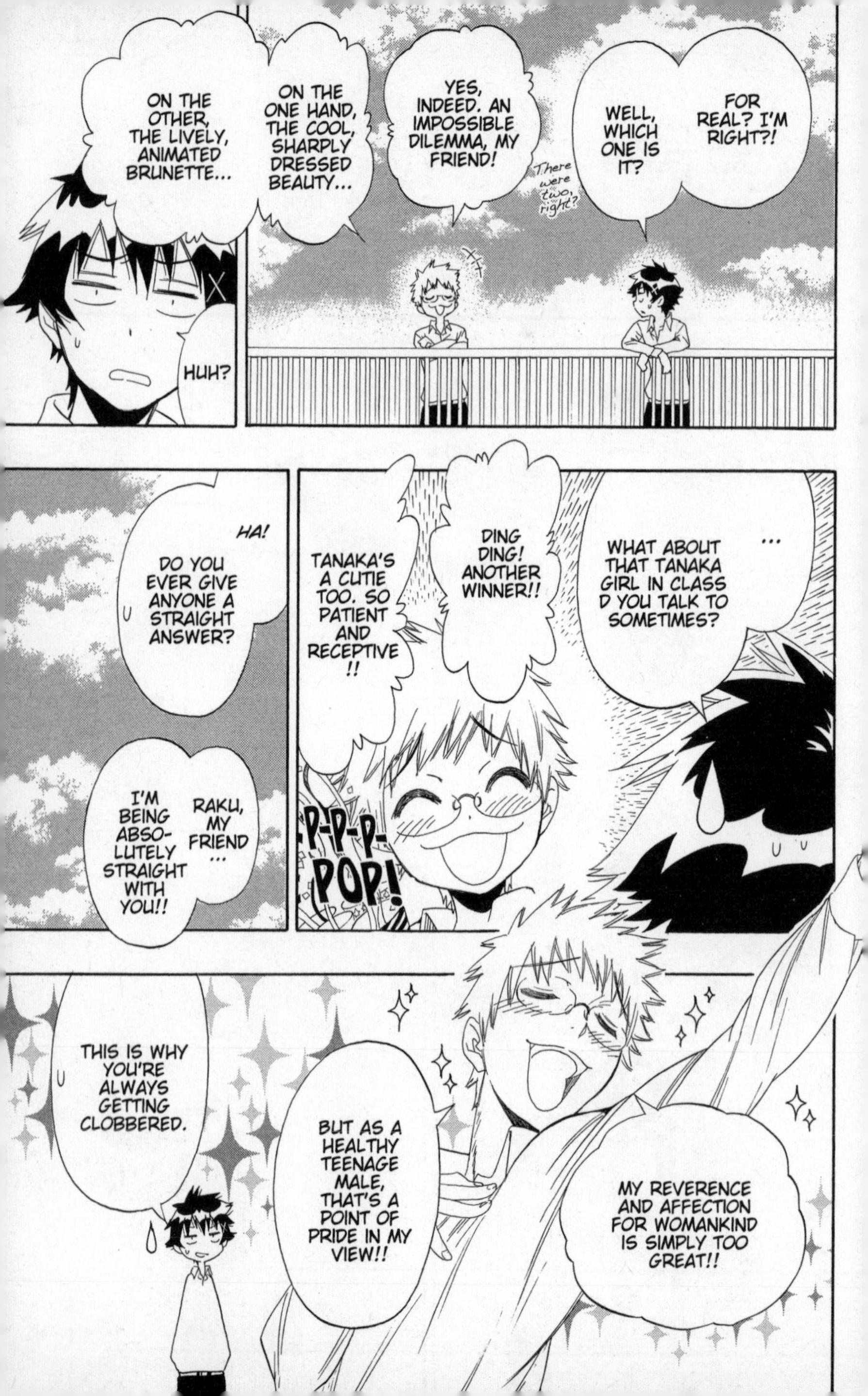
FOR REAL? I'M RIGHT?!
WELL, WHICH ONE IS IT?
There were two, right?
YES, INDEED. AN IMPOSSIBLE DILEMMA, MY FRIEND!
ON THE ONE HAND, THE COOL, SHARPLY DRESSED BEAUTY...
ON THE OTHER, THE LIVELY, ANIMATED BRUNETTE...
HUH?
...
WHAT ABOUT THAT TANAKA GIRL IN CLASS D YOU TALK TO SOMETIMES?
DING DING! ANOTHER WINNER!!
TANAKA'S A CUTIE TOO. SO PATIENT AND RECEPTIVE!!
P-P-P-POP!
HA!
DO YOU EVER GIVE ANYONE A STRAIGHT ANSWER?
RAKU, MY FRIEND...
I'M BEING ABSOLUTELY STRAIGHT WITH YOU!!
MY REVERENCE AND AFFECTION FOR WOMANKIND IS SIMPLY TOO GREAT!!
BUT AS A HEALTHY TEENAGE MALE, THAT'S A POINT OF PRIDE IN MY VIEW!!
THIS IS WHY YOU'RE ALWAYS GETTING CLOBBERED.

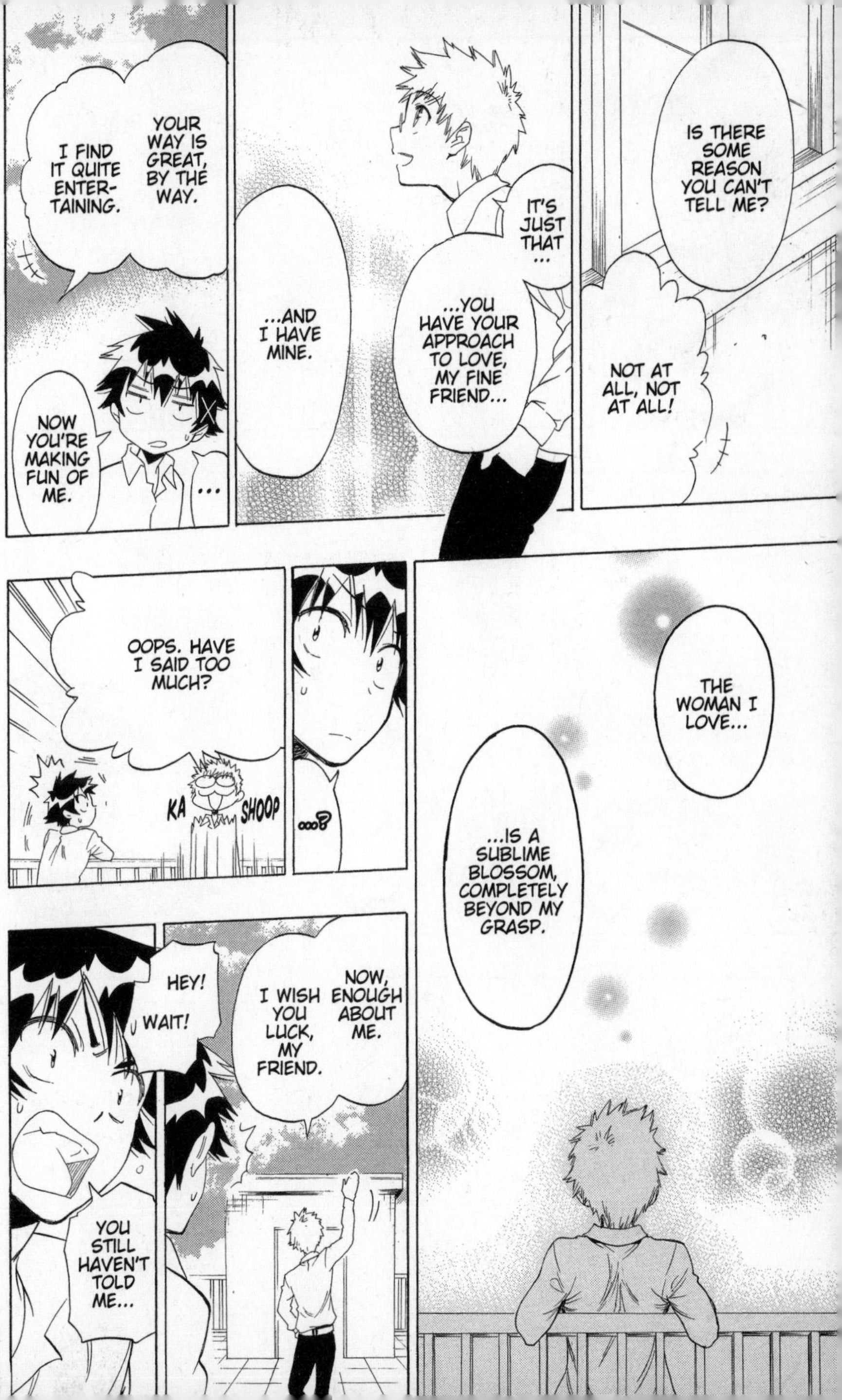
IS THERE SOME REASON YOU CAN'T TELL ME?
NOT AT ALL, NOT AT ALL!
IT'S JUST THAT...
...YOU HAVE YOUR APPROACH TO LOVE, MY FINE FRIEND...
...AND I HAVE MINE.
YOUR WAY IS GREAT, BY THE WAY.
I FIND IT QUITE ENTER-TAINING.
NOW YOU'RE MAKING FUN OF ME.
...
THE WOMAN I LOVE...
...IS A SUBLIME BLOSSOM, COMPLETELY BEYOND MY GRASP.
...?
OOPS. HAVE I SAID TOO MUCH?
KA
SHOOP
NOW, ENOUGH ABOUT ME.
I WISH YOU LUCK, MY FRIEND.
HEY!
WAIT!
YOU STILL HAVEN'T TOLD ME...

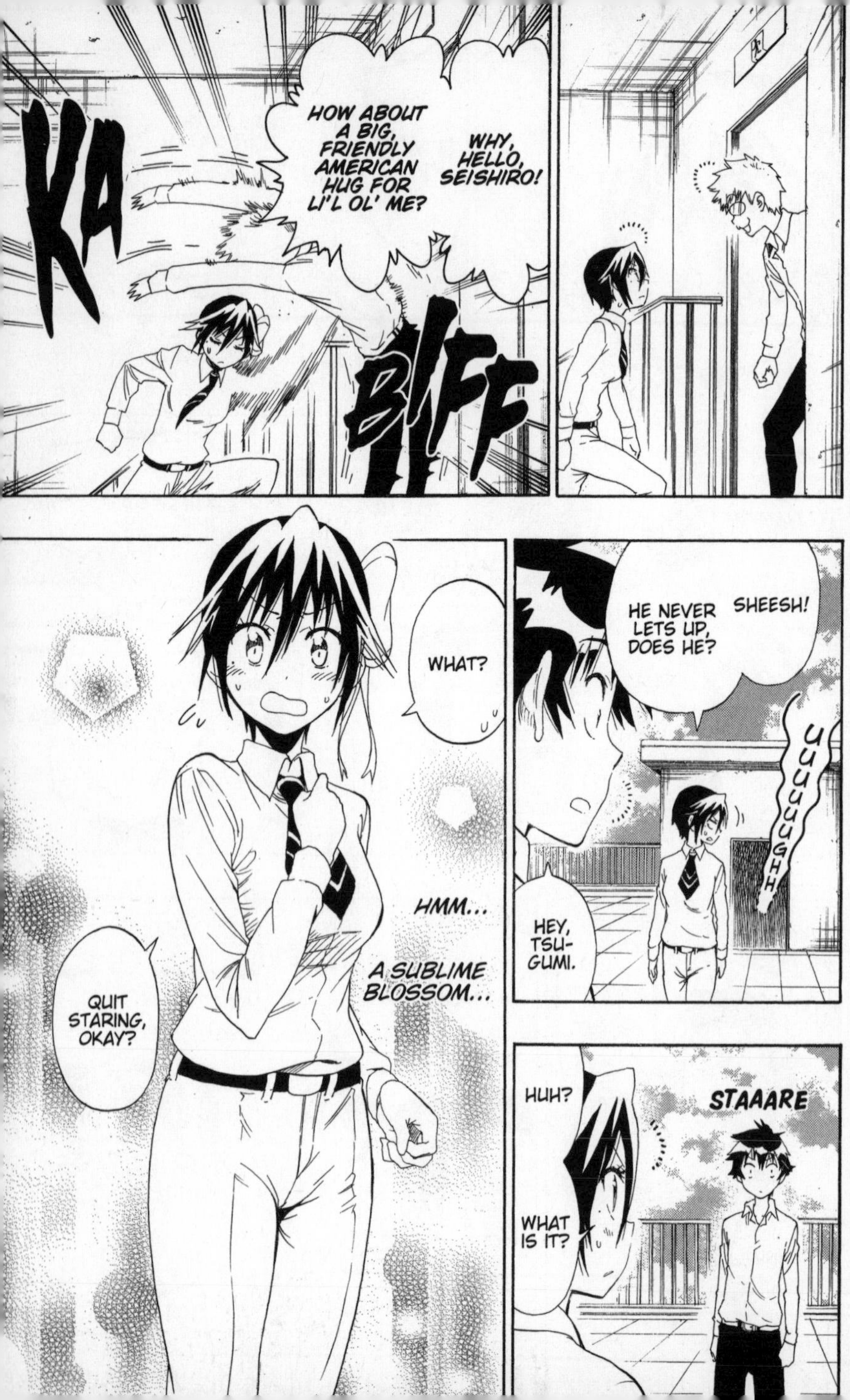
WHY, HELLO, SEISHIRO!
HOW ABOUT A BIG, FRIENDLY AMERICAN HUG FOR LI'L OL' ME?
KA
BIFF
SHEESH!
HE NEVER LETS UP, DOES HE?
UUUUUUGHH
HEY, TSU-GUMI.
HUH?
STAAARE
WHAT IS IT?
WHAT?
HMM...
A SUBLIME BLOSSOM...
QUIT STARING, OKAY?

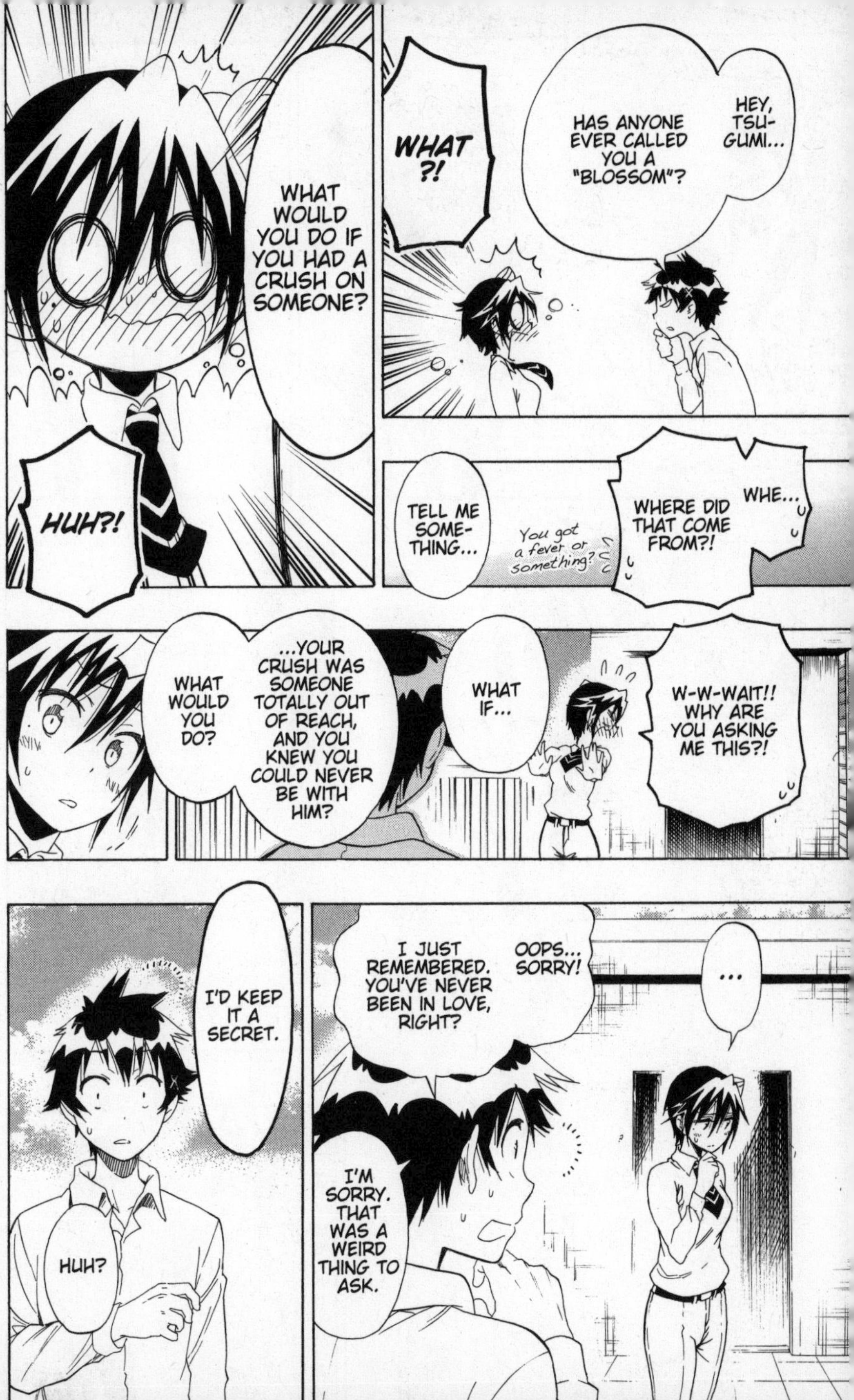
HEY, TSUGUMI...
HAS ANYONE EVER CALLED YOU A "BLOSSOM"?
WHAT?!
WHE...
WHERE DID THAT COME FROM?!
You got a fever or something?
TELL ME SOMETHING...
WHAT WOULD YOU DO IF YOU HAD A CRUSH ON SOMEONE?
HUH?!
W-W-WAIT!! WHY ARE YOU ASKING ME THIS?!
WHAT IF...
...YOUR CRUSH WAS SOMEONE TOTALLY OUT OF REACH, AND YOU KNEW YOU COULD NEVER BE WITH HIM?
WHAT WOULD YOU DO?
...
OOPS... SORRY!
I JUST REMEMBERED. YOU'VE NEVER BEEN IN LOVE, RIGHT?
I'M SORRY. THAT WAS A WEIRD THING TO ASK.
I'D KEEP IT A SECRET.
HUH?

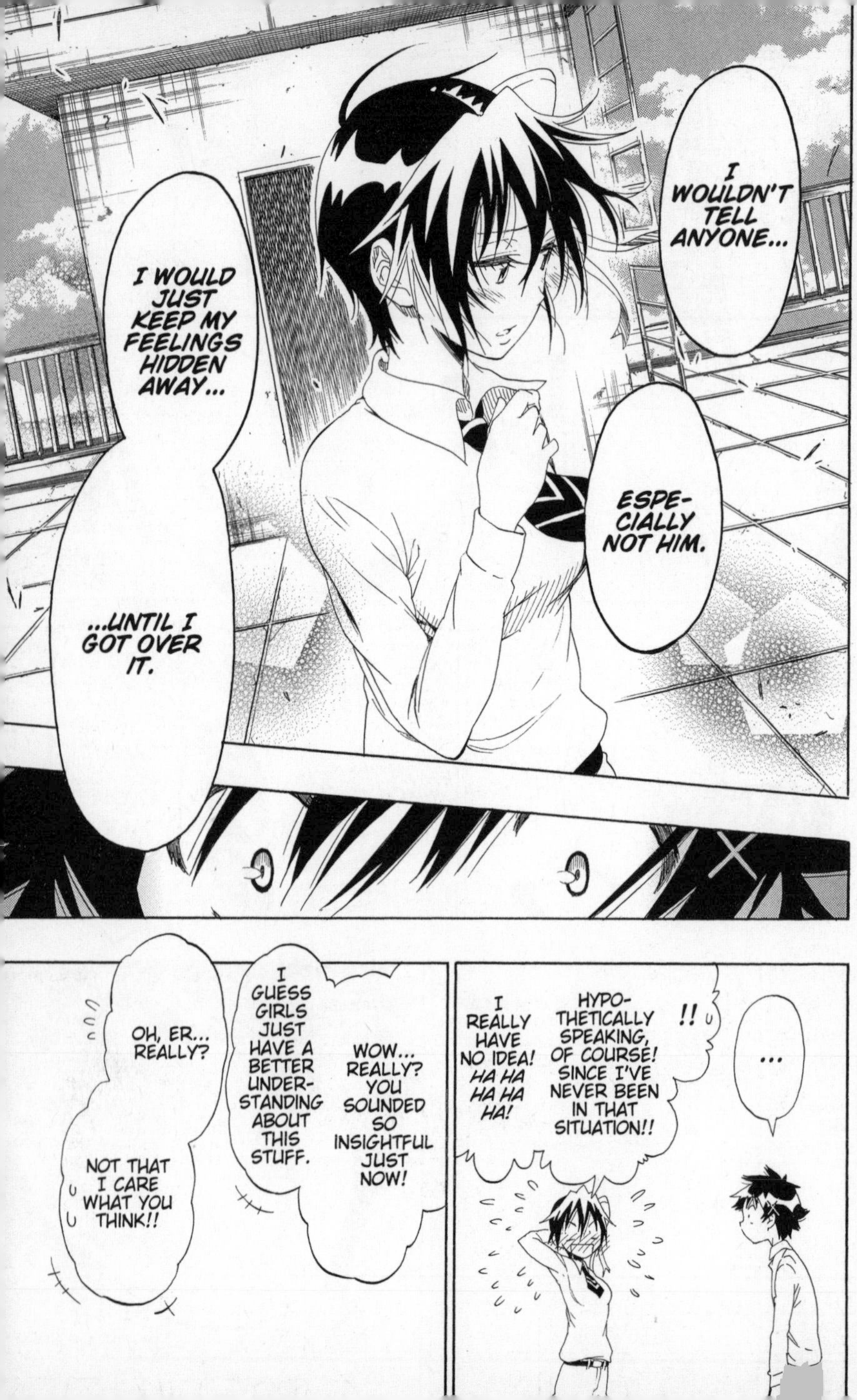
I WOULDN'T TELL ANYONE...
ESPE-CIALLY NOT HIM.
I WOULD JUST KEEP MY FEELINGS HIDDEN AWAY...
...UNTIL I GOT OVER IT.
...
!!
HYPO-THETICALLY SPEAKING, OF COURSE! SINCE I'VE NEVER BEEN IN THAT SITUATION!!
I REALLY HAVE NO IDEA! HA HA HA HA HA!
WOW... REALLY? YOU SOUNDED SO INSIGHTFUL JUST NOW!
I GUESS GIRLS JUST HAVE A BETTER UNDER-STANDING ABOUT THIS STUFF.
OH, ER... REALLY?
NOT THAT I CARE WHAT YOU THINK!!

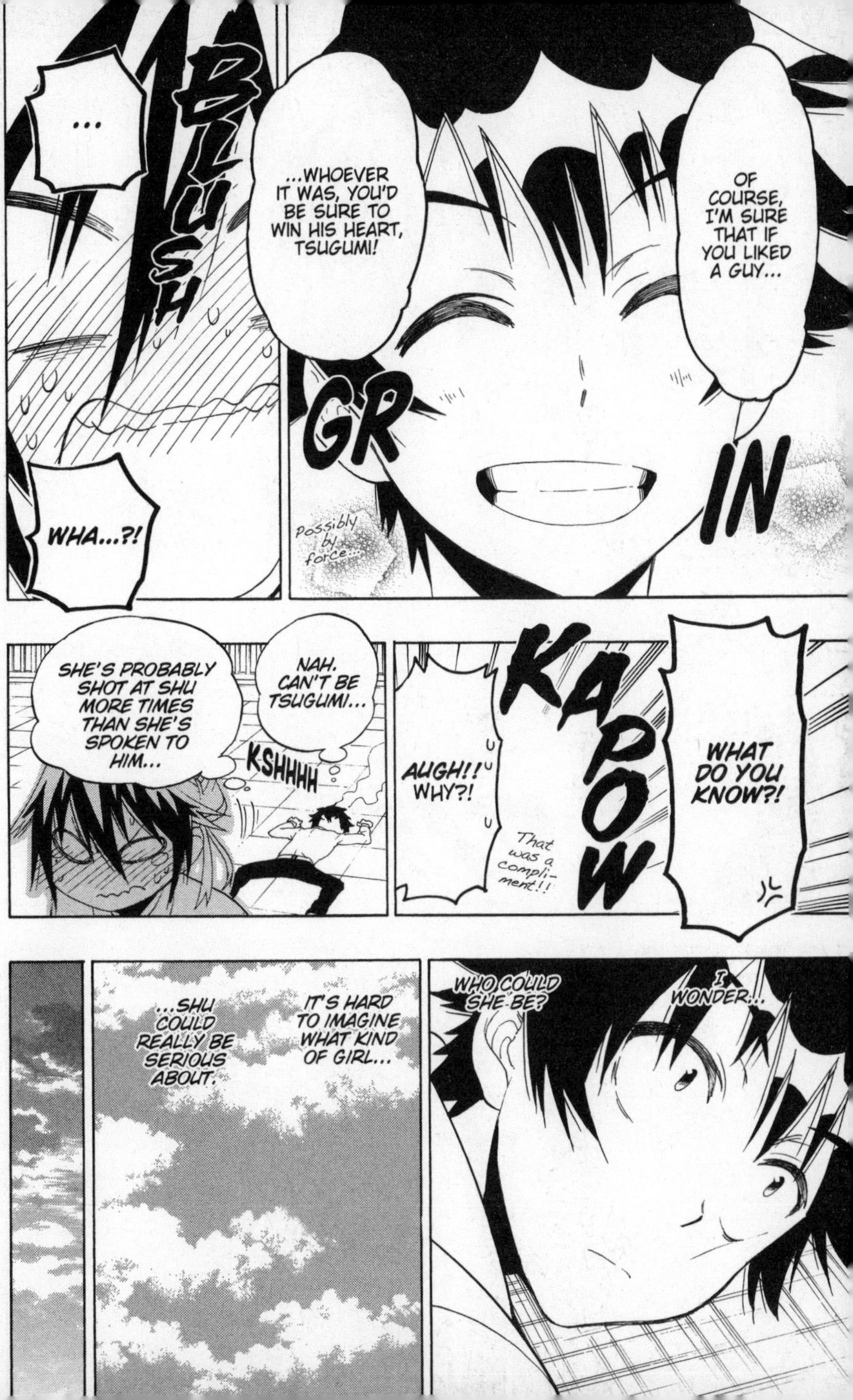
OF COURSE, I'M SURE THAT IF YOU LIKED A GUY...
...WHOEVER IT WAS, YOU'D BE SURE TO WIN HIS HEART, TSUGUMI!
GRIN
Possibly by force...
...
BLUSH
WHA...?!
WHAT DO YOU KNOW?!
KAPOW
AUGH!! WHY?!
That was a compli-ment!!
NAH. CAN'T BE TSUGUMI...
SHE'S PROBABLY SHOT AT SHU MORE TIMES THAN SHE'S SPOKEN TO HIM...
KSHHHH
I WONDER...
WHO COULD SHE BE?
IT'S HARD TO IMAGINE WHAT KIND OF GIRL...
...SHU COULD REALLY BE SERIOUS ABOUT.

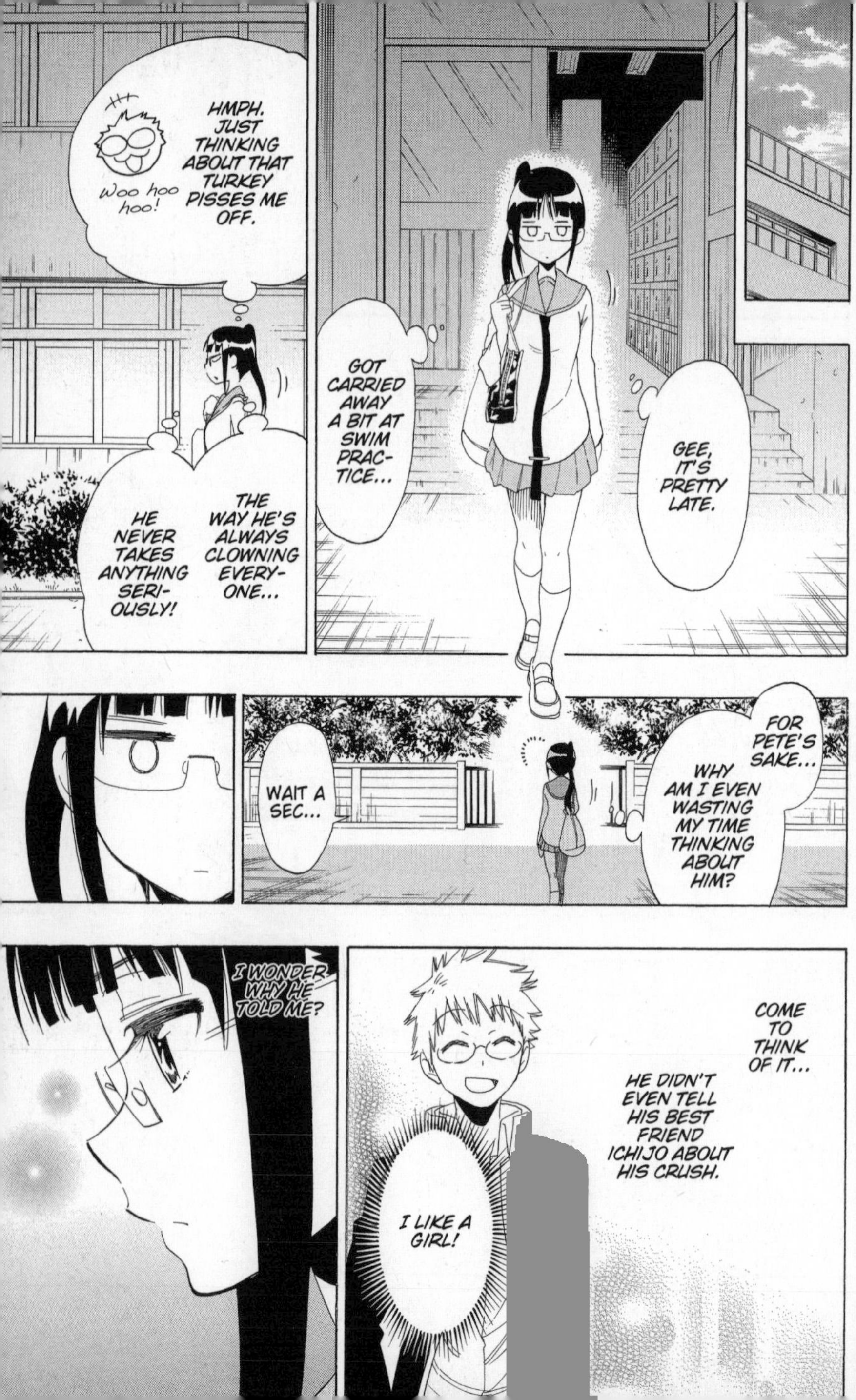
GEE, IT'S PRETTY LATE.
GOT CARRIED AWAY A BIT AT SWIM PRACTICE...
HMPH. JUST THINKING ABOUT THAT TURKEY PISSES ME OFF.
Woo hoo hoo!
THE WAY HE'S ALWAYS CLOWNING EVERYONE...
HE NEVER TAKES ANYTHING SERIOUSLY!
FOR PETE'S SAKE...
WHY AM I EVEN WASTING MY TIME THINKING ABOUT HIM?
WAIT A SEC...
COME TO THINK OF IT...
HE DIDN'T EVEN TELL HIS BEST FRIEND ICHIJO ABOUT HIS CRUSH.
I LIKE A GIRL!
I WONDER WHY HE TOLD ME?

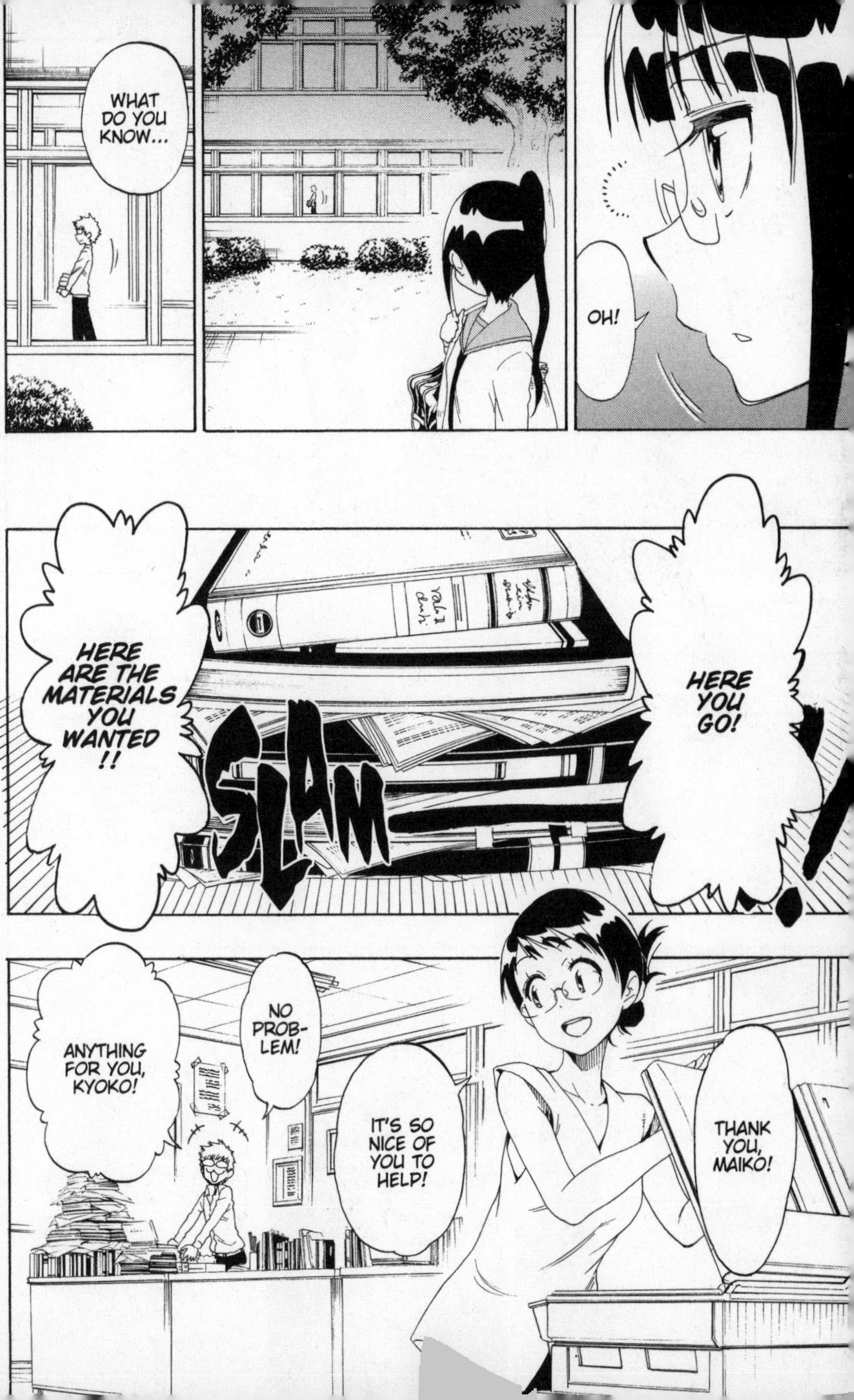
OH!
WHAT DO YOU KNOW...
HERE YOU GO!
HERE ARE THE MATERIALS YOU WANTED!!
SLAM
THANK YOU, MAIKO!
IT'S SO NICE OF YOU TO HELP!
NO PROBLEM!
ANYTHING FOR YOU, KYOKO!

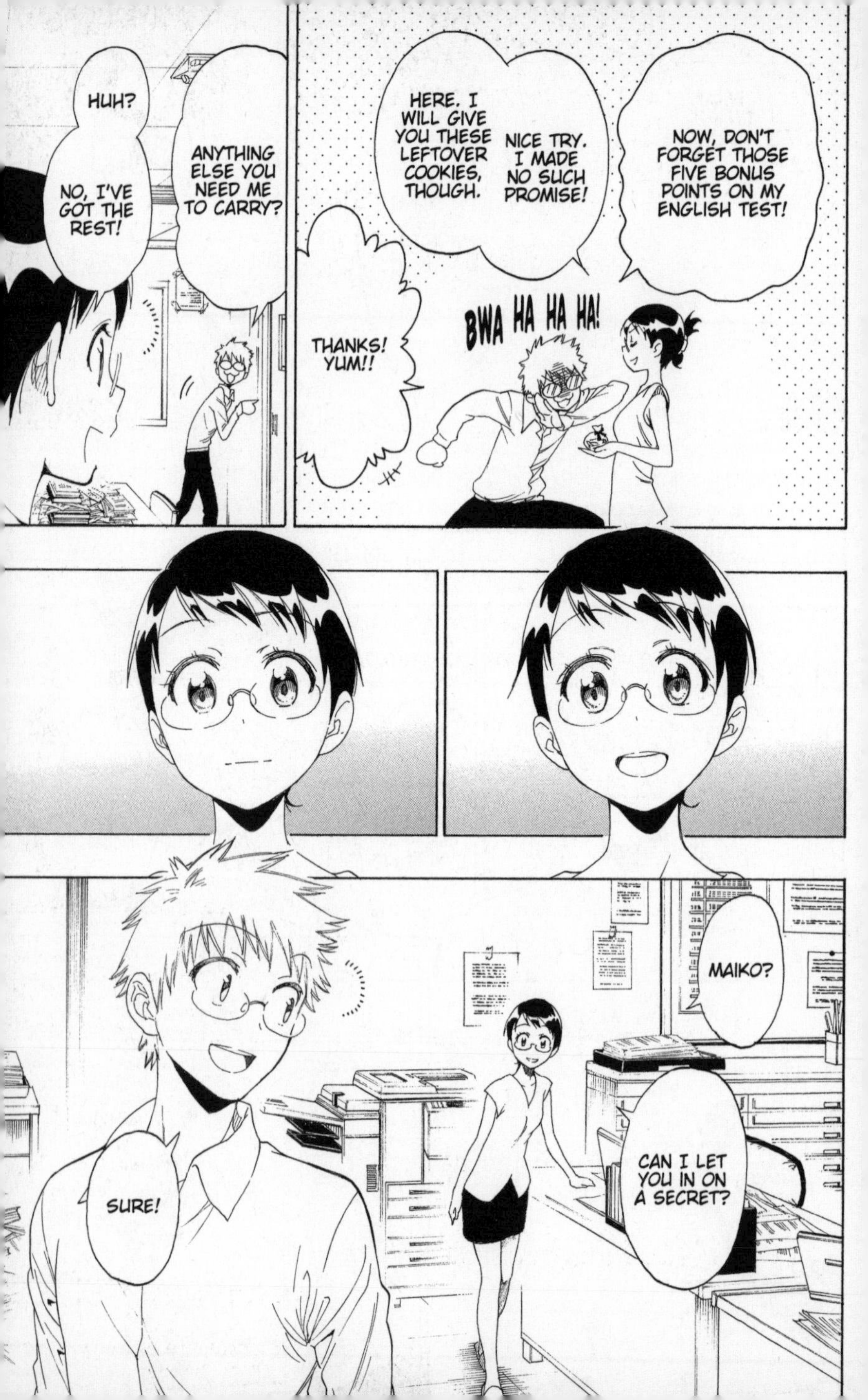
NOW, DON'T FORGET THOSE FIVE BONUS POINTS ON MY ENGLISH TEST!
NICE TRY. I MADE NO SUCH PROMISE!
HERE. I WILL GIVE YOU THESE LEFTOVER COOKIES, THOUGH.
BWA HA HA HA!
THANKS! YUM!!
ANYTHING ELSE YOU NEED ME TO CARRY?
HUH?
NO, I'VE GOT THE REST!
MAIKO?
CAN I LET YOU IN ON A SECRET?
SURE!

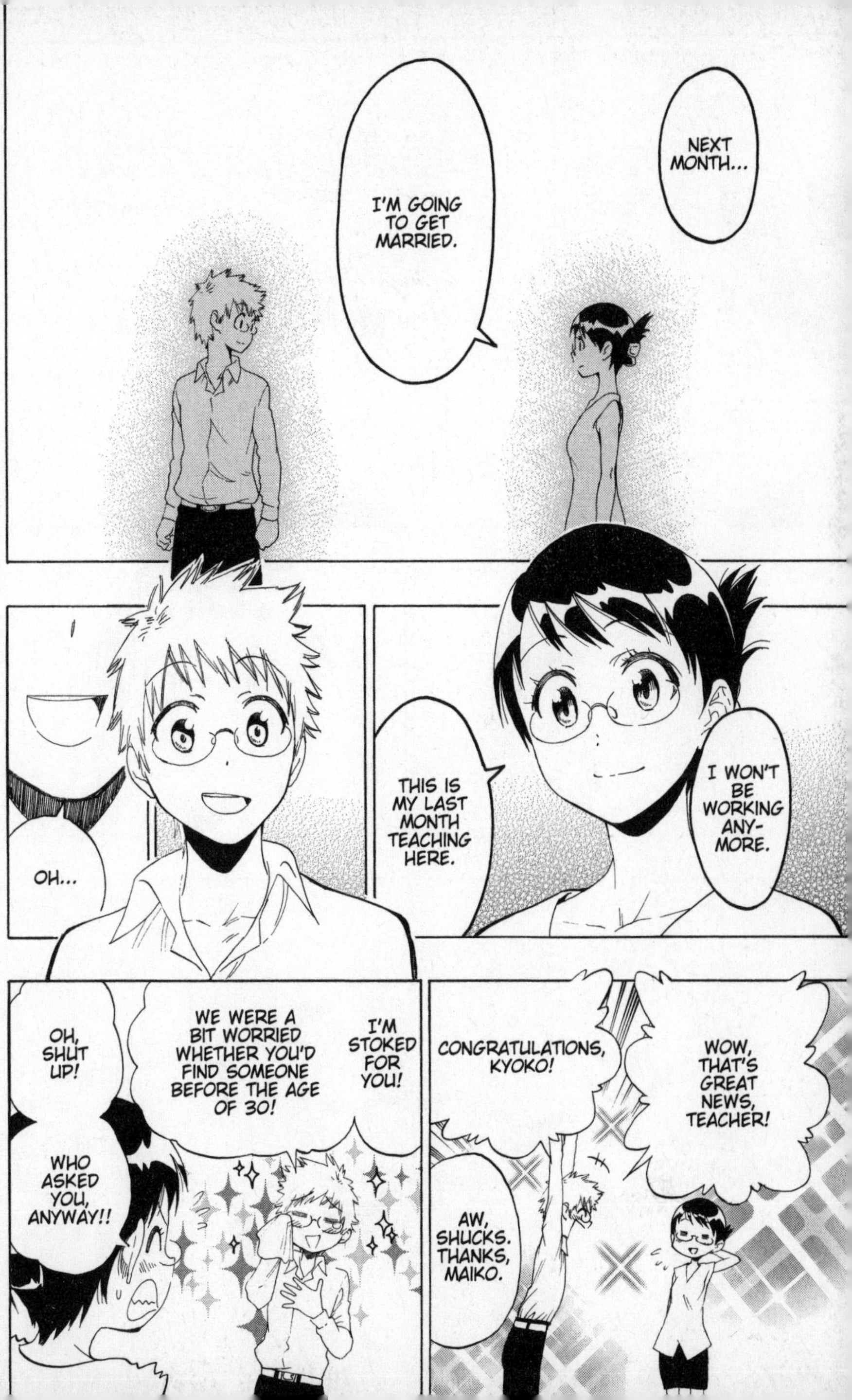
NEXT MONTH...
I'M GOING TO GET MARRIED.
I WON'T BE WORKING ANY-MORE.
THIS IS MY LAST MONTH TEACHING HERE.
OH...
WOW, THAT'S GREAT NEWS, TEACHER!
CONGRATULATIONS, KYOKO!
AW, SHUCKS. THANKS, MAIKO.
I'M STOKED FOR YOU!
WE WERE A BIT WORRIED WHETHER YOU'D FIND SOMEONE BEFORE THE AGE OF 30!
OH, SHUT UP!
WHO ASKED YOU, ANYWAY!!

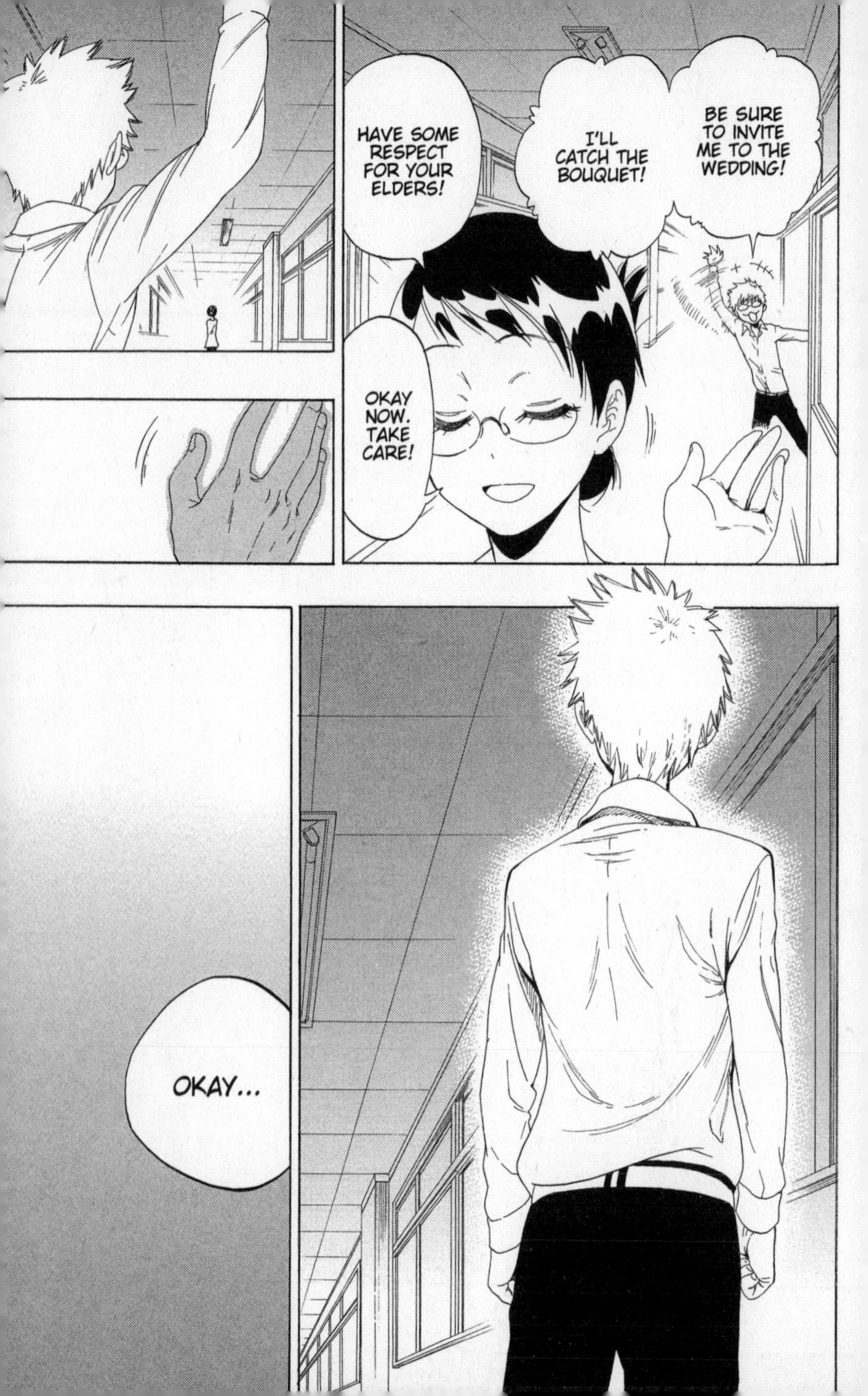
BE SURE TO INVITE ME TO THE WEDDING!
I'LL CATCH THE BOUQUET!
HAVE SOME RESPECT FOR YOUR ELDERS!
OKAY NOW. TAKE CARE!
OKAY...

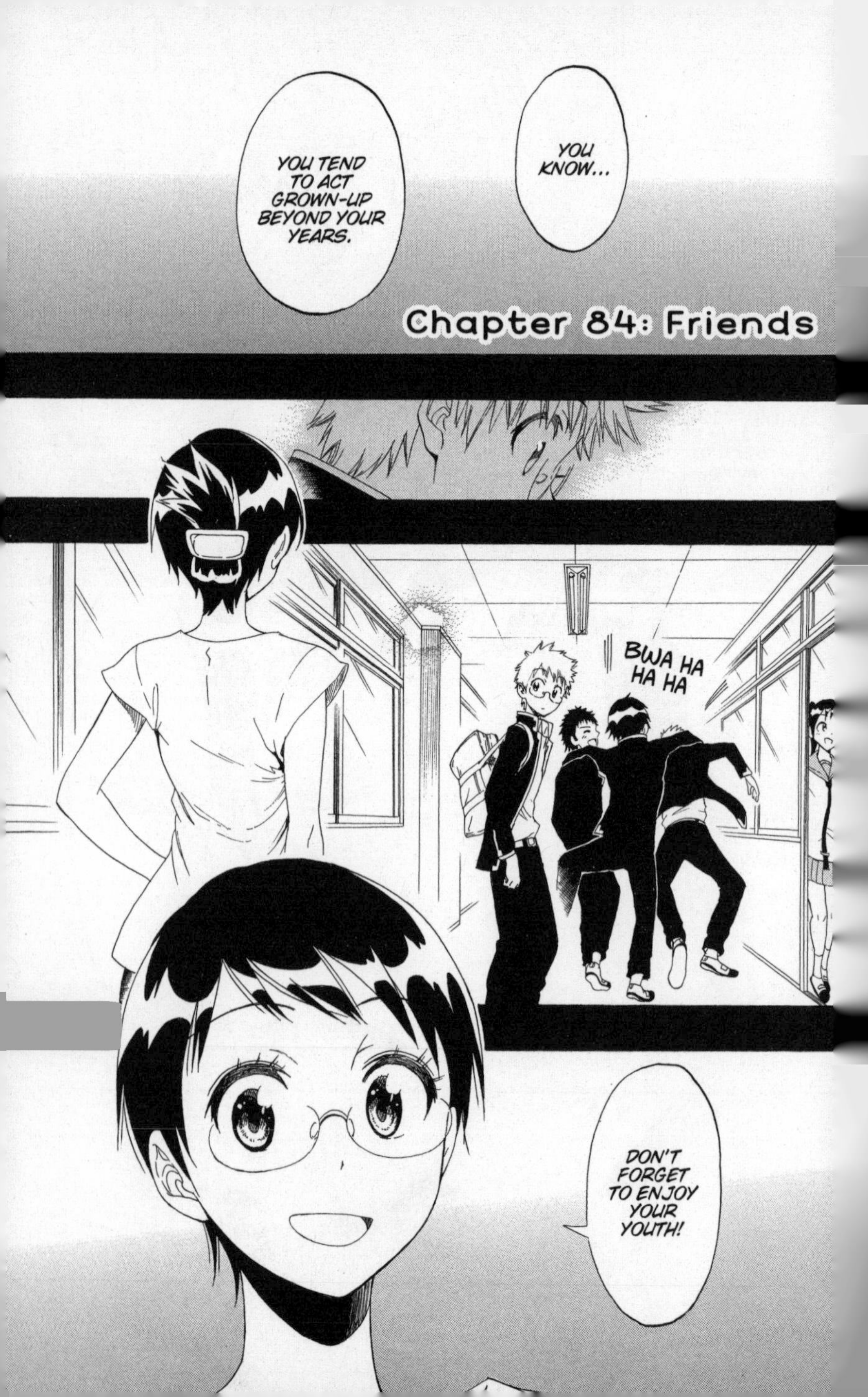
YOU KNOW...
YOU TEND TO ACT GROWN-UP BEYOND YOUR YEARS.
Chapter 84: Friends
BWA HA HA HA
DON'T FORGET TO ENJOY YOUR YOUTH!

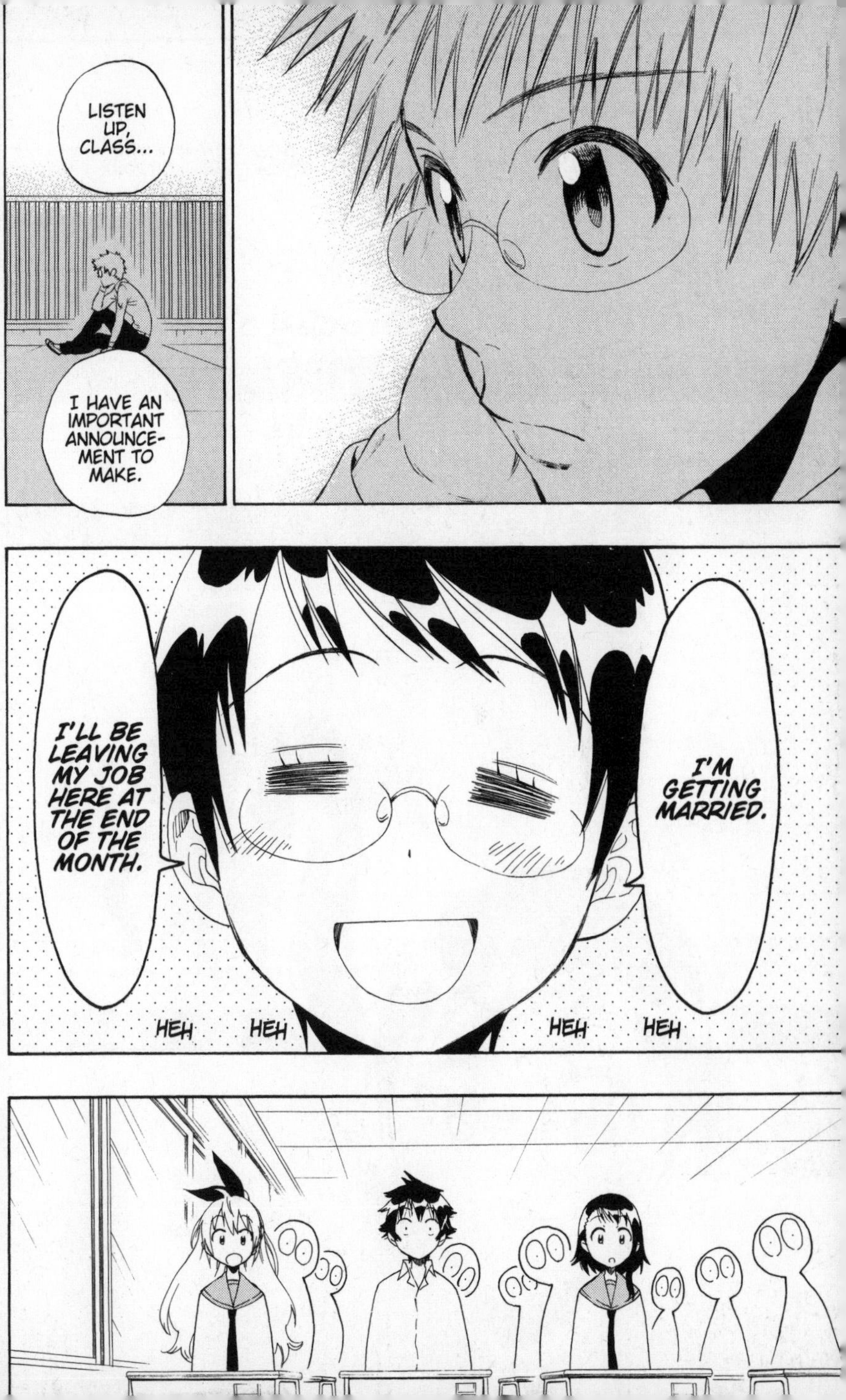
LISTEN UP, CLASS...
I HAVE AN IMPORTANT ANNOUNCE-MENT TO MAKE.
I'M GETTING MARRIED.
I'LL BE LEAVING MY JOB HERE AT THE END OF THE MONTH.
HEH HEH HEH HEH

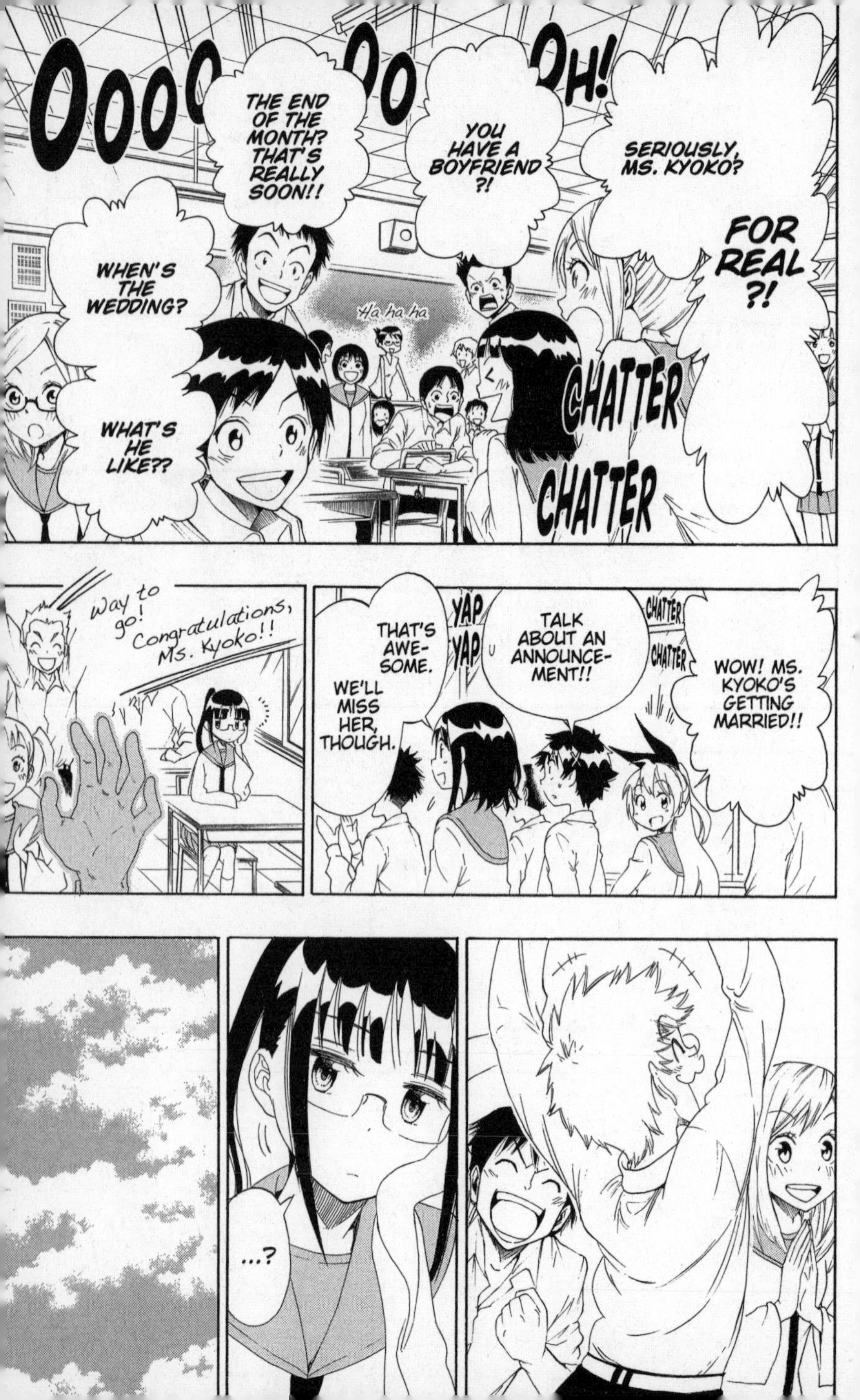
SERIOUSLY, MS. KYOKO?
FOR REAL?!
OOOO OO OH!
YOU HAVE A BOYFRIEND?!
THE END OF THE MONTH? THAT'S REALLY SOON!!
CHATTER CHATTER
Ha ha ha
WHEN'S THE WEDDING?
WHAT'S HE LIKE??
WOW! MS. KYOKO'S GETTING MARRIED!!
CHATTER CHATTER
TALK ABOUT AN ANNOUNCE-MENT!!
YAP YAP
THAT'S AWE-SOME.
WE'LL MISS HER, THOUGH.
Way to go!
Congratulations, Ms. Kyoko!!
...?

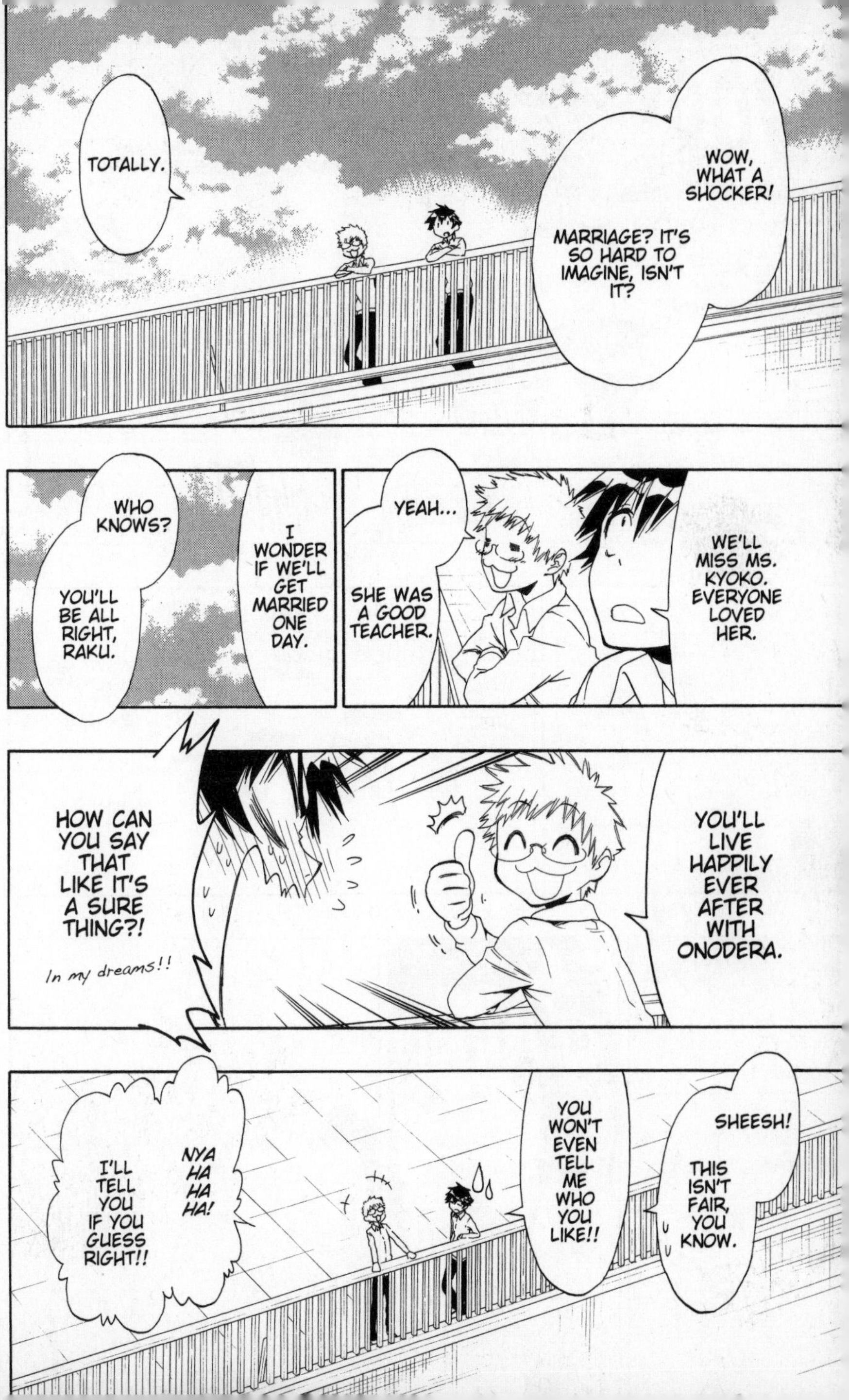
WOW, WHAT A SHOCKER!
MARRIAGE? IT'S SO HARD TO IMAGINE, ISN'T IT?
TOTALLY.
WE'LL MISS MS. KYOKO. EVERYONE LOVED HER.
YEAH...
SHE WAS A GOOD TEACHER.
I WONDER IF WE'LL GET MARRIED ONE DAY.
WHO KNOWS?
YOU'LL BE ALL RIGHT, RAKU.
YOU'LL LIVE HAPPILY EVER AFTER WITH ONODERA.
HOW CAN YOU SAY THAT LIKE IT'S A SURE THING?!
In my dreams!!
SHEESH!
THIS ISN'T FAIR, YOU KNOW.
YOU WON'T EVEN TELL ME WHO YOU LIKE!!
NYA HA HA HA!
I'LL TELL YOU IF YOU GUESS RIGHT!!

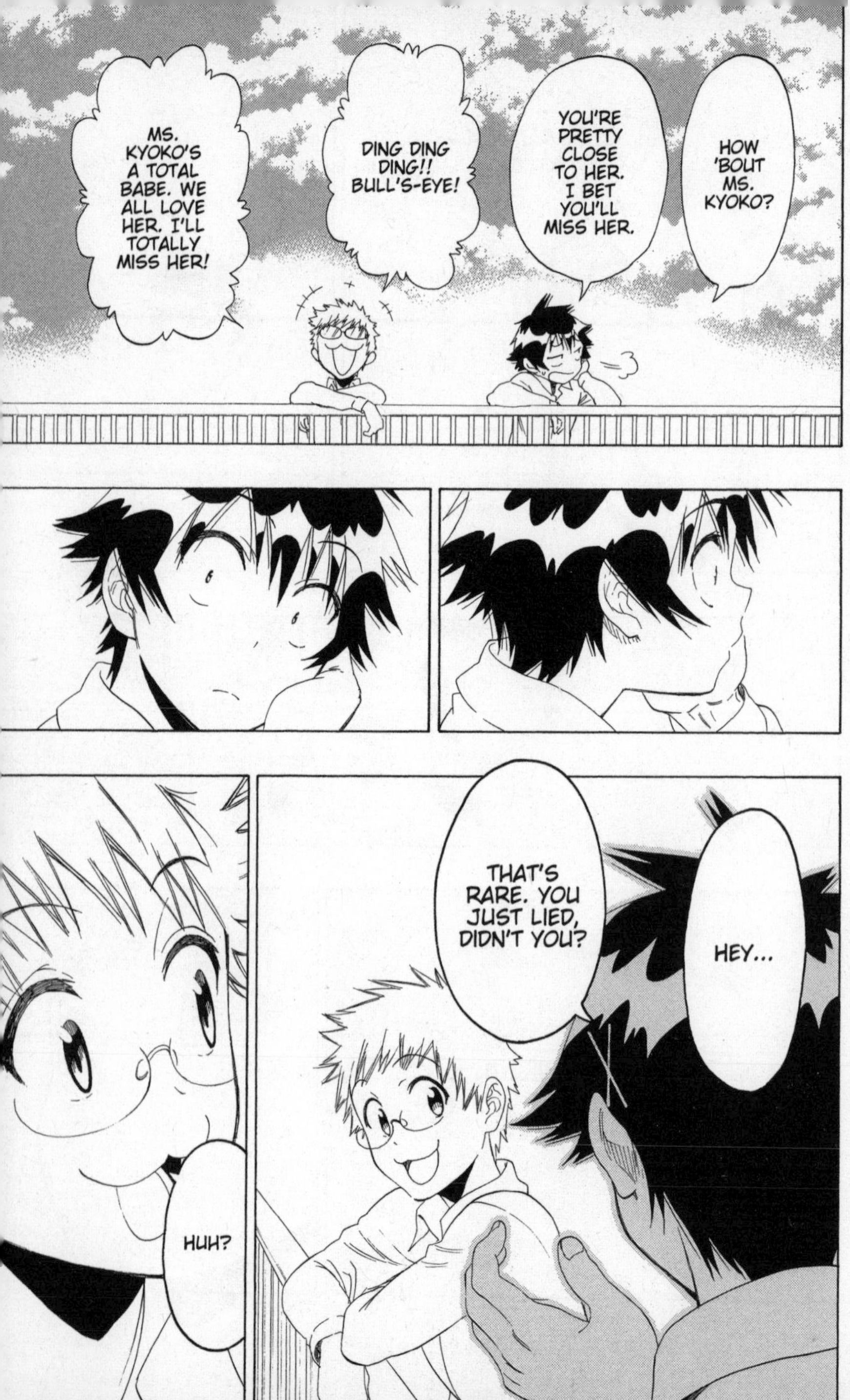
HOW 'BOUT MS. KYOKO?
YOU'RE PRETTY CLOSE TO HER. I BET YOU'LL MISS HER.
DING DING DING!! BULL'S-EYE!
MS. KYOKO'S A TOTAL BABE. WE ALL LOVE HER. I'LL TOTALLY MISS HER!
HEY...
THAT'S RARE. YOU JUST LIED, DIDN'T YOU?
HUH?

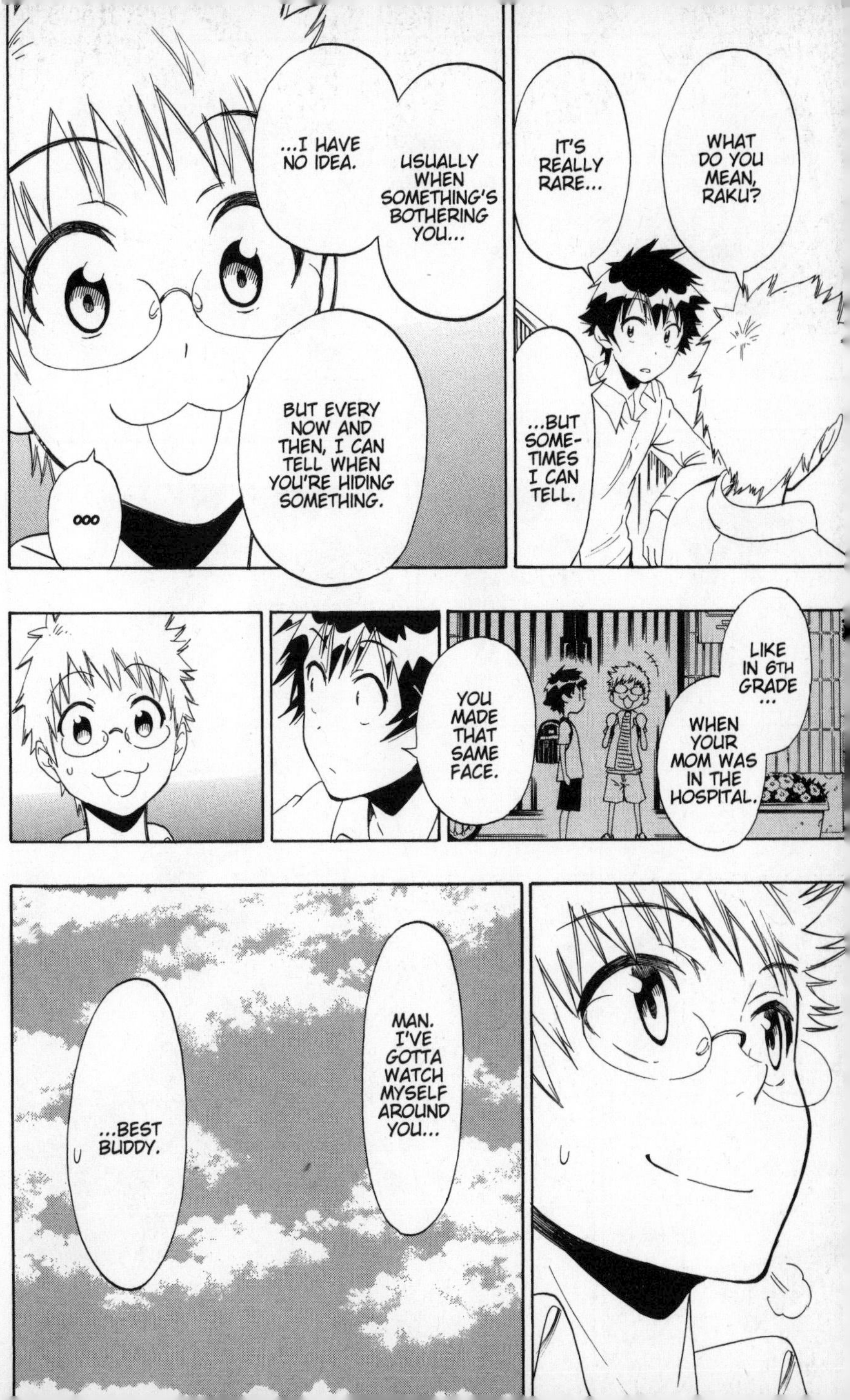
WHAT DO YOU MEAN, RAKU?
IT'S REALLY RARE...
...BUT SOME-TIMES I CAN TELL.
USUALLY WHEN SOMETHING'S BOTHERING YOU...
...I HAVE NO IDEA.
BUT EVERY NOW AND THEN, I CAN TELL WHEN YOU'RE HIDING SOMETHING.
ooo
LIKE IN 6TH GRADE...
WHEN YOUR MOM WAS IN THE HOSPITAL.
YOU MADE THAT SAME FACE.
MAN. I'VE GOTTA WATCH MYSELF AROUND YOU...
...BEST BUDDY.

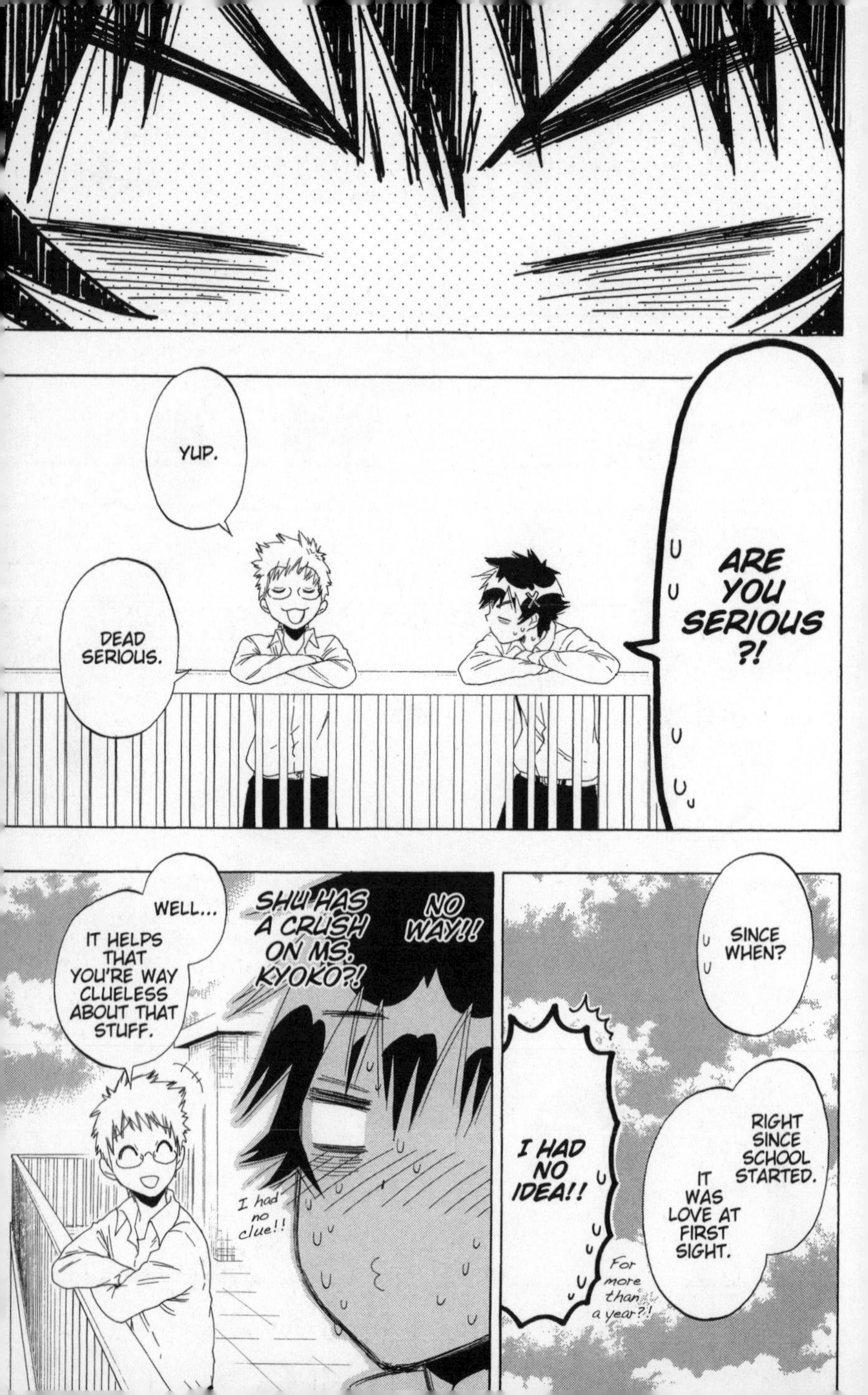
ARE YOU SERIOUS?!
YUP.
DEAD SERIOUS.
SINCE WHEN?
RIGHT SINCE SCHOOL STARTED.
IT WAS LOVE AT FIRST SIGHT.
I HAD NO IDEA!!
For more than a year?!
NO WAY!!
SHU HAS A CRUSH ON MS. KYOKO?!
I had no clue!!
WELL...
IT HELPS THAT YOU'RE WAY CLUELESS ABOUT THAT STUFF.

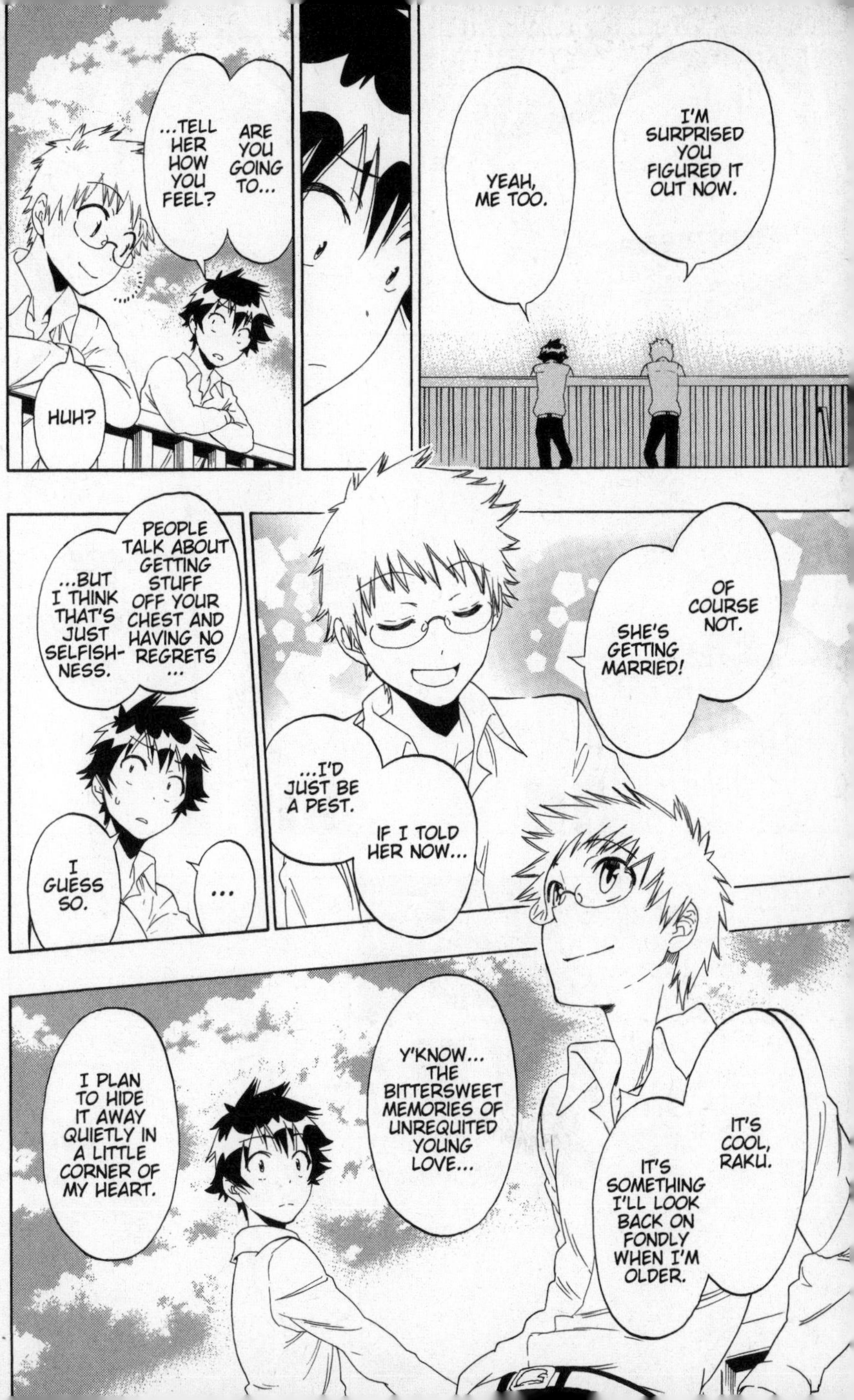
I'M SURPRISED YOU FIGURED IT OUT NOW.
YEAH, ME TOO.
ARE YOU GOING TO...
...TELL HER HOW YOU FEEL?
HUH?
OF COURSE NOT.
SHE'S GETTING MARRIED!
IF I TOLD HER NOW...
...I'D JUST BE A PEST.
PEOPLE TALK ABOUT GETTING STUFF OFF YOUR CHEST AND HAVING NO REGRETS...
...BUT I THINK THAT'S JUST SELFISH-NESS.
...
I GUESS SO.
IT'S COOL, RAKU.
IT'S SOMETHING I'LL LOOK BACK ON FONDLY WHEN I'M OLDER.
Y'KNOW... THE BITTERSWEET MEMORIES OF UNREQUITED YOUNG LOVE...
I PLAN TO HIDE IT AWAY QUIETLY IN A LITTLE CORNER OF MY HEART.

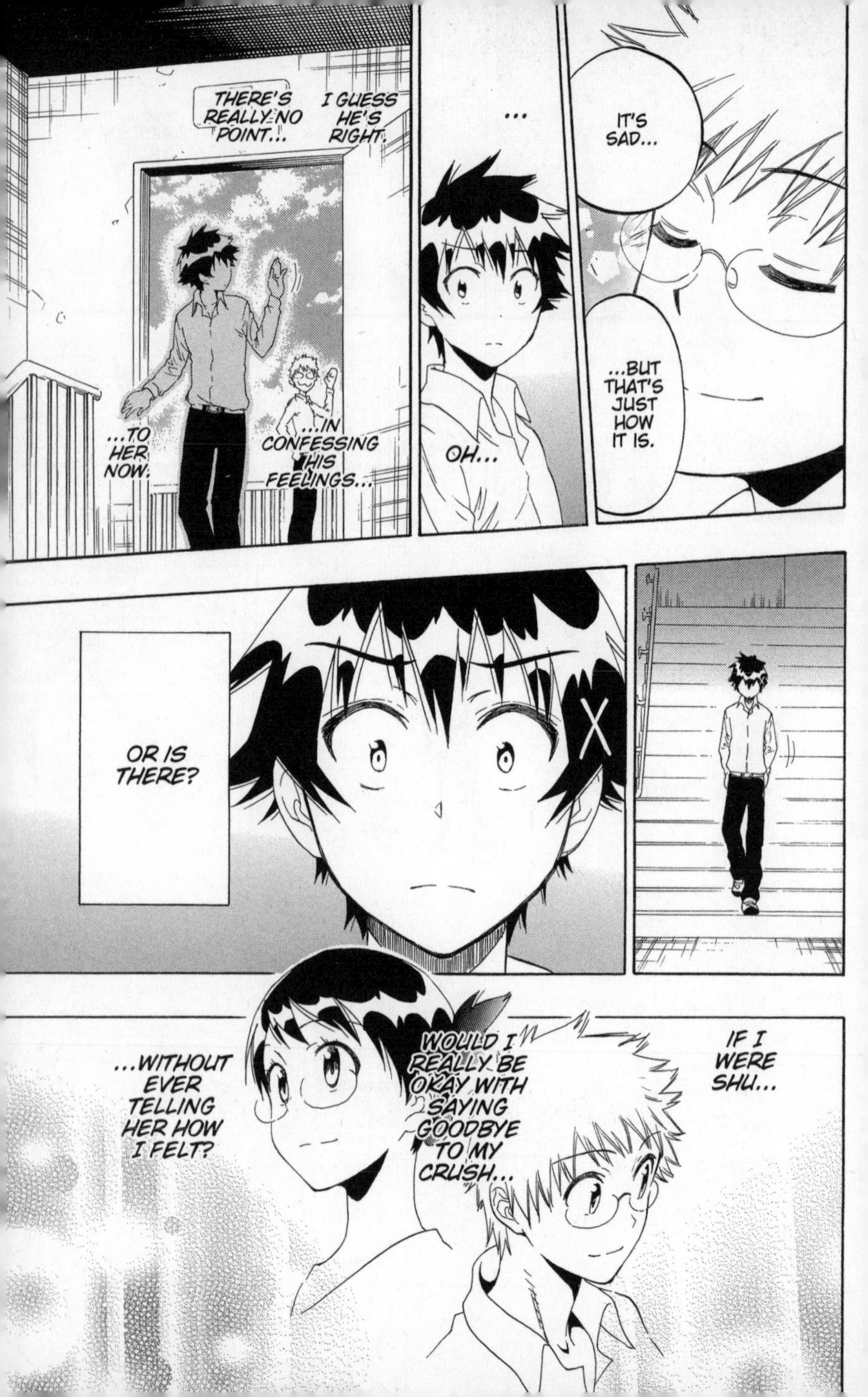
IT'S SAD...
...BUT THAT'S JUST HOW IT IS.
...
OH...
I GUESS HE'S RIGHT.
THERE'S REALLY NO POINT...
...IN CONFESSING THIS FEELINGS...
...TO HER NOW.
OR IS THERE?
IF I WERE SHU...
WOULD I REALLY BE OKAY WITH SAYING GOODBYE TO MY CRUSH...
...WITHOUT EVER TELLING HER HOW I FELT?

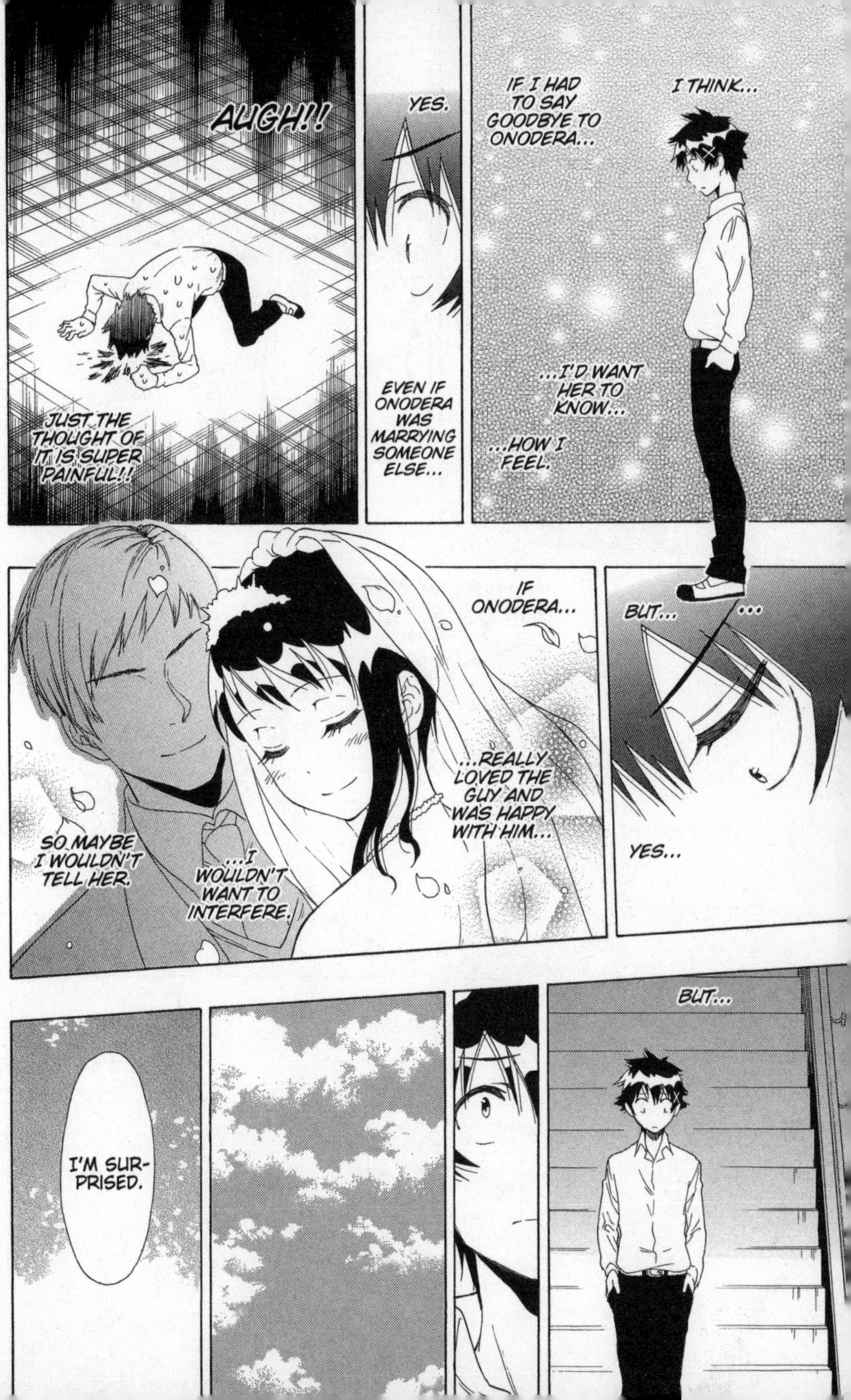
I THINK...
IF I HAD TO SAY GOODBYE TO ONODERA...
...I'D WANT HER TO KNOW...
...HOW I FEEL.
YES.
EVEN IF ONODERA WAS MARRYING SOMEONE ELSE...
AUGH!!
JUST THE THOUGHT OF IT IS SUPER PAINFUL!!
BUT...
...
YES...
IF ONODERA...
...REALLY LOVED THE GUY AND WAS HAPPY WITH HIM...
...I WOULDN'T WANT TO INTERFERE.
SO MAYBE I WOULDN'T TELL HER.
BUT...
I'M SUR-PRISED.

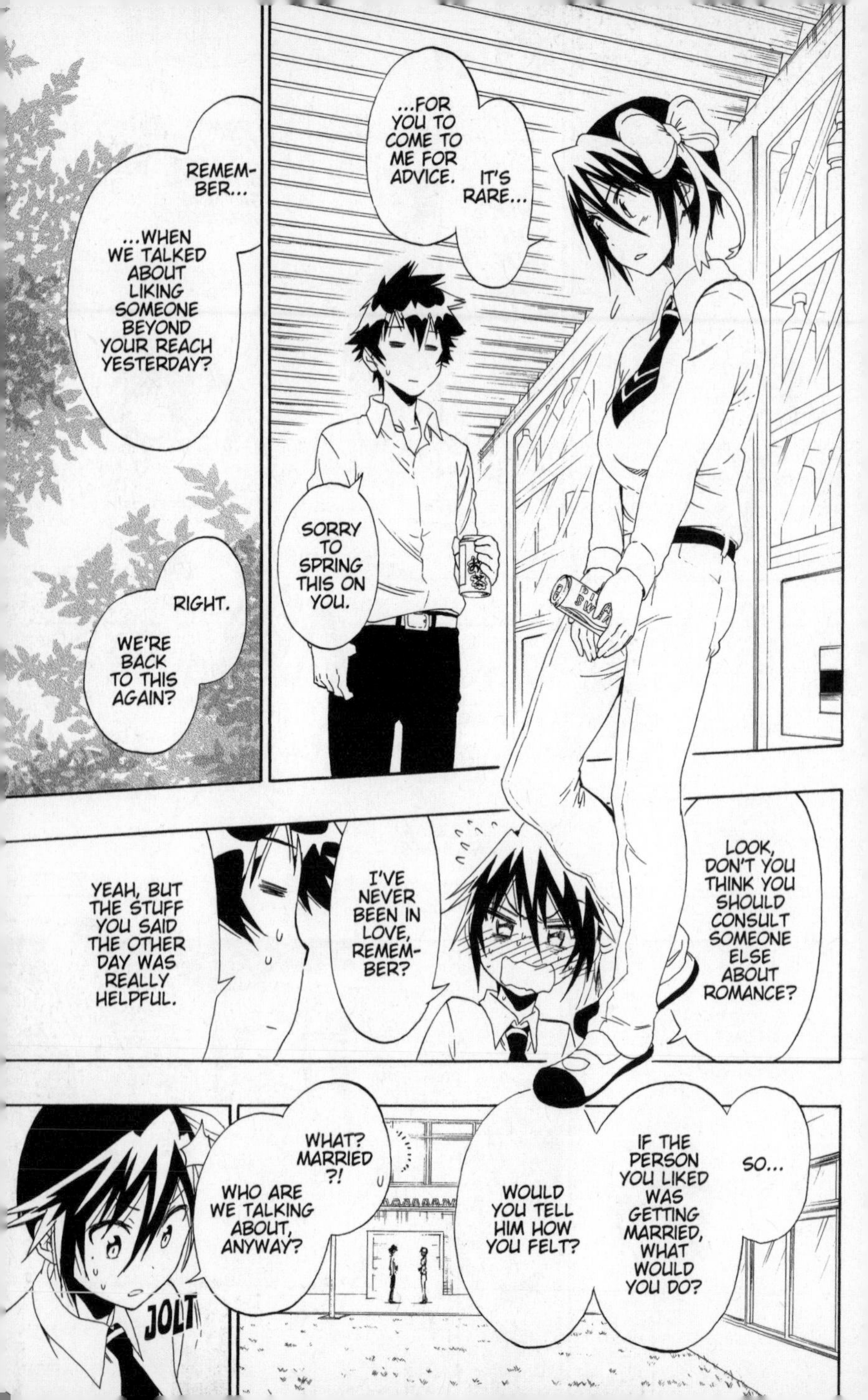
IT'S RARE... ...FOR YOU TO COME TO ME FOR ADVICE.
SORRY TO SPRING THIS ON YOU.
REMEMBER... ...WHEN WE TALKED ABOUT LIKING SOMEONE BEYOND YOUR REACH YESTERDAY?
RIGHT. WE'RE BACK TO THIS AGAIN?
LOOK, DON'T YOU THINK YOU SHOULD CONSULT SOMEONE ELSE ABOUT ROMANCE?
I'VE NEVER BEEN IN LOVE, REMEMBER?
YEAH, BUT THE STUFF YOU SAID THE OTHER DAY WAS REALLY HELPFUL.
SO... IF THE PERSON YOU LIKED WAS GETTING MARRIED, WHAT WOULD YOU DO?
WOULD YOU TELL HIM HOW YOU FELT?
WHAT? MARRIED ?!
WHO ARE WE TALKING ABOUT, ANYWAY?
JOLT

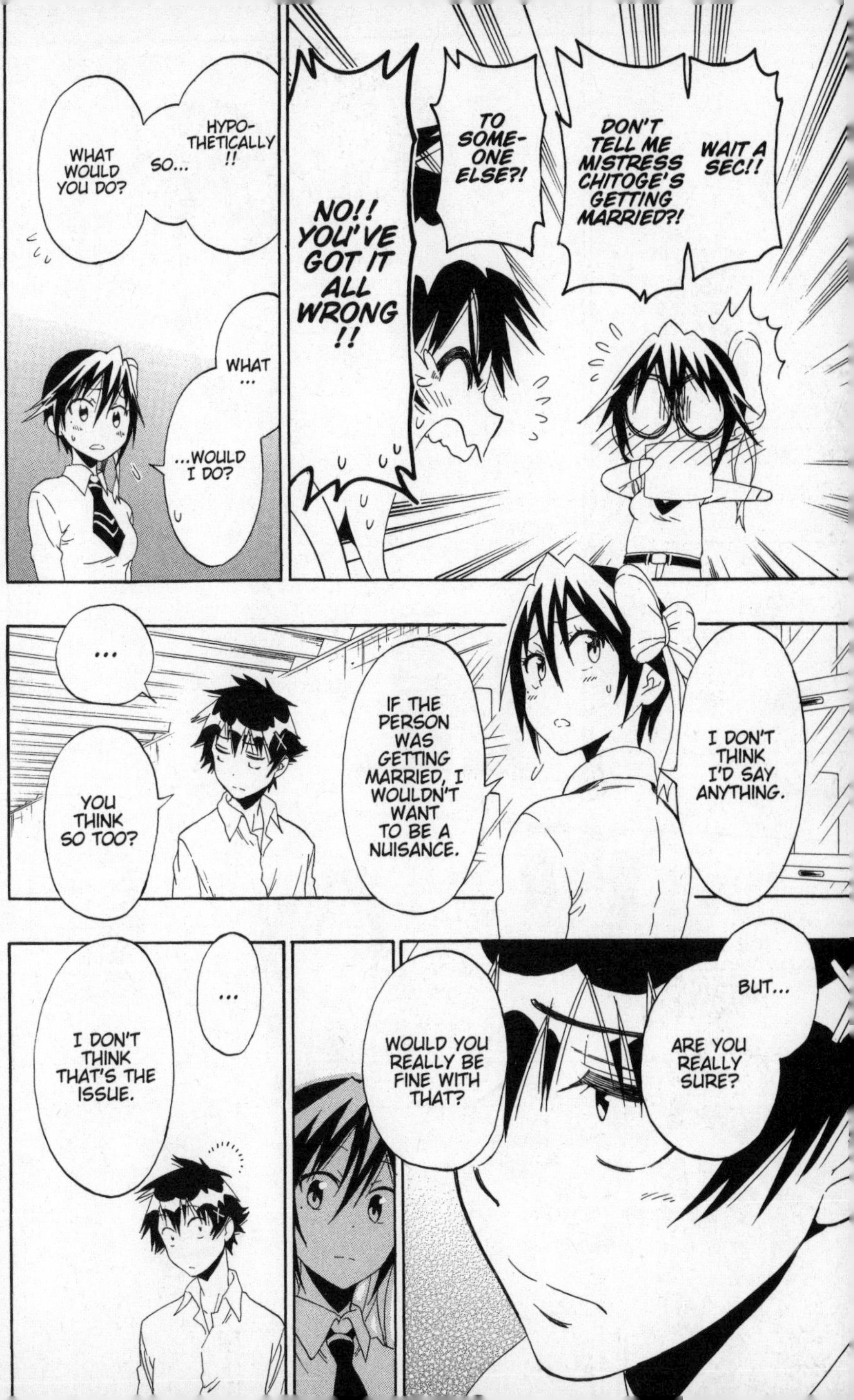
WAIT A SEC!!
DON'T TELL ME MISTRESS CHITOGE'S GETTING MARRIED?!
TO SOME-ONE ELSE?!
NO!! YOU'VE GOT IT ALL WRONG!!
HYPO-THETICALLY!!
SO...
WHAT WOULD YOU DO?
WHAT...
...WOULD I DO?
I DON'T THINK I'D SAY ANYTHING.
IF THE PERSON WAS GETTING MARRIED, I WOULDN'T WANT TO BE A NUISANCE.
...
YOU THINK SO TOO?
BUT...
ARE YOU REALLY SURE?
WOULD YOU REALLY BE FINE WITH THAT?
...
I DON'T THINK THAT'S THE ISSUE.

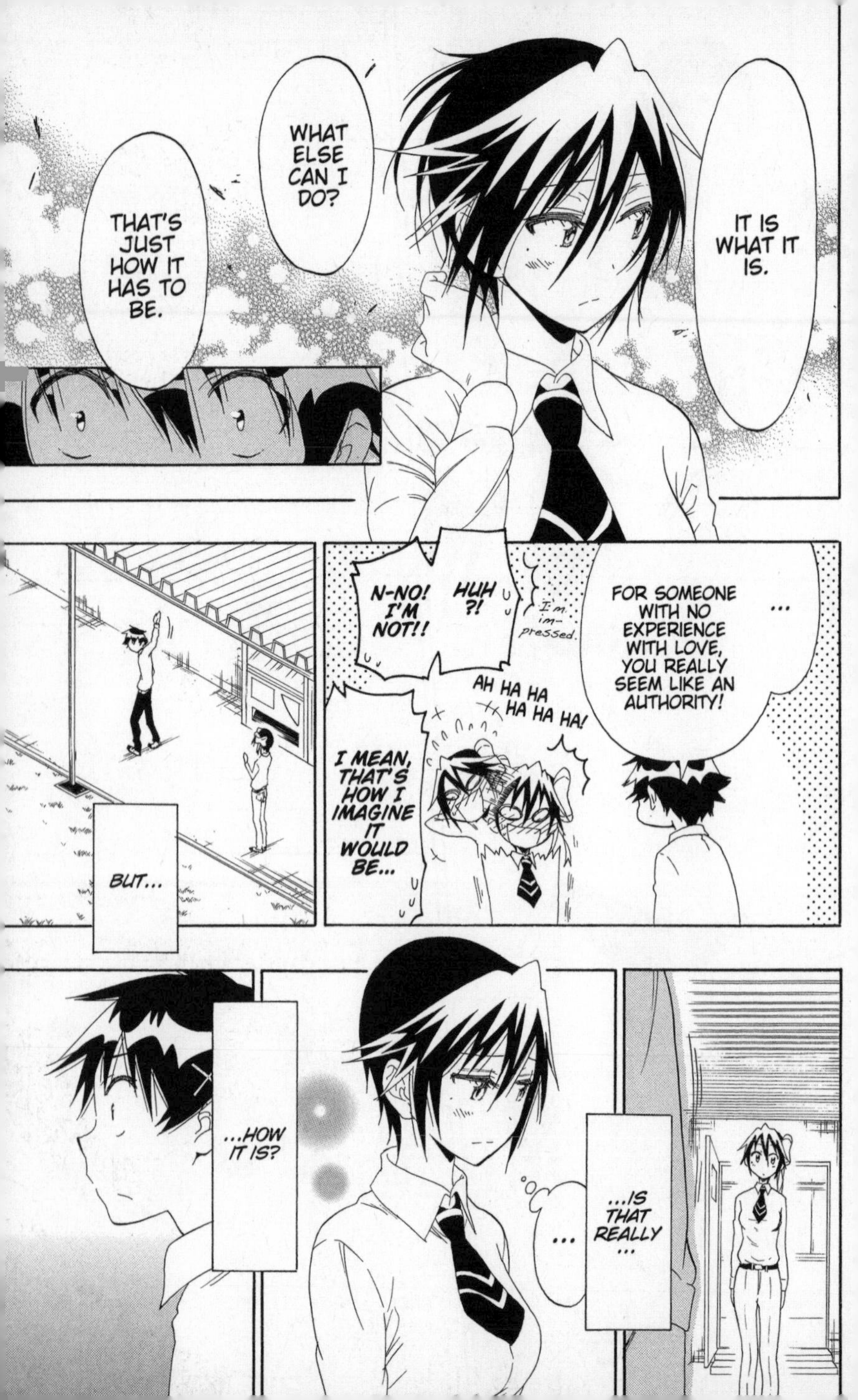
IT IS WHAT IT IS.
WHAT ELSE CAN I DO?
THAT'S JUST HOW IT HAS TO BE.
...
FOR SOMEONE WITH NO EXPERIENCE WITH LOVE, YOU REALLY SEEM LIKE AN AUTHORITY!
I'm im-pressed.
HUH?!
N-NO! I'M NOT!!
AH HA HA HA HA HA!
I MEAN, THAT'S HOW I IMAGINE IT WOULD BE...
BUT...
...IS THAT REALLY...
...
...HOW IT IS?

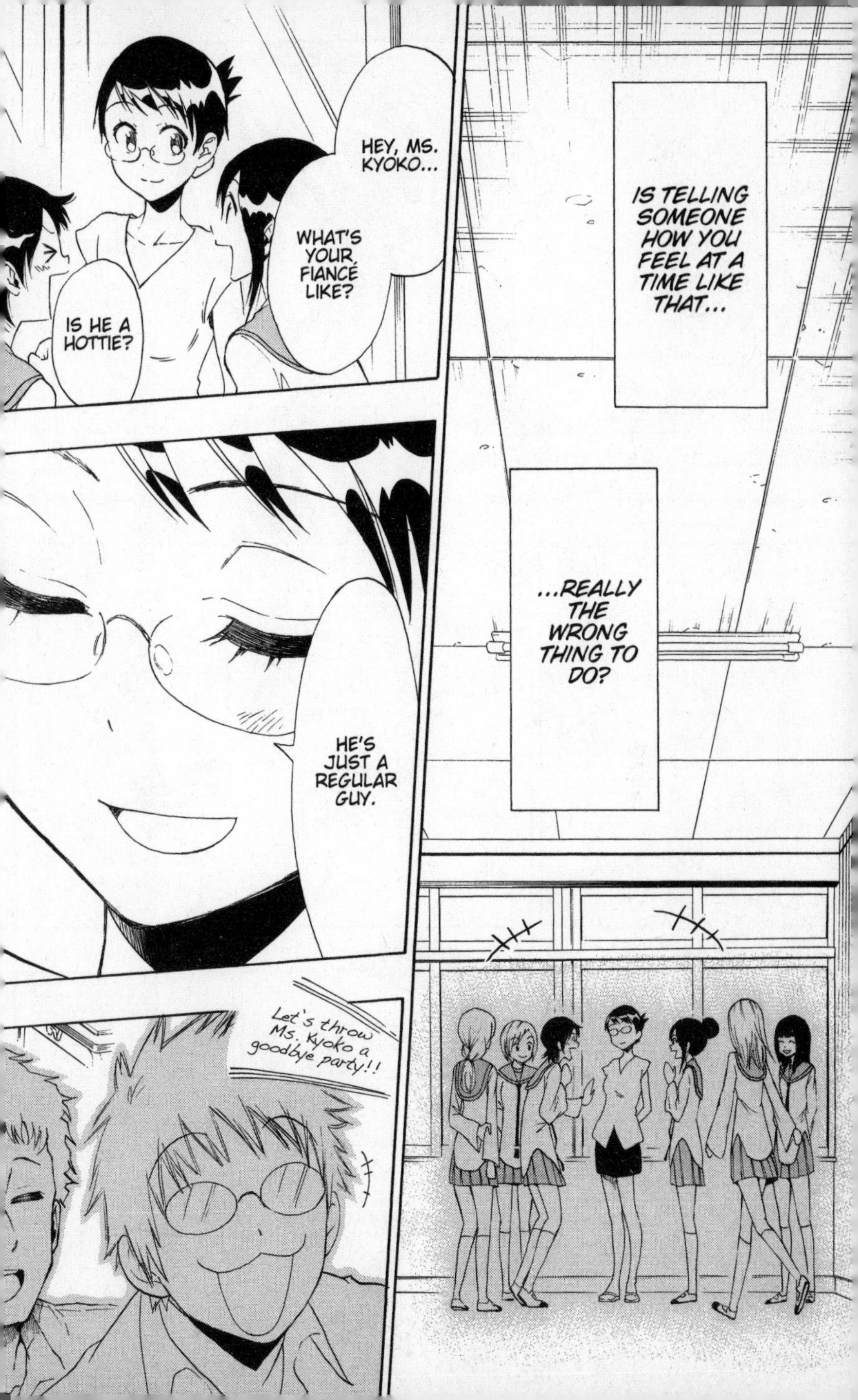
IS TELLING SOMEONE HOW YOU FEEL AT A TIME LIKE THAT...
...REALLY THE WRONG THING TO DO?
HEY, MS. KYOKO...
WHAT'S YOUR FIANCÉ LIKE?
IS HE A HOTTIE?
HE'S JUST A REGULAR GUY.
Let's throw Ms. Kyoko a goodbye party!!

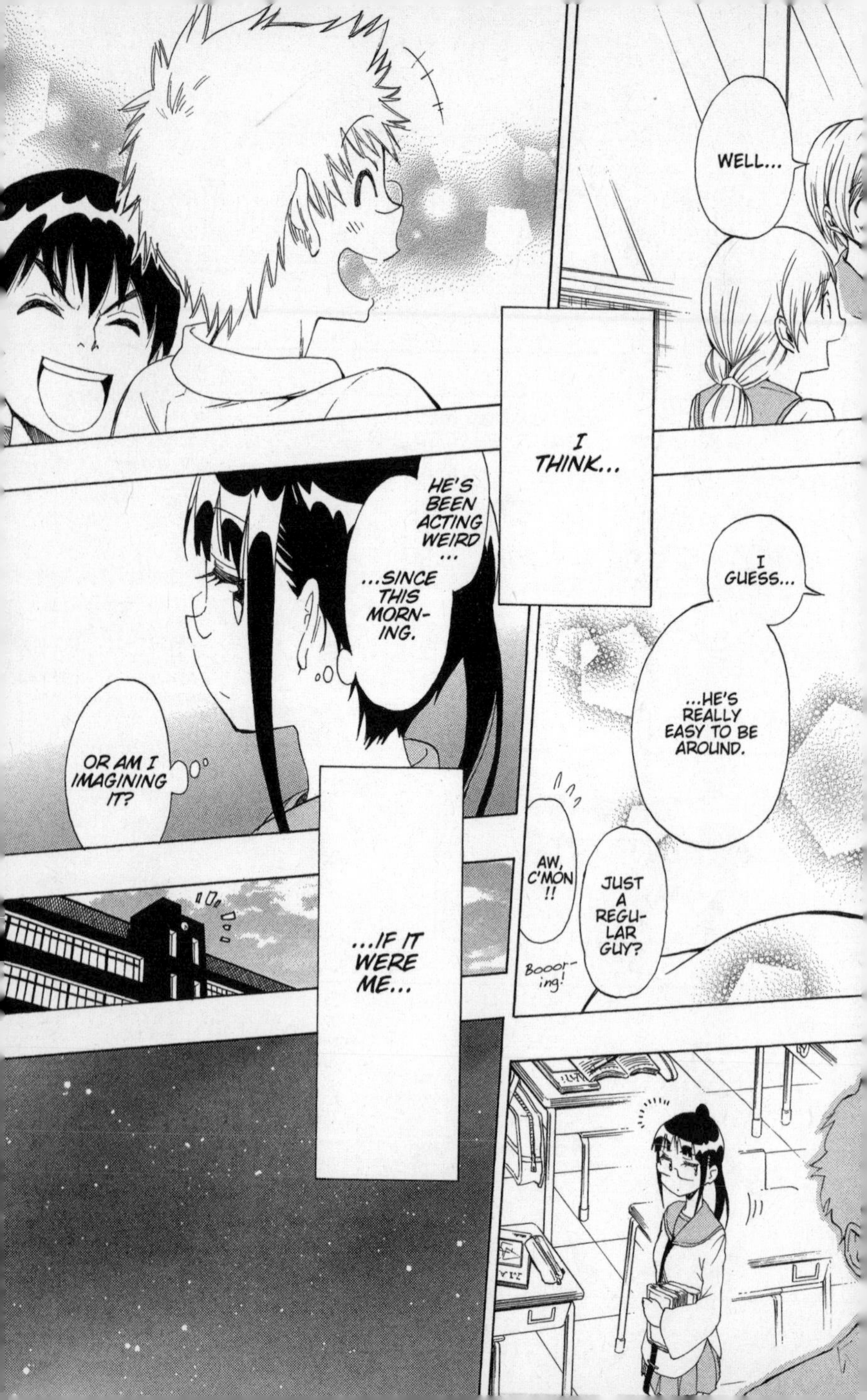
WELL...
I THINK...
I GUESS...
...HE'S REALLY EASY TO BE AROUND.
JUST A REGULAR GUY?
AW, C'MON!!
Booor-ing!
HE'S BEEN ACTING WEIRD...
...SINCE THIS MORNING.
OR AM I IMAGINING IT?
...IF IT WERE ME...

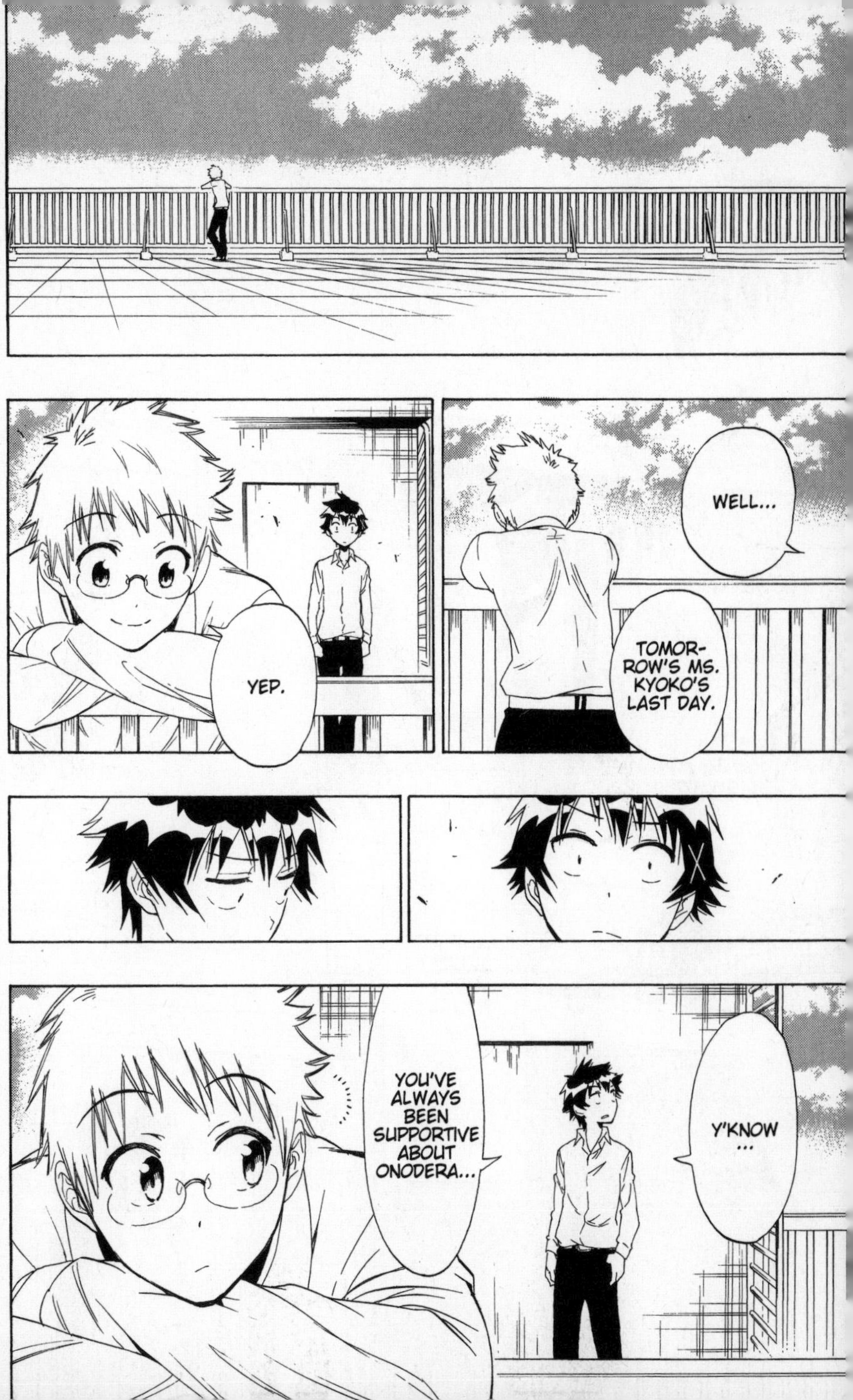
WELL...
TOMOR-ROW'S MS. KYOKO'S LAST DAY.
YEP.
Y'KNOW ...
YOU'VE ALWAYS BEEN SUPPORTIVE ABOUT ONODERA...

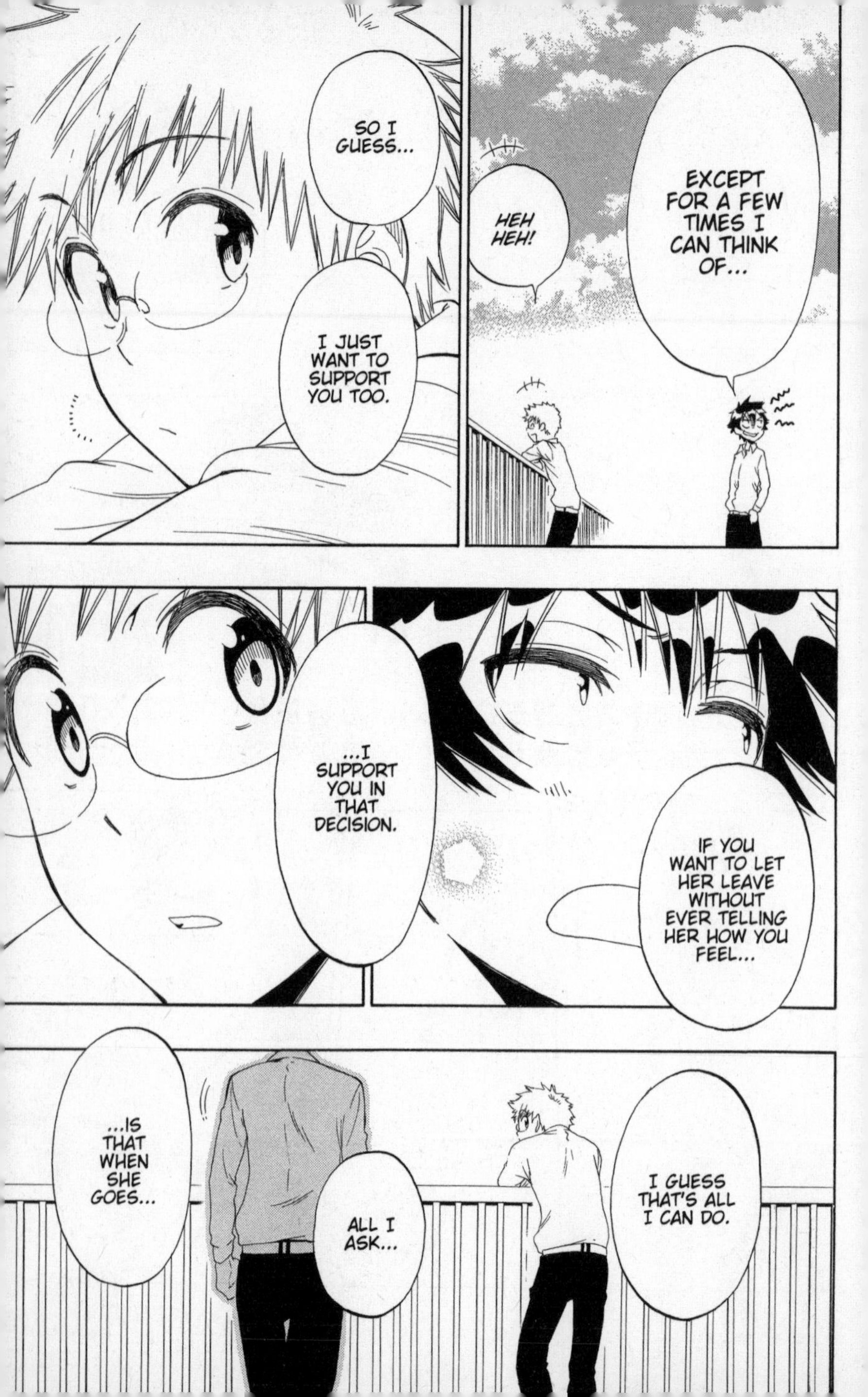
EXCEPT FOR A FEW TIMES I CAN THINK OF...
HEH HEH!
SO I GUESS...
I JUST WANT TO SUPPORT YOU TOO.
IF YOU WANT TO LET HER LEAVE WITHOUT EVER TELLING HER HOW YOU FEEL...
...I SUPPORT YOU IN THAT DECISION.
I GUESS THAT'S ALL I CAN DO.
ALL I ASK...
...IS THAT WHEN SHE GOES...

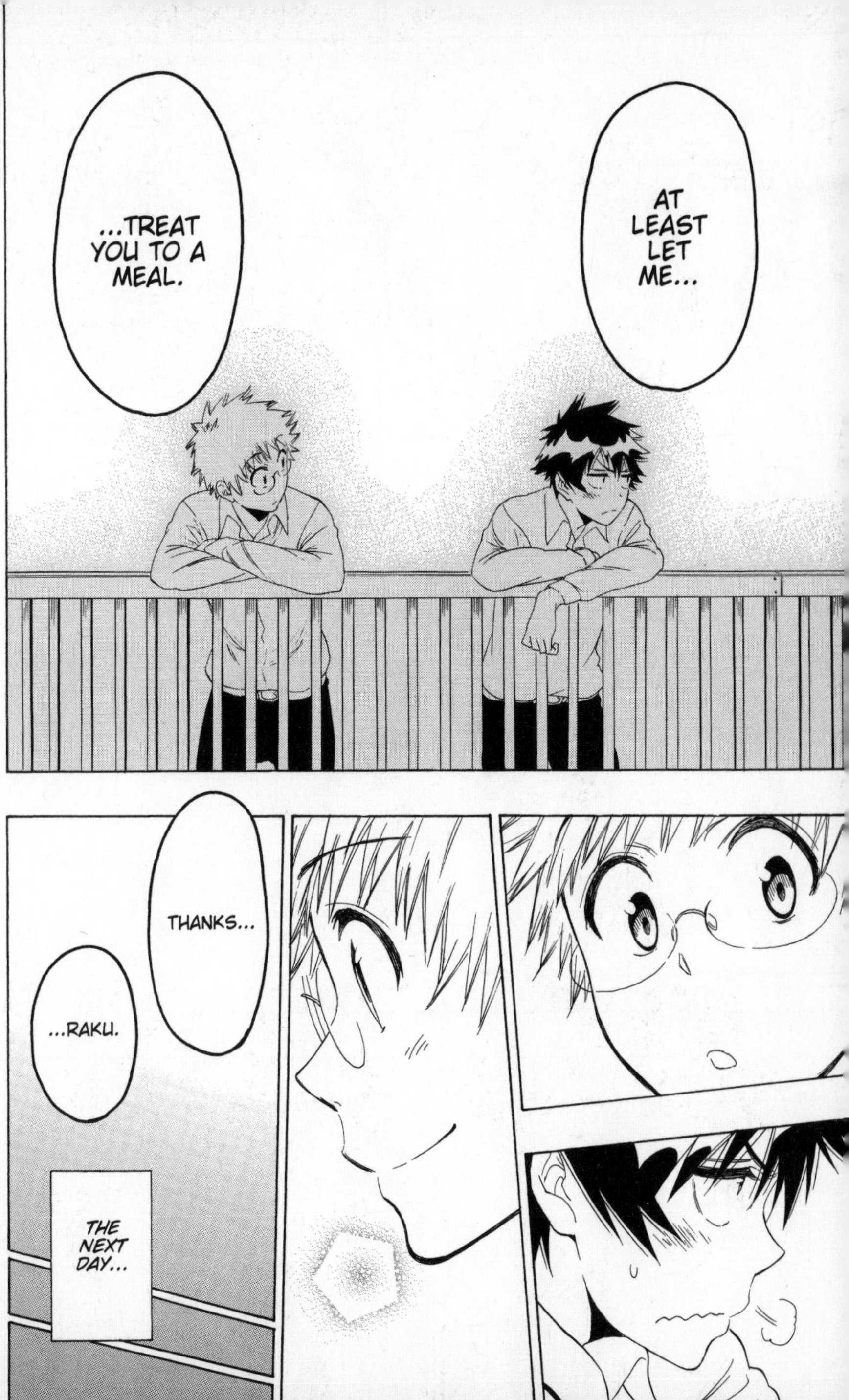
AT LEAST LET ME...
...TREAT YOU TO A MEAL.
THANKS...
...RAKU.
THE NEXT DAY...

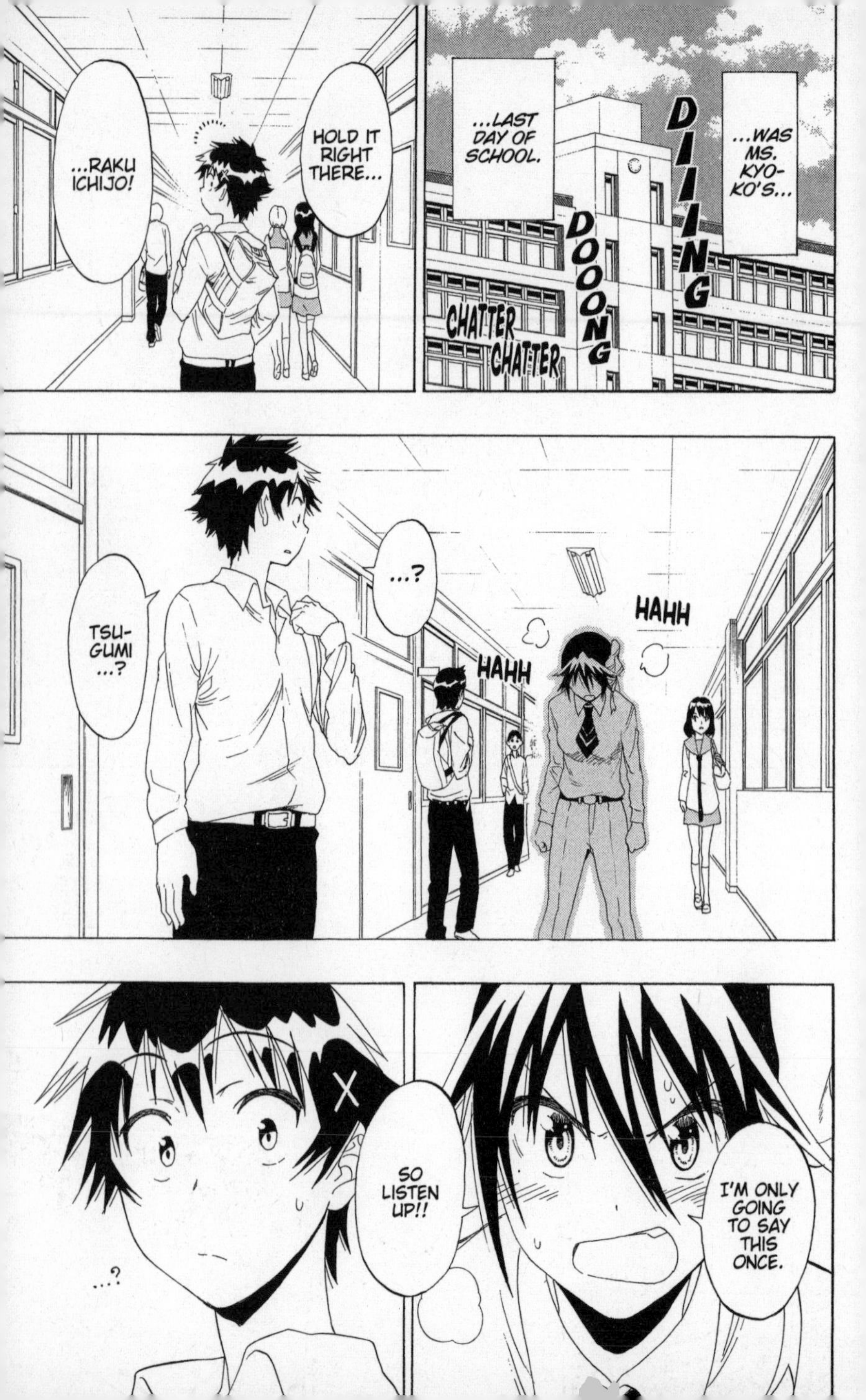
...WAS MS. KYO-KO'S...
DIIING
...LAST DAY OF SCHOOL.
DOOONG
CHATTER CHATTER
HOLD IT RIGHT THERE...
...RAKU ICHIJO!
HAHH
HAHH
...?
TSU-GUMI ...?
I'M ONLY GOING TO SAY THIS ONCE.
SO LISTEN UP!!
...?

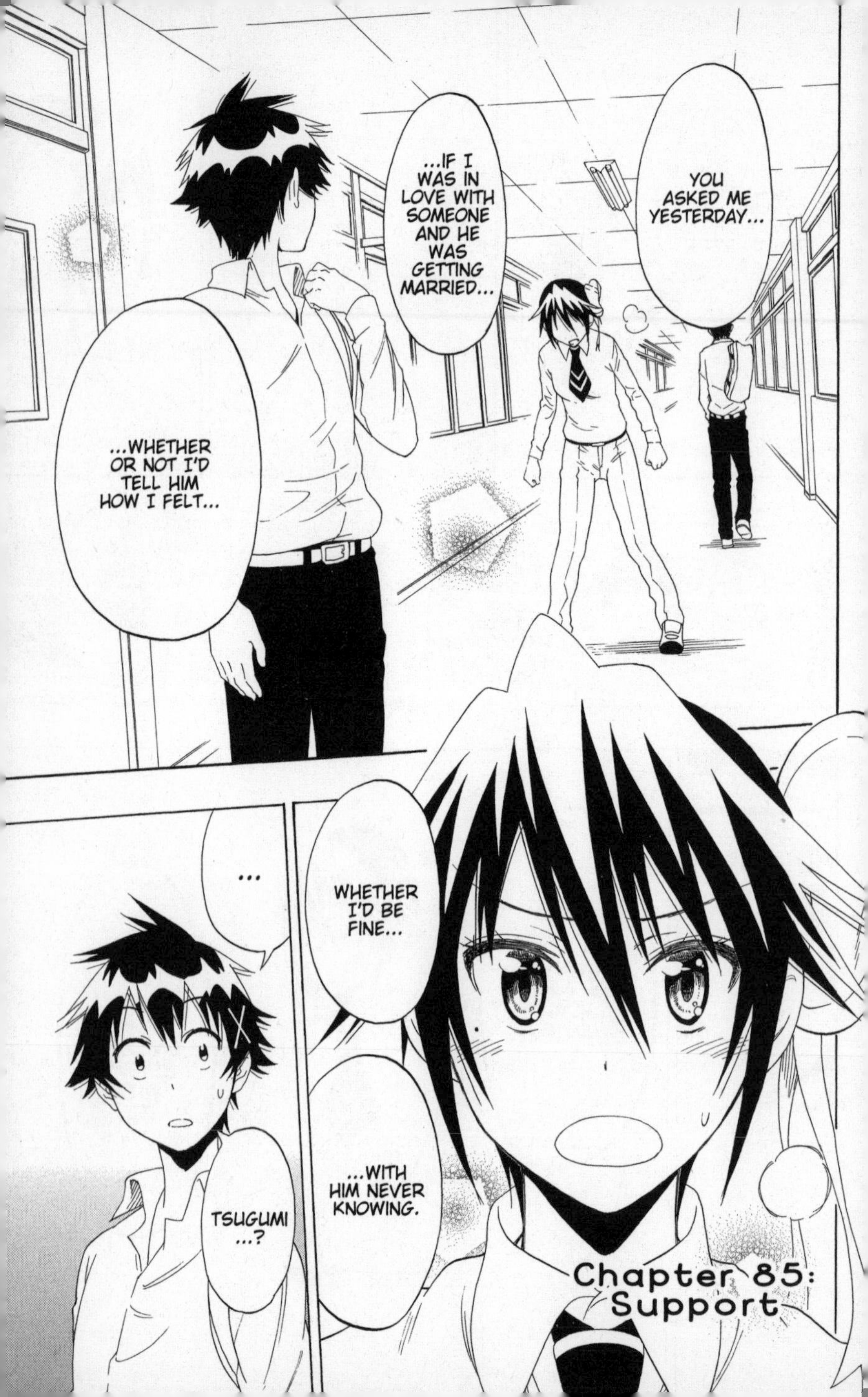
YOU ASKED ME YESTERDAY...
...IF I WAS IN LOVE WITH SOMEONE AND HE WAS GETTING MARRIED...
...WHETHER OR NOT I'D TELL HIM HOW I FELT...
WHETHER I'D BE FINE...
...WITH HIM NEVER KNOWING.
Chapter 85: Support
...
TSUGUMI ...?

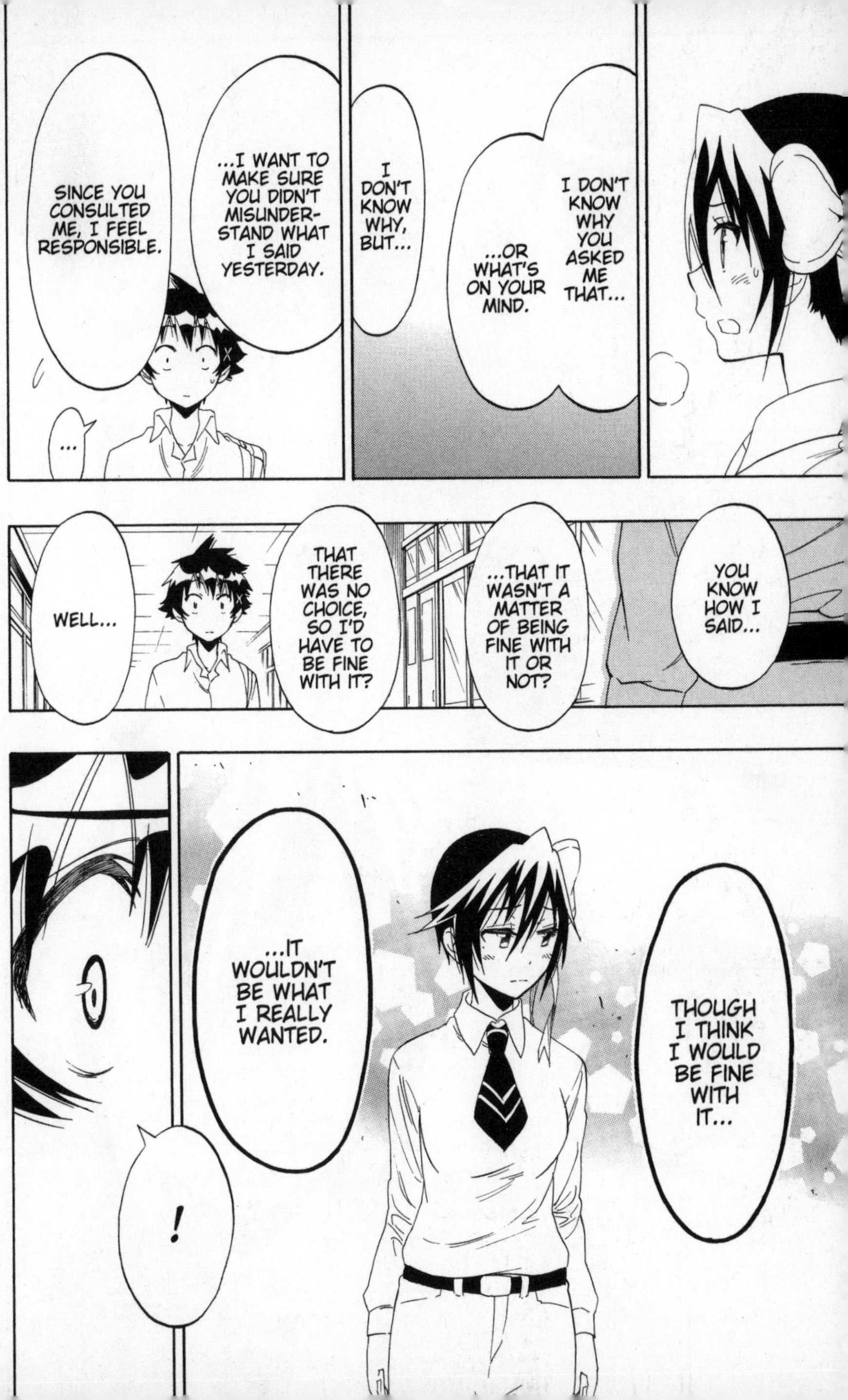
I DON'T KNOW WHY YOU ASKED ME THAT...
...OR WHAT'S ON YOUR MIND.
I DON'T KNOW WHY, BUT...
...I WANT TO MAKE SURE YOU DIDN'T MISUNDER-STAND WHAT I SAID YESTERDAY.
SINCE YOU CONSULTED ME, I FEEL RESPONSIBLE.
...
YOU KNOW HOW I SAID...
...THAT IT WASN'T A MATTER OF BEING FINE WITH IT OR NOT?
THAT THERE WAS NO CHOICE, SO I'D HAVE TO BE FINE WITH IT?
WELL...
THOUGH I THINK I WOULD BE FINE WITH IT...
...IT WOULDN'T BE WHAT I REALLY WANTED.
!

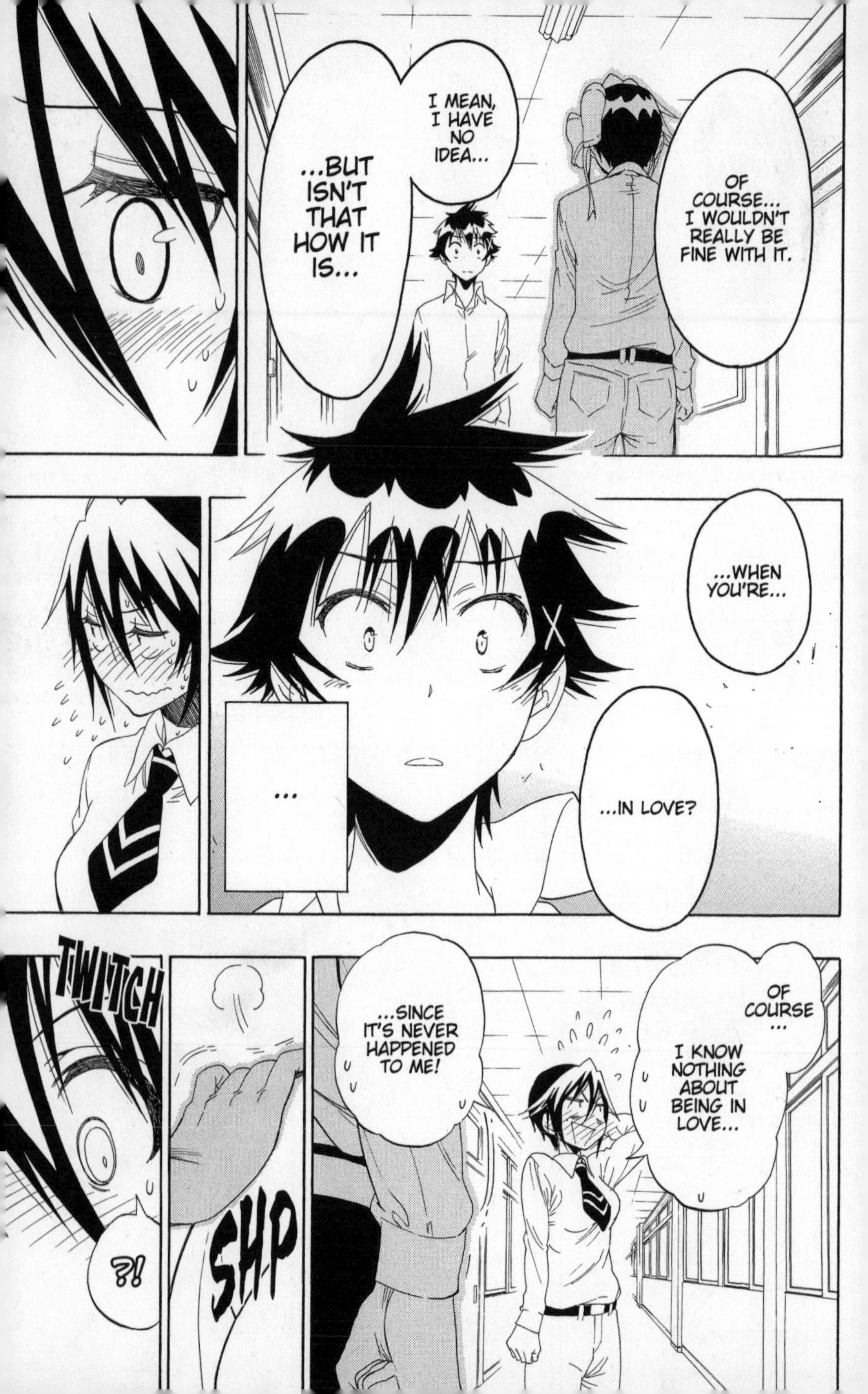
OF COURSE... I WOULDN'T REALLY BE FINE WITH IT.
I MEAN, I HAVE NO IDEA...
...BUT ISN'T THAT HOW IT IS...
...WHEN YOU'RE...
...IN LOVE?
...
OF COURSE...
I KNOW NOTHING ABOUT BEING IN LOVE...
...SINCE IT'S NEVER HAPPENED TO ME!
SHP
TWITCH
?!

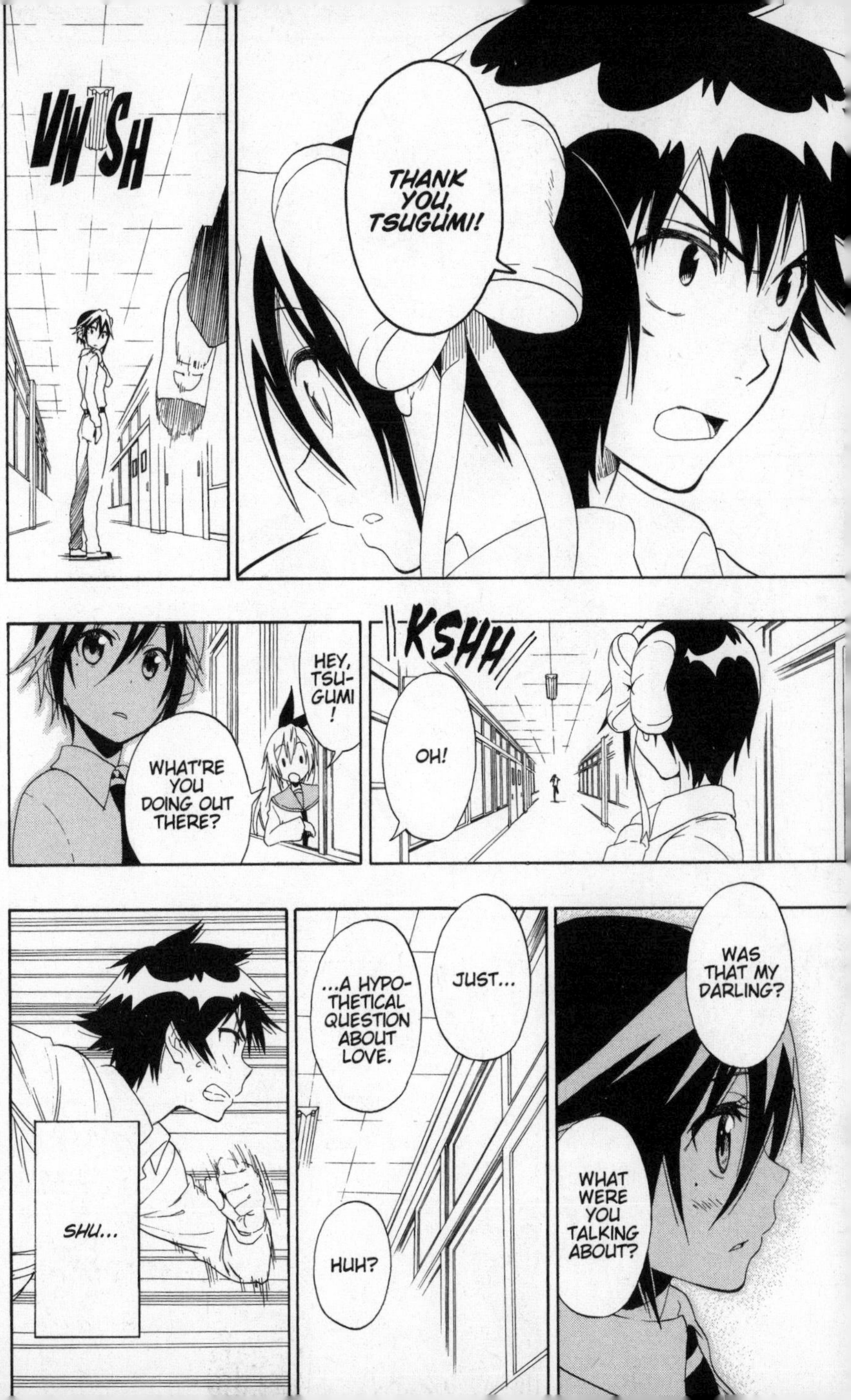
THANK YOU, TSUGUMI!
VWISH
KSHH
OH!
HEY, TSU-GUMI!
WHAT'RE YOU DOING OUT THERE?
WAS THAT MY DARLING?
WHAT WERE YOU TALKING ABOUT?
JUST...
...A HYPO-THETICAL QUESTION ABOUT LOVE.
HUH?
SHU...

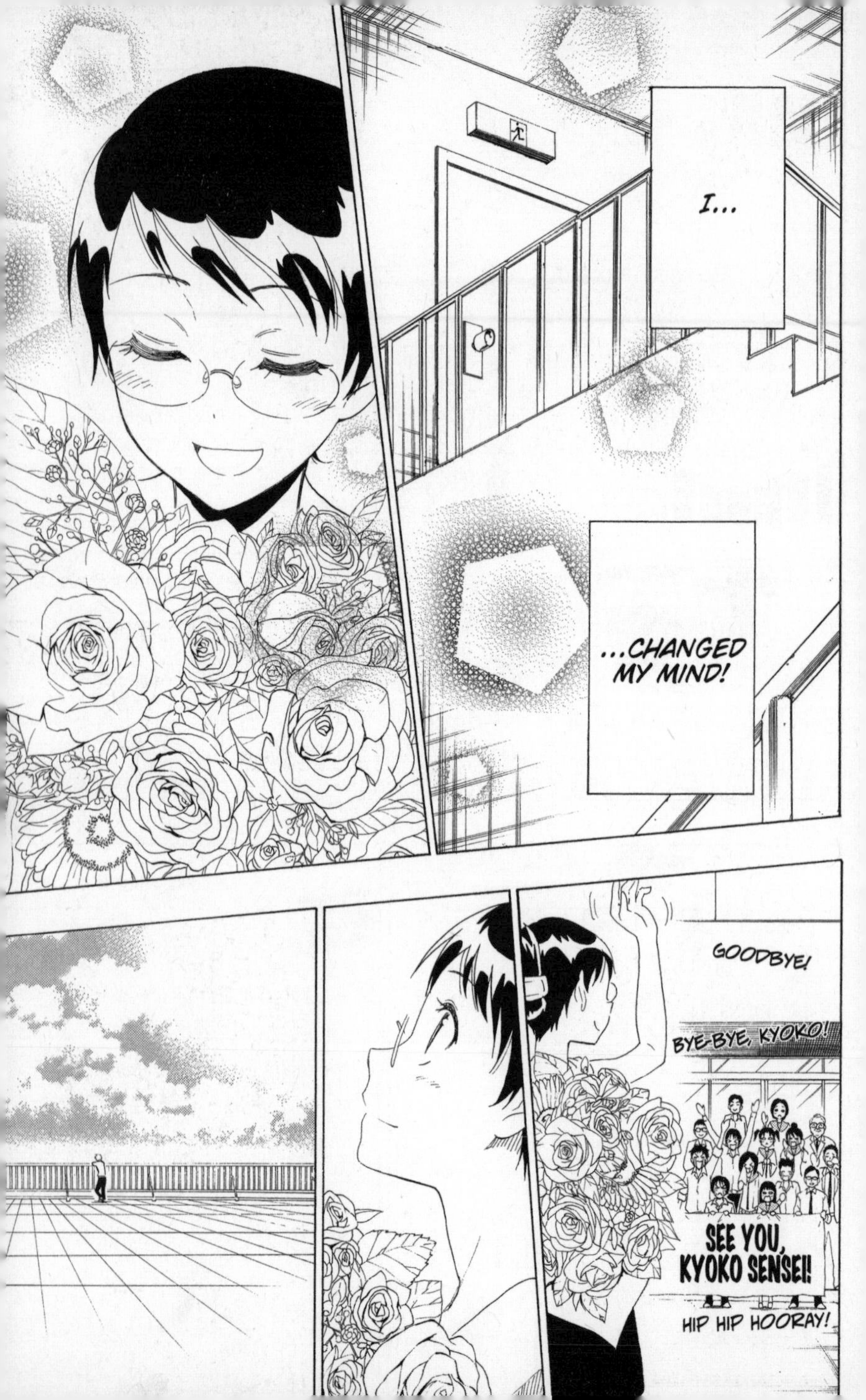
I...
...CHANGED MY MIND!
GOODBYE!
BYE-BYE, KYOKO!
SEE YOU, KYOKO SENSEI!
HIP HIP HOORAY!

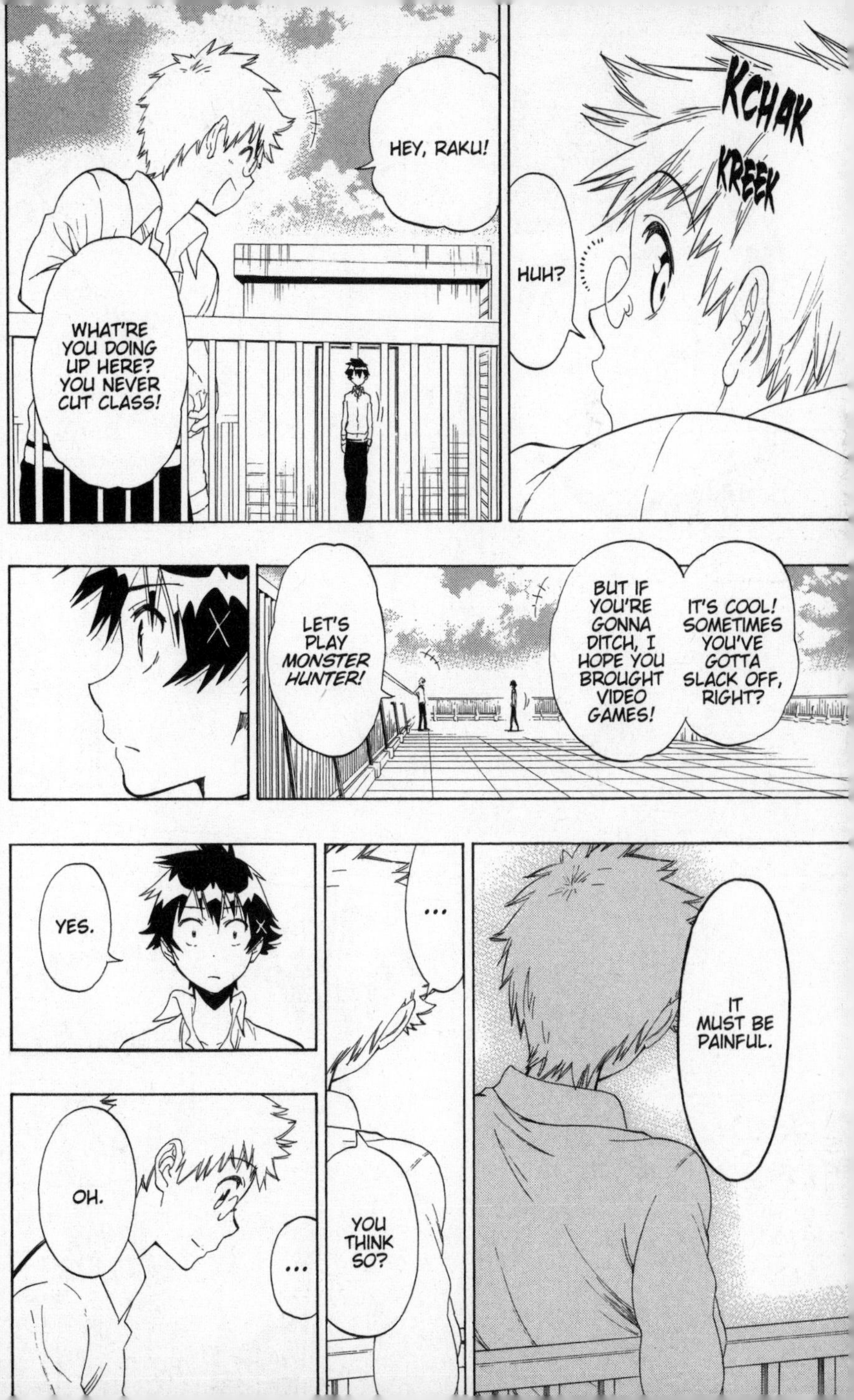
KCHAK
KREEK
HUH?
HEY, RAKU!
WHAT'RE YOU DOING UP HERE? YOU NEVER CUT CLASS!
IT'S COOL! SOMETIMES YOU'VE GOTTA SLACK OFF, RIGHT?
BUT IF YOU'RE GONNA DITCH, I HOPE YOU BROUGHT VIDEO GAMES!
LET'S PLAY MONSTER HUNTER!
IT MUST BE PAINFUL.
...
YOU THINK SO?
YES.
OH.
...

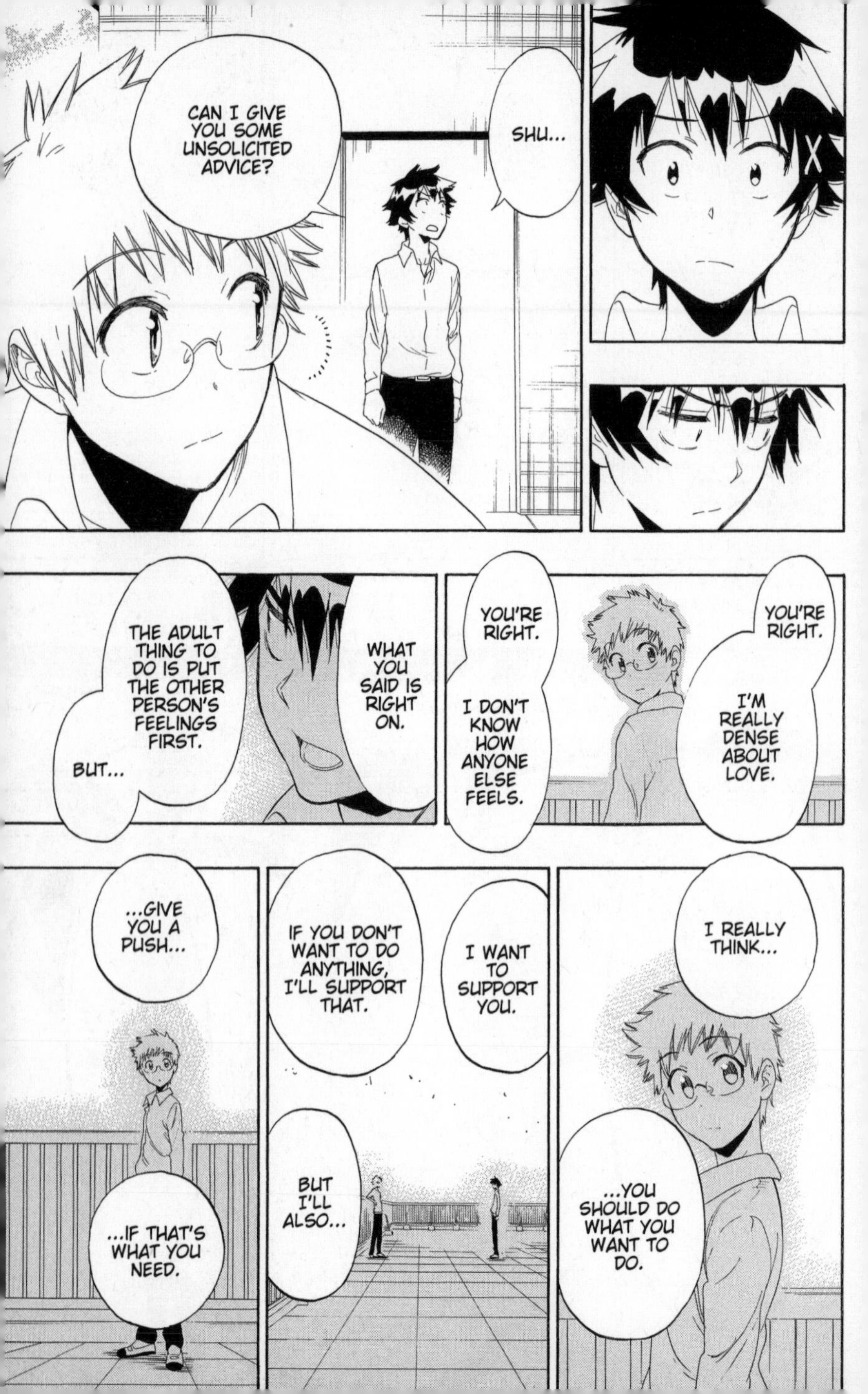
SHU...
CAN I GIVE YOU SOME UNSOLICITED ADVICE?
YOU'RE RIGHT.
I'M REALLY DENSE ABOUT LOVE.
YOU'RE RIGHT.
I DON'T KNOW HOW ANYONE ELSE FEELS.
WHAT YOU SAID IS RIGHT ON.
THE ADULT THING TO DO IS PUT THE OTHER PERSON'S FEELINGS FIRST.
BUT...
I REALLY THINK...
...YOU SHOULD DO WHAT YOU WANT TO DO.
I WANT TO SUPPORT YOU.
IF YOU DON'T WANT TO DO ANYTHING, I'LL SUPPORT THAT.
BUT I'LL ALSO...
...GIVE YOU A PUSH...
...IF THAT'S WHAT YOU NEED.

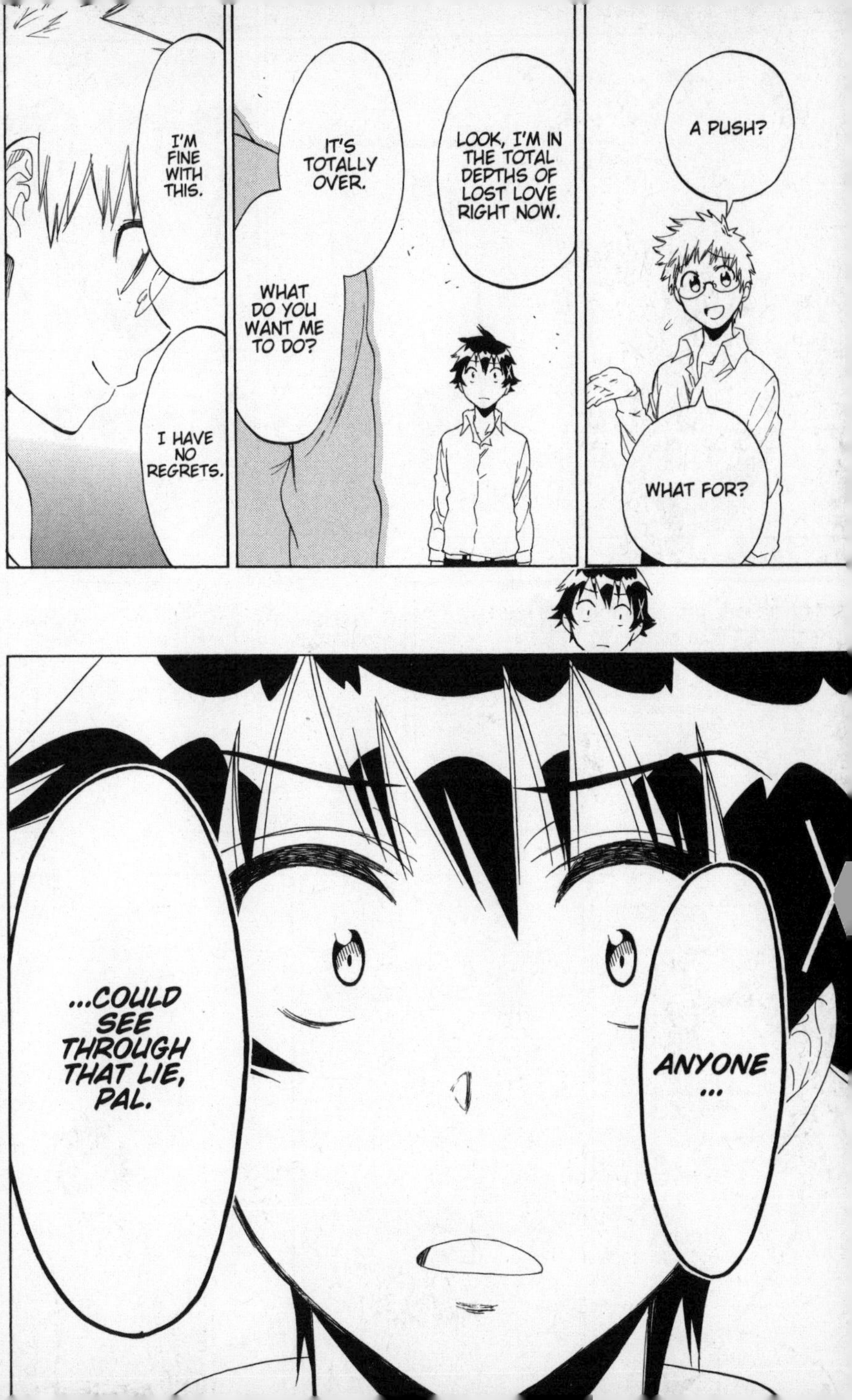
A PUSH?
WHAT FOR?
LOOK, I'M IN THE TOTAL DEPTHS OF LOST LOVE RIGHT NOW.
IT'S TOTALLY OVER.
WHAT DO YOU WANT ME TO DO?
I'M FINE WITH THIS.
I HAVE NO REGRETS.
ANYONE...
...COULD SEE THROUGH THAT LIE, PAL.

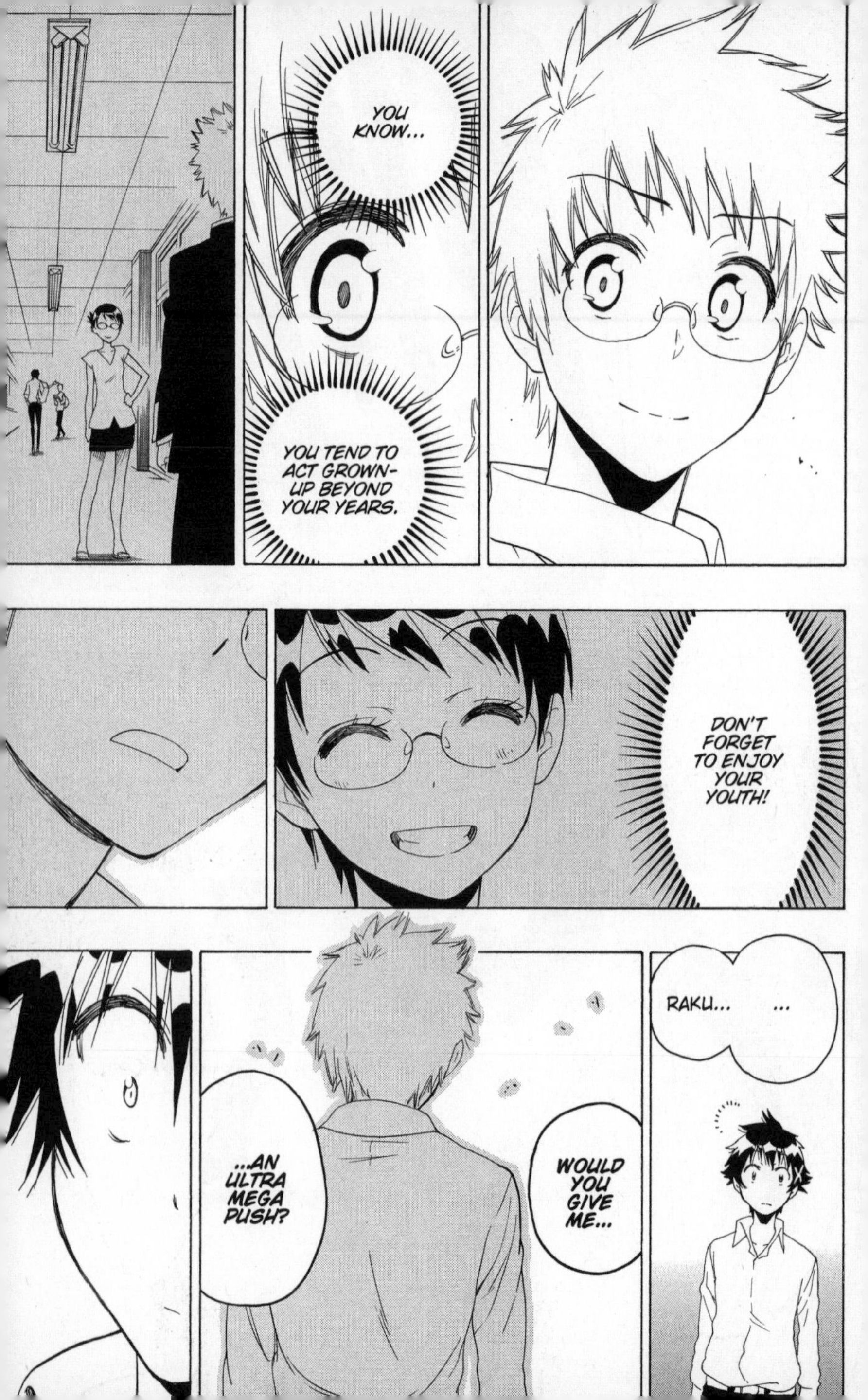
YOU KNOW...
YOU TEND TO ACT GROWN-UP BEYOND YOUR YEARS.
DON'T FORGET TO ENJOY YOUR YOUTH!
RAKU... ...
WOULD YOU GIVE ME...
...AN ULTRA MEGA PUSH?

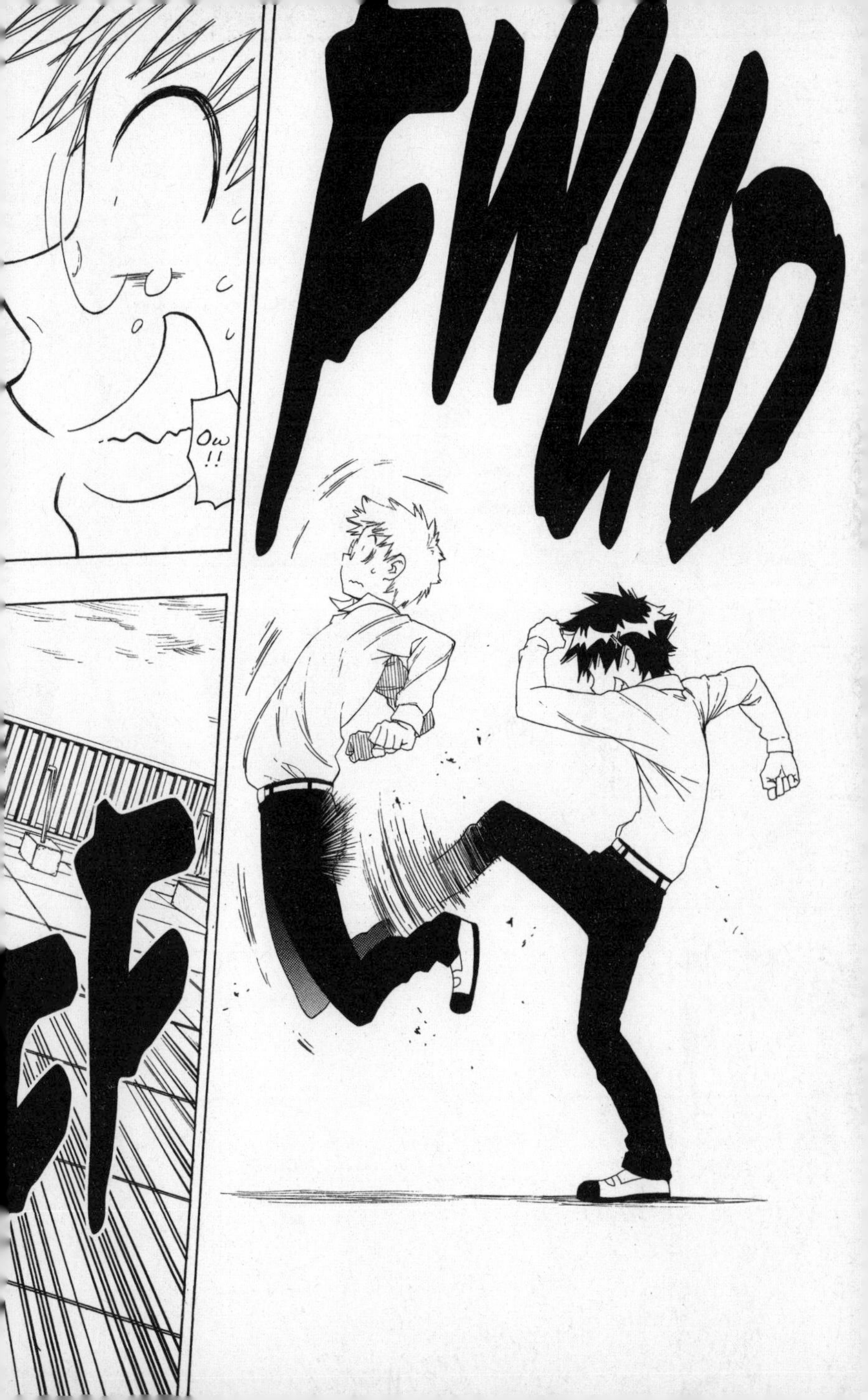
FWUD
Ow !!

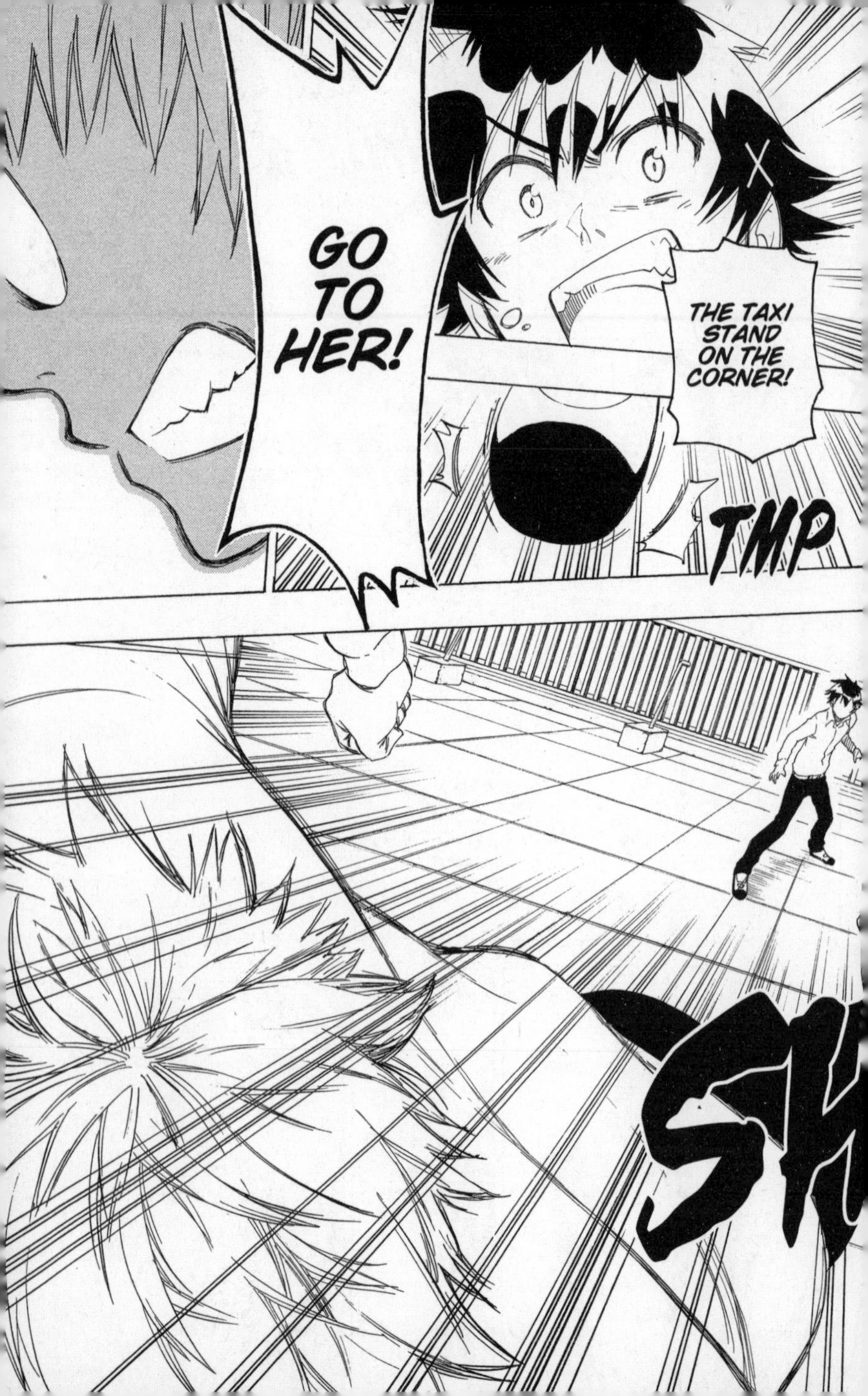
THE TAXI STAND ON THE CORNER!
TMP
GO TO HER!
SH

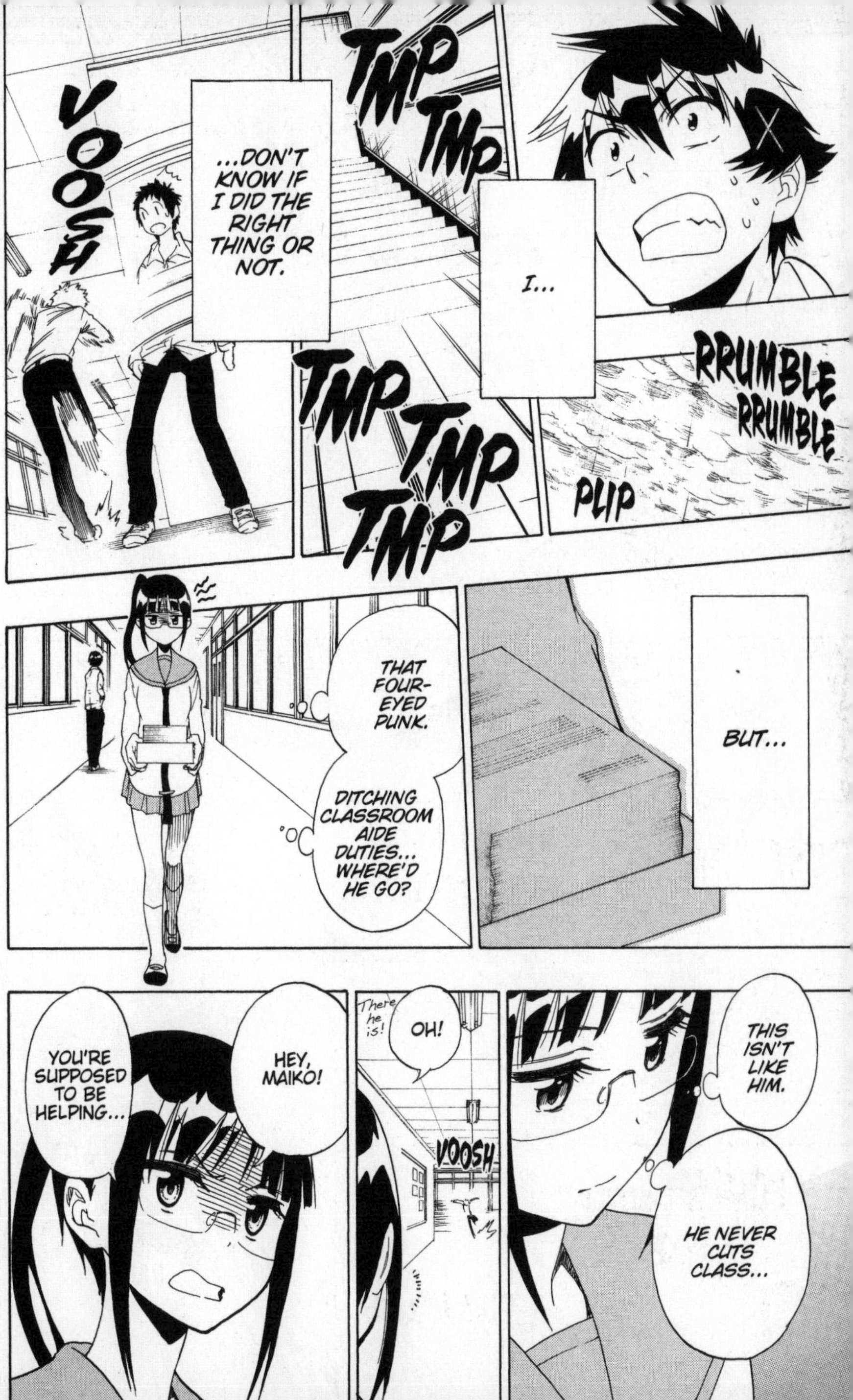
I...
RRUMBLE
RRUMBLE
PLIP
TMP TMP
TMP TMP TMP
...DON'T KNOW IF I DID THE RIGHT THING OR NOT.
VOOSH
BUT...
THAT FOUR-EYED PUNK.
DITCHING CLASSROOM AIDE DUTIES... WHERE'D HE GO?
THIS ISN'T LIKE HIM.
HE NEVER CUTS CLASS...
There he is!
OH!
VOOSH
HEY, MAIKO!
YOU'RE SUPPOSED TO BE HELPING...

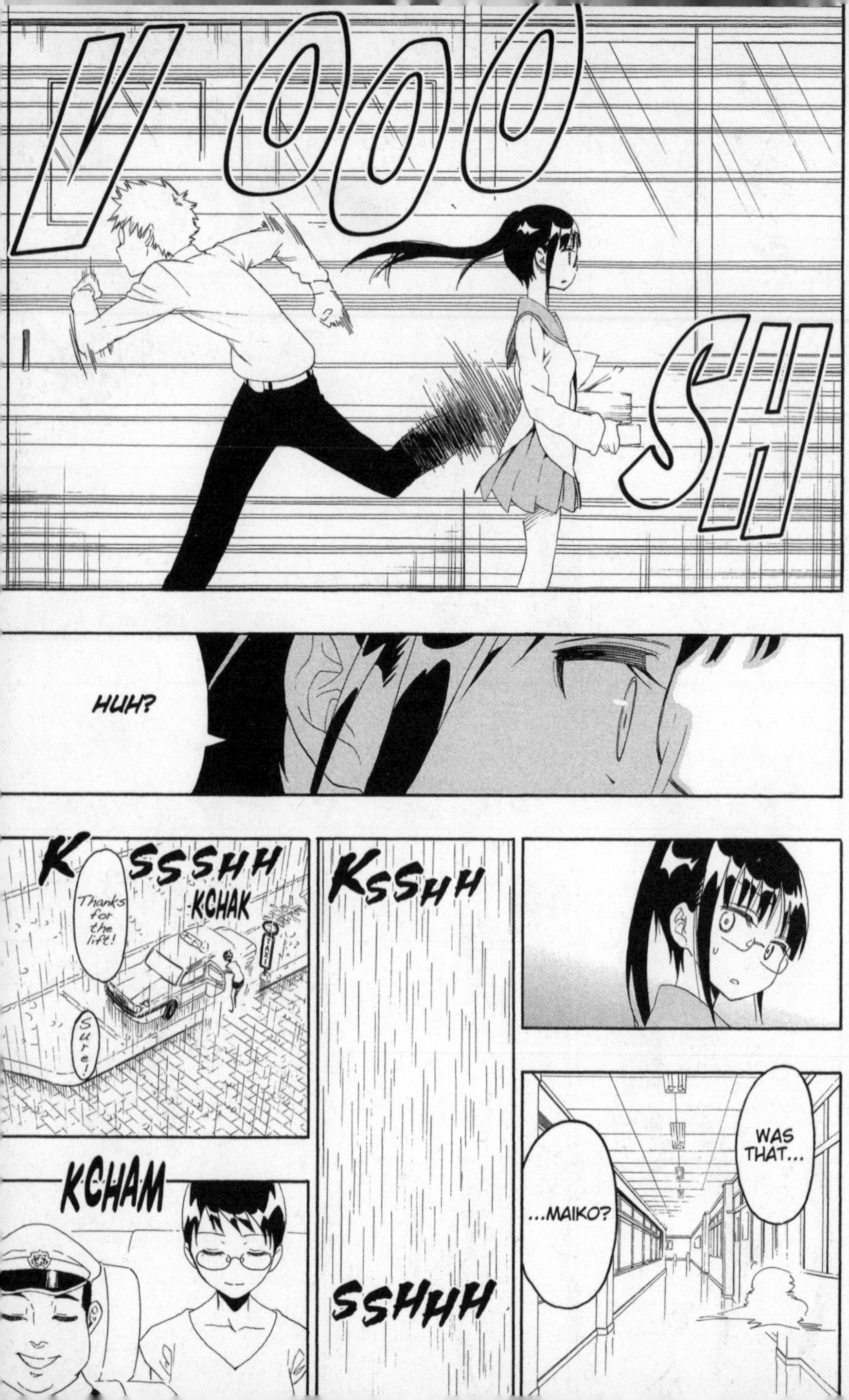
VOOOOSH
HUH?
WAS THAT...
...MAIKO?
KSSHH
SSHHH
KSSSHH
KCHAK
Thanks for the lift!
Sure!
KCHAM

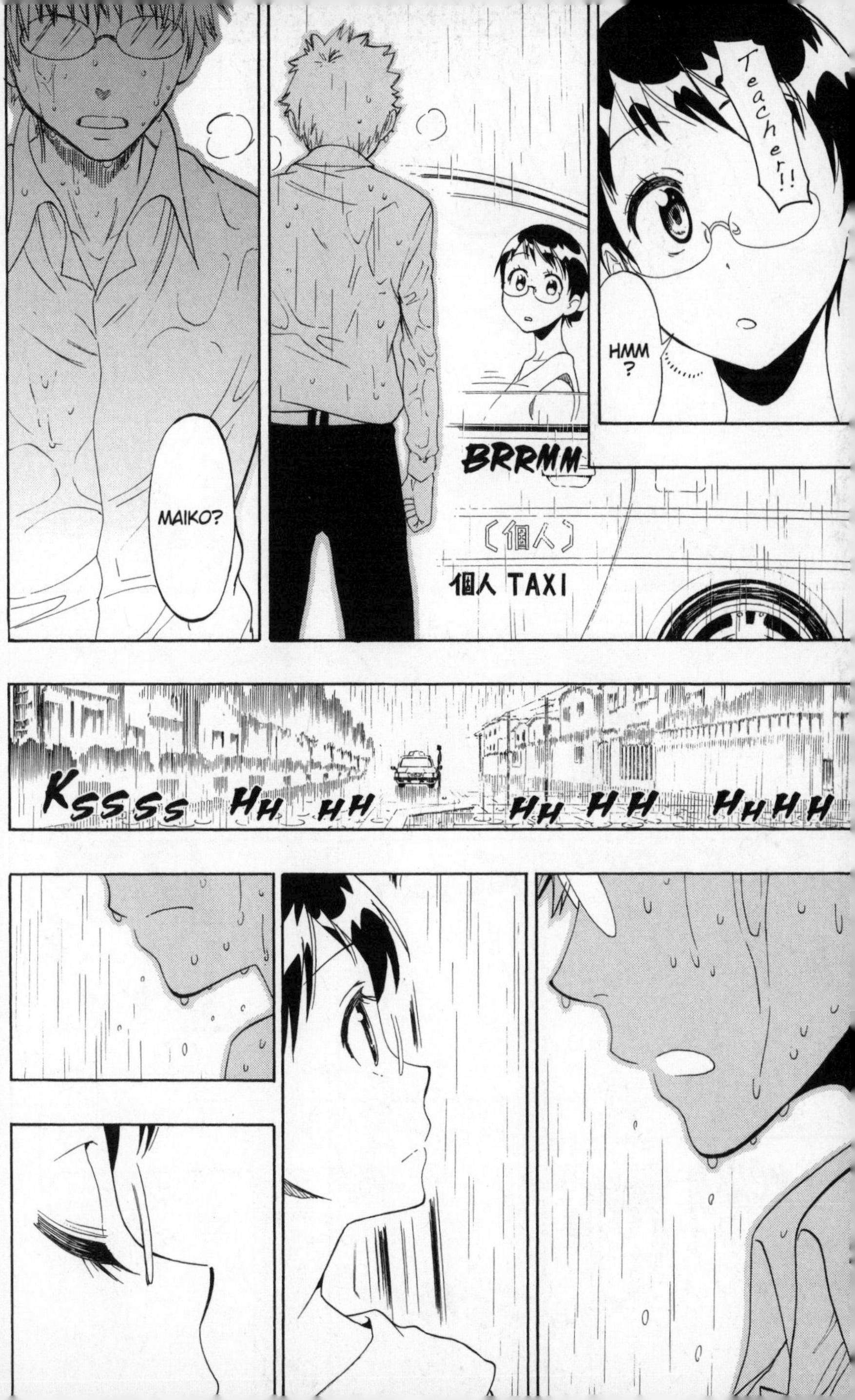
Teacher!!
HMM?
BRRMM
〔個人〕
個人 TAXI
MAIKO?
KSSSSS HH HH HH HH HHHH

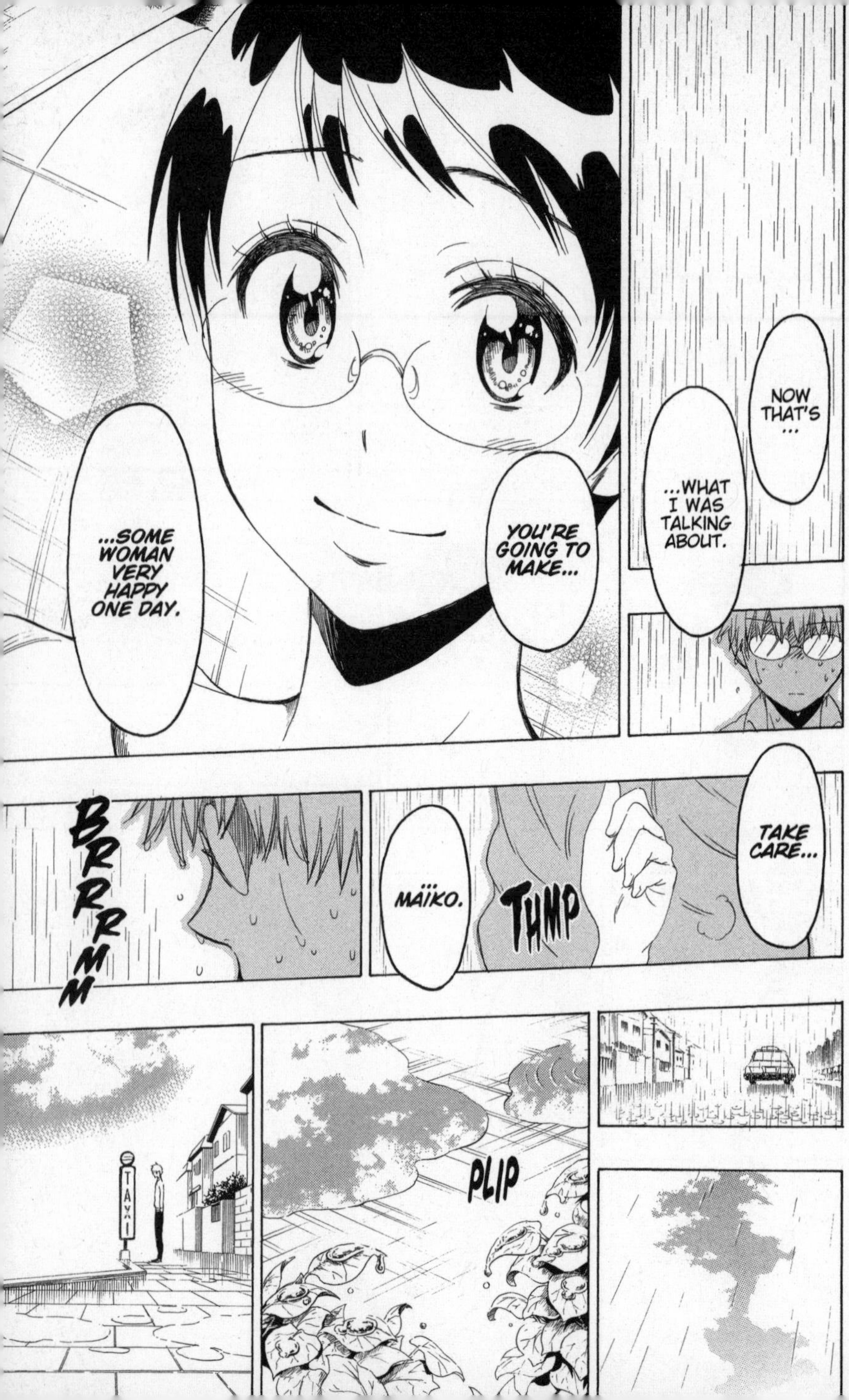
NOW THAT'S ...
...WHAT I WAS TALKING ABOUT.
YOU'RE GOING TO MAKE...
...SOME WOMAN VERY HAPPY ONE DAY.
TAKE CARE...
THMP
... MAÏKO.
BRRRRMM
PLIP
TAXI

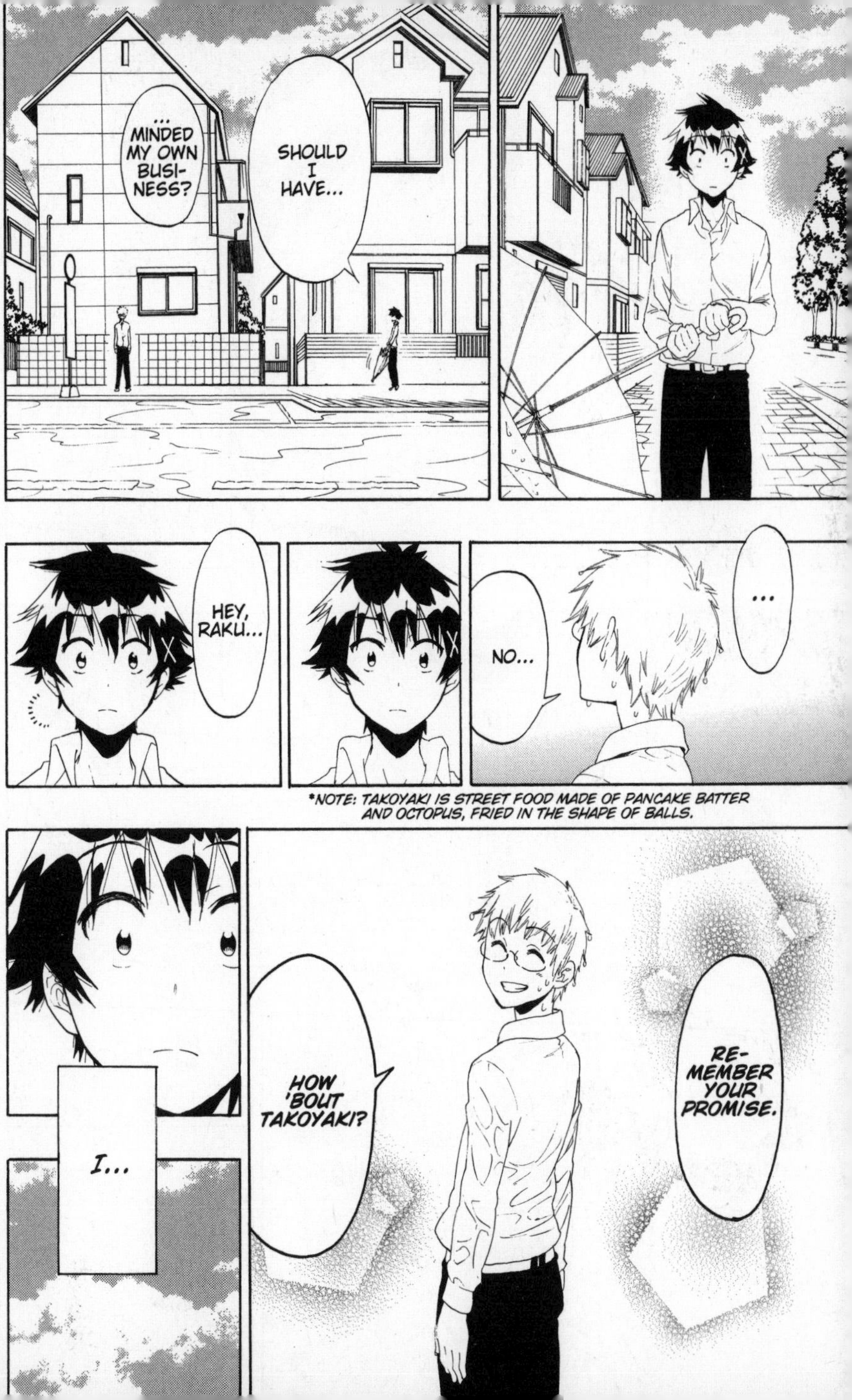
SHOULD I HAVE...
...MINDED MY OWN BUSI-NESS?
...
NO...
HEY, RAKU...
RE-MEMBER YOUR PROMISE.
HOW 'BOUT TAKOYAKI?
I...

*NOTE: TAKOYAKI IS STREET FOOD MADE OF PANCAKE BATTER AND OCTOPUS, FRIED IN THE SHAPE OF BALLS.

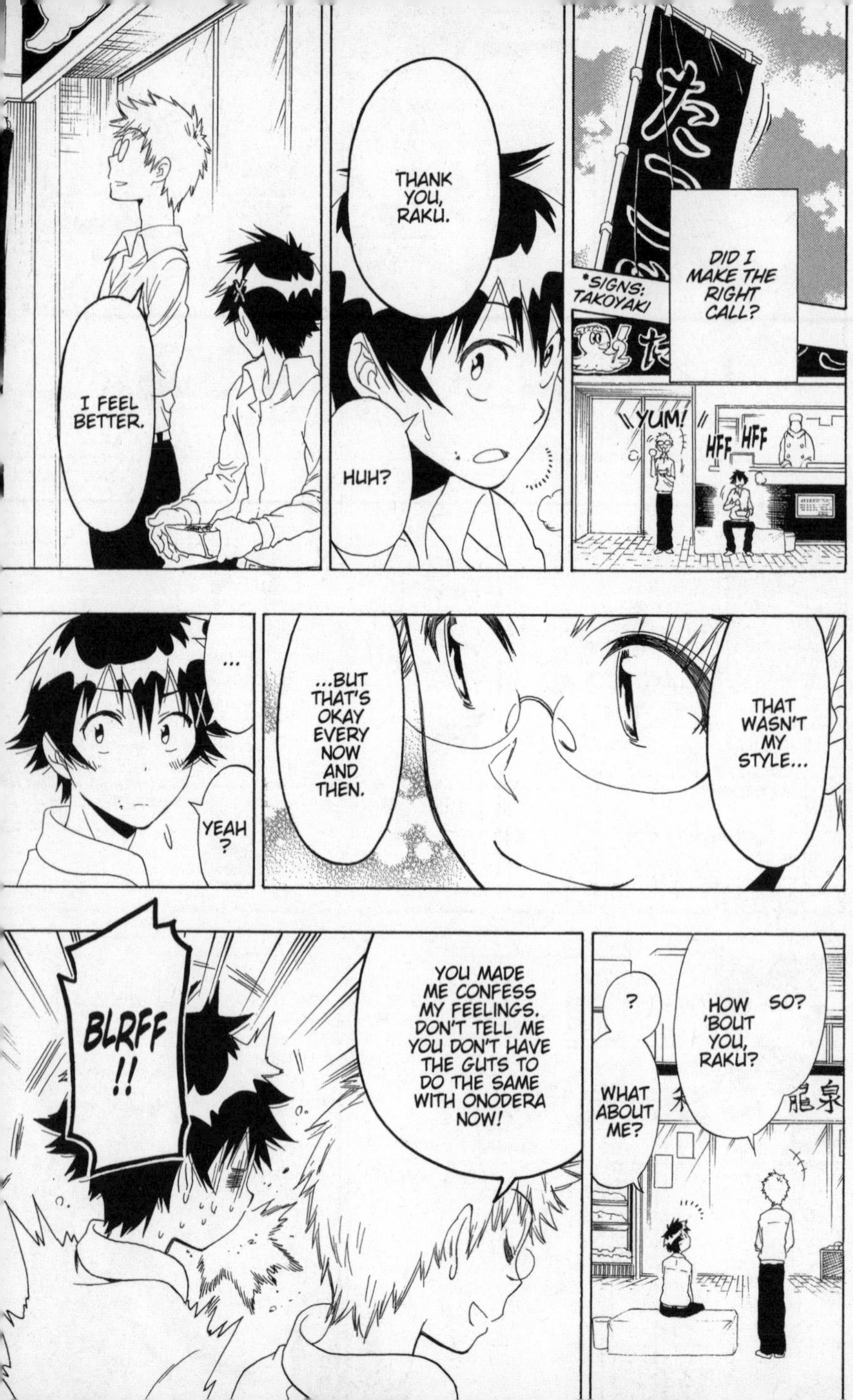
DID I MAKE THE RIGHT CALL?
*SIGNS: TAKOYAKI
YUM!
HFF HFF
THANK YOU, RAKU.
HUH?
I FEEL BETTER.
THAT WASN'T MY STYLE...
...BUT THAT'S OKAY EVERY NOW AND THEN.
...
YEAH?
SO?
HOW 'BOUT YOU, RAKU?
?
WHAT ABOUT ME?
YOU MADE ME CONFESS MY FEELINGS. DON'T TELL ME YOU DON'T HAVE THE GUTS TO DO THE SAME WITH ONODERA NOW!
BLRFF!!

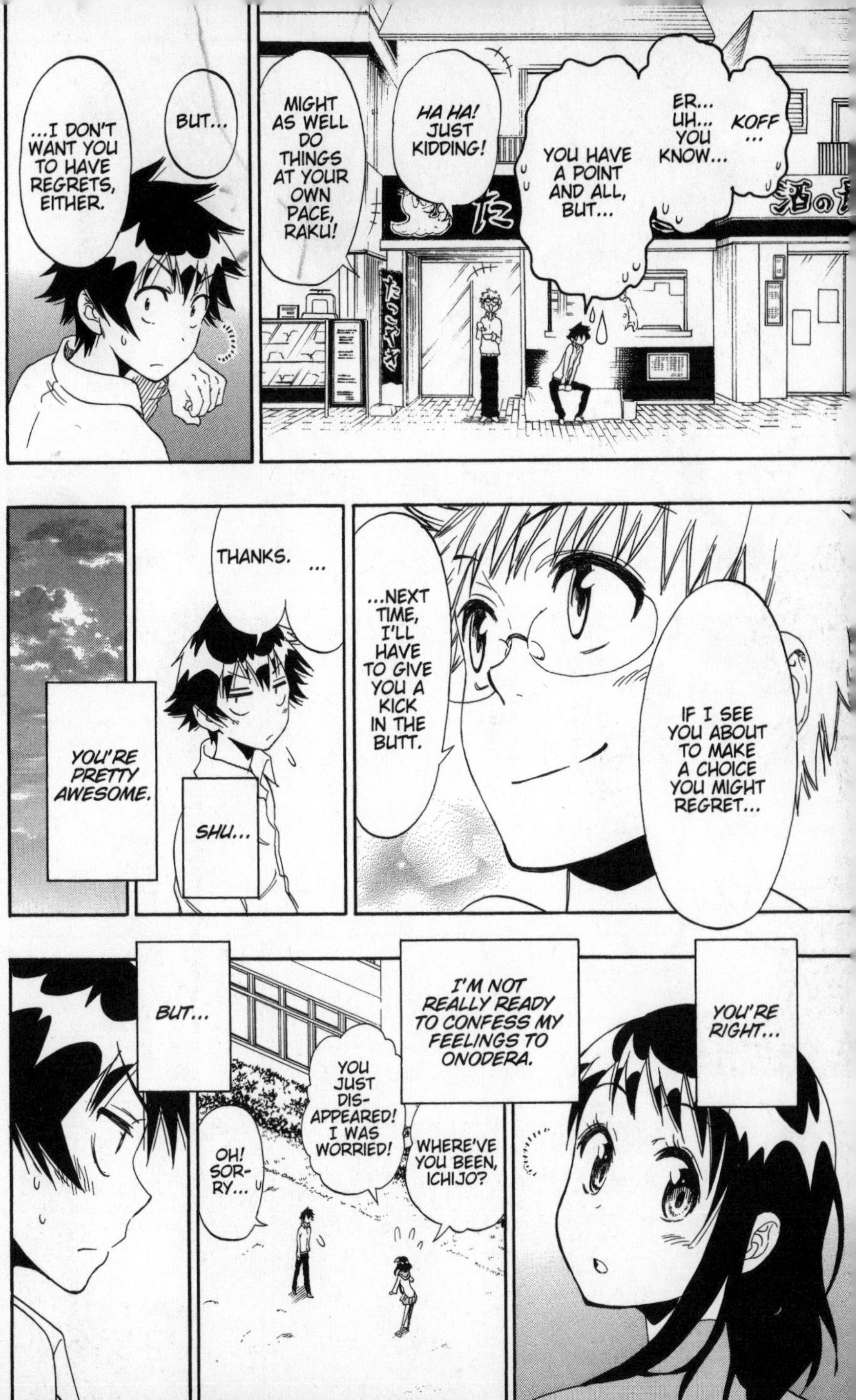
KOFF...
ER... UH... YOU KNOW...
YOU HAVE A POINT AND ALL, BUT...
HA HA! JUST KIDDING!
MIGHT AS WELL DO THINGS AT YOUR OWN PACE, RAKU!
BUT...
...I DON'T WANT YOU TO HAVE REGRETS, EITHER.
IF I SEE YOU ABOUT TO MAKE A CHOICE YOU MIGHT REGRET...
...NEXT TIME, I'LL HAVE TO GIVE YOU A KICK IN THE BUTT.
THANKS.
...
SHU...
YOU'RE PRETTY AWESOME.
YOU'RE RIGHT...
I'M NOT REALLY READY TO CONFESS MY FEELINGS TO ONODERA.
WHERE'VE YOU BEEN, ICHIJO?
YOU JUST DIS-APPEARED! I WAS WORRIED!
OH! SOR-RY...
BUT...

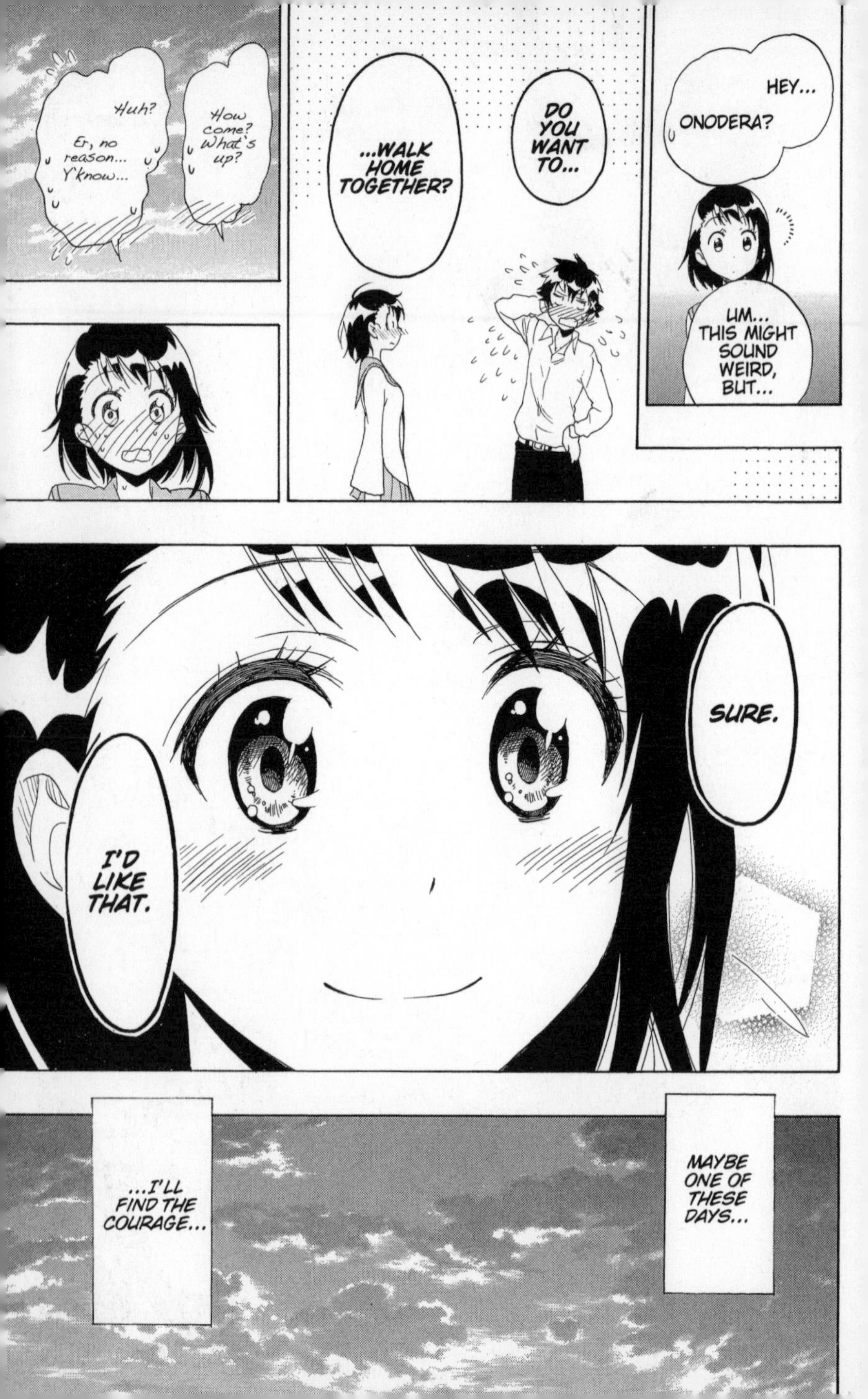
HEY... ONODERA?
UM... THIS MIGHT SOUND WEIRD, BUT...
DO YOU WANT TO...
...WALK HOME TOGETHER?
How come? What's up?
Huh? Er, no reason... Y'know...
SURE.
I'D LIKE THAT.
MAYBE ONE OF THESE DAYS...
...I'LL FIND THE COURAGE...

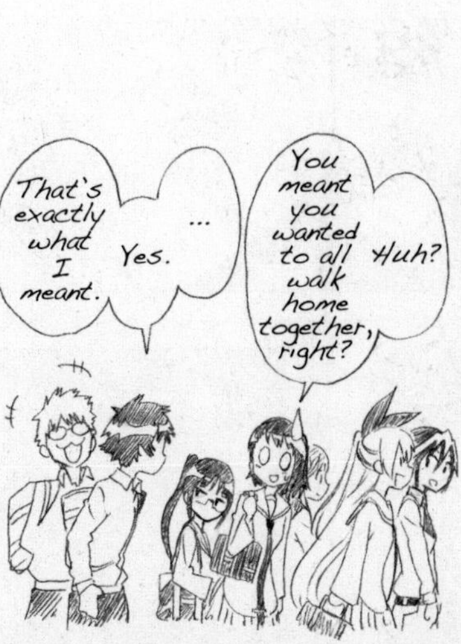
Huh?
You meant you wanted to all walk home together, right?
...
Yes.
That's exactly what I meant.

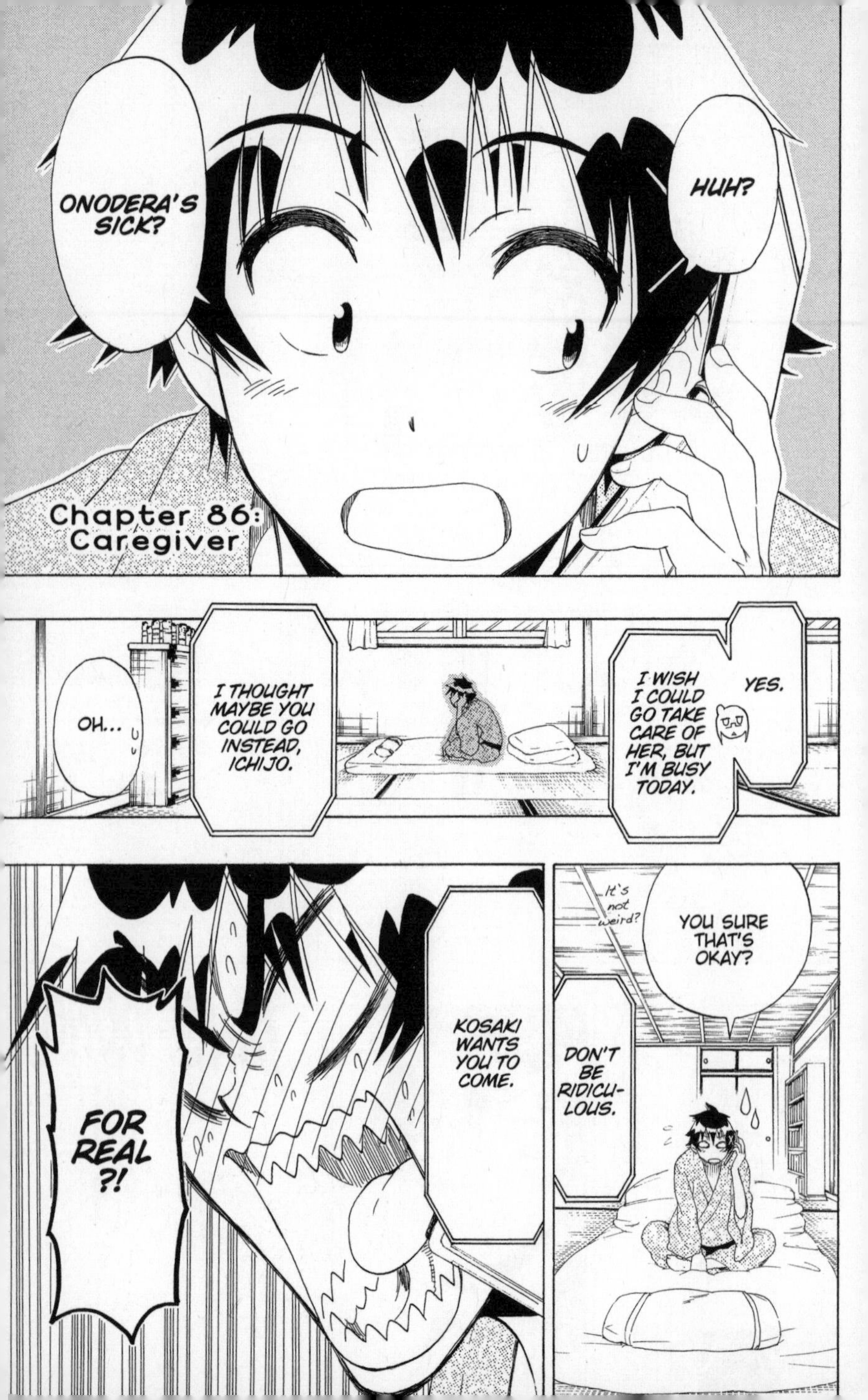
HUH?
ONODERA'S SICK?
Chapter 86: Caregiver
YES.
I WISH I COULD GO TAKE CARE OF HER, BUT I'M BUSY TODAY.
I THOUGHT MAYBE YOU COULD GO INSTEAD, ICHIJO.
OH...
YOU SURE THAT'S OKAY?
...It's not weird?
DON'T BE RIDICULOUS.
KOSAKI WANTS YOU TO COME.
FOR REAL?!

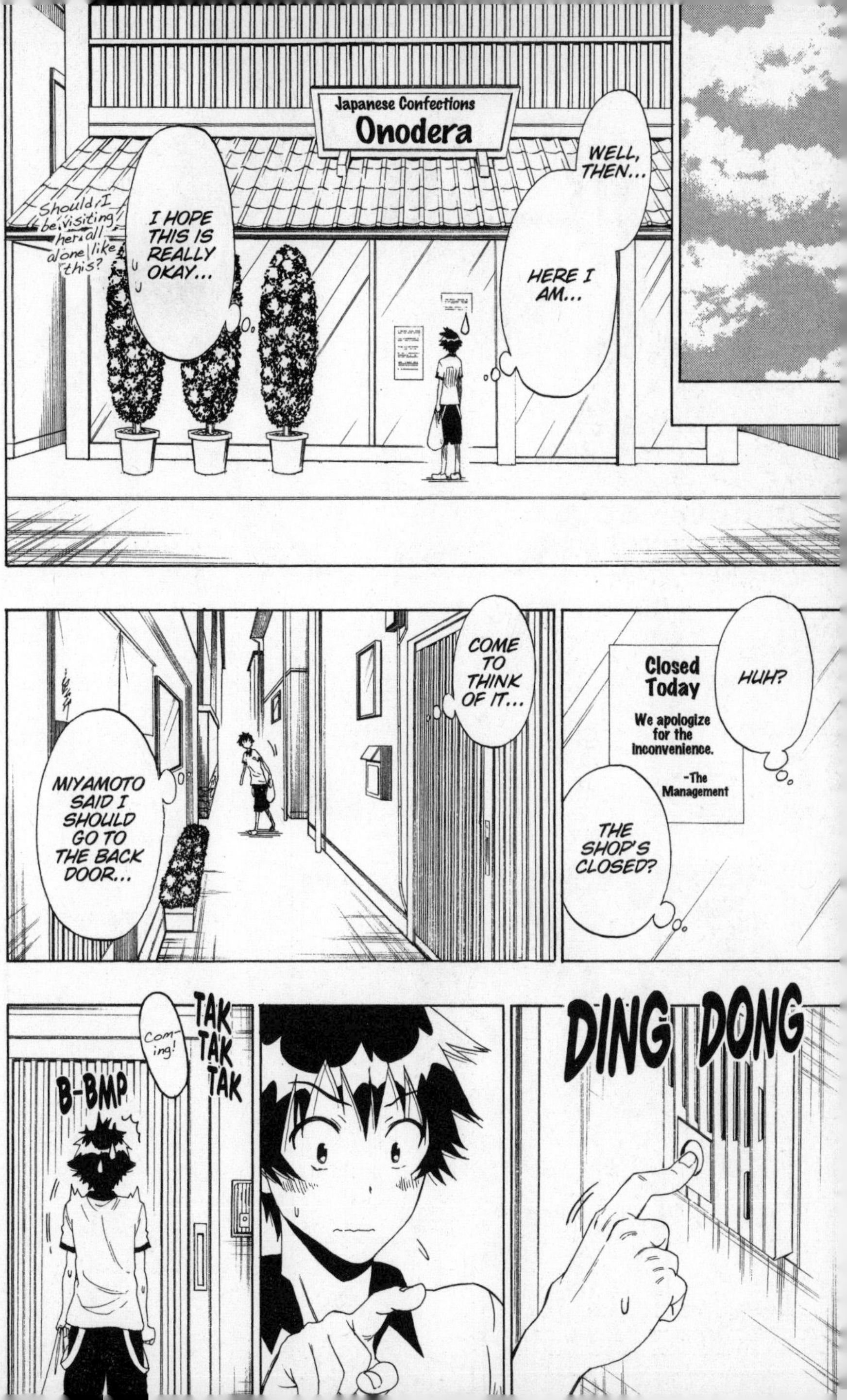
Japanese Confections
Onodera
WELL, THEN...
HERE I AM...
I HOPE THIS IS REALLY OKAY...
Should I be visiting her all alone like this?
HUH?
Closed Today
We apologize for the inconvenience.
-The Management
THE SHOP'S CLOSED?
COME TO THINK OF IT...
MIYAMOTO SAID I SHOULD GO TO THE BACK DOOR...
DING DONG
TAK TAK TAK
Com-ing!
B-BMP

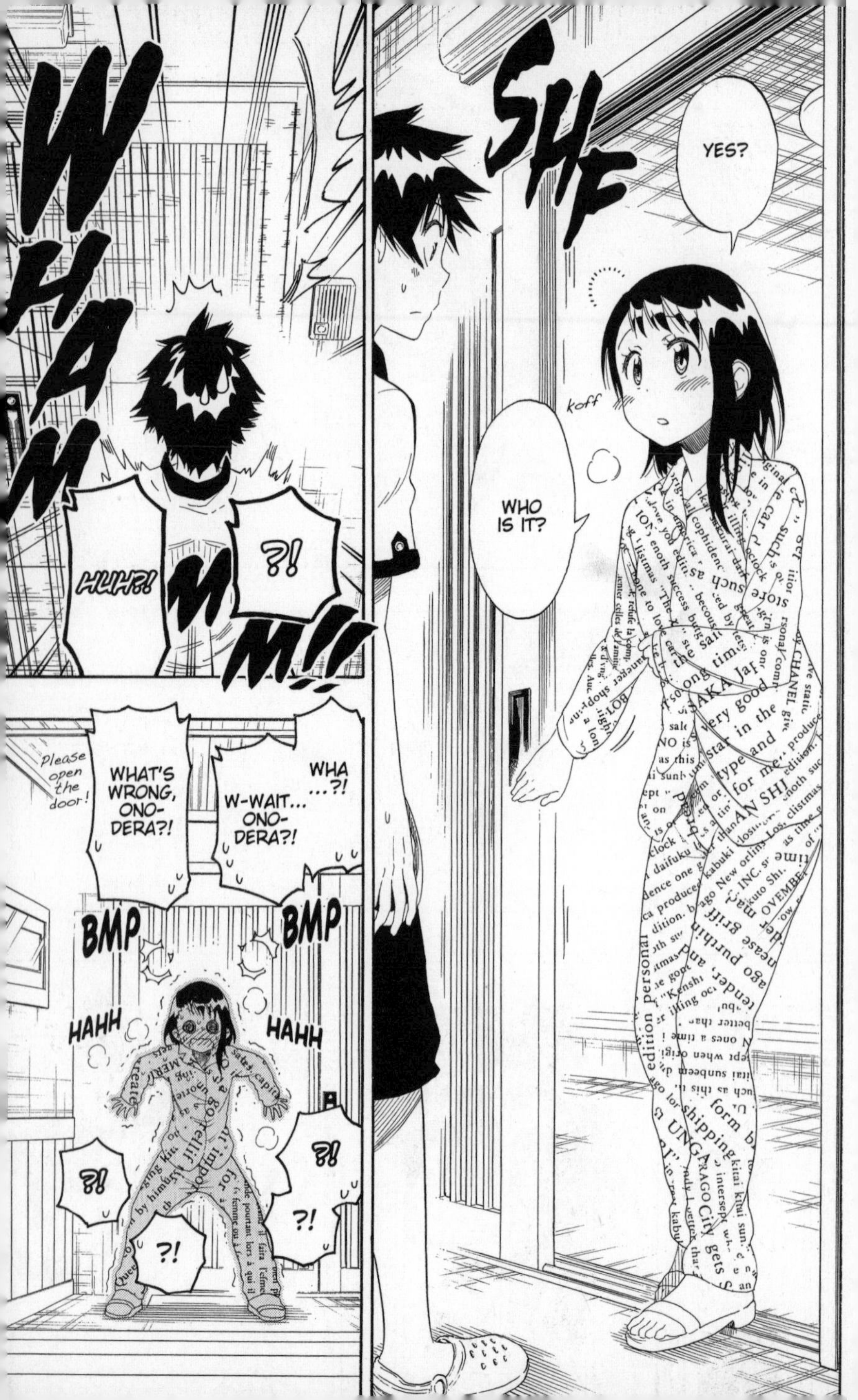

YES?
SHF
koff
WHO IS IT?
?!
MM!!
WHAM
HUH?!
WHA ...?!
W-WAIT... ONO-DERA?!
WHAT'S WRONG, ONO-DERA?!
Please open the door!
BMP
BMP
HAHH
HAHH
?!
?!
?!
?!

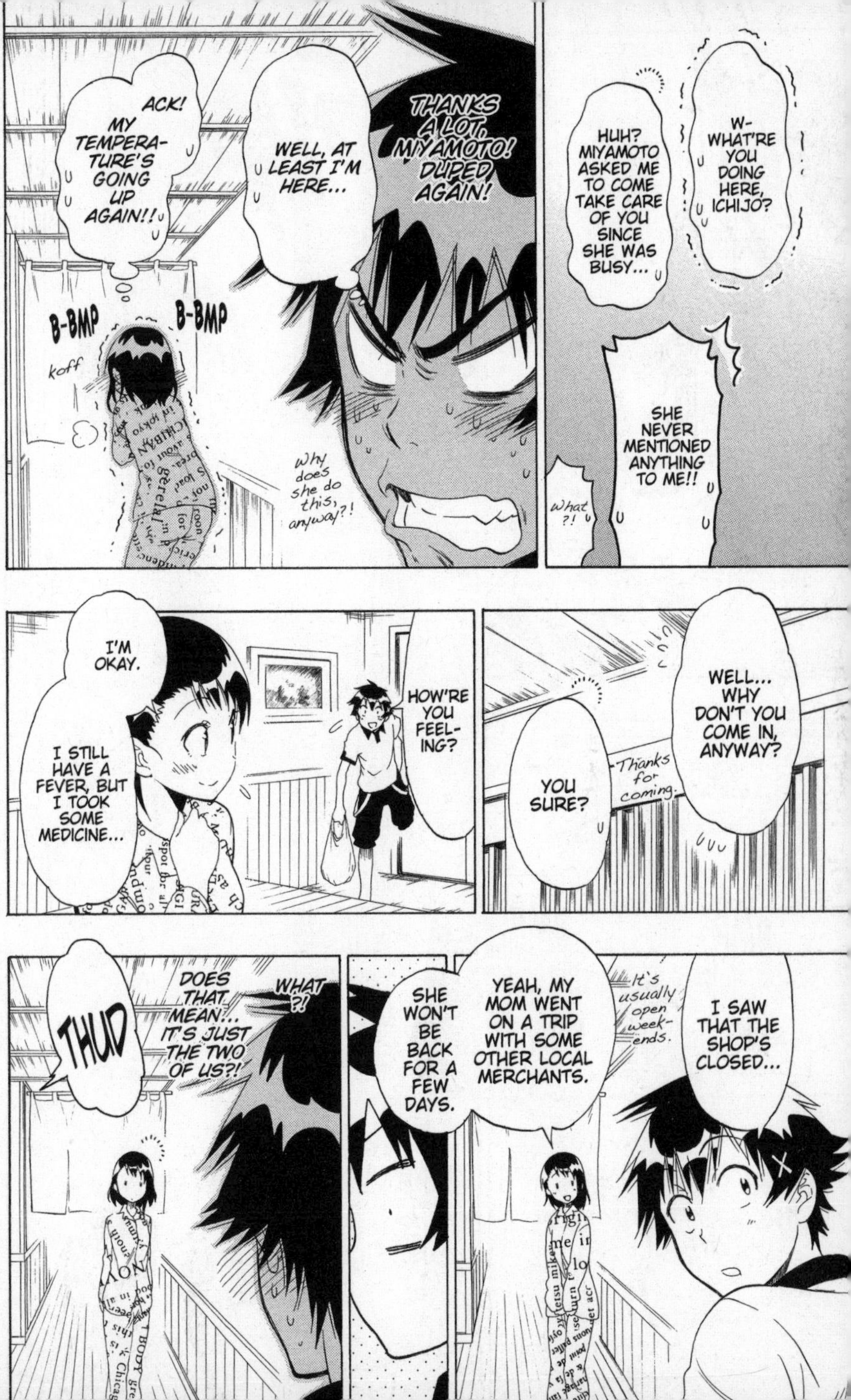
W-WHAT'RE YOU DOING HERE, ICHIJO?
HUH? MIYAMOTO ASKED ME TO COME TAKE CARE OF YOU SINCE SHE WAS BUSY...
SHE NEVER MENTIONED ANYTHING TO ME!!
What?!
THANKS A LOT, MIYAMOTO! DUPED AGAIN!
WELL, AT LEAST I'M HERE...
Why does she do this, anyway?!
ACK! MY TEMPERA-TURE'S GOING UP AGAIN!!
B-BMP
B-BMP
koff
WELL... WHY DON'T YOU COME IN, ANYWAY?
Thanks for coming.
YOU SURE?
HOW'RE YOU FEELING?
I'M OKAY.
I STILL HAVE A FEVER, BUT I TOOK SOME MEDICINE...
I SAW THAT THE SHOP'S CLOSED...
It's usually open weekends.
YEAH, MY MOM WENT ON A TRIP WITH SOME OTHER LOCAL MERCHANTS.
SHE WON'T BE BACK FOR A FEW DAYS.
WHAT?!
DOES THAT MEAN... IT'S JUST THE TWO OF US?!
THUD

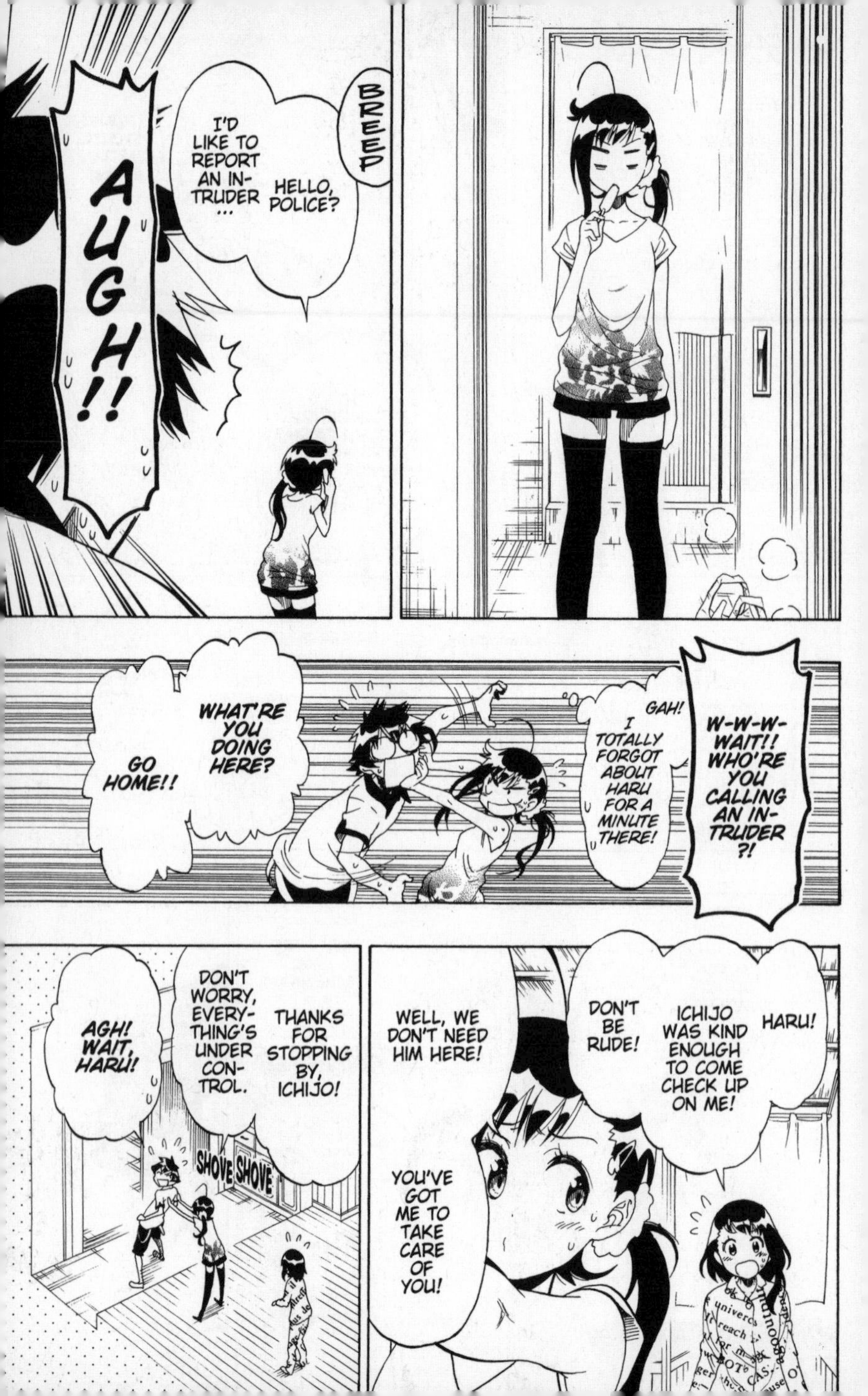
BREEP
HELLO, POLICE?
I'D LIKE TO REPORT AN INTRUDER...
AUGH!!
W-W-W-WAIT!! WHO'RE YOU CALLING AN INTRUDER?!
GAH! I TOTALLY FORGOT ABOUT HARU FOR A MINUTE THERE!
WHAT'RE YOU DOING HERE?
GO HOME!!
HARU!
ICHIJO WAS KIND ENOUGH TO COME CHECK UP ON ME!
DON'T BE RUDE!
WELL, WE DON'T NEED HIM HERE!
YOU'VE GOT ME TO TAKE CARE OF YOU!
THANKS FOR STOPPING BY, ICHIJO!
DON'T WORRY, EVERYTHING'S UNDER CONTROL.
SHOVE SHOVE
AGH! WAIT, HARU!

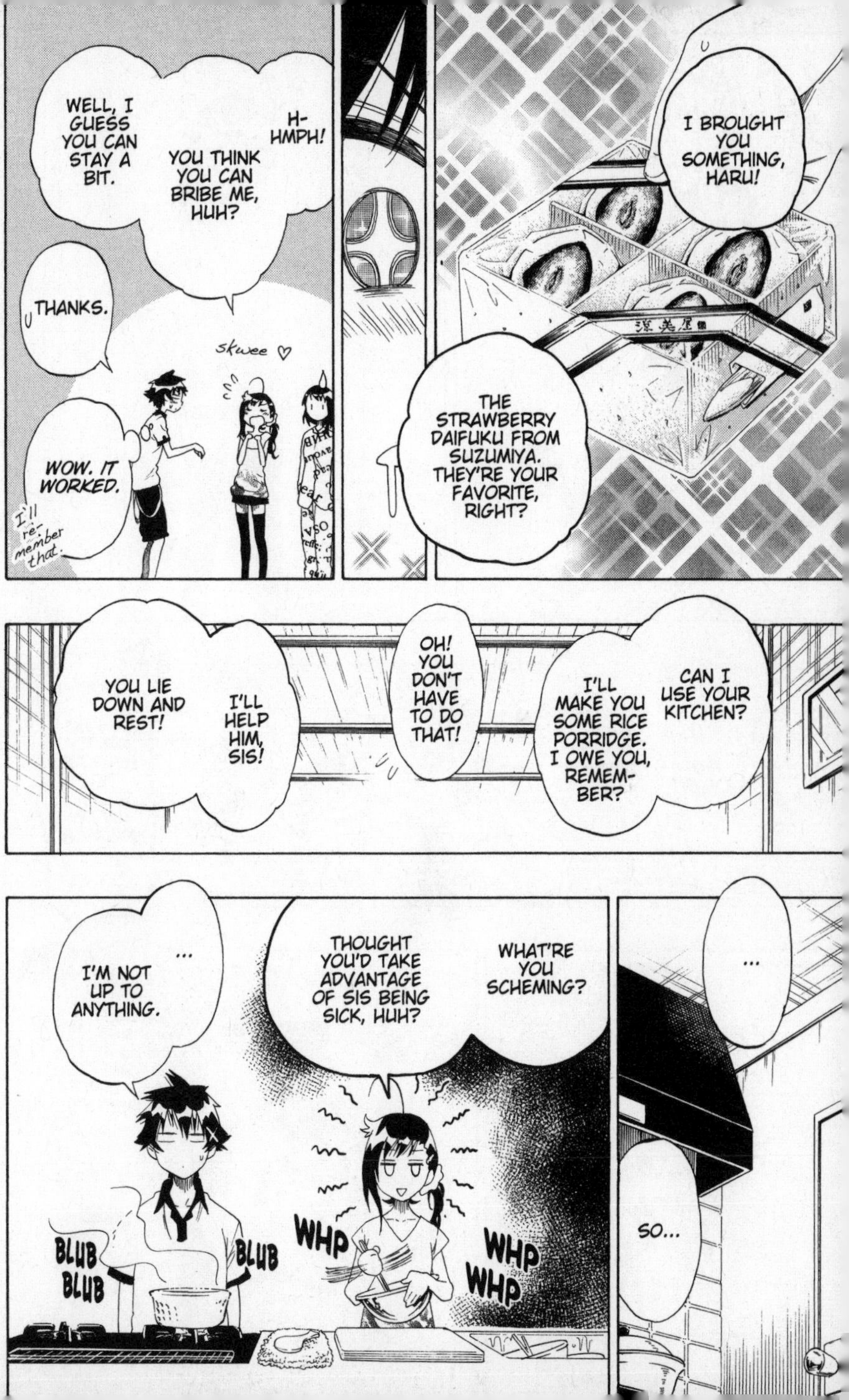
I BROUGHT YOU SOMETHING, HARU!
THE STRAWBERRY DAIFUKU FROM SUZUMIYA. THEY'RE YOUR FAVORITE, RIGHT?
H-HMPH!
YOU THINK YOU CAN BRIBE ME, HUH?
WELL, I GUESS YOU CAN STAY A BIT.
THANKS.
skwee ♡
WOW. IT WORKED.
I'll re-member that.
CAN I USE YOUR KITCHEN?
I'LL MAKE YOU SOME RICE PORRIDGE. I OWE YOU, REMEMBER?
OH! YOU DON'T HAVE TO DO THAT!
I'LL HELP HIM, SIS!
YOU LIE DOWN AND REST!
...
SO...
WHAT'RE YOU SCHEMING?
THOUGHT YOU'D TAKE ADVANTAGE OF SIS BEING SICK, HUH?
WHP
WHP WHP
...
I'M NOT UP TO ANYTHING.
BLUB
BLUB BLUB

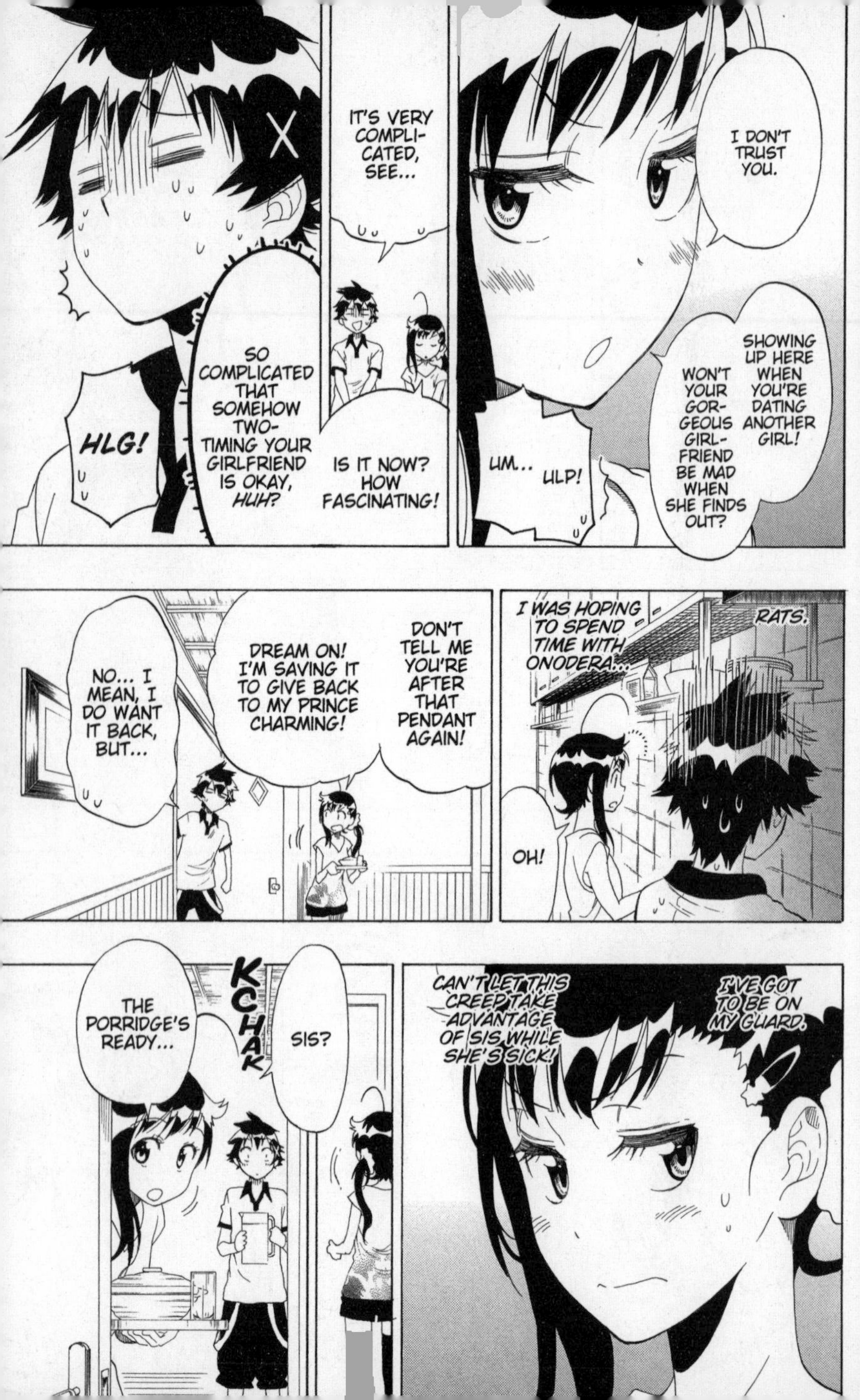
I DON'T TRUST YOU.
SHOWING UP HERE WHEN YOU'RE DATING ANOTHER GIRL!
WON'T YOUR GORGEOUS GIRLFRIEND BE MAD WHEN SHE FINDS OUT?
ULP!
UM...
IT'S VERY COMPLICATED, SEE...
IS IT NOW? HOW FASCINATING!
SO COMPLICATED THAT SOMEHOW TWO-TIMING YOUR GIRLFRIEND IS OKAY, *HUH?*
HLG!
RATS.
I WAS HOPING TO SPEND TIME WITH ONODERA...
OH!
DON'T TELL ME YOU'RE AFTER THAT PENDANT AGAIN!
DREAM ON! I'M SAVING IT TO GIVE BACK TO MY PRINCE CHARMING!
NO... I MEAN, I DO WANT IT BACK, BUT...
I'VE GOT TO BE ON MY GUARD.
CAN'T LET THIS CREEP TAKE ADVANTAGE OF SIS WHILE SHE'S SICK!
SIS?
KCHAK
THE PORRIDGE'S READY...

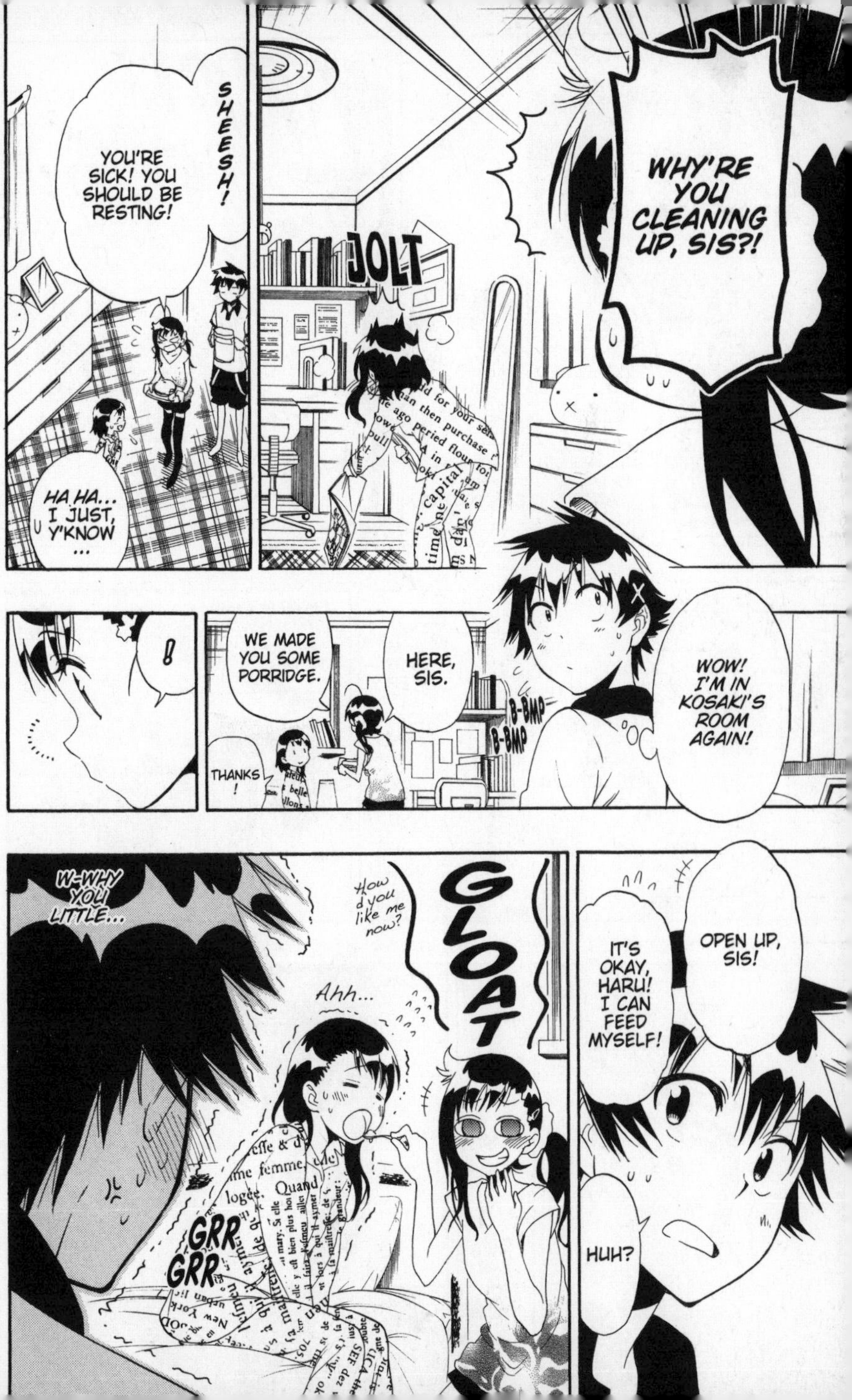
WHY'RE YOU CLEANING UP, SIS?!
JOLT
SHEESH!
YOU'RE SICK! YOU SHOULD BE RESTING!
HA HA... I JUST, Y'KNOW...
WOW! I'M IN KOSAKI'S ROOM AGAIN!
B-BMP
B-BMP
HERE, SIS.
WE MADE YOU SOME PORRIDGE.
THANKS!
!
OPEN UP, SIS!
IT'S OKAY, HARU! I CAN FEED MYSELF!
HUH?
GLOAT
How d you like me now?
Ahh...
W-WHY YOU LITTLE...
GRR
GRR

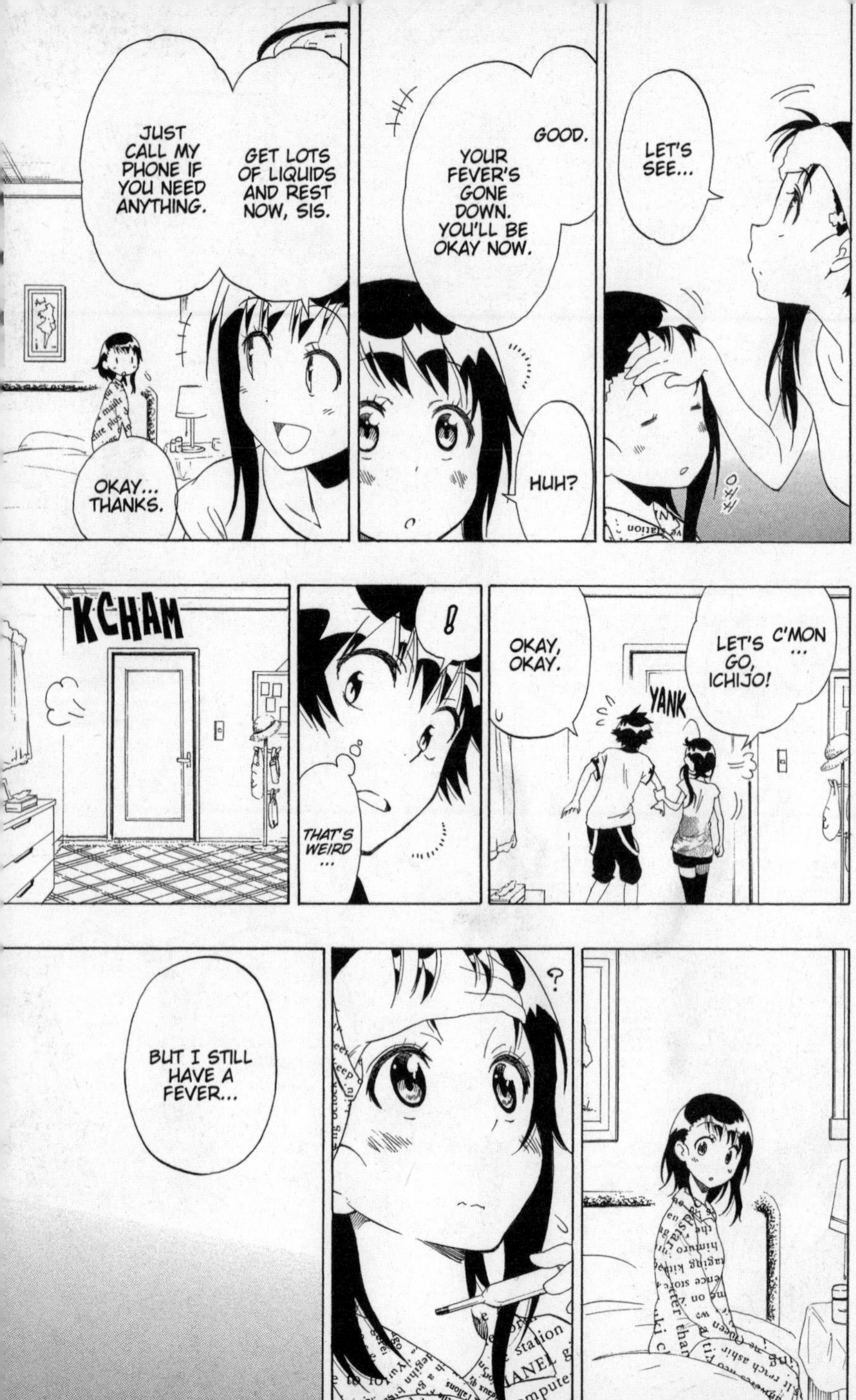
LET'S SEE...
GOOD.
YOUR FEVER'S GONE DOWN. YOU'LL BE OKAY NOW.
HUH?
GET LOTS OF LIQUIDS AND REST NOW, SIS.
JUST CALL MY PHONE IF YOU NEED ANYTHING.
OKAY... THANKS.
C'MON...
LET'S GO, ICHIJO!
YANK
OKAY, OKAY.
!
THAT'S WEIRD...
KCHAM
?
BUT I STILL HAVE A FEVER...

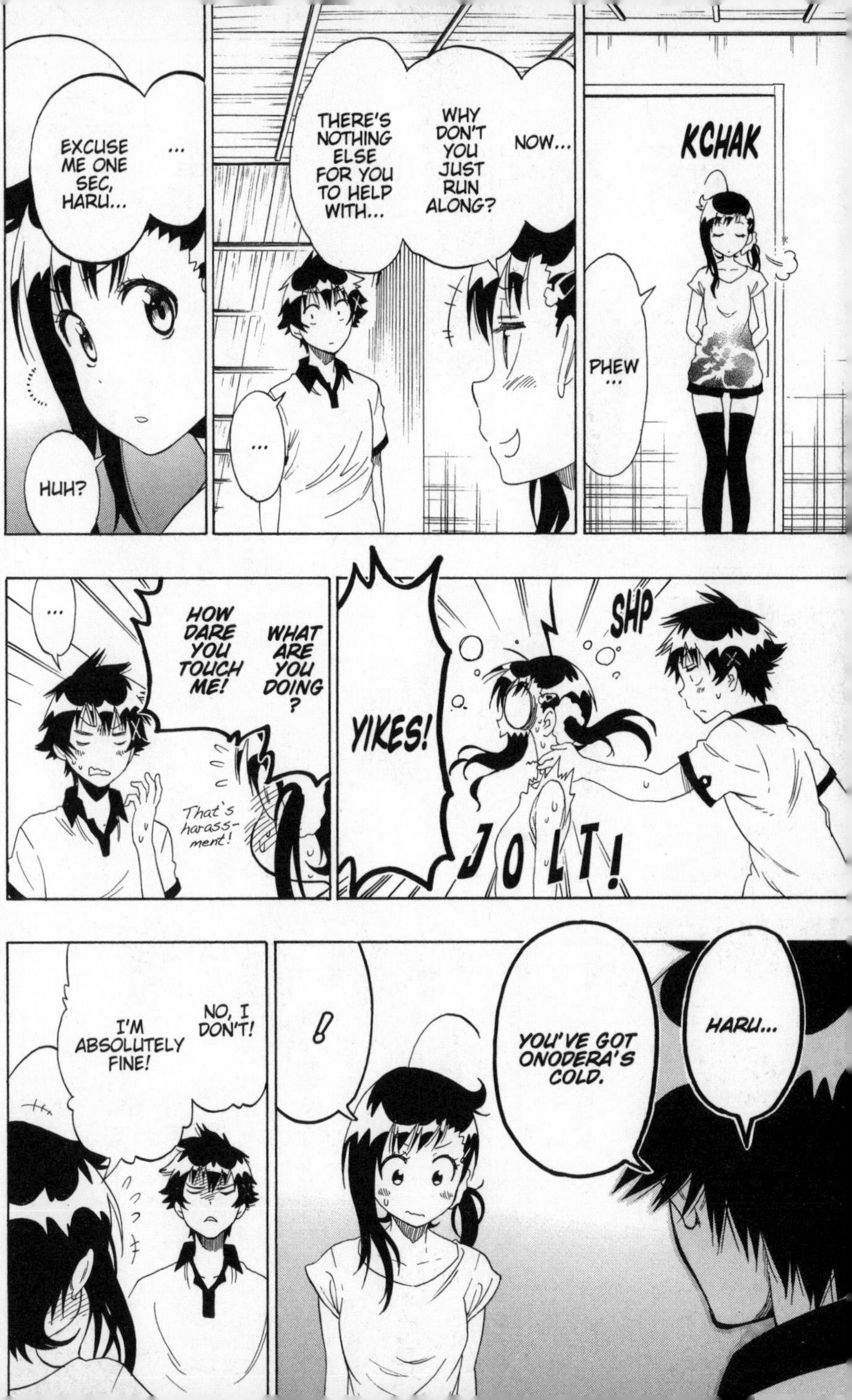
KCHAK
PHEW...
NOW...
WHY DON'T YOU JUST RUN ALONG?
THERE'S NOTHING ELSE FOR YOU TO HELP WITH...
...
...
EXCUSE ME ONE SEC, HARU...
HUH?
SHP
YIKES!
JOLT!
WHAT ARE YOU DOING?
HOW DARE YOU TOUCH ME!
...
That's harassment!
HARU...
YOU'VE GOT ONODERA'S COLD.
!
NO, I DON'T!
I'M ABSOLUTELY FINE!

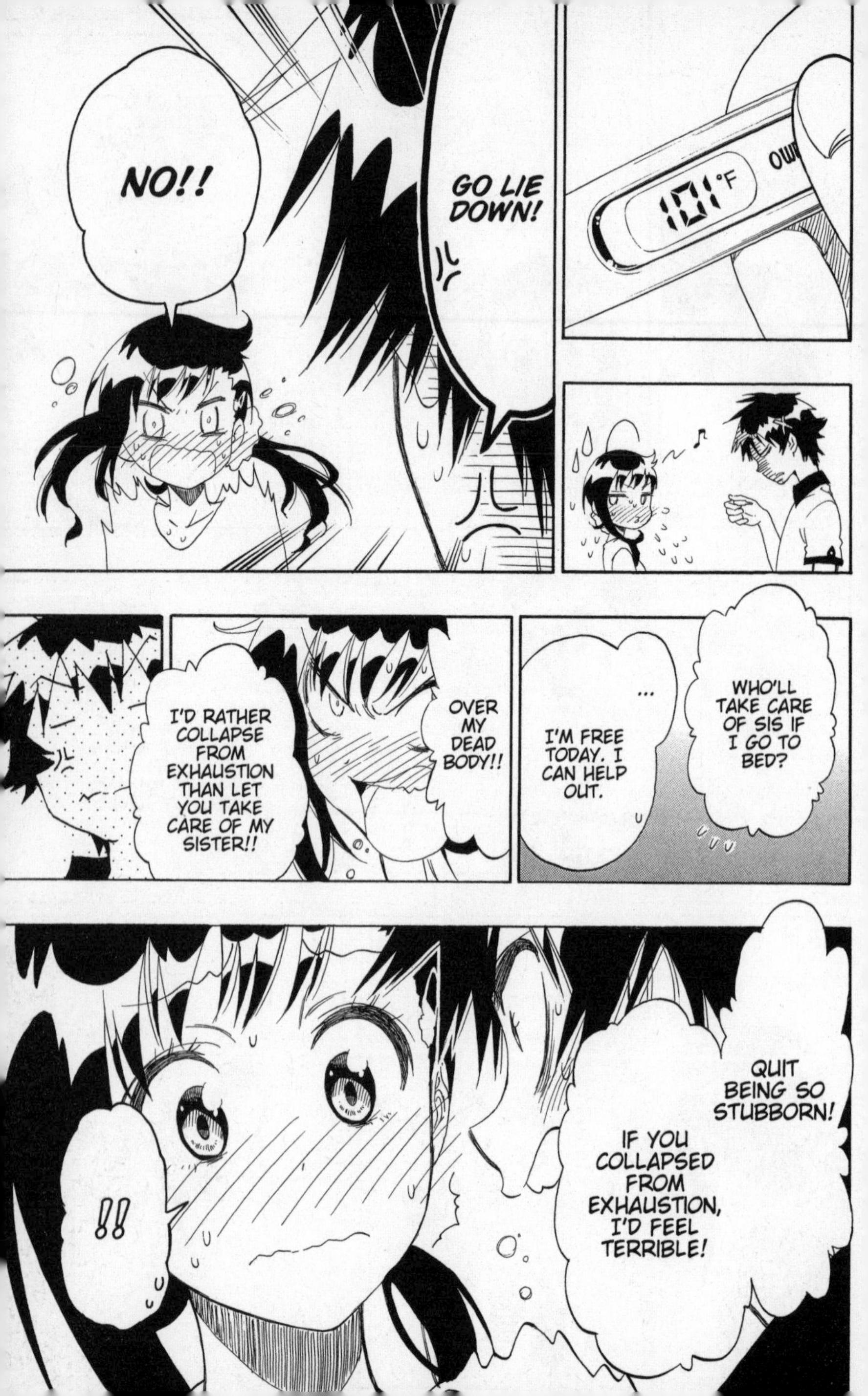
101°F
GO LIE DOWN!
NO!!
WHO'LL TAKE CARE OF SIS IF I GO TO BED?
...
I'M FREE TODAY. I CAN HELP OUT.
OVER MY DEAD BODY!!
I'D RATHER COLLAPSE FROM EXHAUSTION THAN LET YOU TAKE CARE OF MY SISTER!!
QUIT BEING SO STUBBORN!
IF YOU COLLAPSED FROM EXHAUSTION, I'D FEEL TERRIBLE!
!!

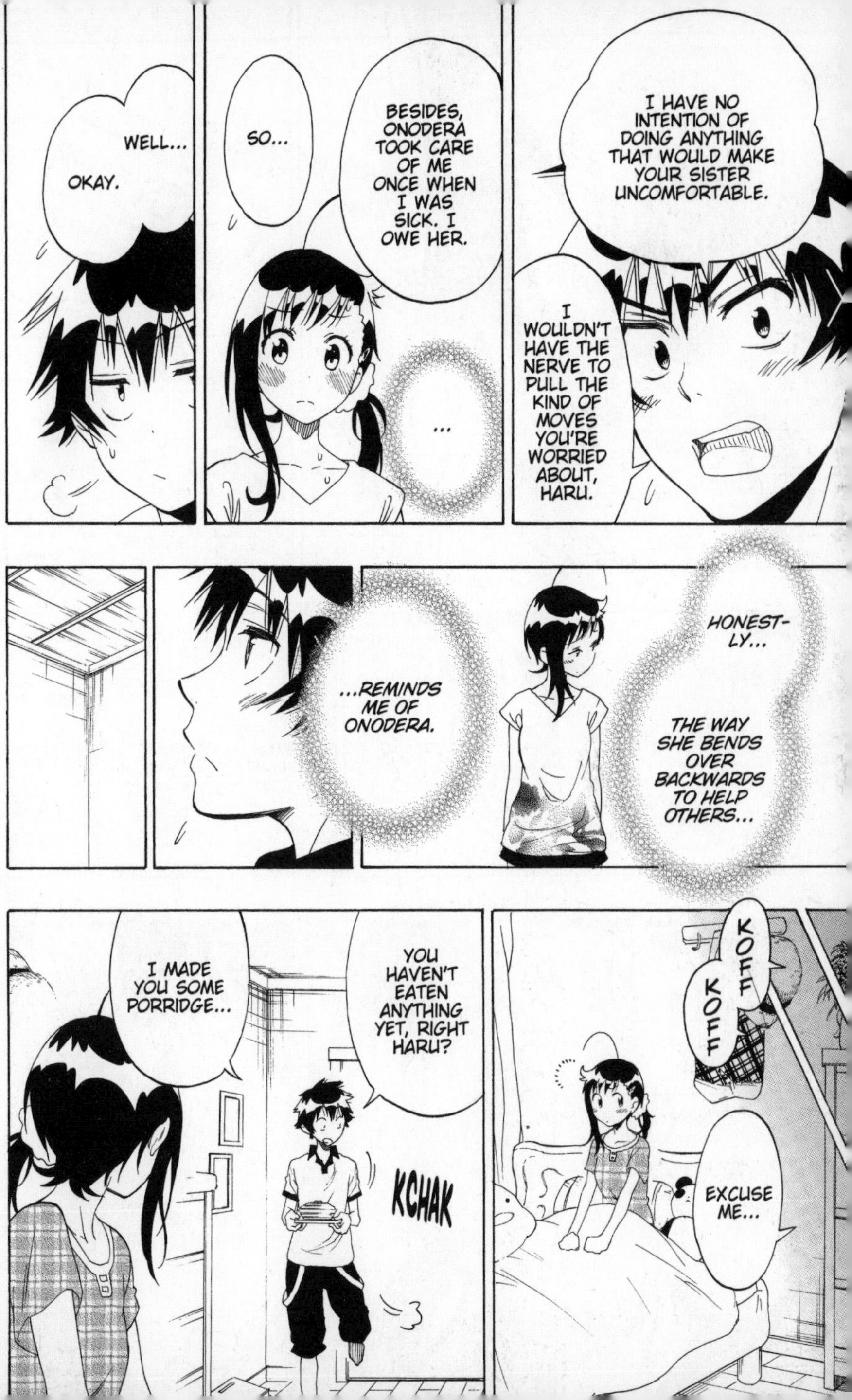
I HAVE NO INTENTION OF DOING ANYTHING THAT WOULD MAKE YOUR SISTER UNCOMFORTABLE.
I WOULDN'T HAVE THE NERVE TO PULL THE KIND OF MOVES YOU'RE WORRIED ABOUT, HARU.
BESIDES, ONODERA TOOK CARE OF ME ONCE WHEN I WAS SICK. I OWE HER.
SO...
...
WELL...
OKAY.
HONEST-LY...
THE WAY SHE BENDS OVER BACKWARDS TO HELP OTHERS...
...REMINDS ME OF ONODERA.
KOFF
KOFF
EXCUSE ME...
YOU HAVEN'T EATEN ANYTHING YET, RIGHT HARU?
KCHAK
I MADE YOU SOME PORRIDGE...

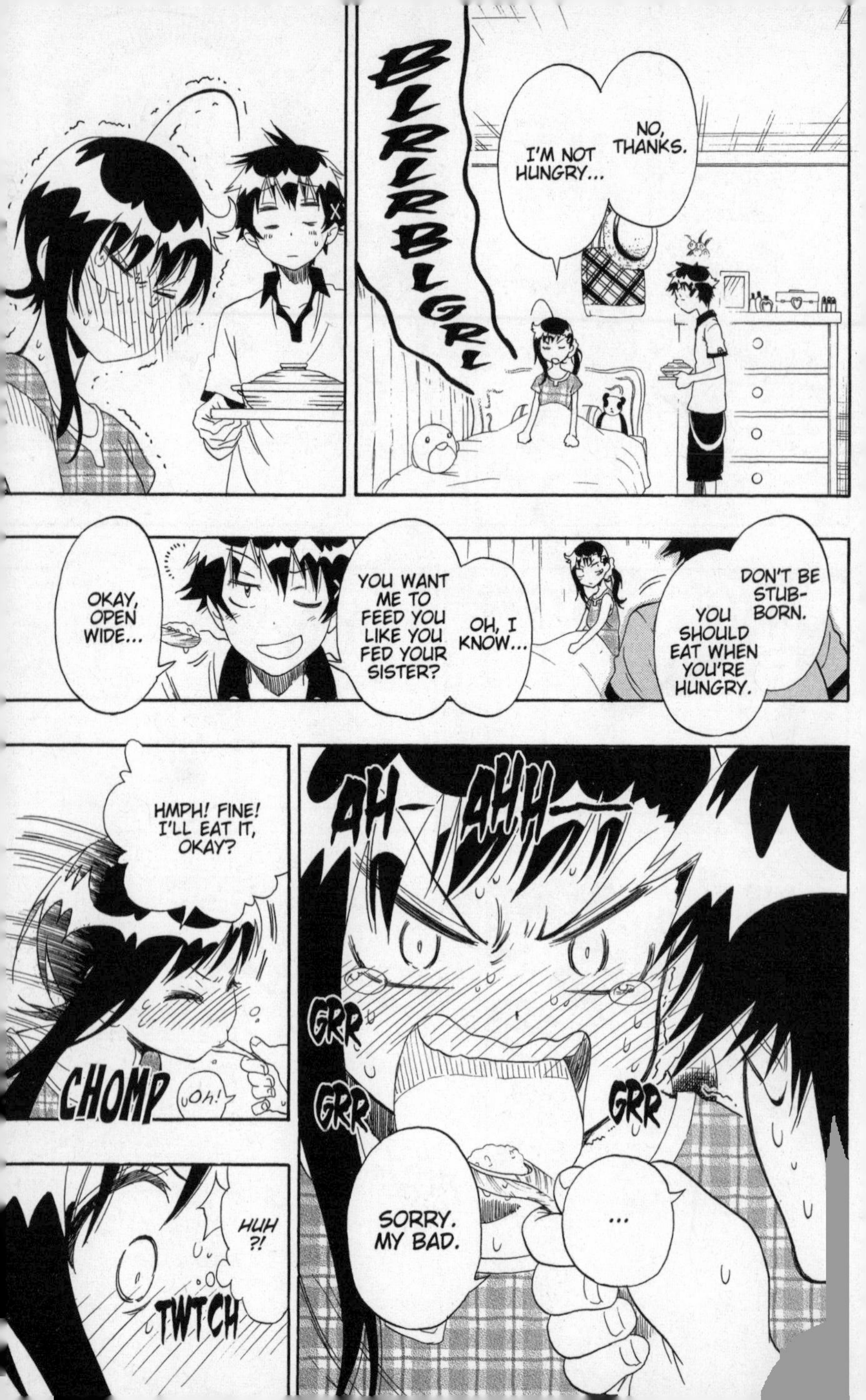
BLRLRBLGRL
NO, THANKS.
I'M NOT HUNGRY...
DON'T BE STUB-BORN.
YOU SHOULD EAT WHEN YOU'RE HUNGRY.
OH, I KNOW...
YOU WANT ME TO FEED YOU LIKE YOU FED YOUR SISTER?
OKAY, OPEN WIDE...
AH- AHH—
GRR
GRR
GRR
...
SORRY. MY BAD.
HMPH! FINE! I'LL EAT IT, OKAY?
CHOMP
Oh!
HUH ?!
TWTCH

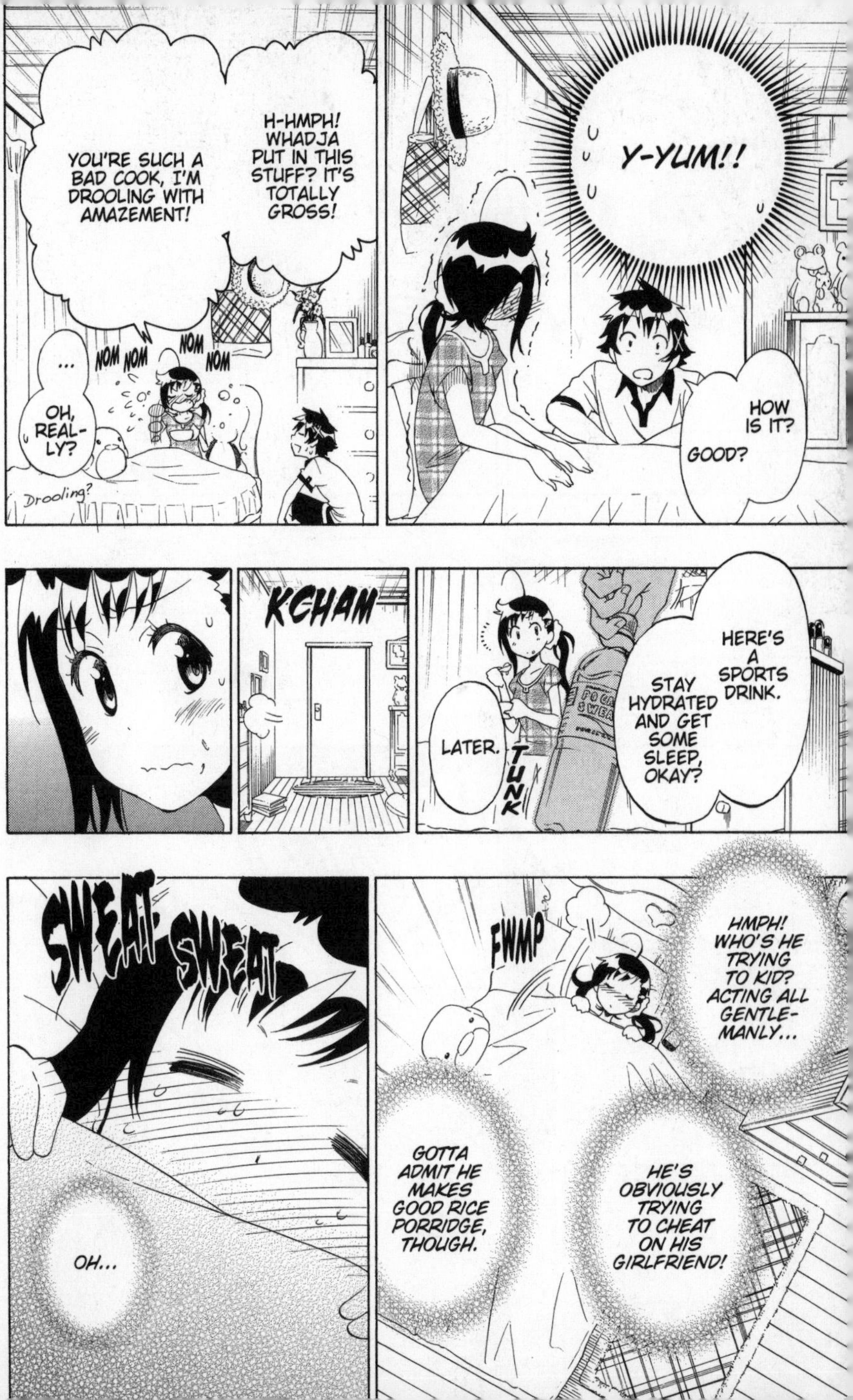
HOW IS IT?
GOOD?
Y-YUM!!
H-HMPH! WHADJA PUT IN THIS STUFF? IT'S TOTALLY GROSS!
YOU'RE SUCH A BAD COOK, I'M DROOLING WITH AMAZEMENT!
NOM NOM NOM NOM
...
OH, REAL-LY?
Drooling?
HERE'S A SPORTS DRINK.
STAY HYDRATED AND GET SOME SLEEP, OKAY?
TUNK
LATER.
KCHAM
FWMP
HMPH! WHO'S HE TRYING TO KID? ACTING ALL GENTLE-MANLY...
HE'S OBVIOUSLY TRYING TO CHEAT ON HIS GIRLFRIEND!
GOTTA ADMIT HE MAKES GOOD RICE PORRIDGE, THOUGH.
SWEAT SWEAT
OH...

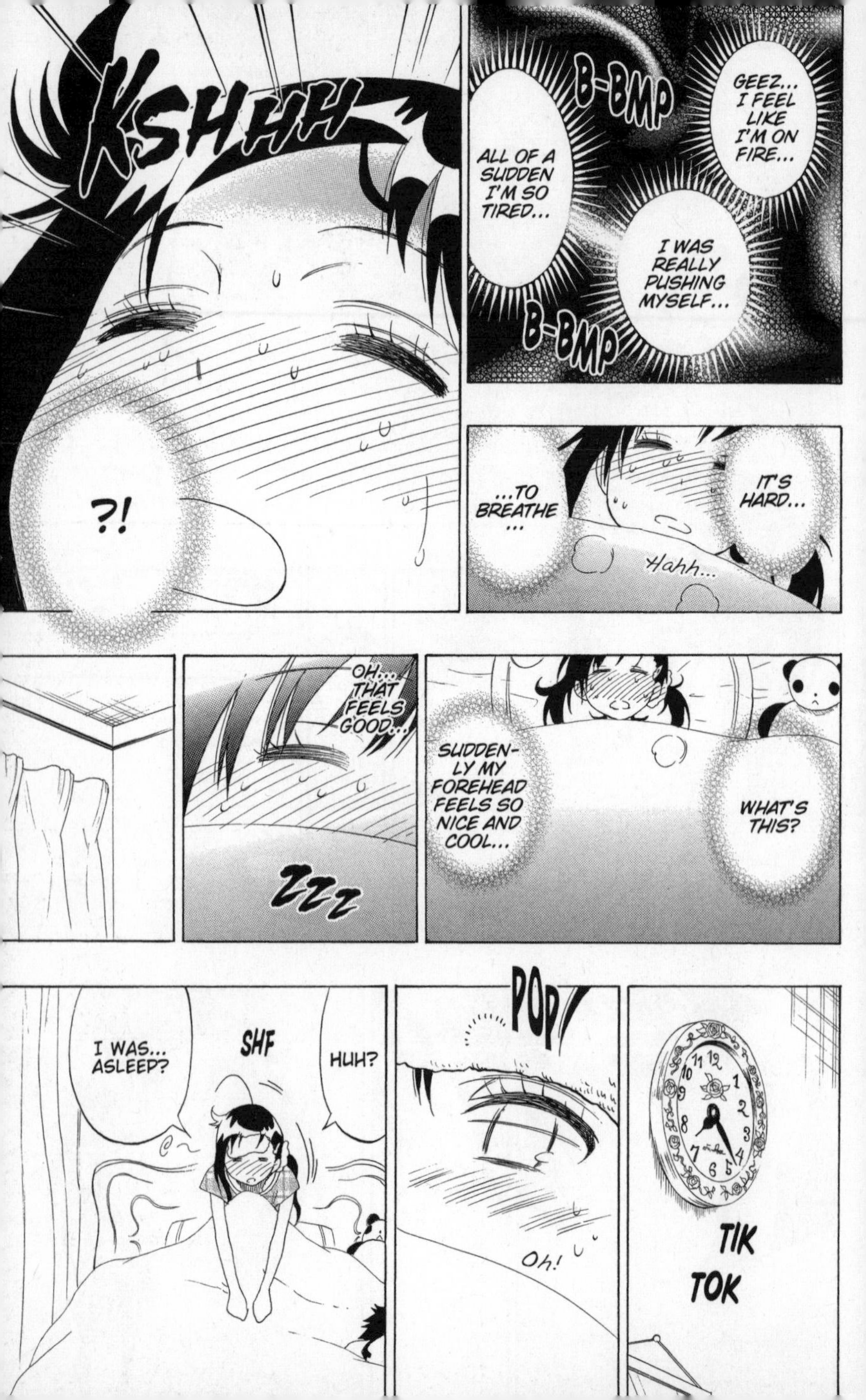
GEEZ... I FEEL LIKE I'M ON FIRE...
B-BMP
ALL OF A SUDDEN I'M SO TIRED...
I WAS REALLY PUSHING MYSELF...
B-BMP
IT'S HARD...
...TO BREATHE...
Hahh...
KSHHH
?!
WHAT'S THIS?
SUDDEN-LY MY FOREHEAD FEELS SO NICE AND COOL...
OH... THAT FEELS GOOD...
ZZZ
TIK
TOK
POP
Oh!
HUH?
SHF
I WAS... ASLEEP?

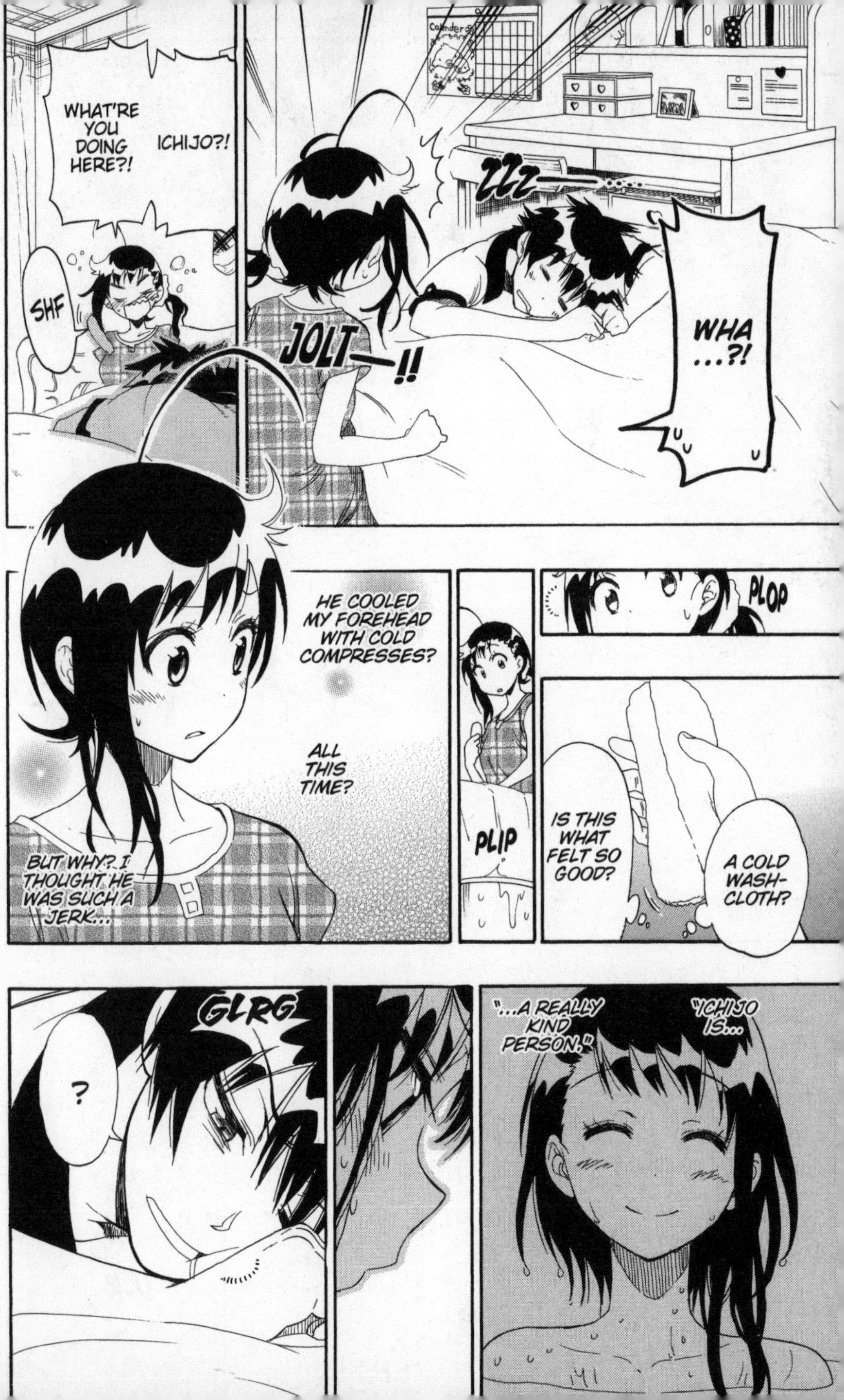
ZZZ—...
WHA...?!
JOLT—!!
SHF
ICHIJO?!
WHAT'RE YOU DOING HERE?!
PLOP
A COLD WASH-CLOTH?
IS THIS WHAT FELT SO GOOD?
PLIP
HE COOLED MY FOREHEAD WITH COLD COMPRESSES?
ALL THIS TIME?
BUT WHY? I THOUGHT HE WAS SUCH A JERK...
"ICHIJO IS...
...A REALLY KIND PERSON."
GLRG
?

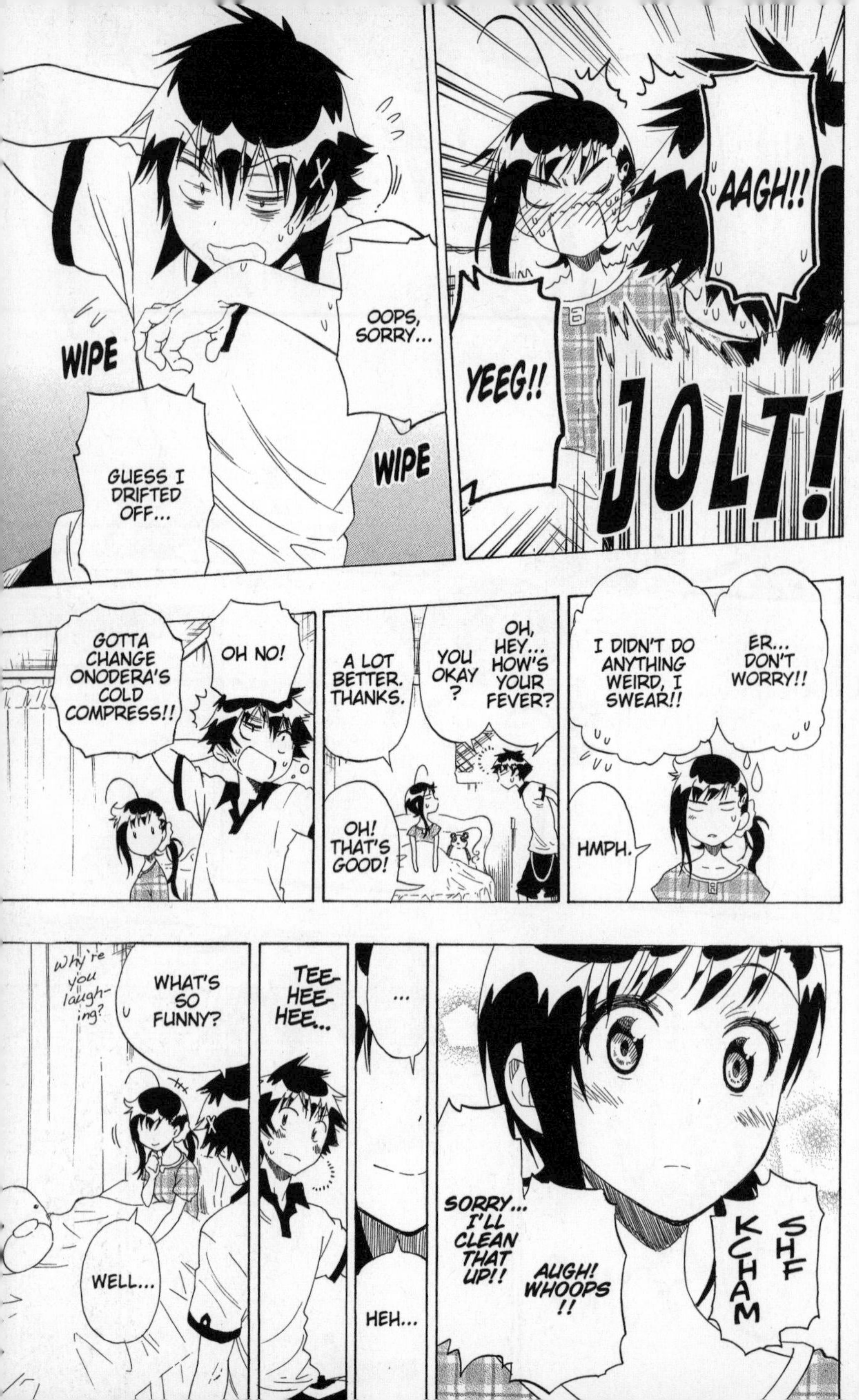

AAGH!!
YEEG!!
JOLT!
OOPS, SORRY...
WIPE
WIPE
GUESS I DRIFTED OFF...
ER... DON'T WORRY!!
I DIDN'T DO ANYTHING WEIRD, I SWEAR!!
HMPH.
OH, HEY... HOW'S YOUR FEVER?
YOU OKAY?
A LOT BETTER. THANKS.
OH! THAT'S GOOD!
OH NO!
GOTTA CHANGE ONODERA'S COLD COMPRESS!!
SHF
KCHAM
AUGH! WHOOPS!!
SORRY... I'LL CLEAN THAT UP!!
...
HEH...
TEE-HEE-HEE...
WHAT'S SO FUNNY?
Why're you laughing?
WELL...

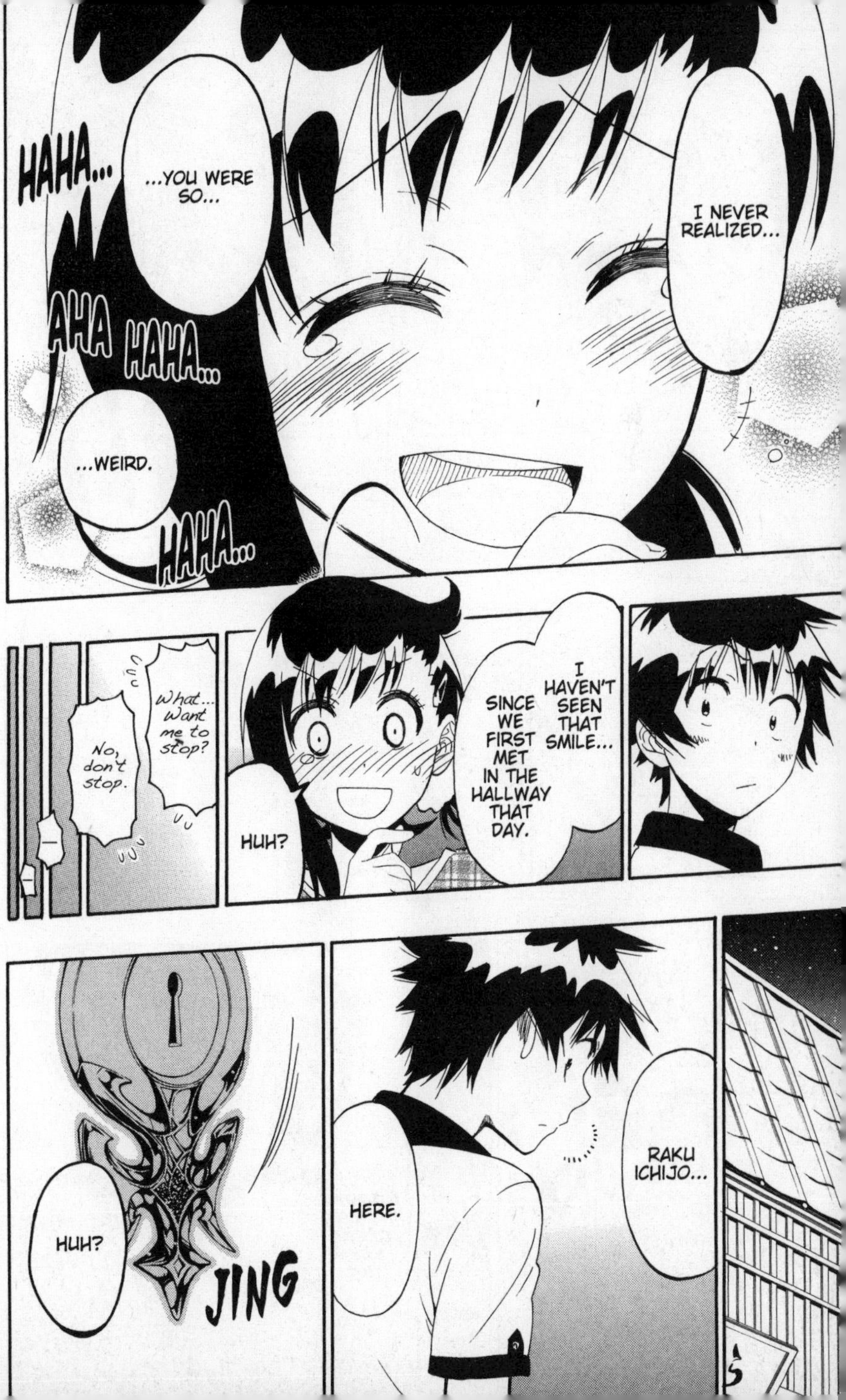
I NEVER REALIZED...
...YOU WERE SO...
HAHA...
AHA HAHA...
...WEIRD.
HAHA...
I HAVEN'T SEEN THAT SMILE... SINCE WE FIRST MET IN THE HALLWAY THAT DAY.
HUH?
What... Want me to stop?
No, don't stop.
RAKU ICHIJO...
......
HERE.
HUH?
JING

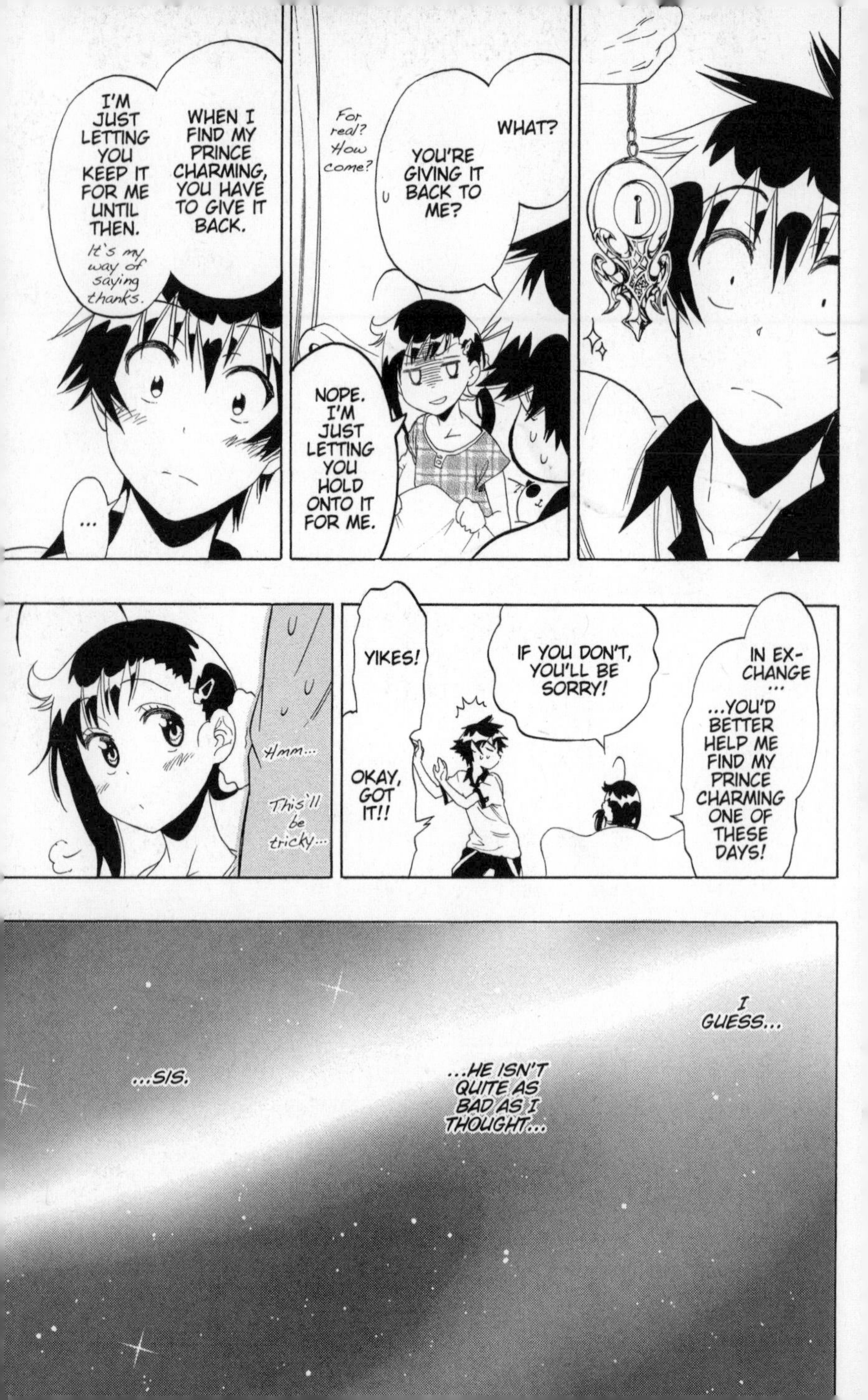
WHAT?
YOU'RE GIVING IT BACK TO ME?
For real? How come?
NOPE. I'M JUST LETTING YOU HOLD ONTO IT FOR ME.
WHEN I FIND MY PRINCE CHARMING, YOU HAVE TO GIVE IT BACK.
I'M JUST LETTING YOU KEEP IT FOR ME UNTIL THEN.
It's my way of saying thanks.
...
IN EX-CHANGE... ...YOU'D BETTER HELP ME FIND MY PRINCE CHARMING ONE OF THESE DAYS!
IF YOU DON'T, YOU'LL BE SORRY!
YIKES!
OKAY, GOT IT!!
Hmm...
This'll be tricky...
I GUESS...
...HE ISN'T QUITE AS BAD AS I THOUGHT...
...SIS.

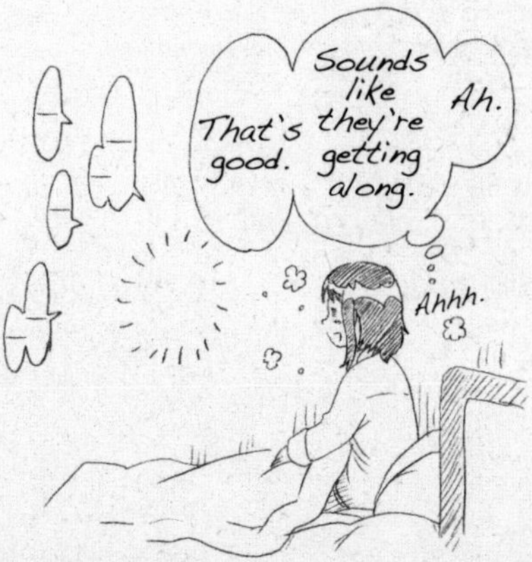
Ah.
Sounds like they're getting along.
That's good.
Ahhh.

Chapter 87: Special Day

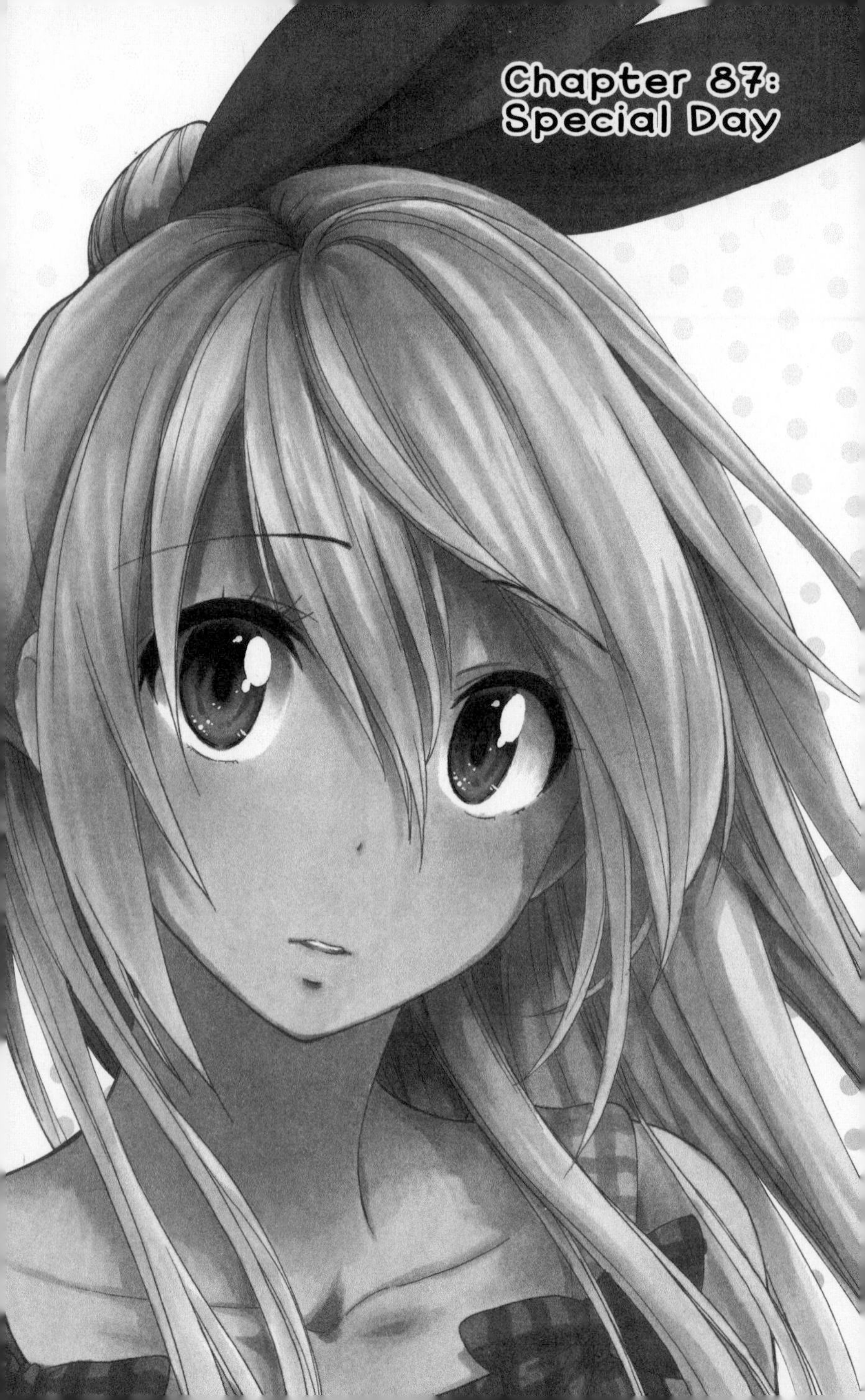

NISEKOI

False Love

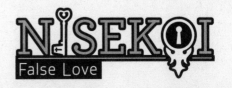

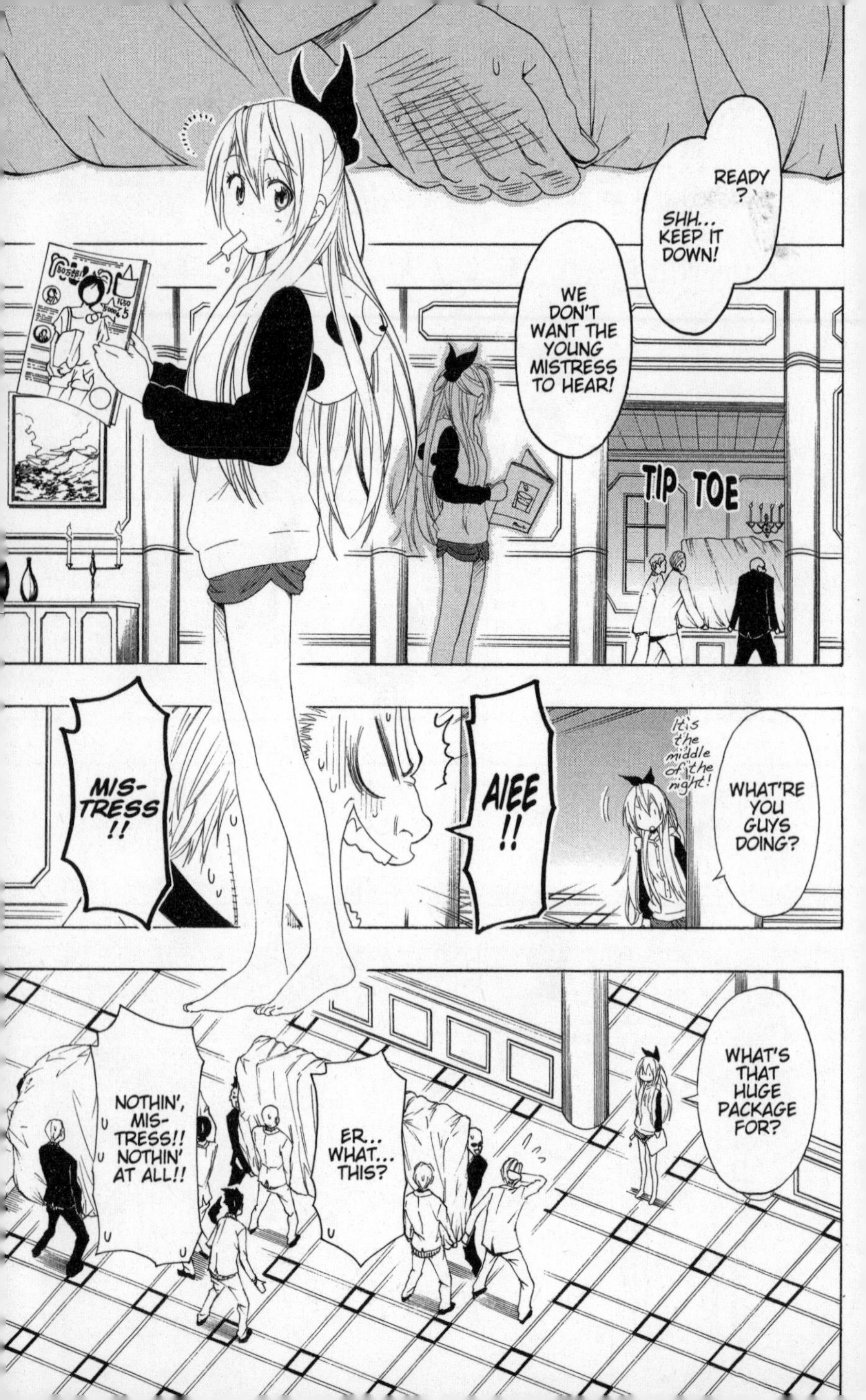

READY?
SHH... KEEP IT DOWN!
WE DON'T WANT THE YOUNG MISTRESS TO HEAR!
TIP TOE
It's the middle of the night!
WHAT'RE YOU GUYS DOING?
AIEE!!
MIS-TRESS!!
WHAT'S THAT HUGE PACKAGE FOR?
ER... WHAT... THIS?
NOTHIN', MIS-TRESS!! NOTHIN' AT ALL!!

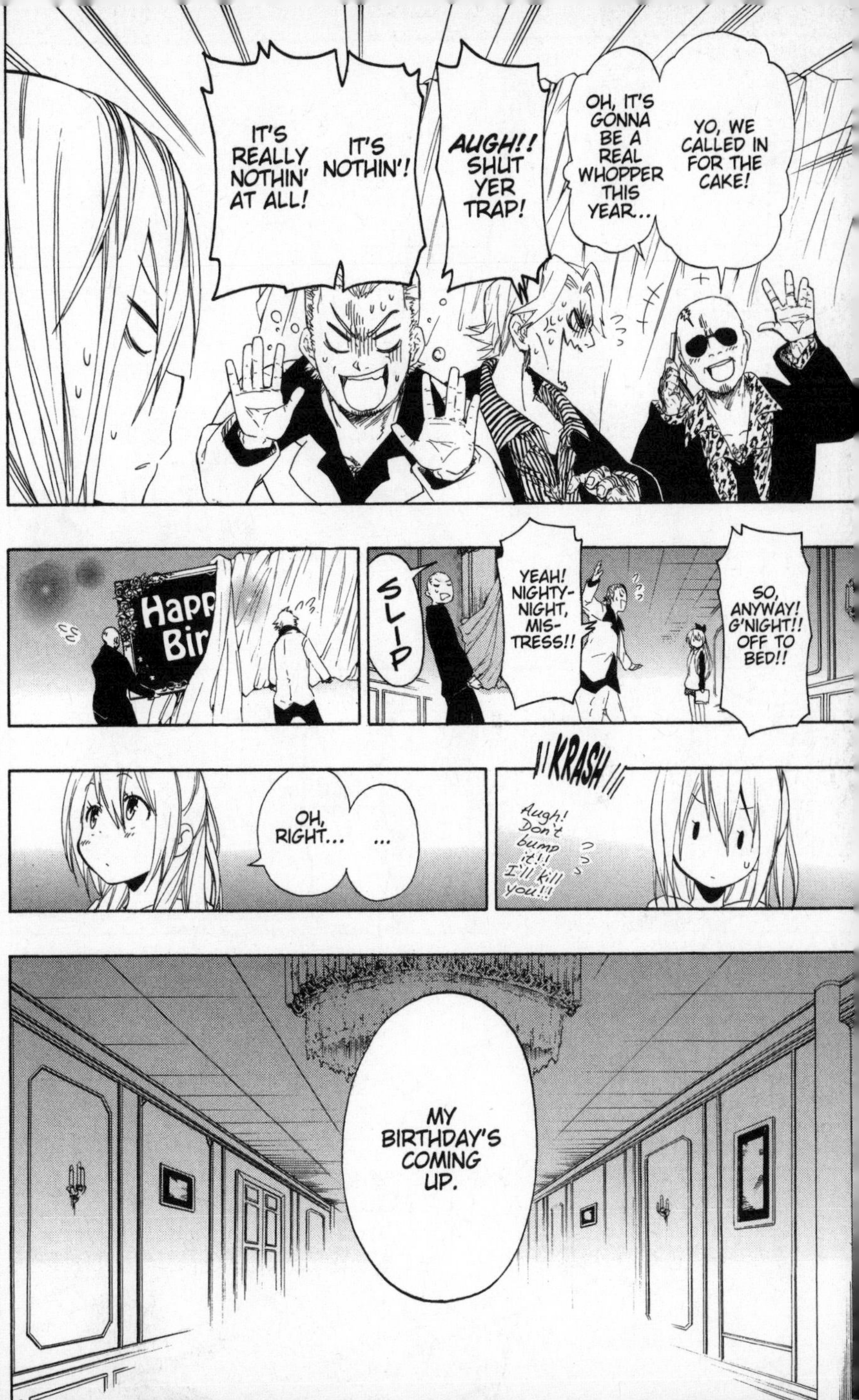
YO, WE CALLED IN FOR THE CAKE!
OH, IT'S GONNA BE A REAL WHOPPER THIS YEAR...
AUGH!! SHUT YER TRAP!
IT'S NOTHIN'!
IT'S REALLY NOTHIN' AT ALL!
SO, ANYWAY! G'NIGHT!! OFF TO BED!!
YEAH! NIGHTY-NIGHT, MIS-TRESS!!
SLIP
Happ Bir
KRASH
Augh! Don't bump it!! I'll kill you!!
OH, RIGHT...
...
MY BIRTHDAY'S COMING UP.

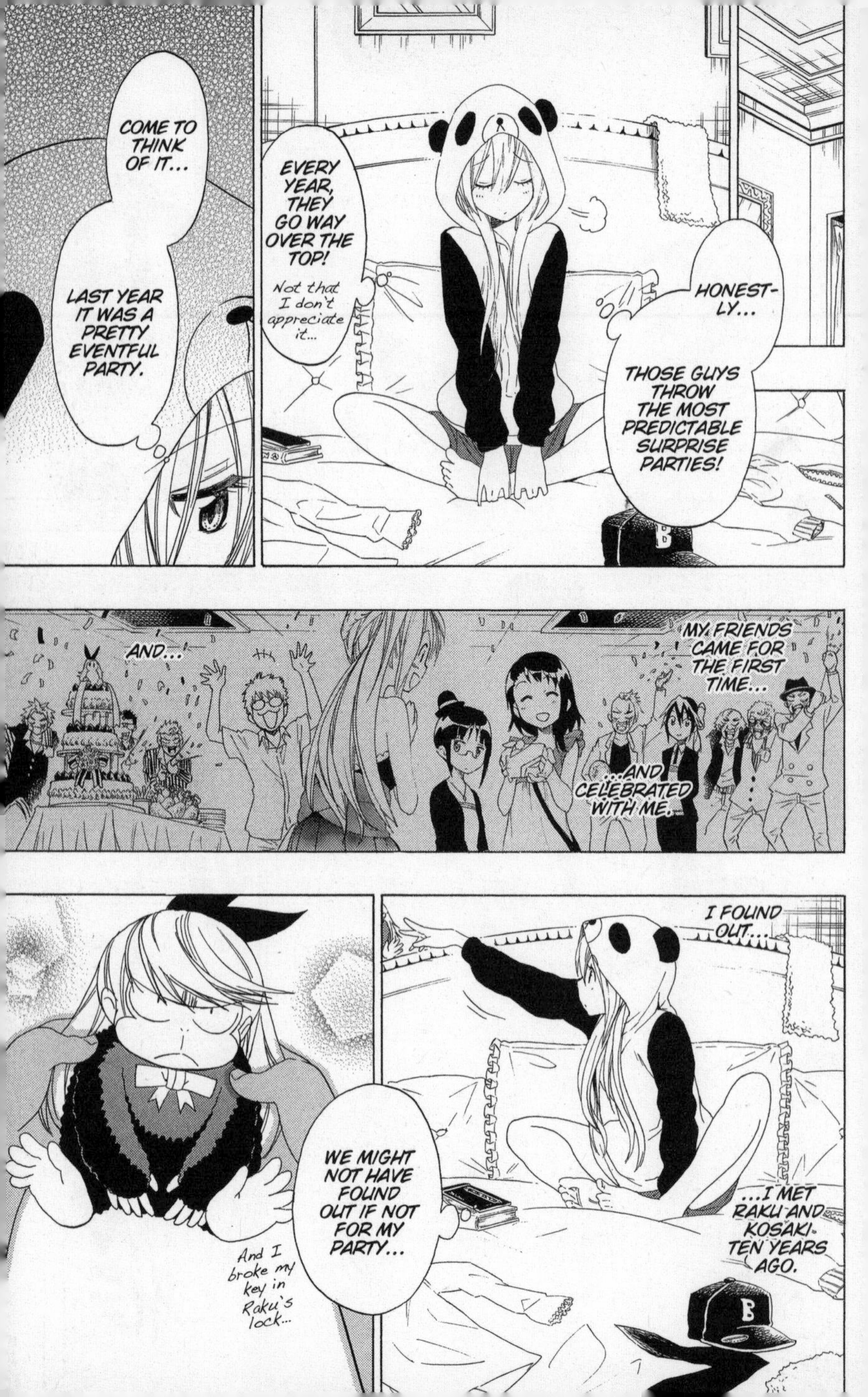
HONESTLY...
THOSE GUYS THROW THE MOST PREDICTABLE SURPRISE PARTIES!
EVERY YEAR, THEY GO WAY OVER THE TOP!
Not that I don't appreciate it...
COME TO THINK OF IT...
LAST YEAR IT WAS A PRETTY EVENTFUL PARTY.
AND...
MY FRIENDS CAME FOR THE FIRST TIME...
...AND CELEBRATED WITH ME.
I FOUND OUT...
...I MET RAKU AND KOSAKI TEN YEARS AGO.
WE MIGHT NOT HAVE FOUND OUT IF NOT FOR MY PARTY...
And I broke my key in Raku's lock...

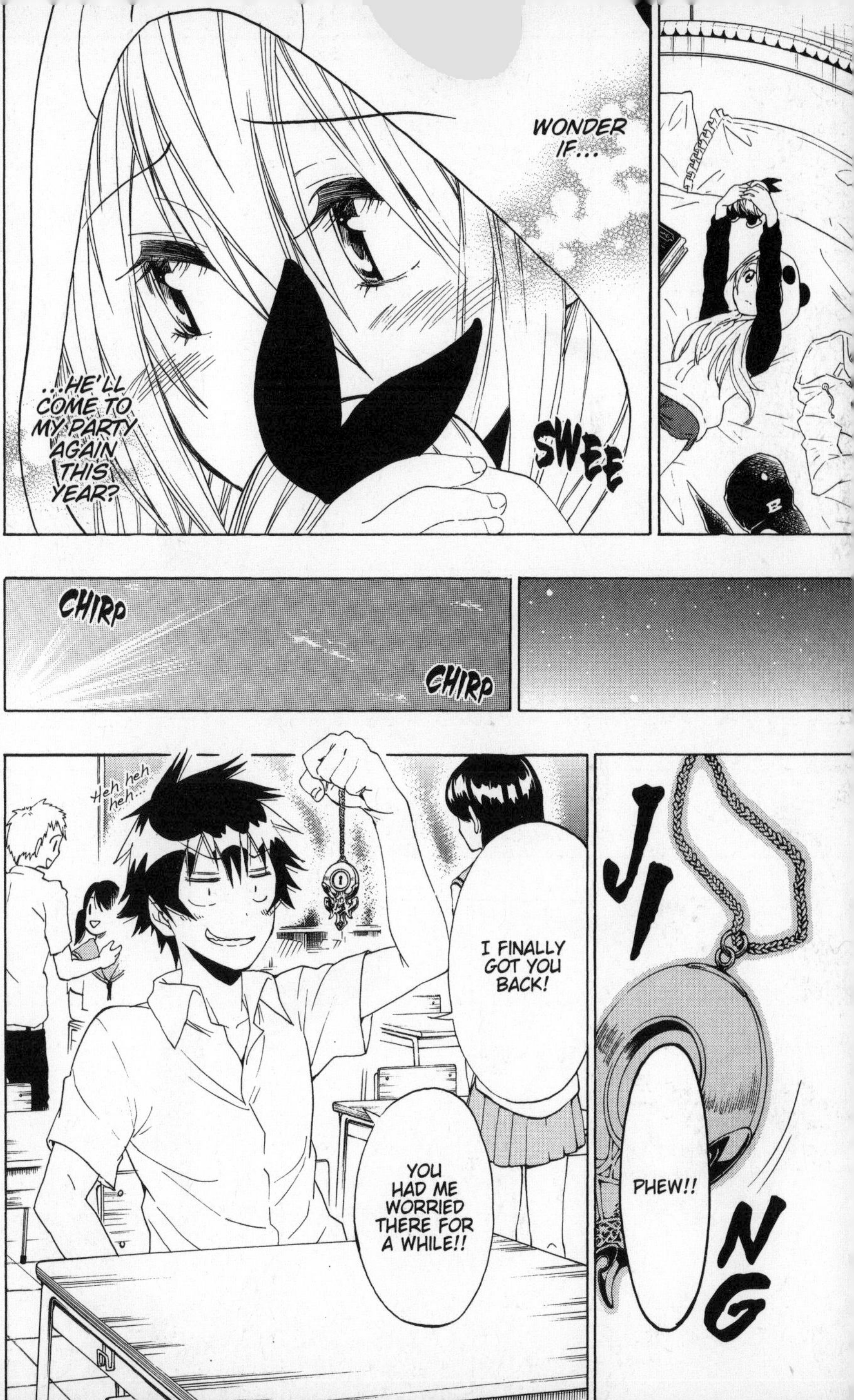
WONDER IF...
...HE'LL COME TO MY PARTY AGAIN THIS YEAR?
SWEE
CHIRP
CHIRP
JING
PHEW!!
Heh heh heh...
I FINALLY GOT YOU BACK!
YOU HAD ME WORRIED THERE FOR A WHILE!!

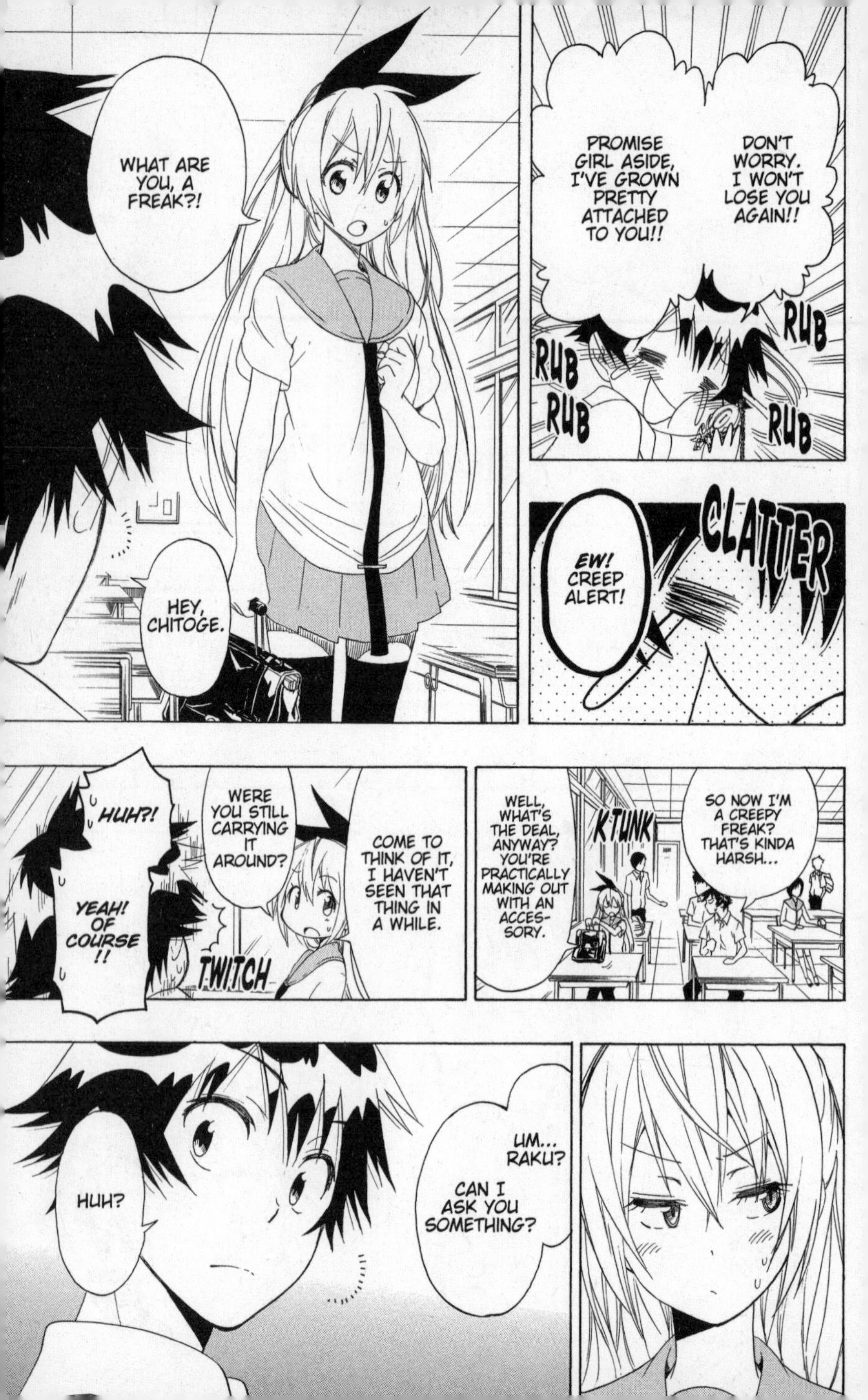
DON'T WORRY. I WON'T LOSE YOU AGAIN!!
PROMISE GIRL ASIDE, I'VE GROWN PRETTY ATTACHED TO YOU!!
RUB
RUB
RUB
RUB
CLATTER
EW! CREEP ALERT!
WHAT ARE YOU, A FREAK?!
HEY, CHITOGE.
SO NOW I'M A CREEPY FREAK? THAT'S KINDA HARSH...
WELL, WHAT'S THE DEAL, ANYWAY? YOU'RE PRACTICALLY MAKING OUT WITH AN ACCES-SORY.
KTUNK
COME TO THINK OF IT, I HAVEN'T SEEN THAT THING IN A WHILE.
WERE YOU STILL CARRYING IT AROUND?
HUH?!
YEAH! OF COURSE!!
TWITCH
UM... RAKU?
CAN I ASK YOU SOMETHING?
HUH?

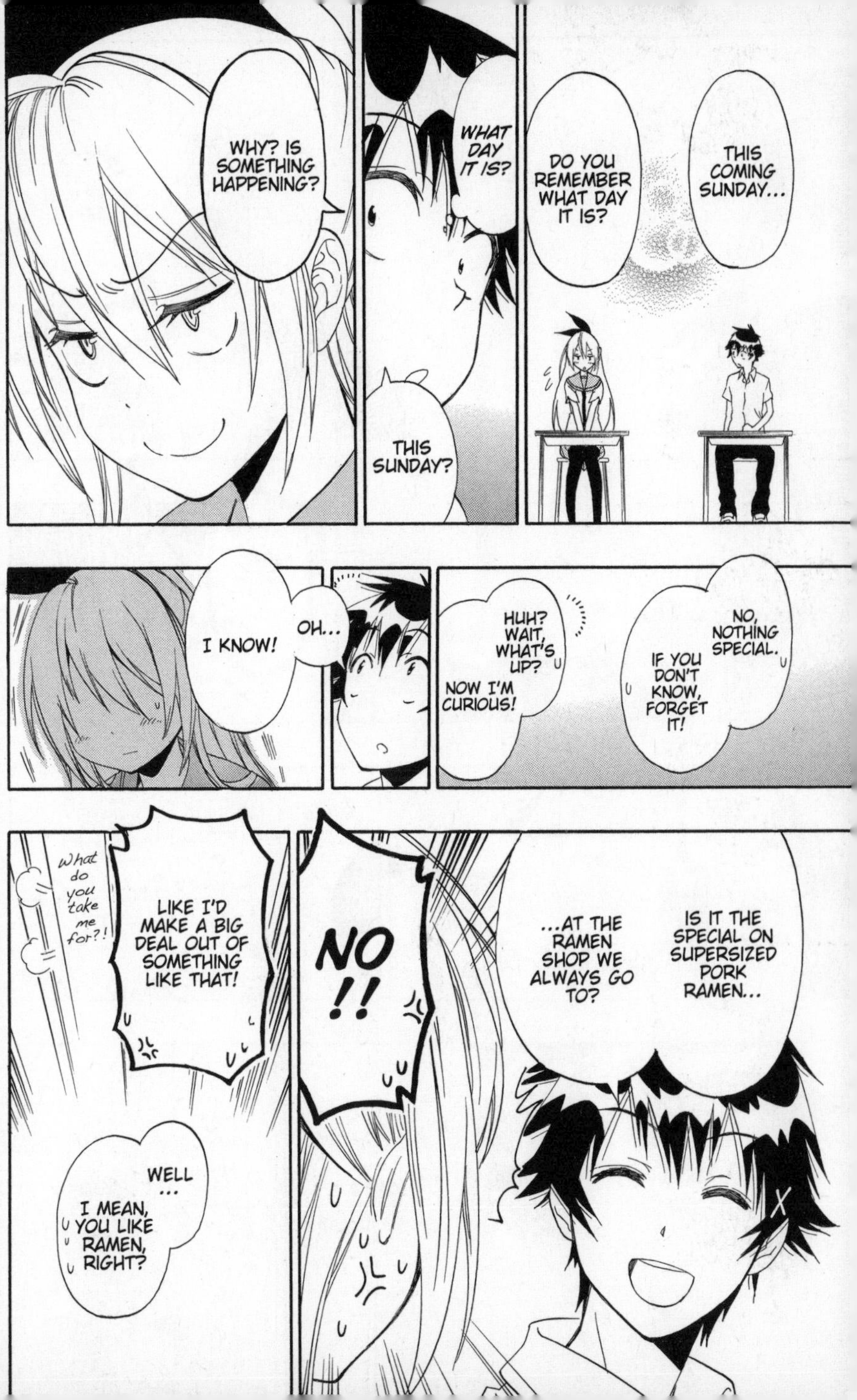
THIS COMING SUNDAY...
DO YOU REMEMBER WHAT DAY IT IS?
WHAT DAY IT IS?
THIS SUNDAY?
WHY? IS SOMETHING HAPPENING?
NO, NOTHING SPECIAL.
IF YOU DON'T KNOW, FORGET IT!
HUH? WAIT, WHAT'S UP?
NOW I'M CURIOUS!
OH...
I KNOW!
IS IT THE SPECIAL ON SUPERSIZED PORK RAMEN...
...AT THE RAMEN SHOP WE ALWAYS GO TO?
NO!!
LIKE I'D MAKE A BIG DEAL OUT OF SOMETHING LIKE THAT!
what do you take me for?!
WELL... I MEAN, YOU LIKE RAMEN, RIGHT?

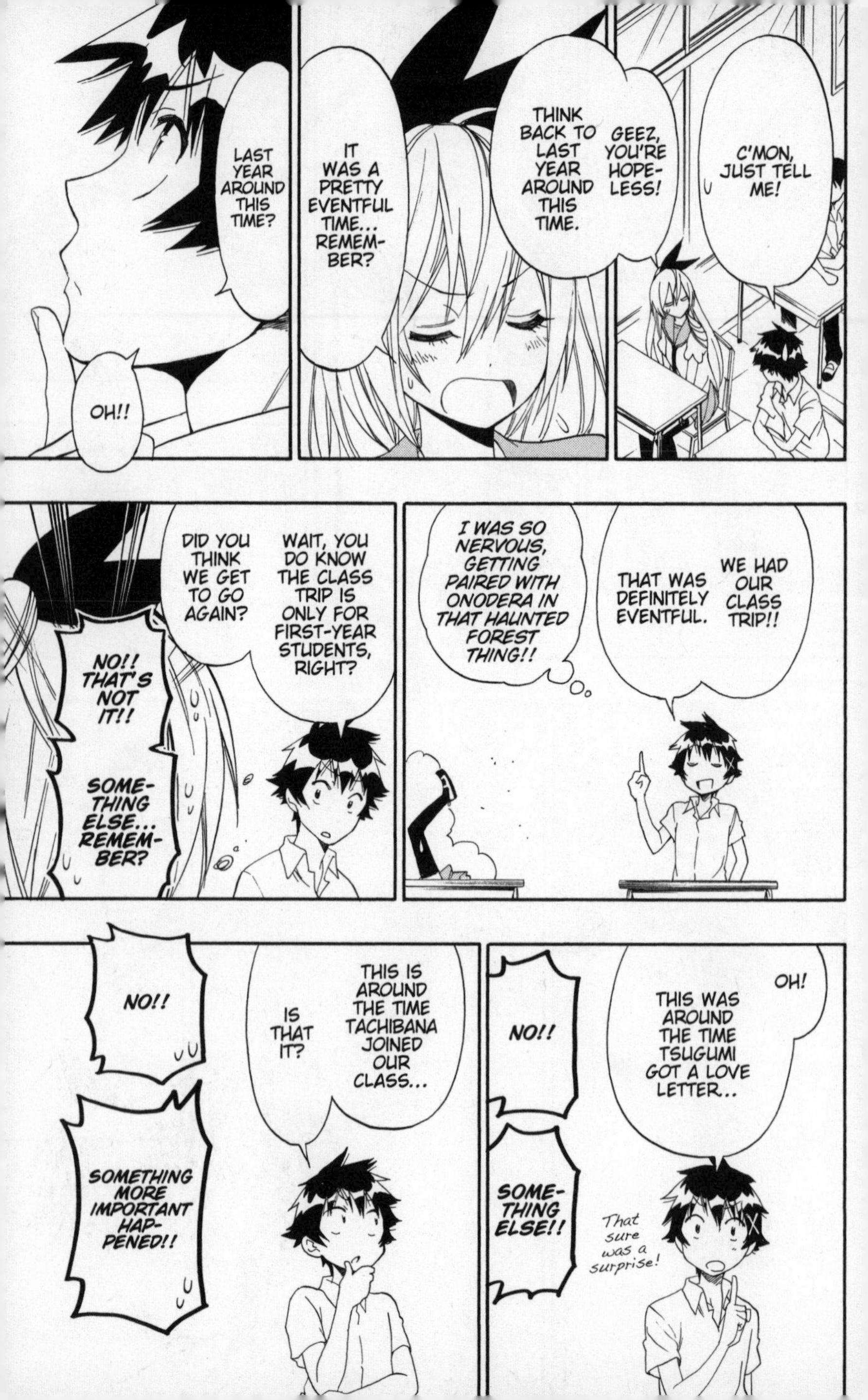
C'MON, JUST TELL ME!
GEEZ, YOU'RE HOPELESS!
THINK BACK TO LAST YEAR AROUND THIS TIME.
IT WAS A PRETTY EVENTFUL TIME... REMEMBER?
LAST YEAR AROUND THIS TIME?
OH!!
WE HAD OUR CLASS TRIP!!
THAT WAS DEFINITELY EVENTFUL.
I WAS SO NERVOUS, GETTING PAIRED WITH ONODERA IN THAT HAUNTED FOREST THING!!
WAIT, YOU DO KNOW THE CLASS TRIP IS ONLY FOR FIRST-YEAR STUDENTS, RIGHT?
DID YOU THINK WE GET TO GO AGAIN?
NO!! THAT'S NOT IT!!
SOMETHING ELSE... REMEMBER?
OH!
THIS WAS AROUND THE TIME TSUGUMI GOT A LOVE LETTER...
That sure was a surprise!
NO!!
SOMETHING ELSE!!
THIS IS AROUND THE TIME TACHIBANA JOINED OUR CLASS...
IS THAT IT?
NO!!
SOMETHING MORE IMPORTANT HAPPENED!!

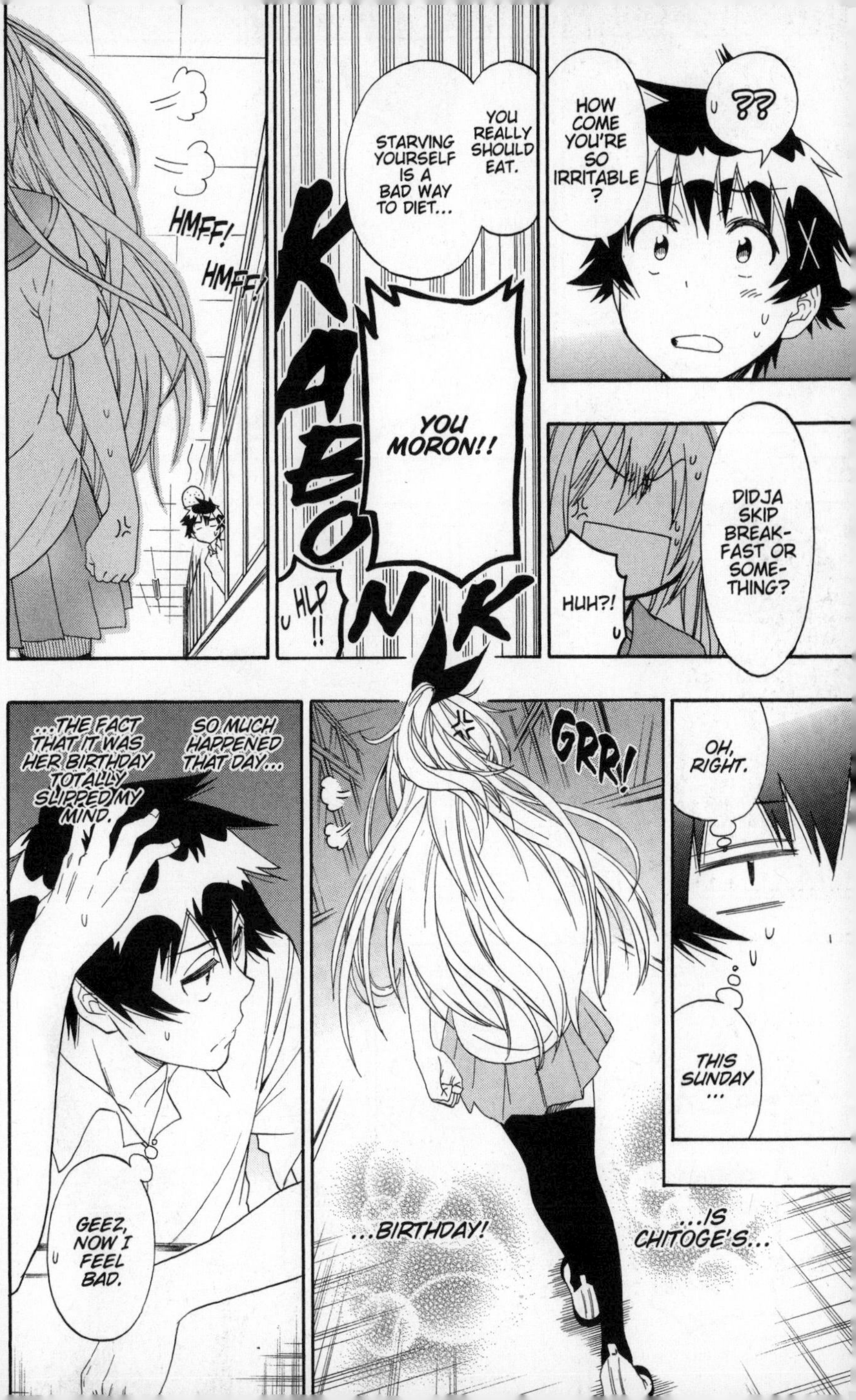
??
HOW COME YOU'RE SO IRRITABLE?
DIDJA SKIP BREAK-FAST OR SOME-THING?
HUH?!
YOU REALLY SHOULD EAT.
STARVING YOURSELF IS A BAD WAY TO DIET...
YOU MORON!!
KABONK
HLP!!
HMFF!
HMFF!
OH, RIGHT.
THIS SUNDAY...
...IS CHITOGE'S...
...BIRTHDAY!
GRR!
SO MUCH HAPPENED THAT DAY...
...THE FACT THAT IT WAS HER BIRTHDAY TOTALLY SLIPPED MY MIND.
GEEZ, NOW I FEEL BAD.

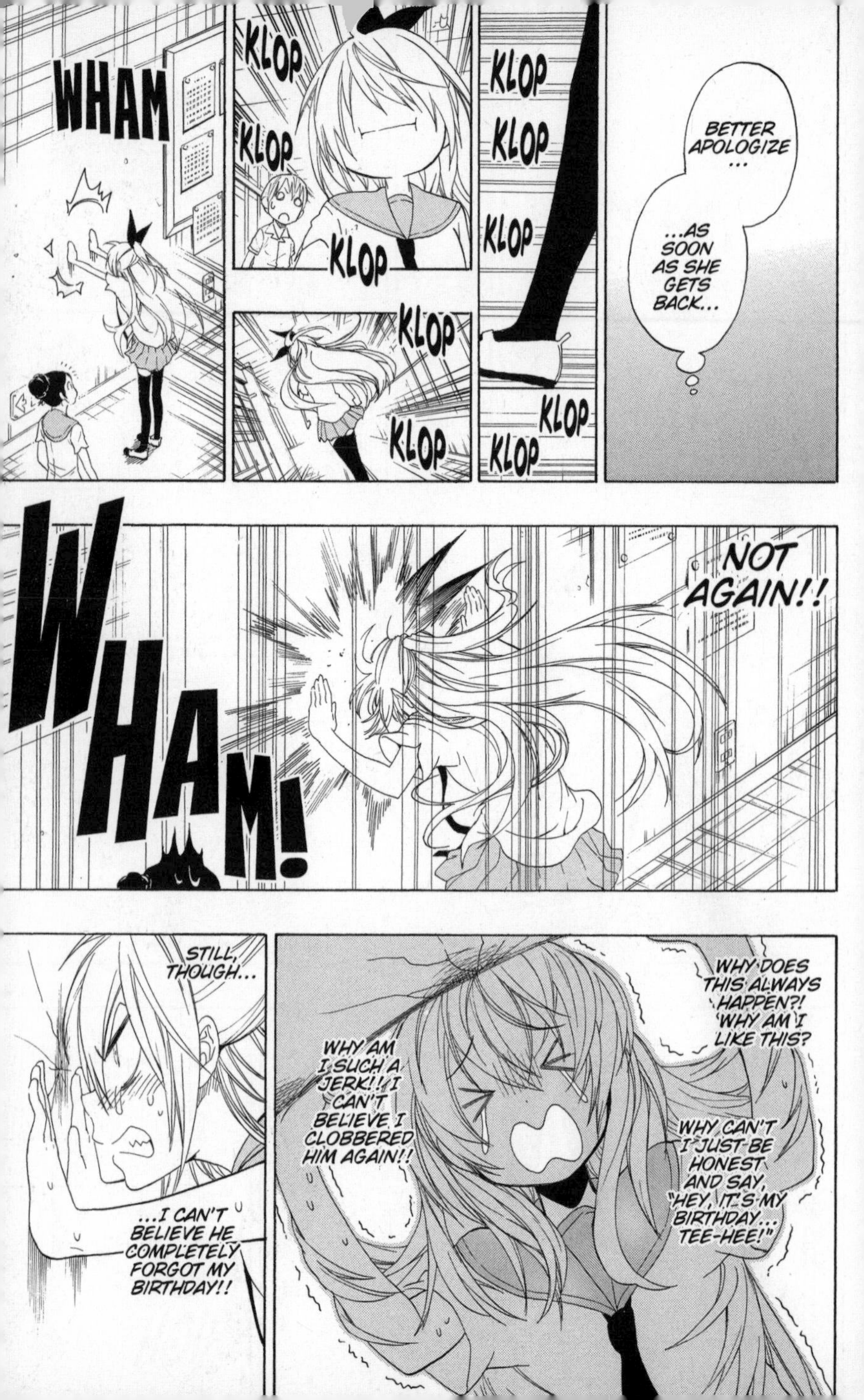
BETTER APOLOGIZE...
...AS SOON AS SHE GETS BACK...
KLOP
KLOP
KLOP
KLOP
KLOP
KLOP
KLOP
KLOP
KLOP
KLOP
WHAM
NOT AGAIN!!
WHAM!
WHY DOES THIS ALWAYS HAPPEN?! WHY AM I LIKE THIS?
WHY AM I SUCH A JERK!! I CAN'T BELIEVE I CLOBBERED HIM AGAIN!!
WHY CAN'T I JUST BE HONEST AND SAY, "HEY, IT'S MY BIRTHDAY... TEE-HEE!"
STILL, THOUGH...
...I CAN'T BELIEVE HE COMPLETELY FORGOT MY BIRTHDAY!!

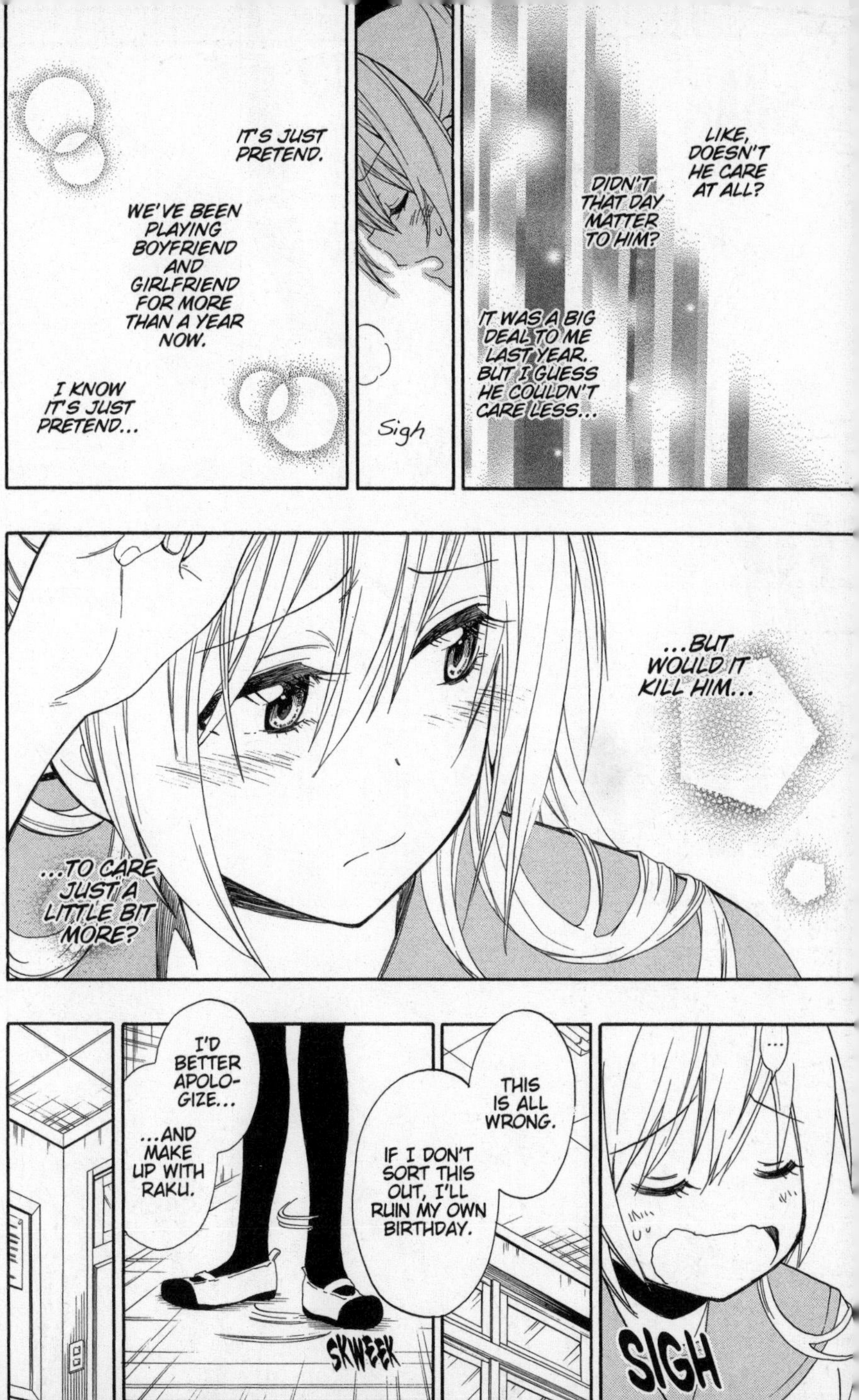
LIKE, DOESN'T HE CARE AT ALL?
DIDN'T THAT DAY MATTER TO HIM?
IT WAS A BIG DEAL TO ME LAST YEAR. BUT I GUESS HE COULDN'T CARE LESS...
Sigh
IT'S JUST PRETEND.
WE'VE BEEN PLAYING BOYFRIEND AND GIRLFRIEND FOR MORE THAN A YEAR NOW.
I KNOW IT'S JUST PRETEND...
...BUT WOULD IT KILL HIM...
...TO CARE JUST A LITTLE BIT MORE?
...
SIGH
THIS IS ALL WRONG.
IF I DON'T SORT THIS OUT, I'LL RUIN MY OWN BIRTHDAY.
I'D BETTER APOLOGIZE...
...AND MAKE UP WITH RAKU.
SKWEEK

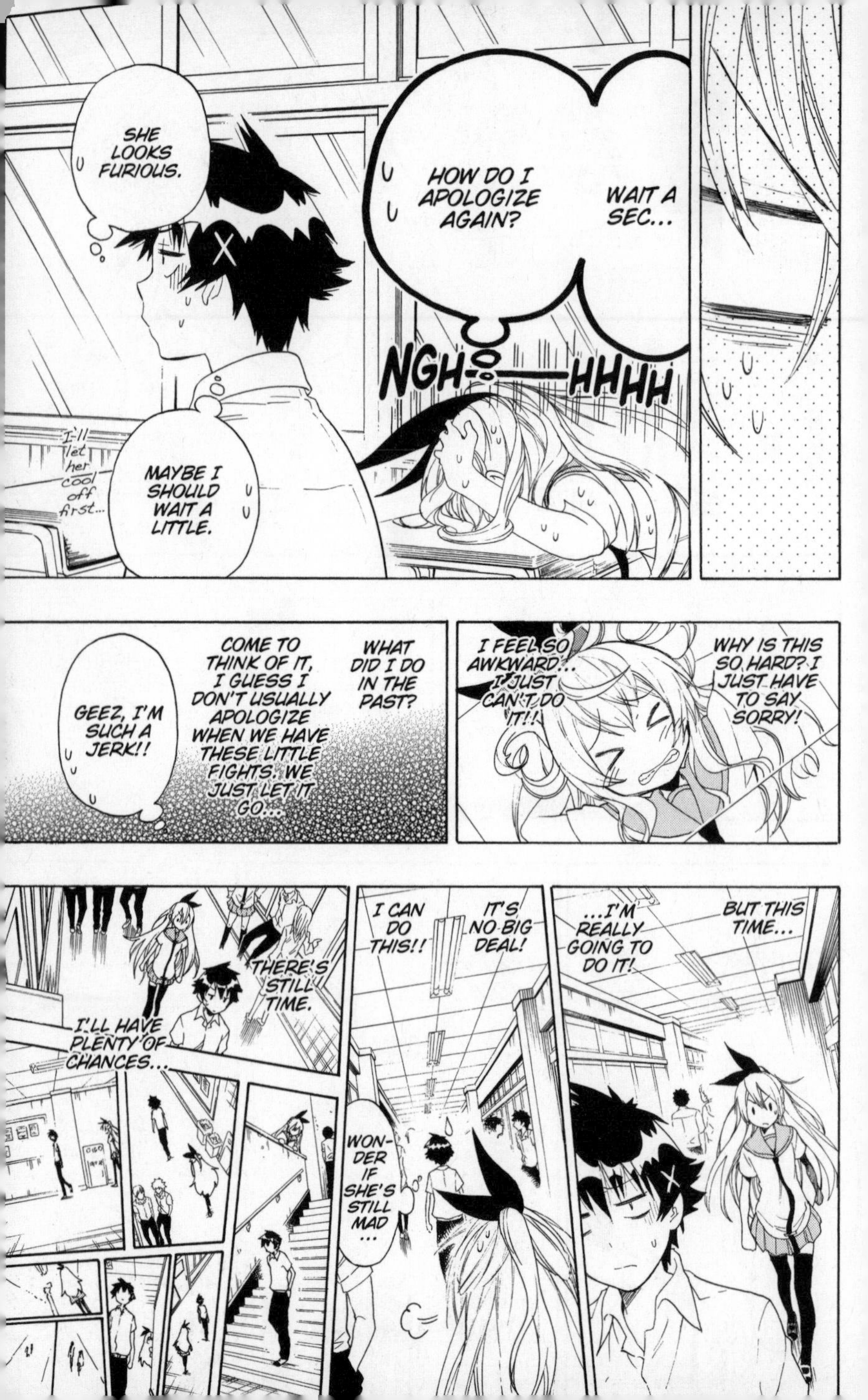
WAIT A SEC...
HOW DO I APOLOGIZE AGAIN?
NGH—HHHH
SHE LOOKS FURIOUS.
MAYBE I SHOULD WAIT A LITTLE.
I'll let her cool off first...
WHY IS THIS SO HARD? I JUST HAVE TO SAY SORRY!
I FEEL SO AWKWARD... I JUST CAN'T DO IT!!
WHAT DID I DO IN THE PAST?
COME TO THINK OF IT, I GUESS I DON'T USUALLY APOLOGIZE WHEN WE HAVE THESE LITTLE FIGHTS. WE JUST LET IT GO...
GEEZ, I'M SUCH A JERK!!
BUT THIS TIME...
...I'M REALLY GOING TO DO IT!
IT'S NO BIG DEAL!
I CAN DO THIS!!
WONDER IF SHE'S STILL MAD...
THERE'S STILL TIME.
I'LL HAVE PLENTY OF CHANCES...

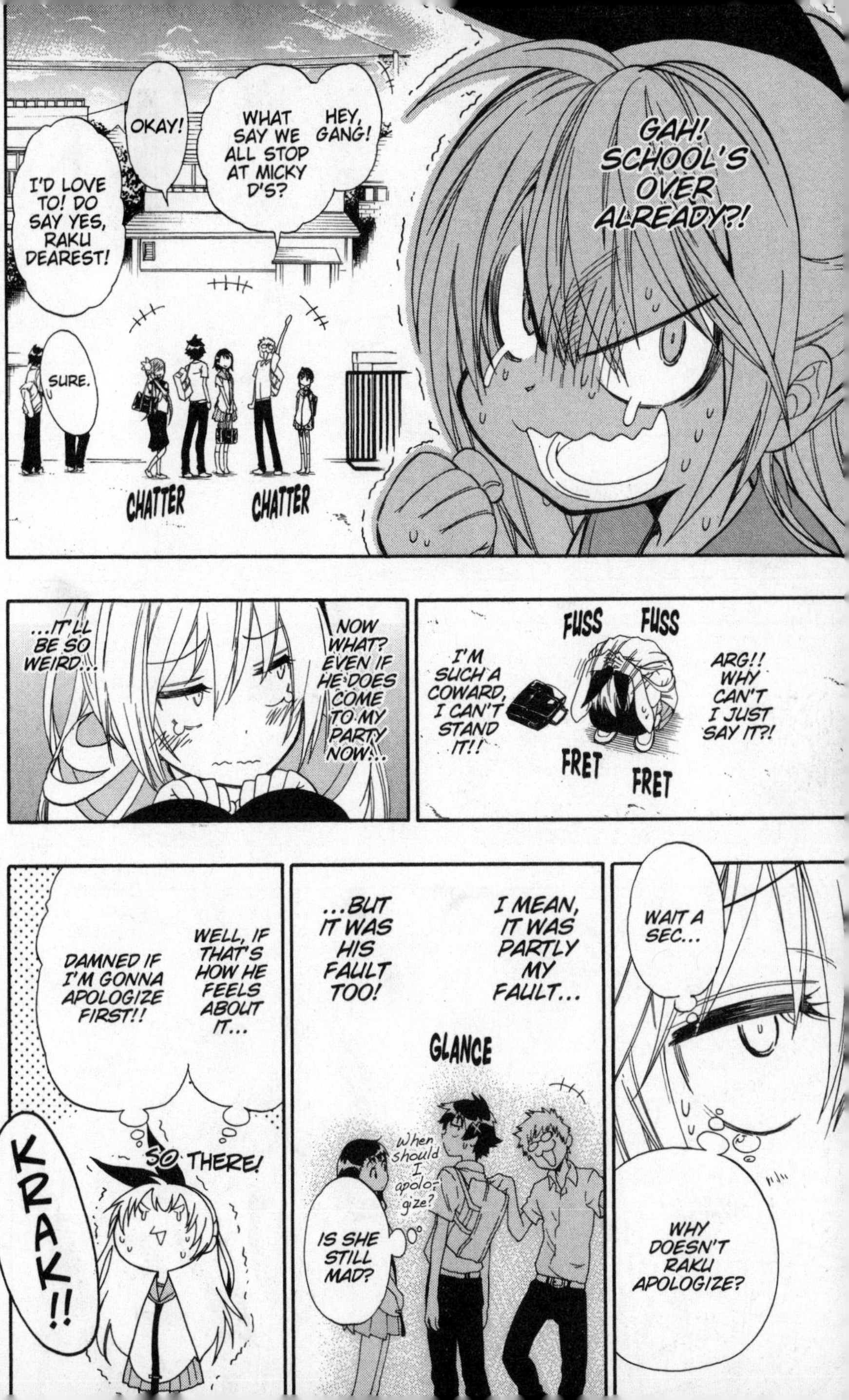
GAH! SCHOOL'S OVER ALREADY?!
HEY, GANG! WHAT SAY WE ALL STOP AT MICKY D'S?
OKAY!
I'D LOVE TO! DO SAY YES, RAKU DEAREST!
SURE.
CHATTER CHATTER
ARG!! WHY CAN'T I JUST SAY IT?!
FUSS FUSS
I'M SUCH A COWARD, I CAN'T STAND IT!!
FRET FRET
NOW WHAT? EVEN IF HE DOES COME TO MY PARTY NOW...
...IT'LL BE SO WEIRD...
WAIT A SEC...
WHY DOESN'T RAKU APOLOGIZE?
I MEAN, IT WAS PARTLY MY FAULT...
...BUT IT WAS HIS FAULT TOO!
GLANCE
When should I apologize?
IS SHE STILL MAD?
WELL, IF THAT'S HOW HE FEELS ABOUT IT...
DAMNED IF I'M GONNA APOLOGIZE FIRST!!
SO THERE!
KRAK!!

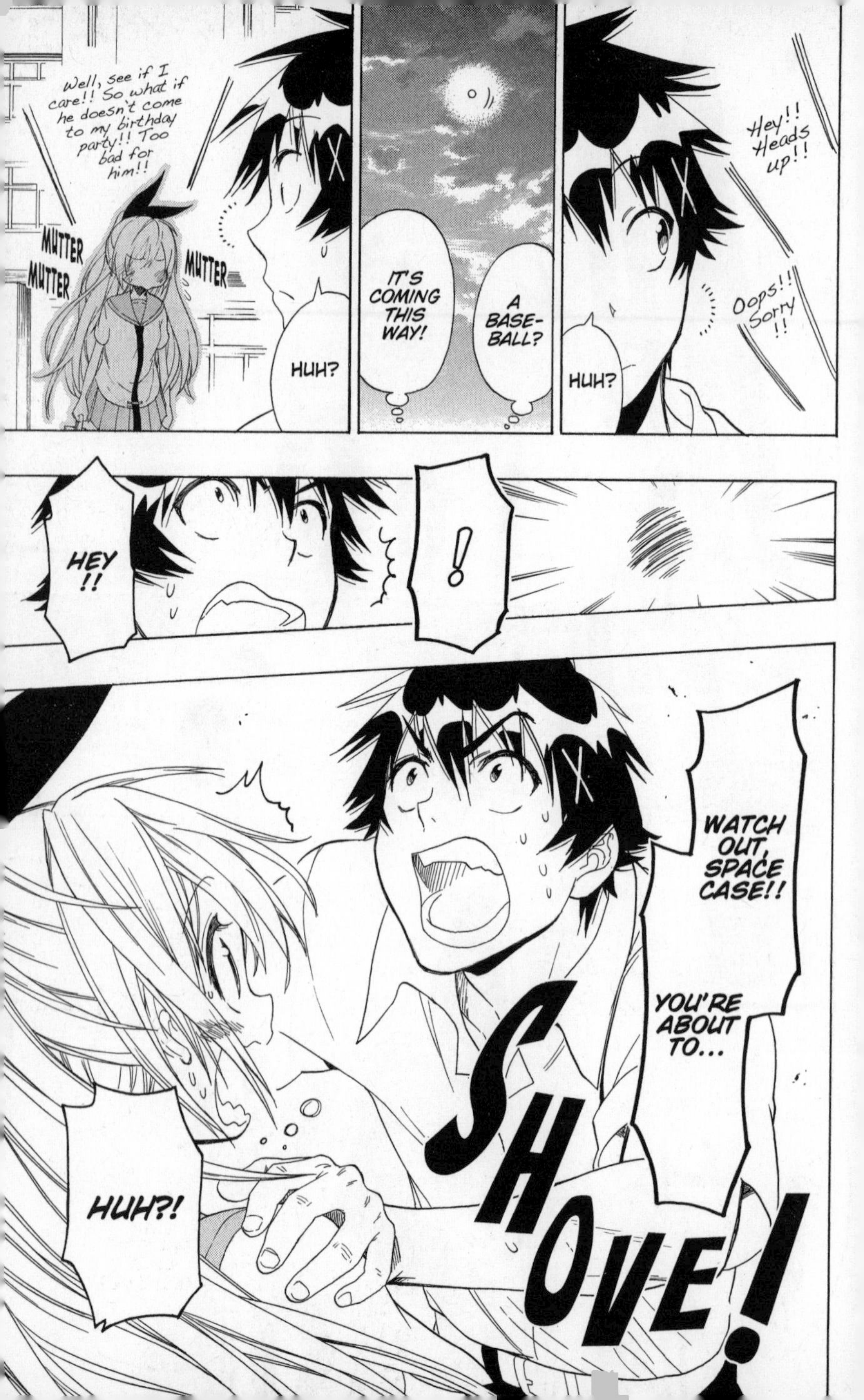
Hey!! Heads up!!
Oops!! Sorry!!
HUH?
A BASE-BALL?
IT'S COMING THIS WAY!
HUH?
Well, see if I care!! So what if he doesn't come to my birthday party!! Too bad for him!!
MUTTER MUTTER
MUTTER
!
HEY!!
WATCH OUT, SPACE CASE!!
YOU'RE ABOUT TO...
SHOVE!
HUH?!

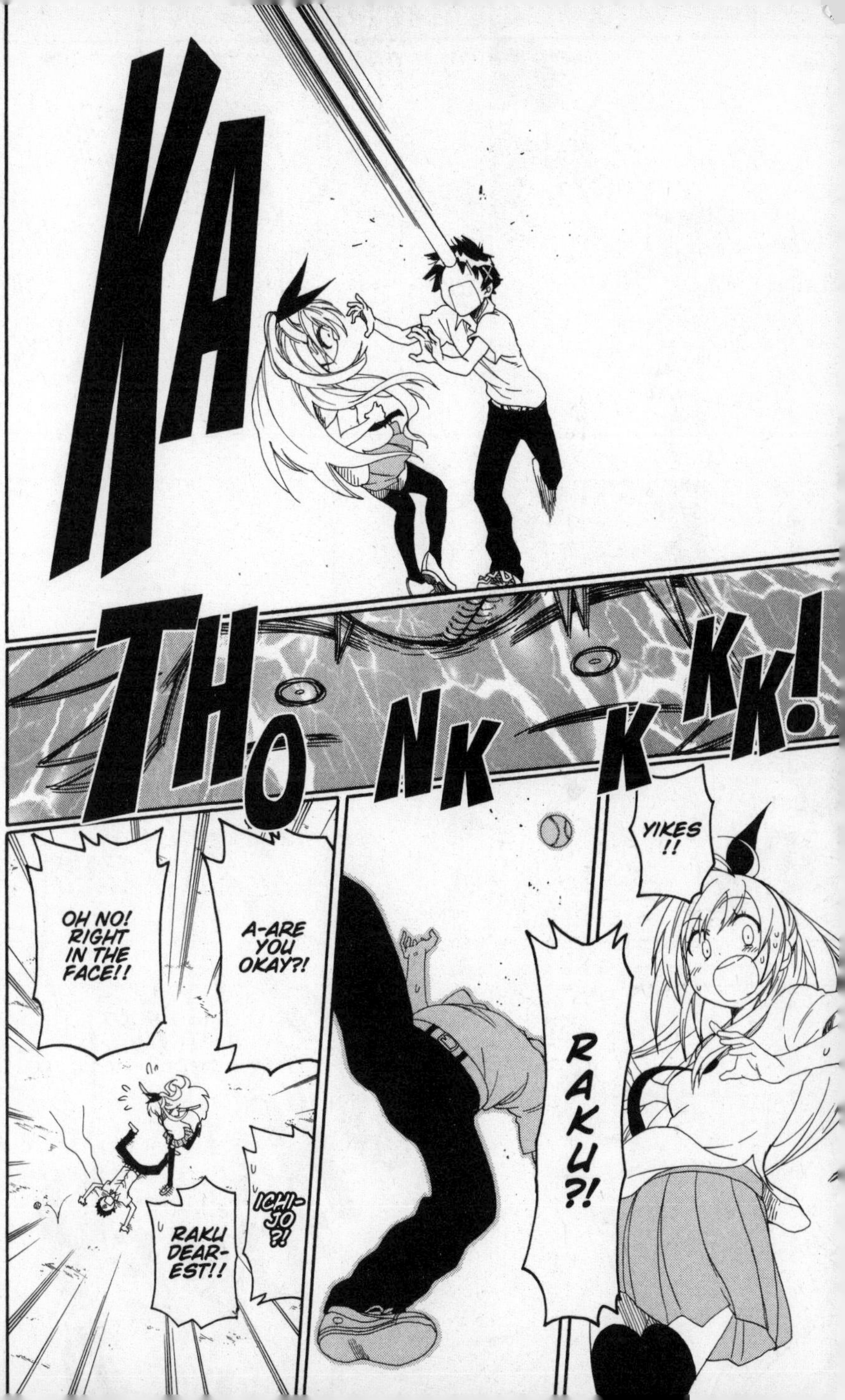

KA
THONK K KK!
YIKES!!
RAKU?!
A-ARE YOU OKAY?!
OH NO! RIGHT IN THE FACE!!
ICHIJO?!
RAKU DEAREST!!

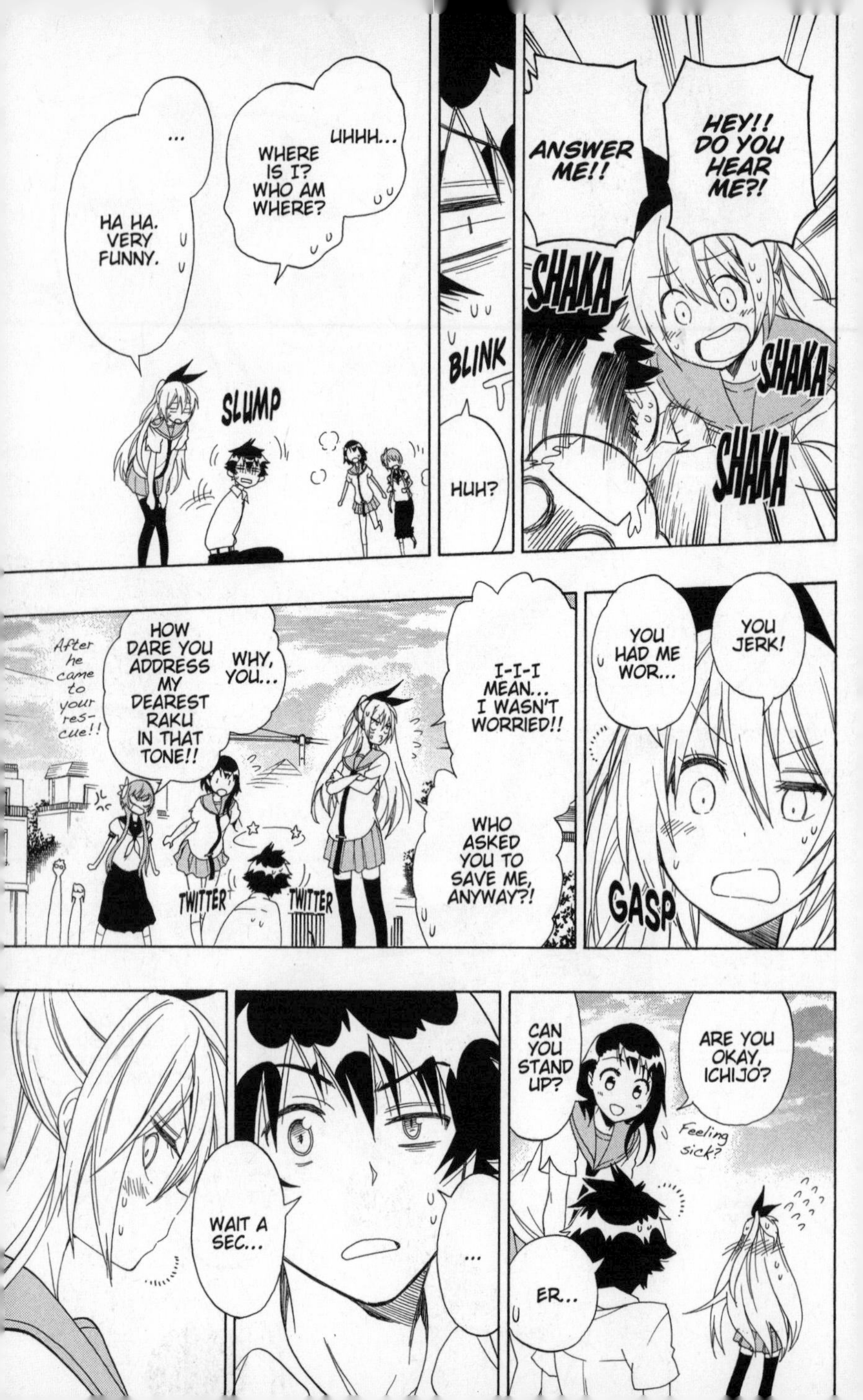
HEY!! DO YOU HEAR ME?!
ANSWER ME!!
SHAKA
SHAKA
SHAKA
BLINK
HUH?
UHHH...
WHERE IS I? WHO AM WHERE?
...
HA HA. VERY FUNNY.
SLUMP
YOU JERK!
YOU HAD ME WOR...
GASP
I-I-I MEAN... I WASN'T WORRIED!!
WHO ASKED YOU TO SAVE ME, ANYWAY?!
WHY, YOU...
HOW DARE YOU ADDRESS MY DEAREST RAKU IN THAT TONE!!
After he came to your rescue!!
TWITTER
TWITTER
ARE YOU OKAY, ICHIJO?
CAN YOU STAND UP?
Feeling sick?
ER...
...
WAIT A SEC...

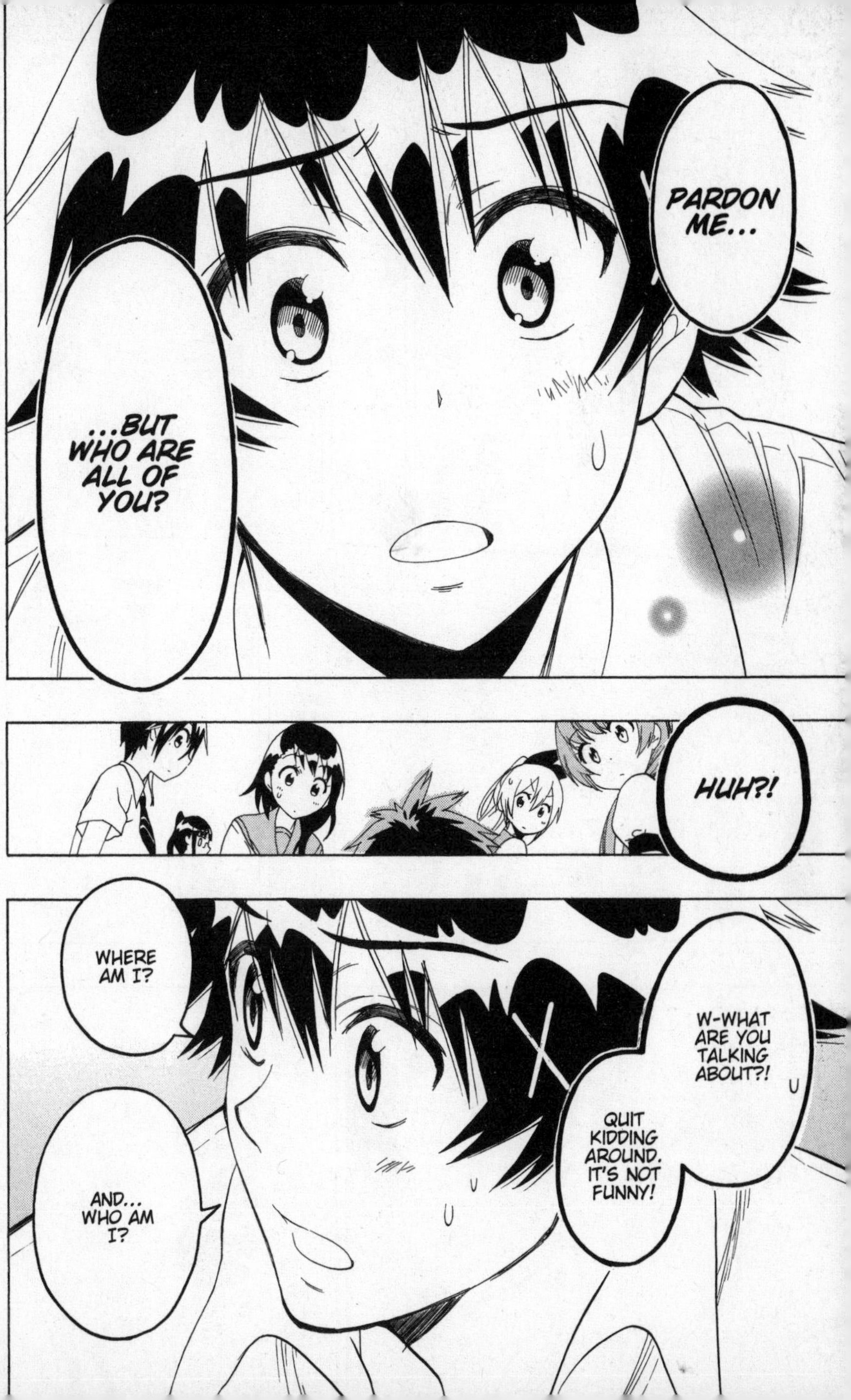
PARDON ME...
...BUT WHO ARE ALL OF YOU?
HUH?!
W-WHAT ARE YOU TALKING ABOUT?!
QUIT KIDDING AROUND. IT'S NOT FUNNY!
WHERE AM I?
AND... WHO AM I?

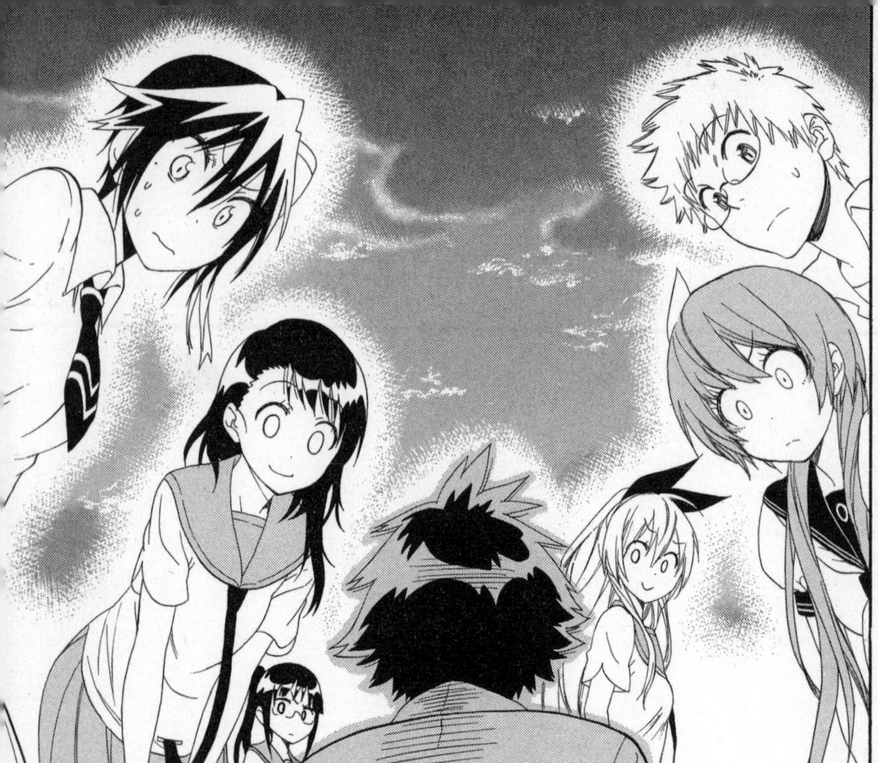
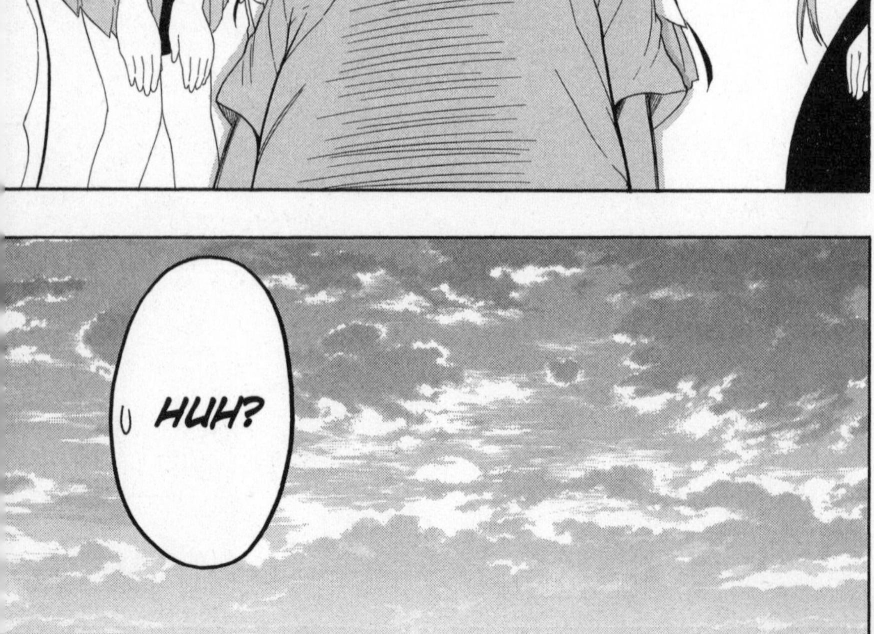
HUH?

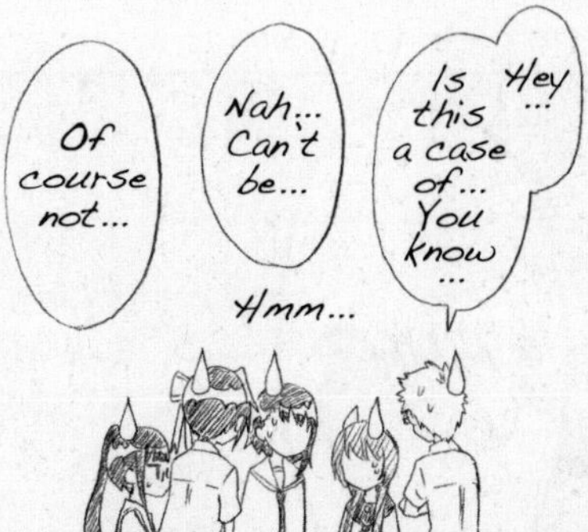
Hey... Is this a case of... You know...
Nah... Can't be...
Of course not...
Hmm...

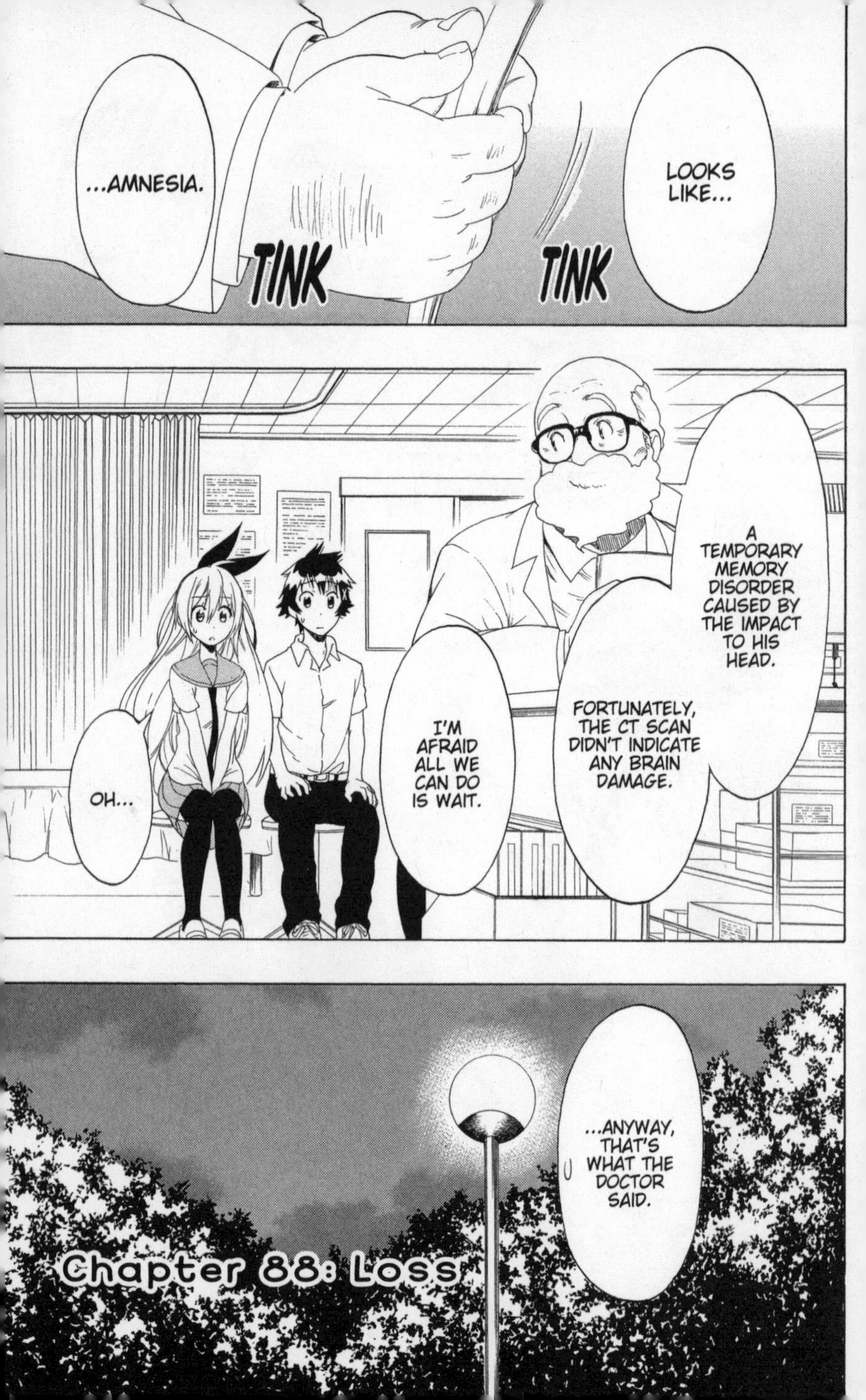
LOOKS LIKE...
TINK
TINK
...AMNESIA.
A TEMPORARY MEMORY DISORDER CAUSED BY THE IMPACT TO HIS HEAD.
FORTUNATELY, THE CT SCAN DIDN'T INDICATE ANY BRAIN DAMAGE.
I'M AFRAID ALL WE CAN DO IS WAIT.
OH...
...ANYWAY, THAT'S WHAT THE DOCTOR SAID.
Chapter 88: Loss

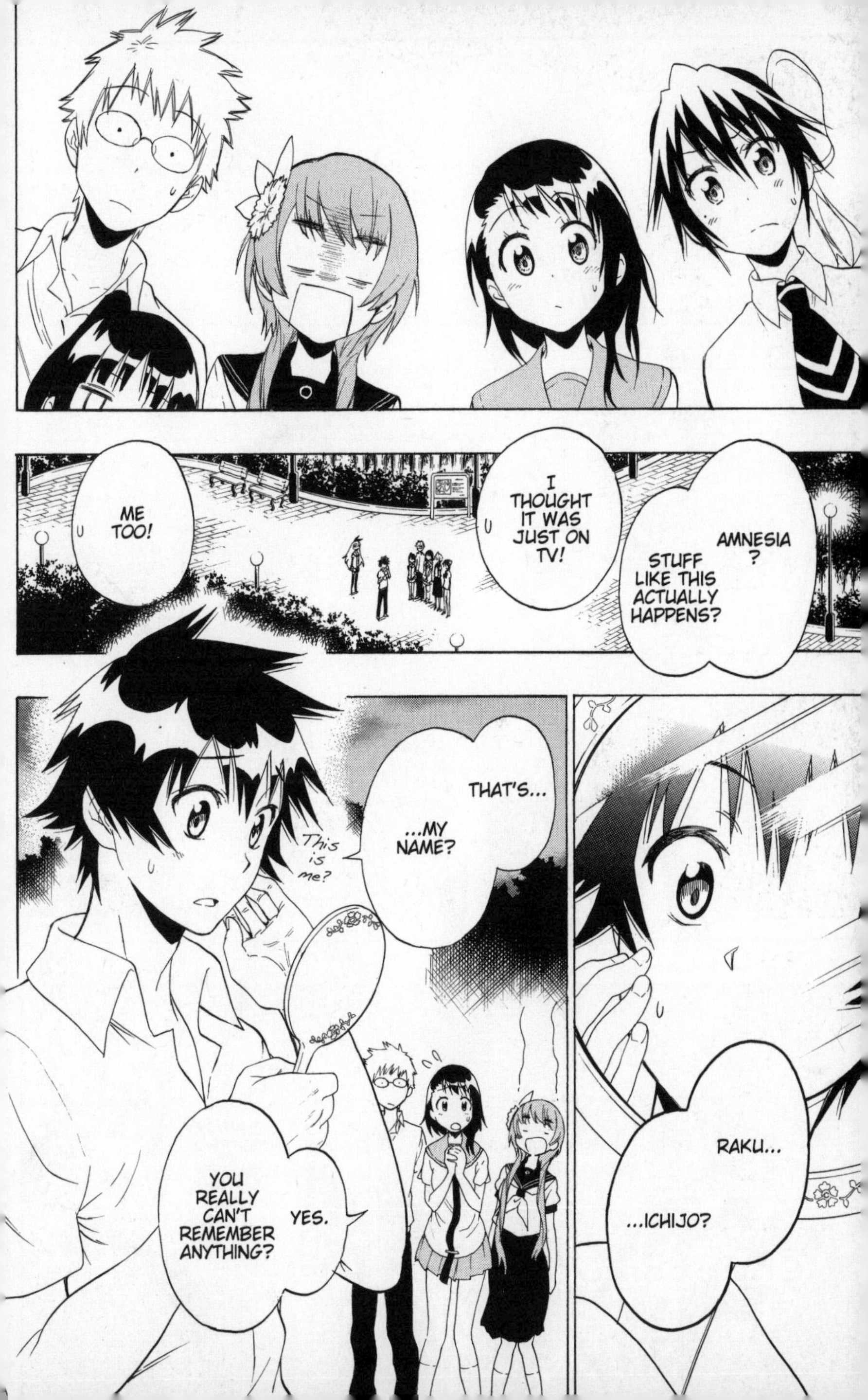
AMNESIA? STUFF LIKE THIS ACTUALLY HAPPENS?
I THOUGHT IT WAS JUST ON TV!
ME TOO!
RAKU... ...ICHIJO?
THAT'S... ...MY NAME?
This is me?
YOU REALLY CAN'T REMEMBER ANYTHING?
YES.

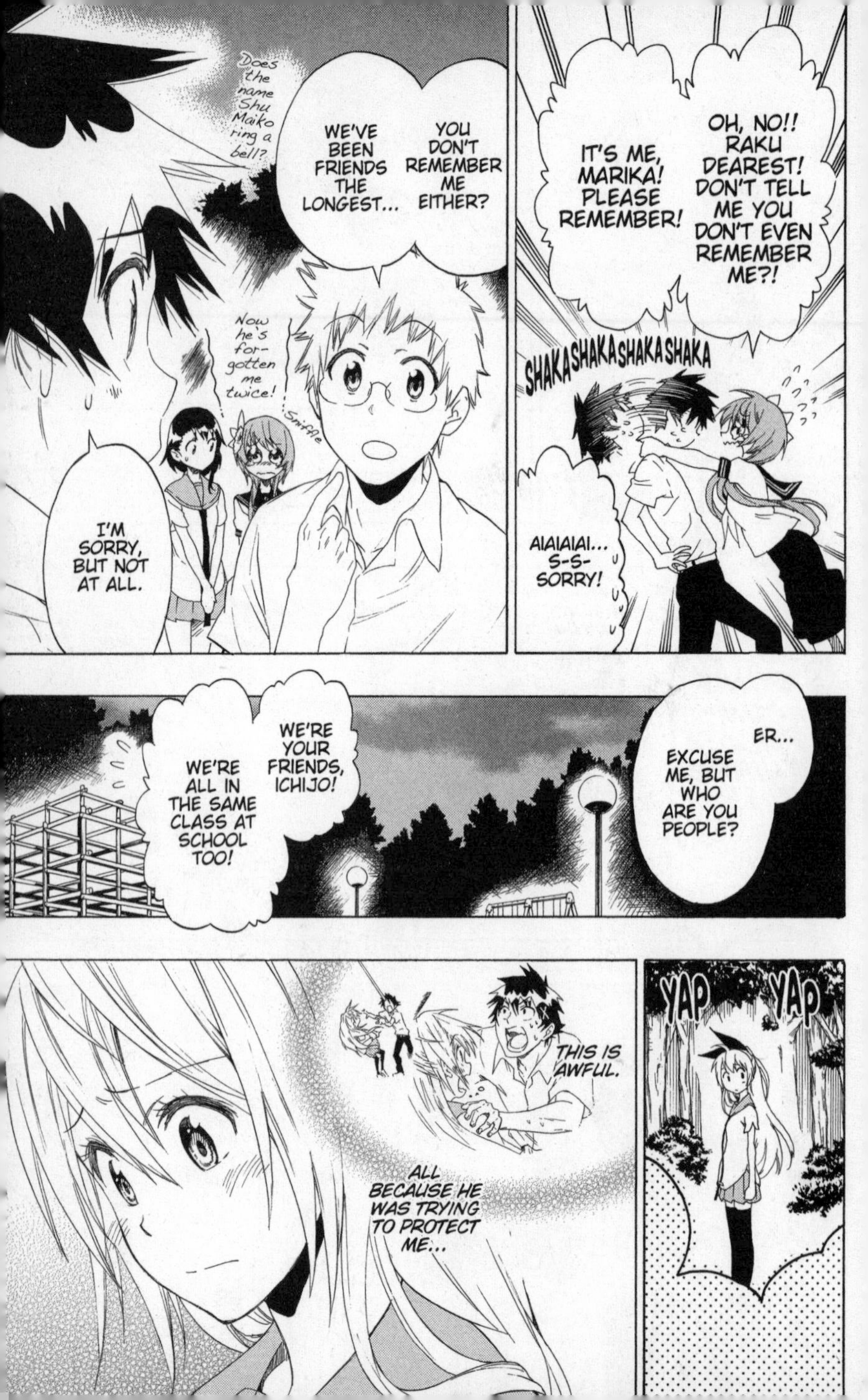
OH, NO!! RAKU DEAREST! DON'T TELL ME YOU DON'T EVEN REMEMBER ME?!
IT'S ME, MARIKA! PLEASE REMEMBER!
SHAKASHAKASHAKASHAKA
AIAIAIAI... S-S-SORRY!
YOU DON'T REMEMBER ME EITHER?
WE'VE BEEN FRIENDS THE LONGEST...
Does the name Shu Maiko ring a bell?
Now he's forgotten me twice!
Sniffle
I'M SORRY, BUT NOT AT ALL.
ER... EXCUSE ME, BUT WHO ARE YOU PEOPLE?
WE'RE YOUR FRIENDS, ICHIJO!
WE'RE ALL IN THE SAME CLASS AT SCHOOL TOO!
YAP YAP
THIS IS AWFUL.
ALL BECAUSE HE WAS TRYING TO PROTECT ME...

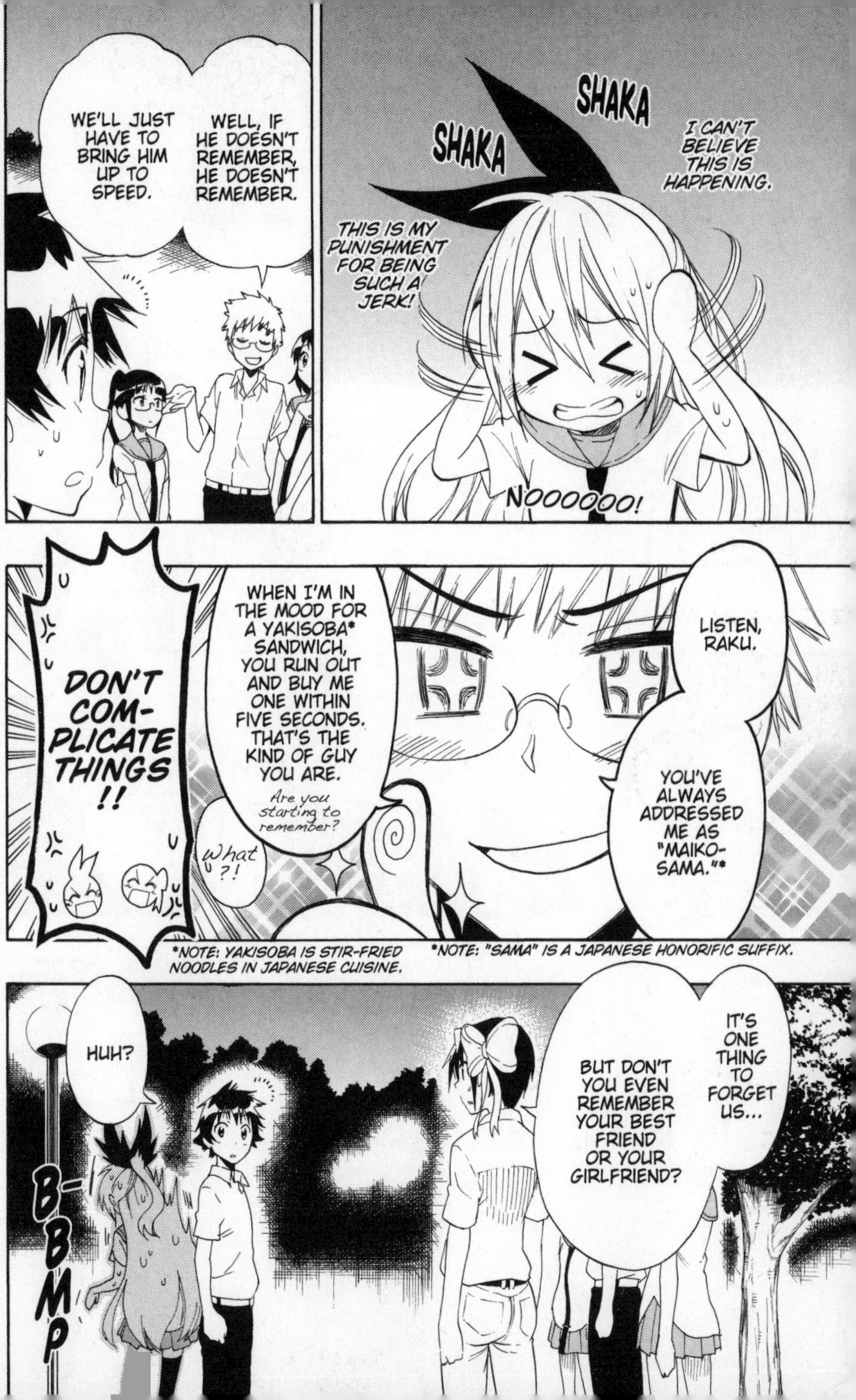
SHAKA
I CAN'T BELIEVE THIS IS HAPPENING.
SHAKA
THIS IS MY PUNISHMENT FOR BEING SUCH A JERK!
NOOOOOO!
WELL, IF HE DOESN'T REMEMBER, HE DOESN'T REMEMBER.
WE'LL JUST HAVE TO BRING HIM UP TO SPEED.
LISTEN, RAKU.
YOU'VE ALWAYS ADDRESSED ME AS "MAIKO-SAMA."*
WHEN I'M IN THE MOOD FOR A YAKISOBA* SANDWICH, YOU RUN OUT AND BUY ME ONE WITHIN FIVE SECONDS. THAT'S THE KIND OF GUY YOU ARE.
Are you starting to remember?
What?!
DON'T COMPLICATE THINGS!!
*NOTE: YAKISOBA IS STIR-FRIED NOODLES IN JAPANESE CUISINE.
*NOTE: "SAMA" IS A JAPANESE HONORIFIC SUFFIX.
IT'S ONE THING TO FORGET US...
BUT DON'T YOU EVEN REMEMBER YOUR BEST FRIEND OR YOUR GIRLFRIEND?
HUH?
B-BUMP

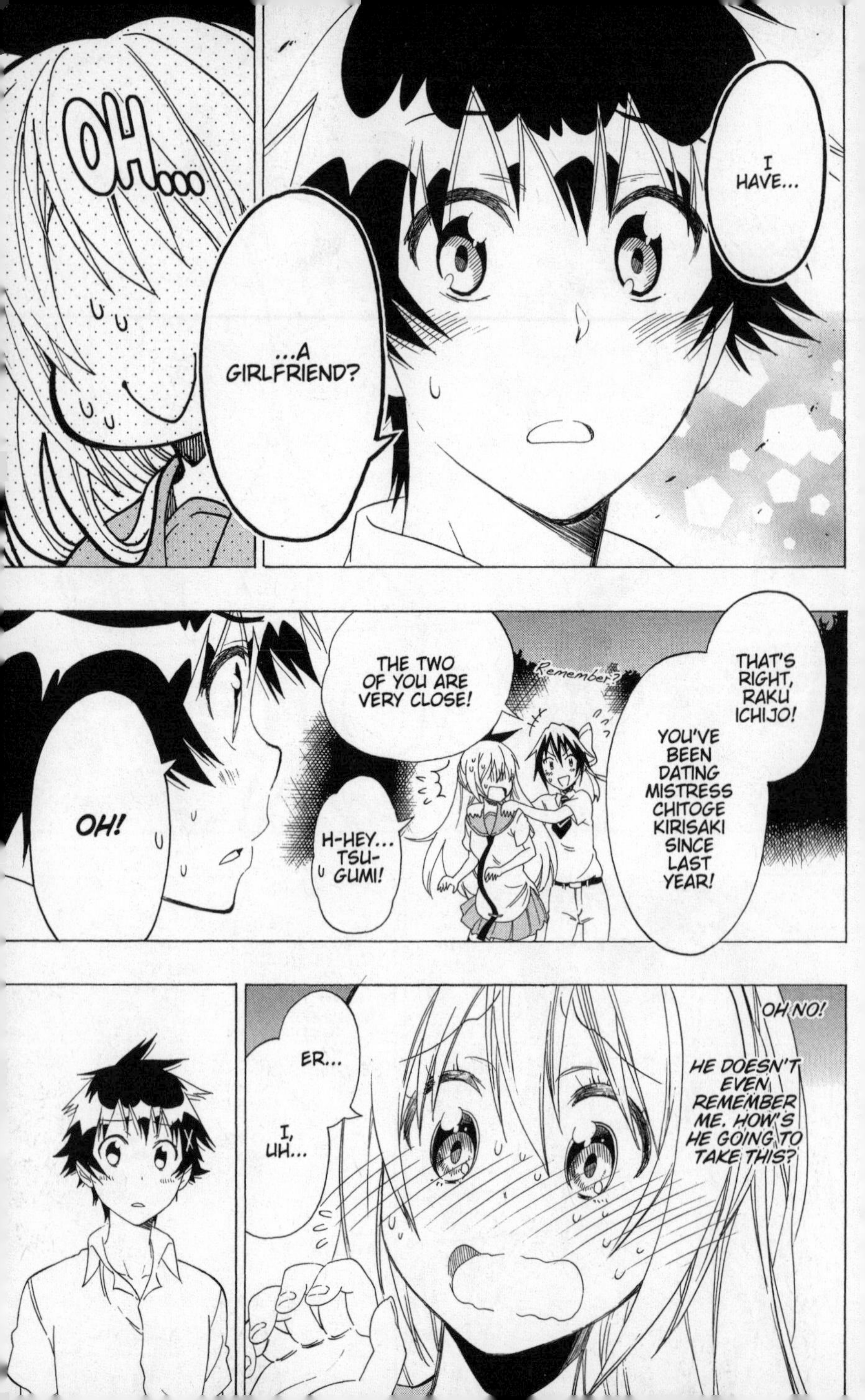
I HAVE...
...A GIRLFRIEND?
OH...
THAT'S RIGHT, RAKU ICHIJO!
YOU'VE BEEN DATING MISTRESS CHITOGE KIRISAKI SINCE LAST YEAR!
Remember?
THE TWO OF YOU ARE VERY CLOSE!
H-HEY... TSU-GUMI!
OH!
OH NO!
HE DOESN'T EVEN REMEMBER ME. HOW'S HE GOING TO TAKE THIS?
ER...
I, UH...

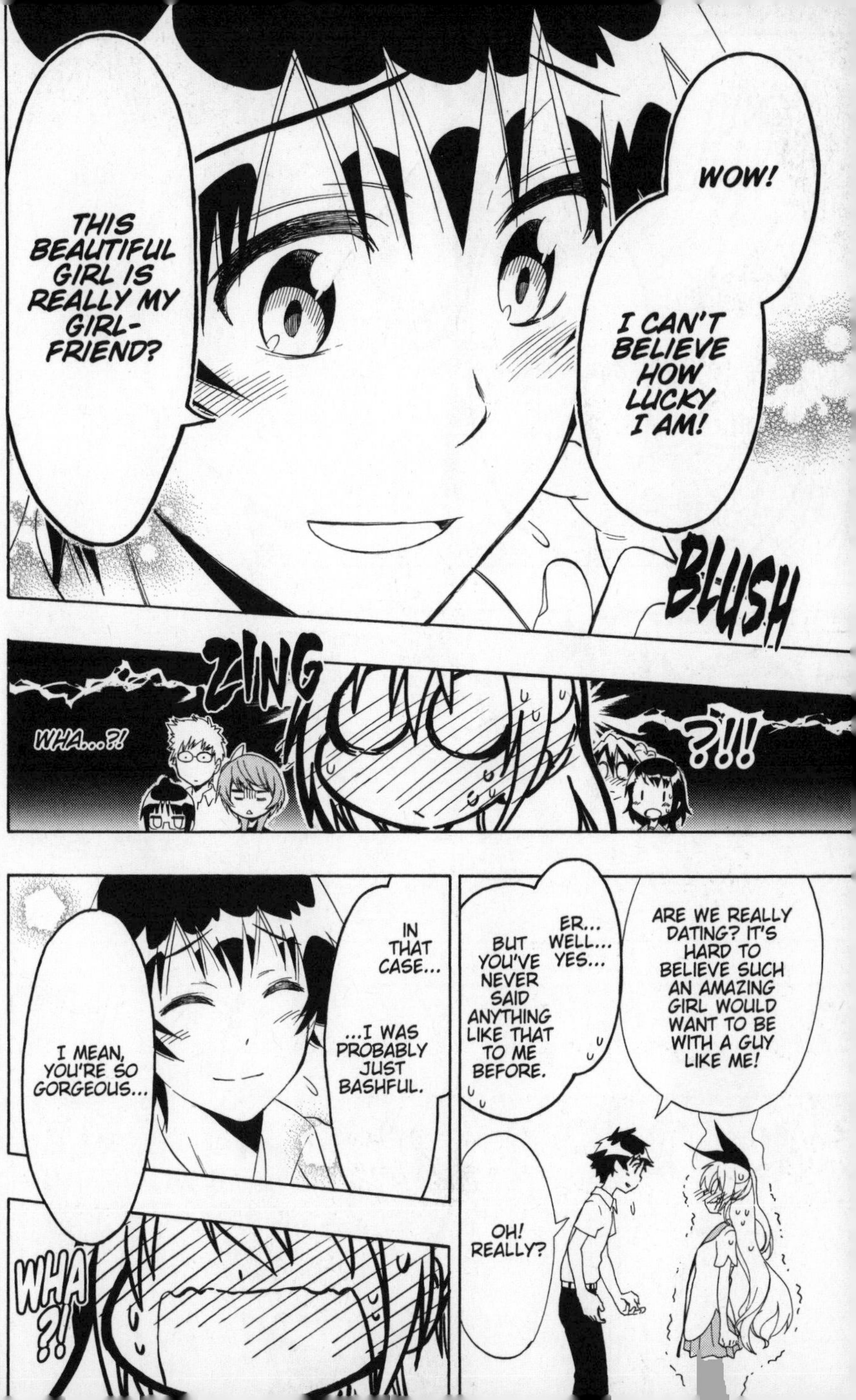
WOW!
I CAN'T BELIEVE HOW LUCKY I AM!
THIS BEAUTIFUL GIRL IS REALLY MY GIRL-FRIEND?
BLUSH
ZING
?!!
WHA...?!
ARE WE REALLY DATING? IT'S HARD TO BELIEVE SUCH AN AMAZING GIRL WOULD WANT TO BE WITH A GUY LIKE ME!
ER... WELL... YES...
BUT YOU'VE NEVER SAID ANYTHING LIKE THAT TO ME BEFORE.
OH! REALLY?
IN THAT CASE...
...I WAS PROBABLY JUST BASHFUL.
I MEAN, YOU'RE SO GORGEOUS...
WHA ?!

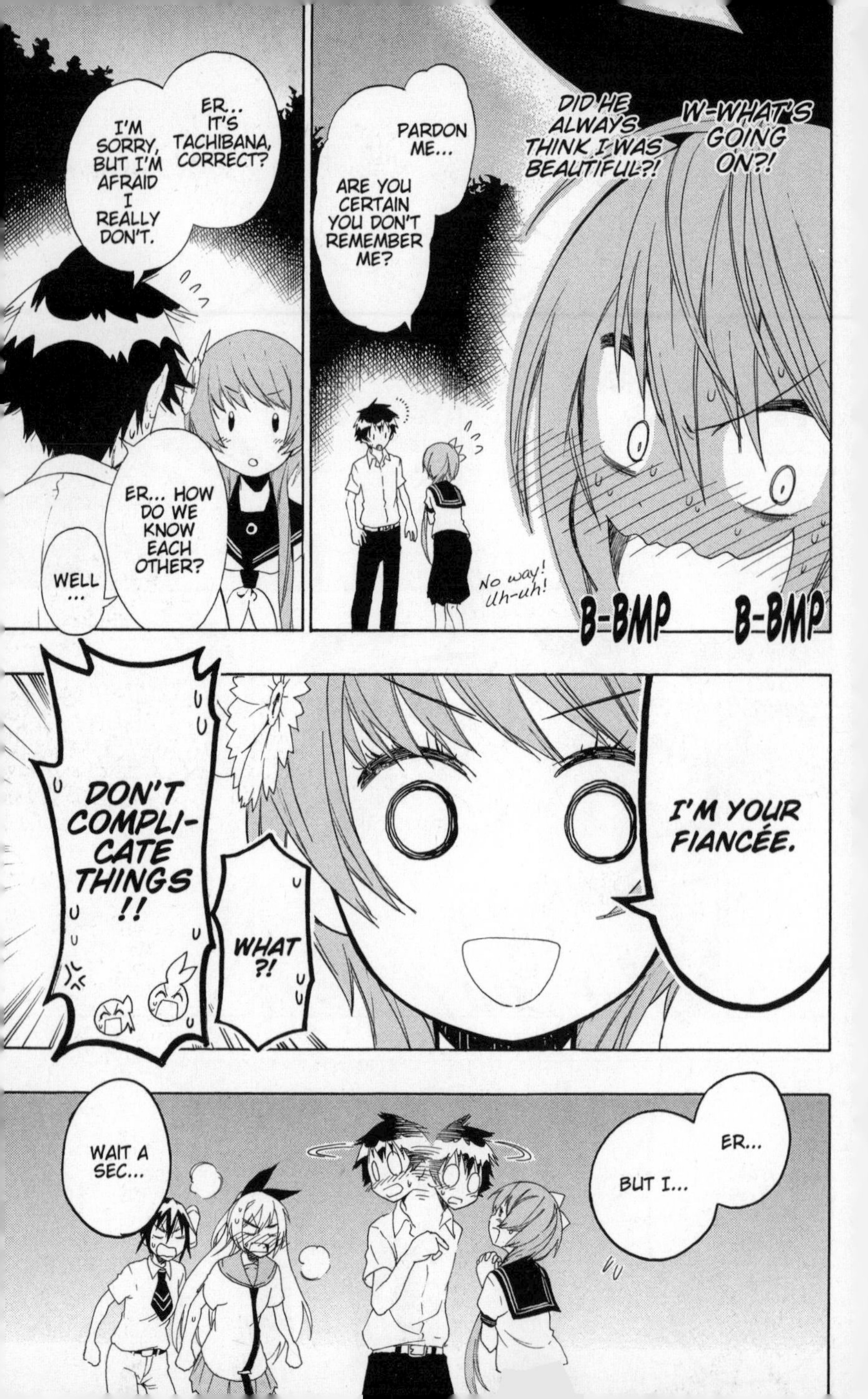
W-WHAT'S GOING ON?!
DID HE ALWAYS THINK I WAS BEAUTIFUL?!
B-BMP
B-BMP
PARDON ME...
ARE YOU CERTAIN YOU DON'T REMEMBER ME?
No way! Uh-uh!
ER... IT'S TACHIBANA, CORRECT?
I'M SORRY, BUT I'M AFRAID I REALLY DON'T.
ER... HOW DO WE KNOW EACH OTHER?
WELL...
I'M YOUR FIANCÉE.
WHAT?!
DON'T COMPLI-CATE THINGS!!
ER...
BUT I...
WAIT A SEC...

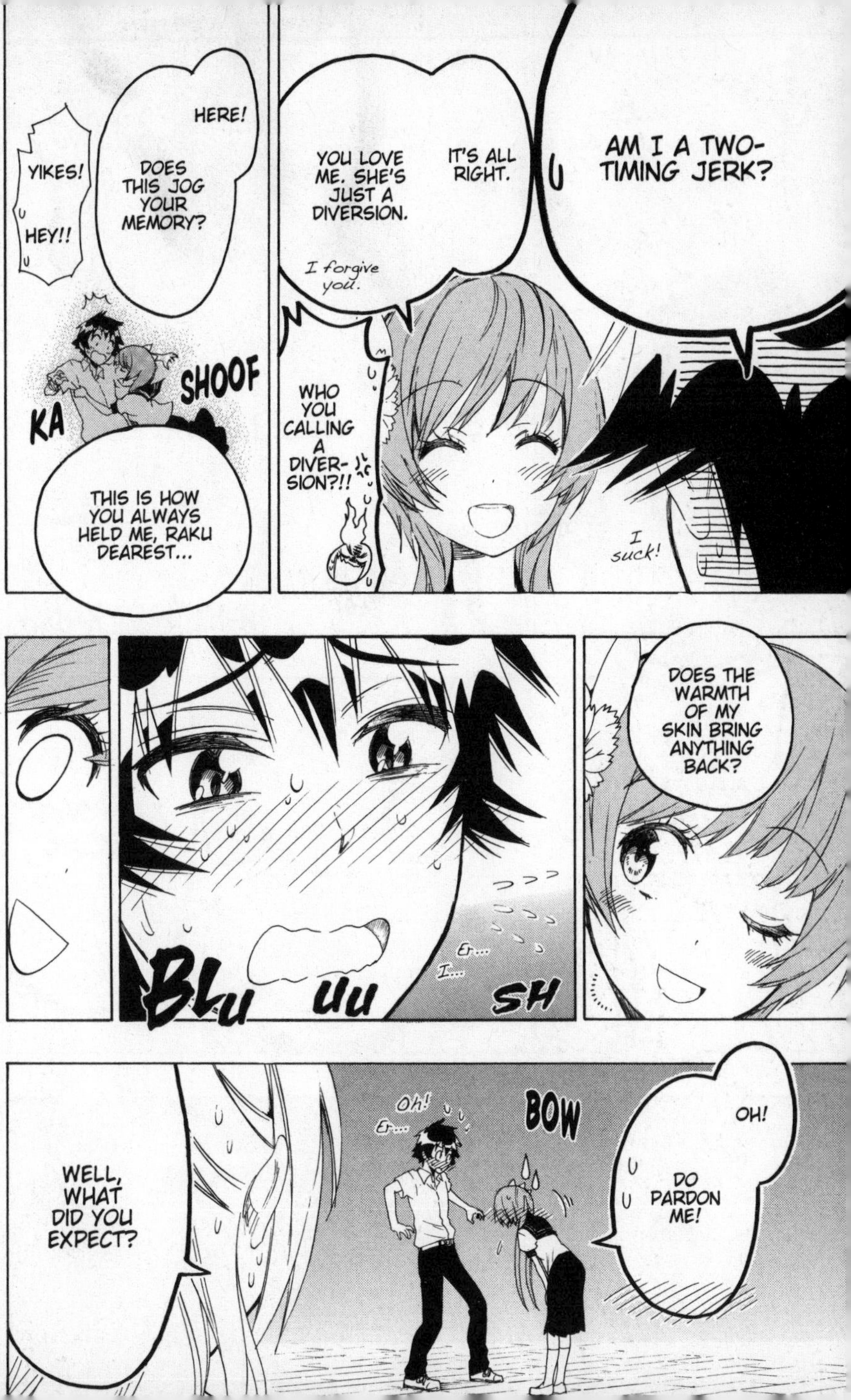
AM I A TWO-TIMING JERK?
I suck!
IT'S ALL RIGHT.
YOU LOVE ME. SHE'S JUST A DIVERSION.
I forgive you.
WHO YOU CALLING A DIVERSION?!!
HERE!
DOES THIS JOG YOUR MEMORY?
YIKES!
HEY!!
SHOOF
KA
THIS IS HOW YOU ALWAYS HELD ME, RAKU DEAREST...
DOES THE WARMTH OF MY SKIN BRING ANYTHING BACK?
Er... I...
BLUUUSH
OH!
DO PARDON ME!
BOW
Oh! Er...
WELL, WHAT DID YOU EXPECT?

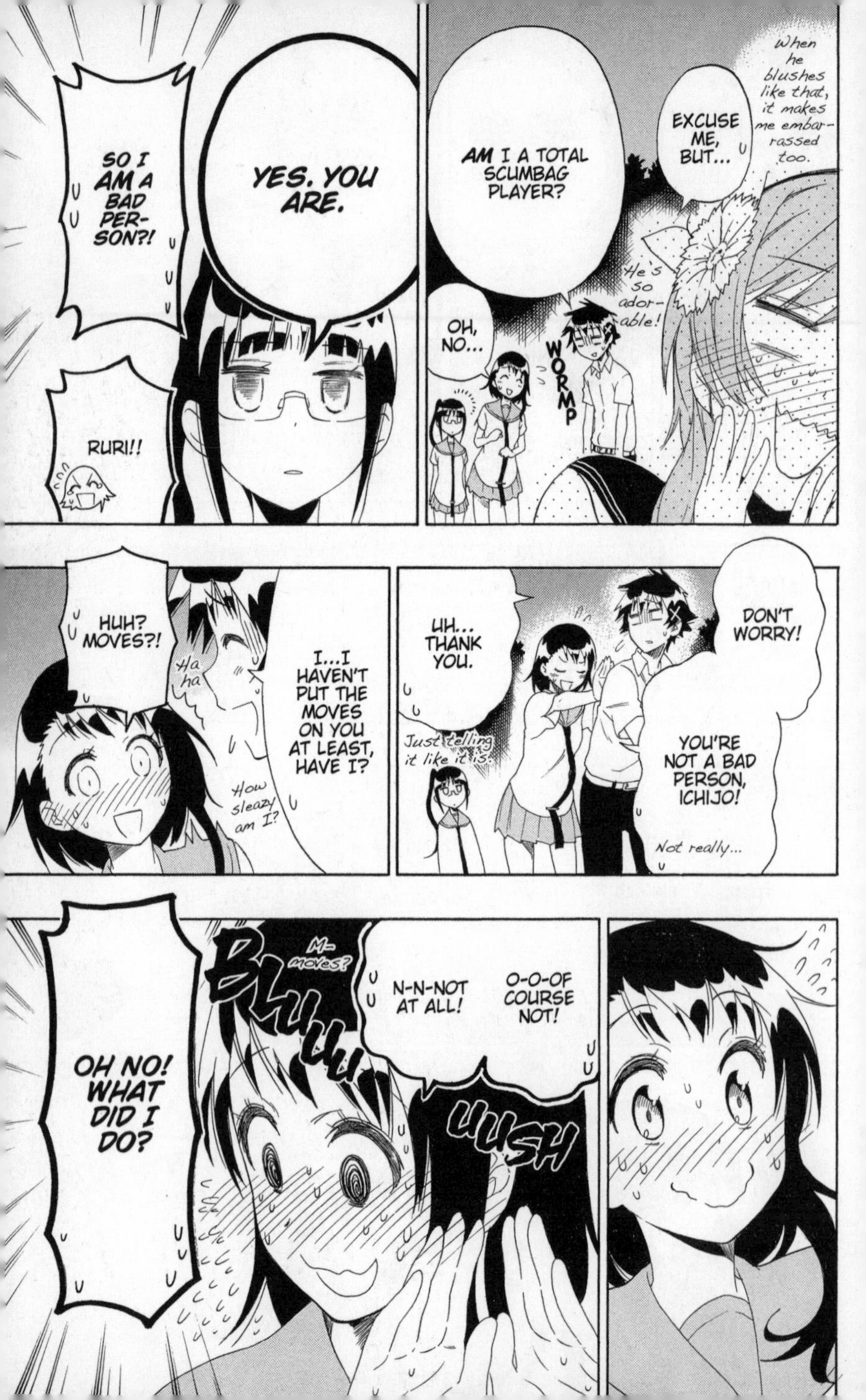
When he blushes like that, it makes me embarrassed too.
EXCUSE ME, BUT...
AM I A TOTAL SCUMBAG PLAYER?
He's so adorable!
OH, NO...
WORMP
YES. YOU ARE.
SO I AM A BAD PERSON?!
RURI!!
DON'T WORRY!
YOU'RE NOT A BAD PERSON, ICHIJO!
Not really...
UH... THANK YOU.
Just telling it like it is.
I...I HAVEN'T PUT THE MOVES ON YOU AT LEAST, HAVE I?
Ha ha
How sleazy am I?
HUH? MOVES?!
O-O-OF COURSE NOT!
N-N-NOT AT ALL!
M-moves?
BLUUUUSH
OH NO! WHAT DID I DO?

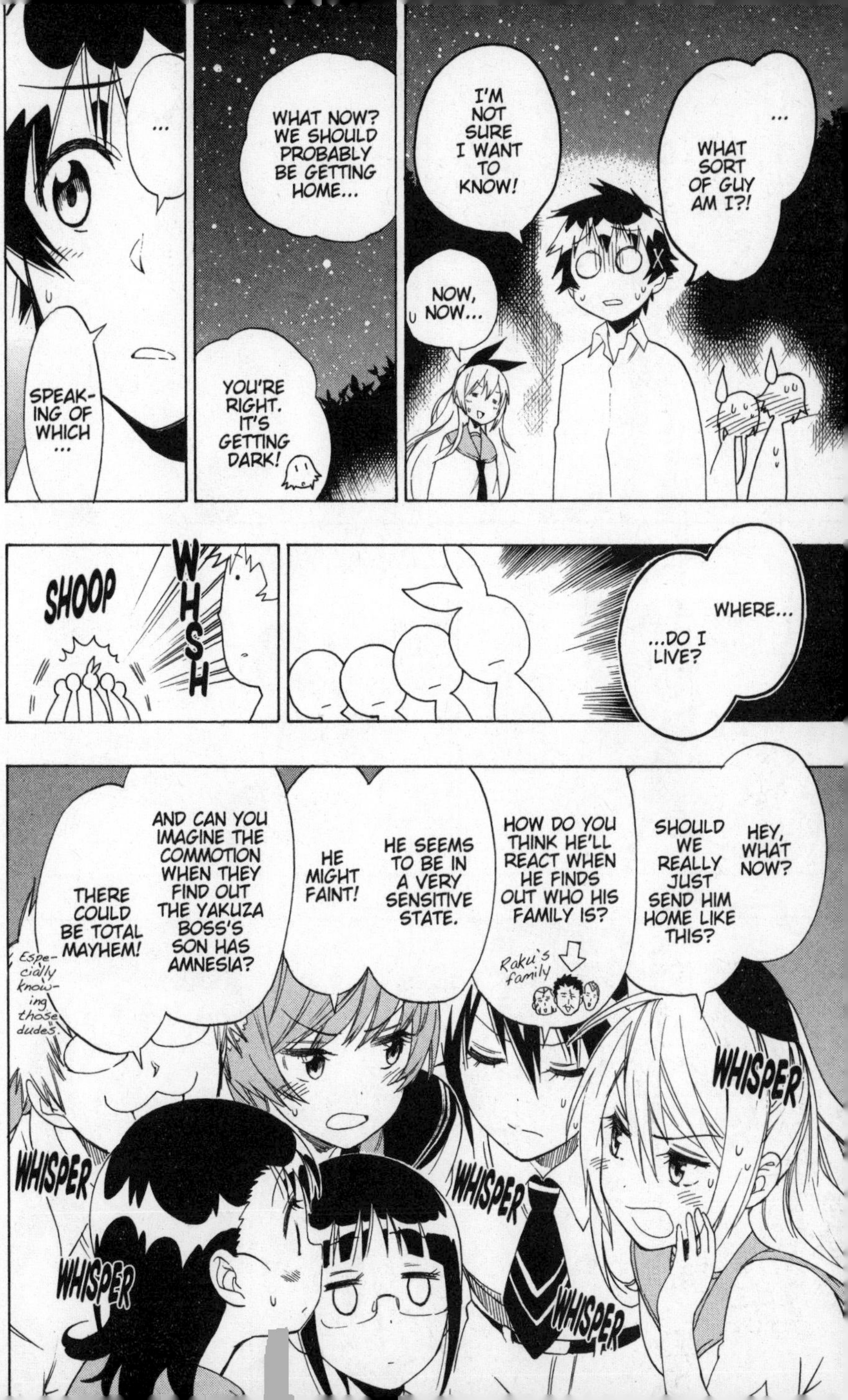
...
WHAT SORT OF GUY AM I?!
I'M NOT SURE I WANT TO KNOW!
NOW, NOW...
WHAT NOW? WE SHOULD PROBABLY BE GETTING HOME...
YOU'RE RIGHT. IT'S GETTING DARK!
...
SPEAK-ING OF WHICH...
WHERE...
...DO I LIVE?
WHSH
SHOOP
HEY, WHAT NOW?
SHOULD WE REALLY JUST SEND HIM HOME LIKE THIS?
HOW DO YOU THINK HE'LL REACT WHEN HE FINDS OUT WHO HIS FAMILY IS?
Raku's family
HE SEEMS TO BE IN A VERY SENSITIVE STATE.
HE MIGHT FAINT!
AND CAN YOU IMAGINE THE COMMOTION WHEN THEY FIND OUT THE YAKUZA BOSS'S SON HAS AMNESIA?
THERE COULD BE TOTAL MAYHEM!
Espe-cially know-ing those dudes.
WHISPER
WHISPER
WHISPER
WHISPER
WHISPER

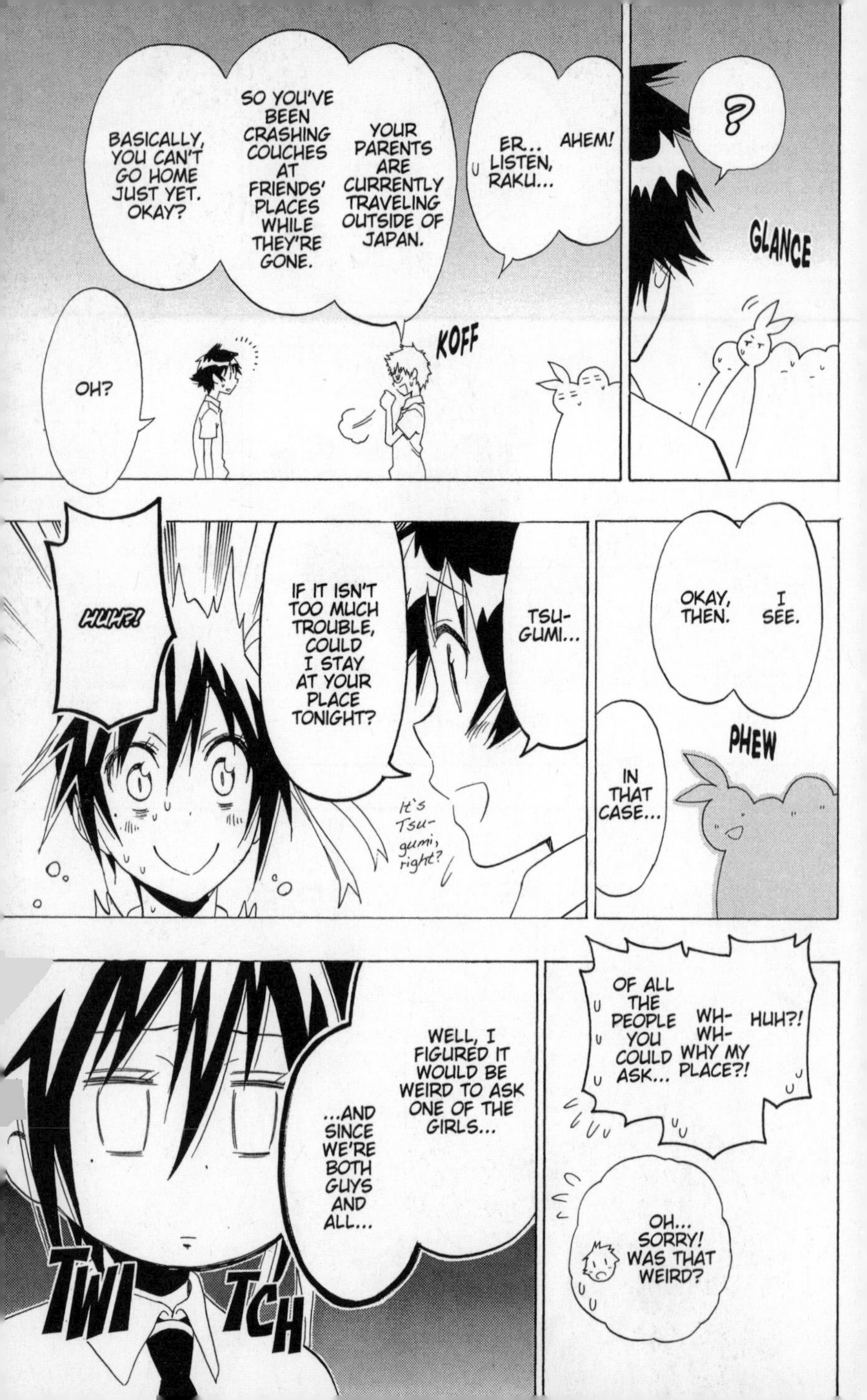
?
GLANCE
AHEM!
ER... LISTEN, RAKU...
YOUR PARENTS ARE CURRENTLY TRAVELING OUTSIDE OF JAPAN.
SO YOU'VE BEEN CRASHING COUCHES AT FRIENDS' PLACES WHILE THEY'RE GONE.
BASICALLY, YOU CAN'T GO HOME JUST YET. OKAY?
KOFF
OH?
I SEE.
OKAY, THEN.
PHEW
IN THAT CASE...
TSU-GUMI...
It's Tsu-gumi, right?
IF IT ISN'T TOO MUCH TROUBLE, COULD I STAY AT YOUR PLACE TONIGHT?
HUH?!
HUH?!
WH- WH- WHY MY PLACE?!
OF ALL THE PEOPLE YOU COULD ASK...
OH... SORRY! WAS THAT WEIRD?
WELL, I FIGURED IT WOULD BE WEIRD TO ASK ONE OF THE GIRLS...
...AND SINCE WE'RE BOTH GUYS AND ALL...
TWITCH

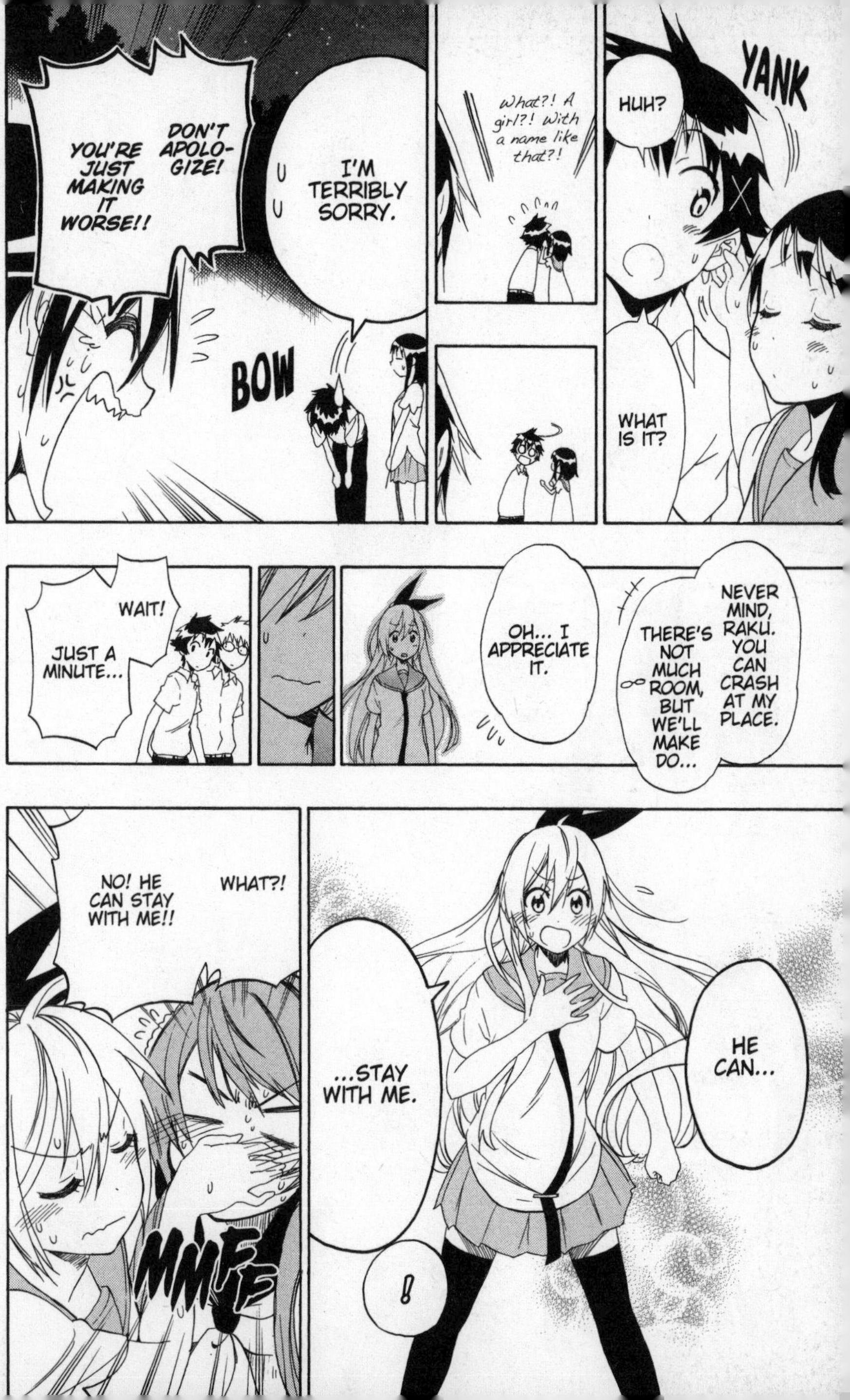
YANK
HUH?
WHAT IS IT?
What?! A girl?! With a name like that?!
I'M TERRIBLY SORRY.
DON'T APOLOGIZE! YOU'RE JUST MAKING IT WORSE!!
BOW
NEVER MIND, RAKU. YOU CAN CRASH AT MY PLACE.
THERE'S NOT MUCH ROOM, BUT WE'LL MAKE DO...
OH... I APPRECIATE IT.
WAIT!
JUST A MINUTE...
HE CAN...
...STAY WITH ME.
!
WHAT?!
NO! HE CAN STAY WITH ME!!
MMF

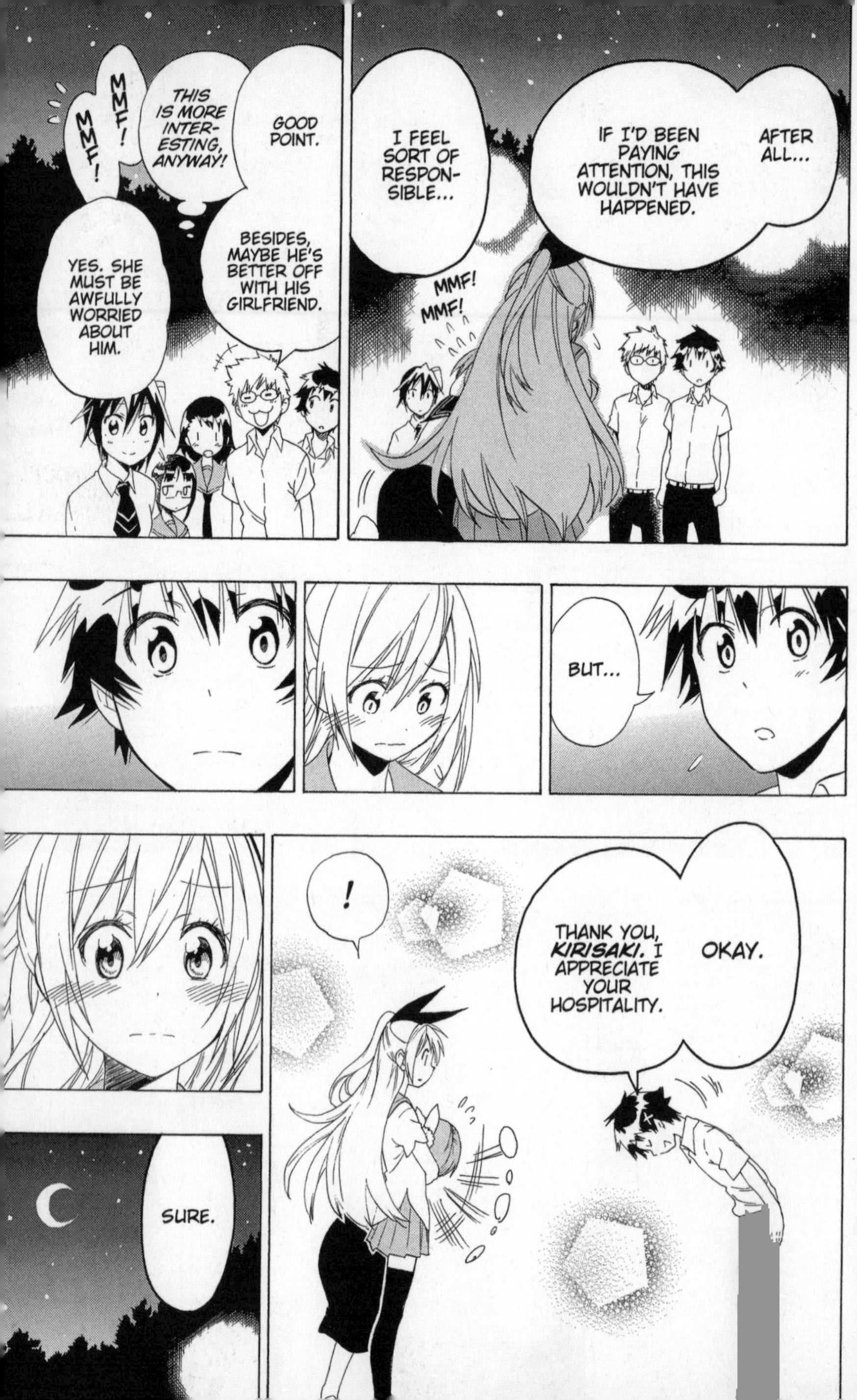
AFTER ALL...
IF I'D BEEN PAYING ATTENTION, THIS WOULDN'T HAVE HAPPENED.
I FEEL SORT OF RESPONSIBLE...
MMF! MMF!
GOOD POINT.
THIS IS MORE INTERESTING, ANYWAY!
MMF! MMF!
BESIDES, MAYBE HE'S BETTER OFF WITH HIS GIRLFRIEND.
YES. SHE MUST BE AWFULLY WORRIED ABOUT HIM.
BUT...
OKAY.
THANK YOU, KIRISAKI. I APPRECIATE YOUR HOSPITALITY.
!
SURE.

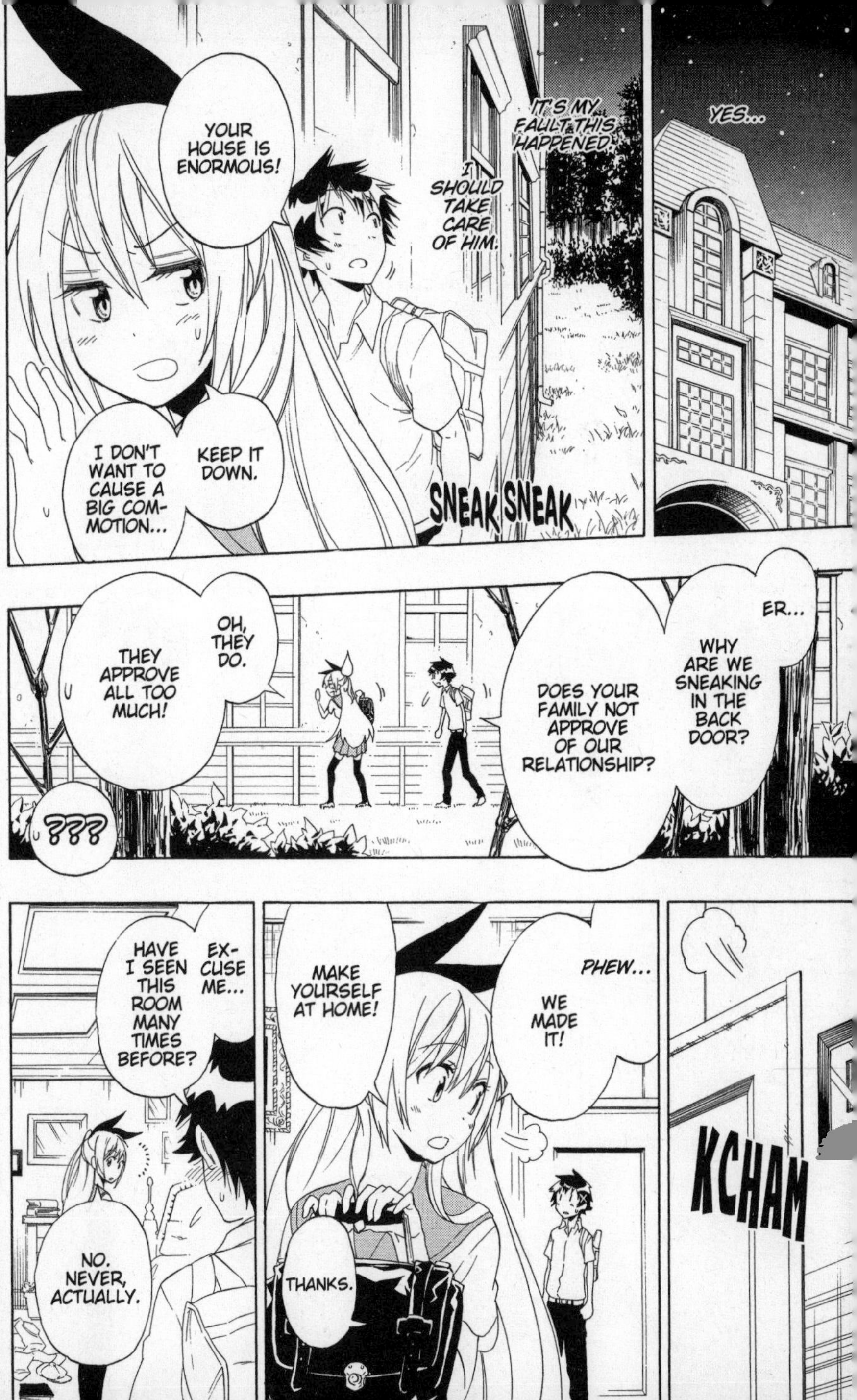
YES...
IT'S MY FAULT THIS HAPPENED.
I SHOULD TAKE CARE OF HIM.
SNEAK SNEAK
YOUR HOUSE IS ENORMOUS!
KEEP IT DOWN.
I DON'T WANT TO CAUSE A BIG COMMOTION...
ER...
WHY ARE WE SNEAKING IN THE BACK DOOR?
DOES YOUR FAMILY NOT APPROVE OF OUR RELATIONSHIP?
OH, THEY DO.
THEY APPROVE ALL TOO MUCH!
???
KCHAM
PHEW...
WE MADE IT!
MAKE YOURSELF AT HOME!
THANKS.
EXCUSE ME...
HAVE I SEEN THIS ROOM MANY TIMES BEFORE?
NO. NEVER, ACTUALLY.

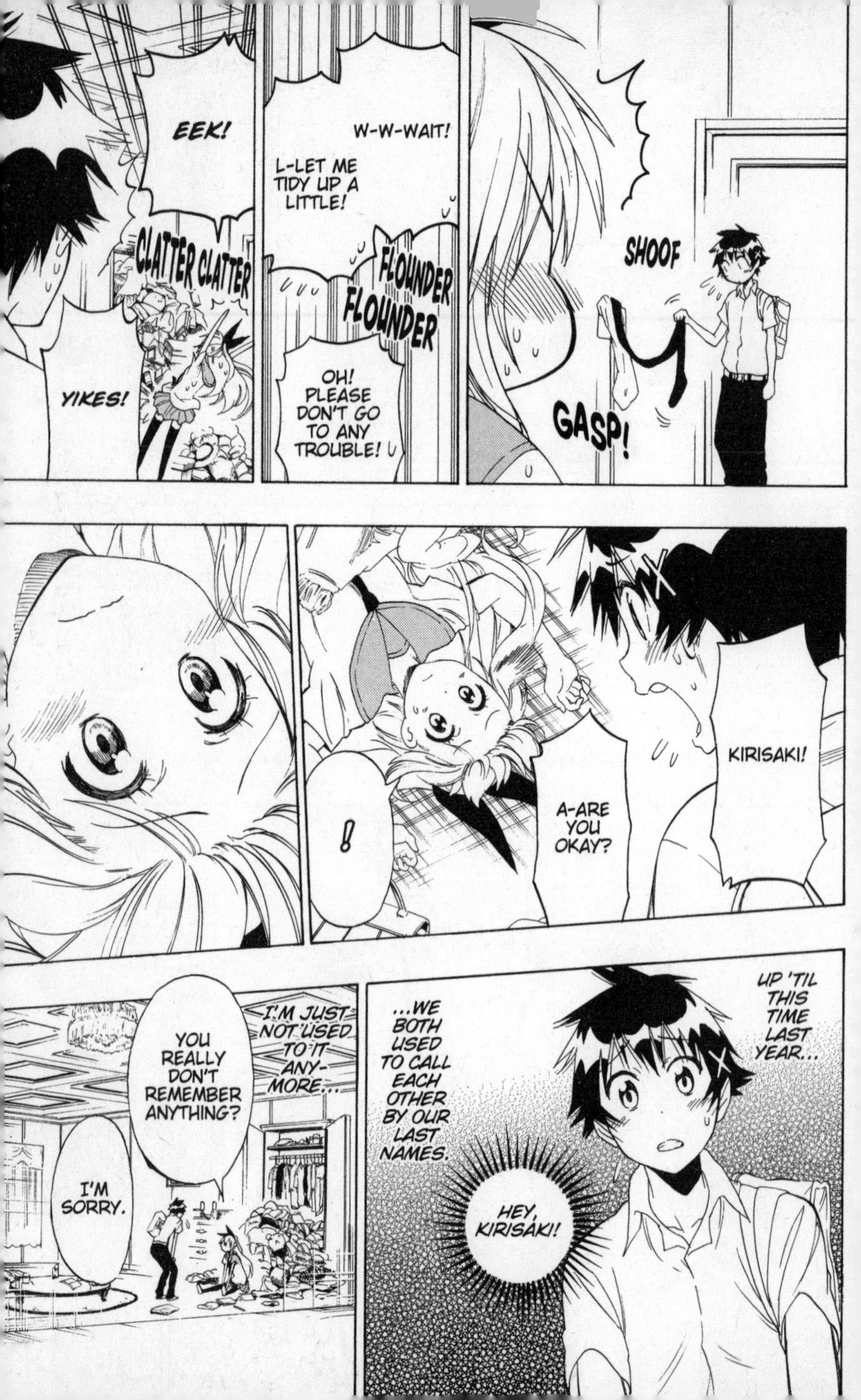
SHOOF
GASP!
W-W-WAIT!
L-LET ME TIDY UP A LITTLE!
FLOUNDER FLOUNDER
OH! PLEASE DON'T GO TO ANY TROUBLE!
EEK!
CLATTER CLATTER
YIKES!
KIRISAKI!
A-ARE YOU OKAY?
!
UP 'TIL THIS TIME LAST YEAR...
...WE BOTH USED TO CALL EACH OTHER BY OUR LAST NAMES.
HEY, KIRISAKI!
I'M JUST NOT USED TO IT ANYMORE...
YOU REALLY DON'T REMEMBER ANYTHING?
I'M SORRY.

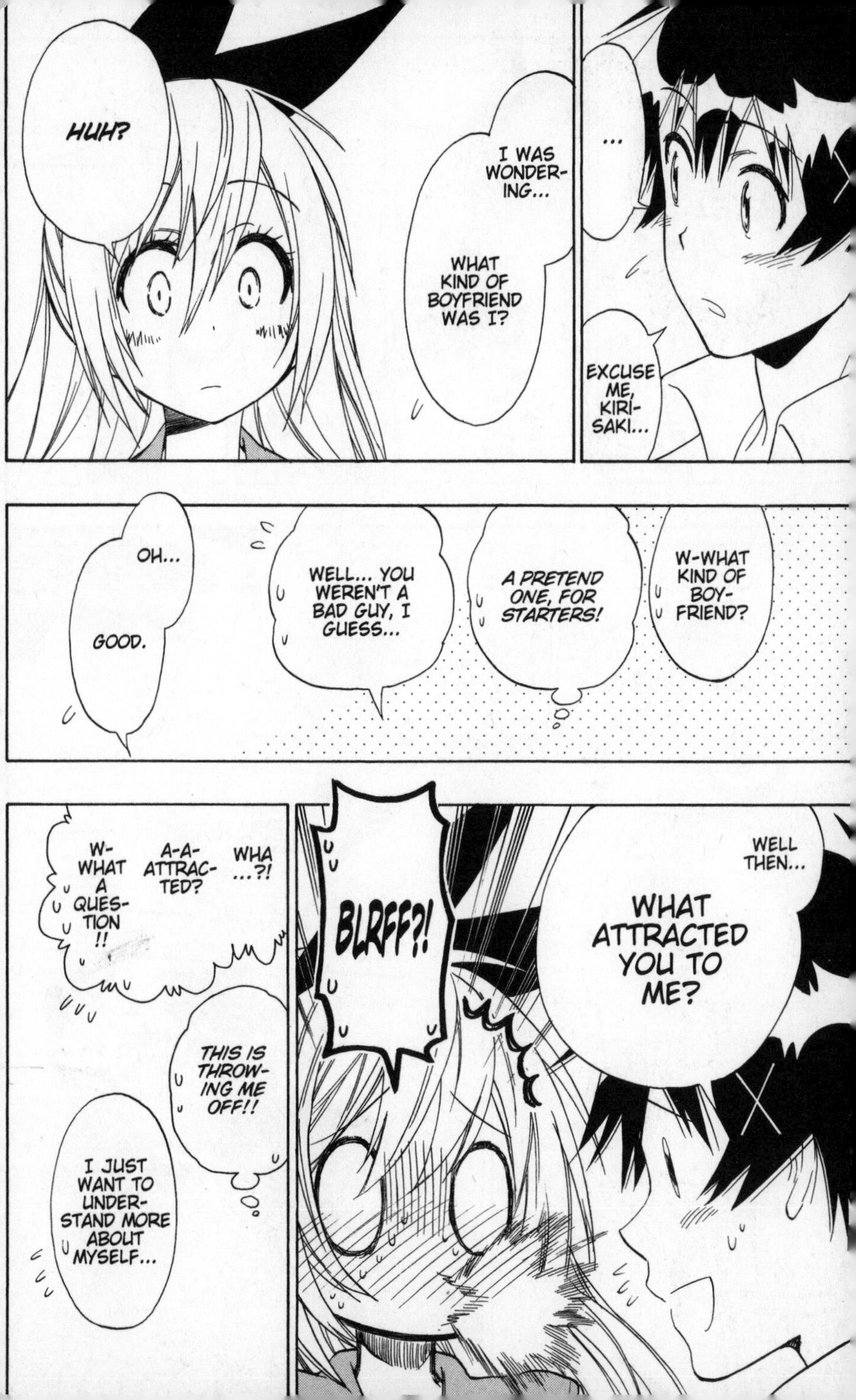
...
EXCUSE ME, KIRISAKI...
I WAS WONDERING...
WHAT KIND OF BOYFRIEND WAS I?
HUH?
W-WHAT KIND OF BOYFRIEND?
A PRETEND ONE, FOR STARTERS!
WELL... YOU WEREN'T A BAD GUY, I GUESS...
OH...
GOOD.
WELL THEN...
WHAT ATTRACTED YOU TO ME?
BLRFF?!
WHA...?!
A-A-ATTRACTED?
W-WHAT A QUESTION!!
THIS IS THROWING ME OFF!!
I JUST WANT TO UNDERSTAND MORE ABOUT MYSELF...

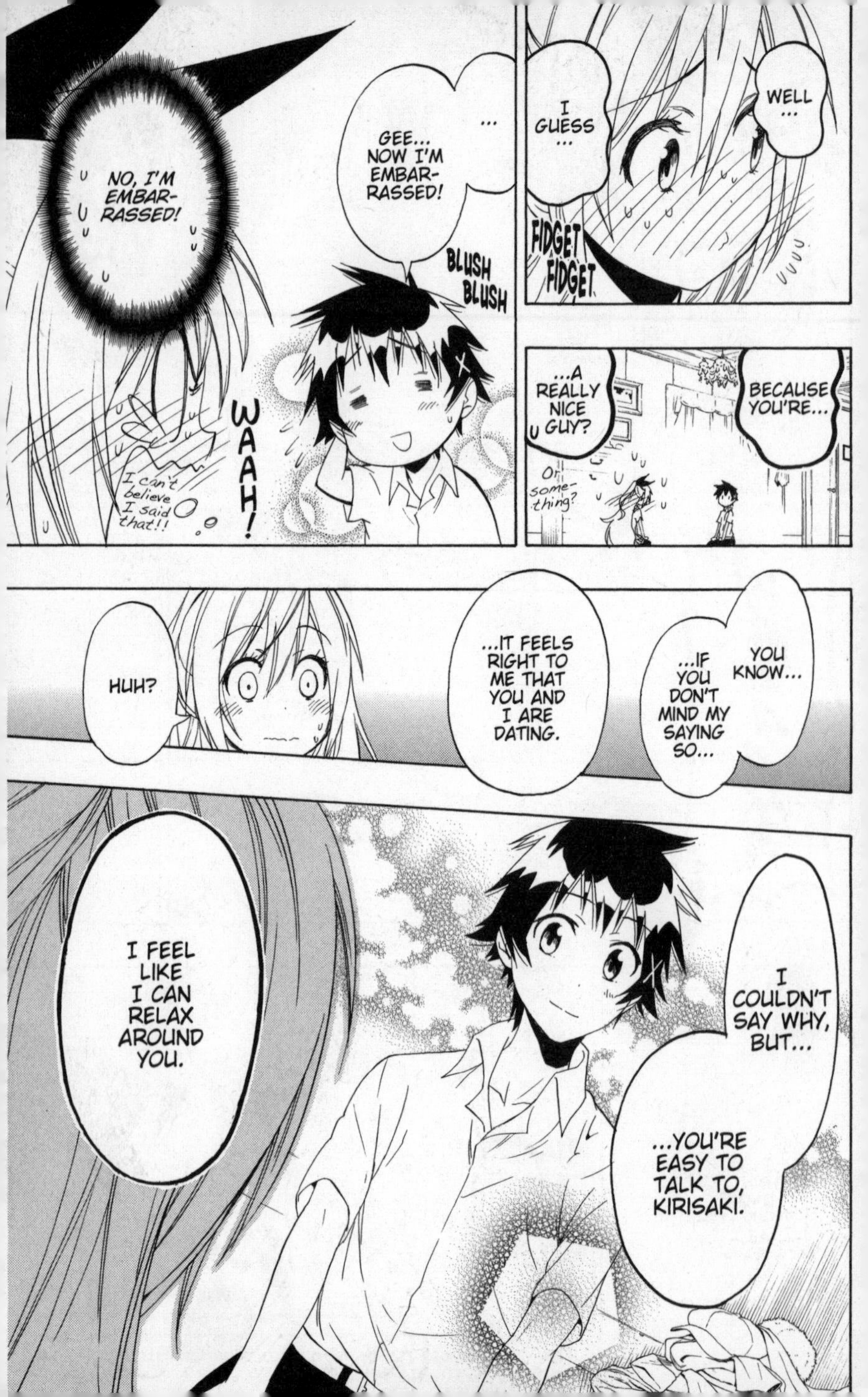
WELL...
I GUESS...
FIDGET FIDGET
BECAUSE YOU'RE...
...A REALLY NICE GUY?
Or something?
...
GEE... NOW I'M EMBARRASSED!
BLUSH BLUSH
NO, I'M EMBARRASSED!
WAAH!
I can't believe I said that!!
YOU KNOW...
...IF YOU DON'T MIND MY SAYING SO...
...IT FEELS RIGHT TO ME THAT YOU AND I ARE DATING.
HUH?
I COULDN'T SAY WHY, BUT...
...YOU'RE EASY TO TALK TO, KIRISAKI.
I FEEL LIKE I CAN RELAX AROUND YOU.

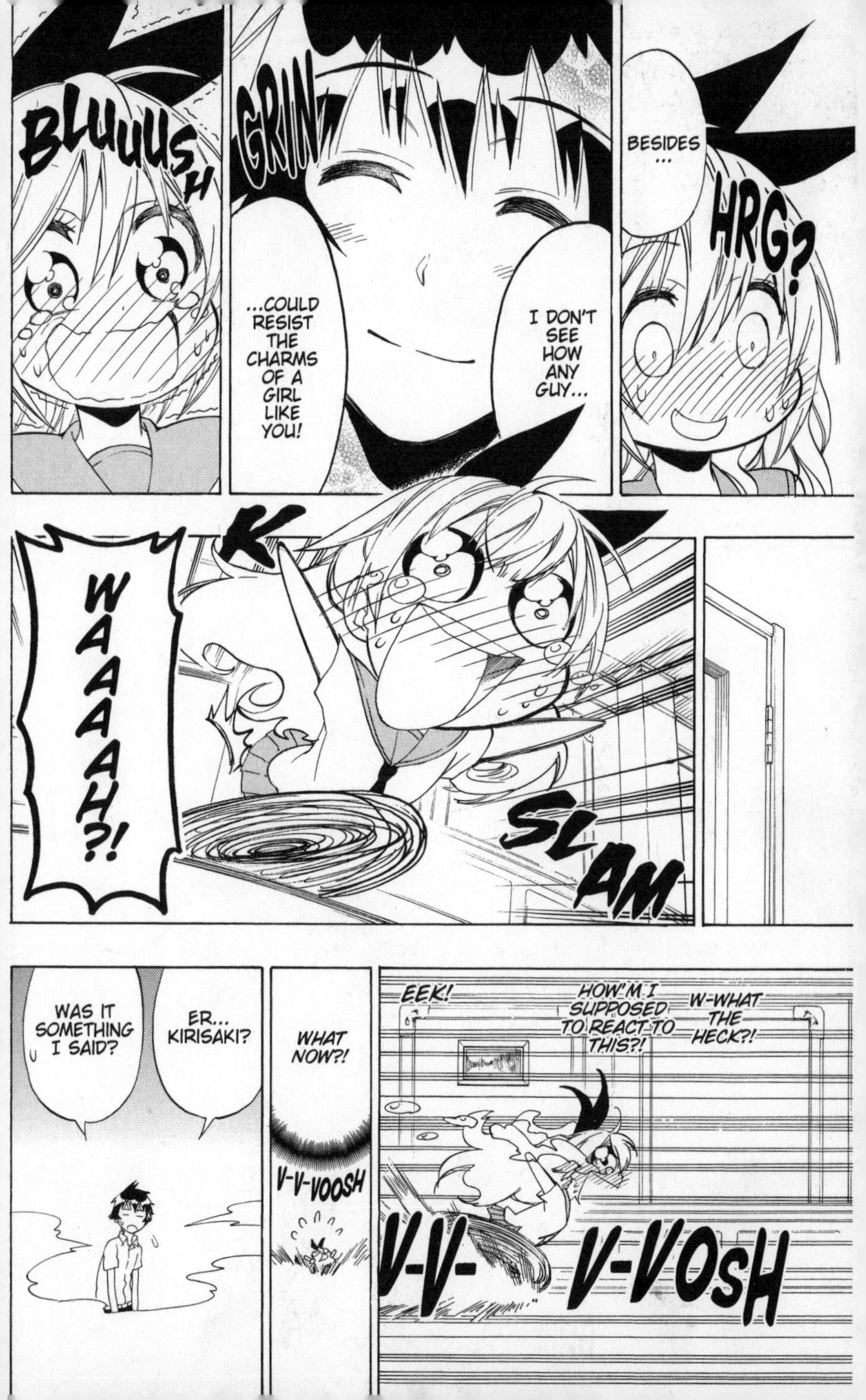
BESIDES...
HRG?
I DON'T SEE HOW ANY GUY...
...COULD RESIST THE CHARMS OF A GIRL LIKE YOU!
GRIN
BLUUUSH
K
WAAAAAH?!
SLAM
W-WHAT THE HECK?!
HOW'M I SUPPOSED TO REACT TO THIS?!
EEK!
V-VOSH
V-V-
WHAT NOW?!
V-V-VOOSH
ER... KIRISAKI?
WAS IT SOMETHING I SAID?

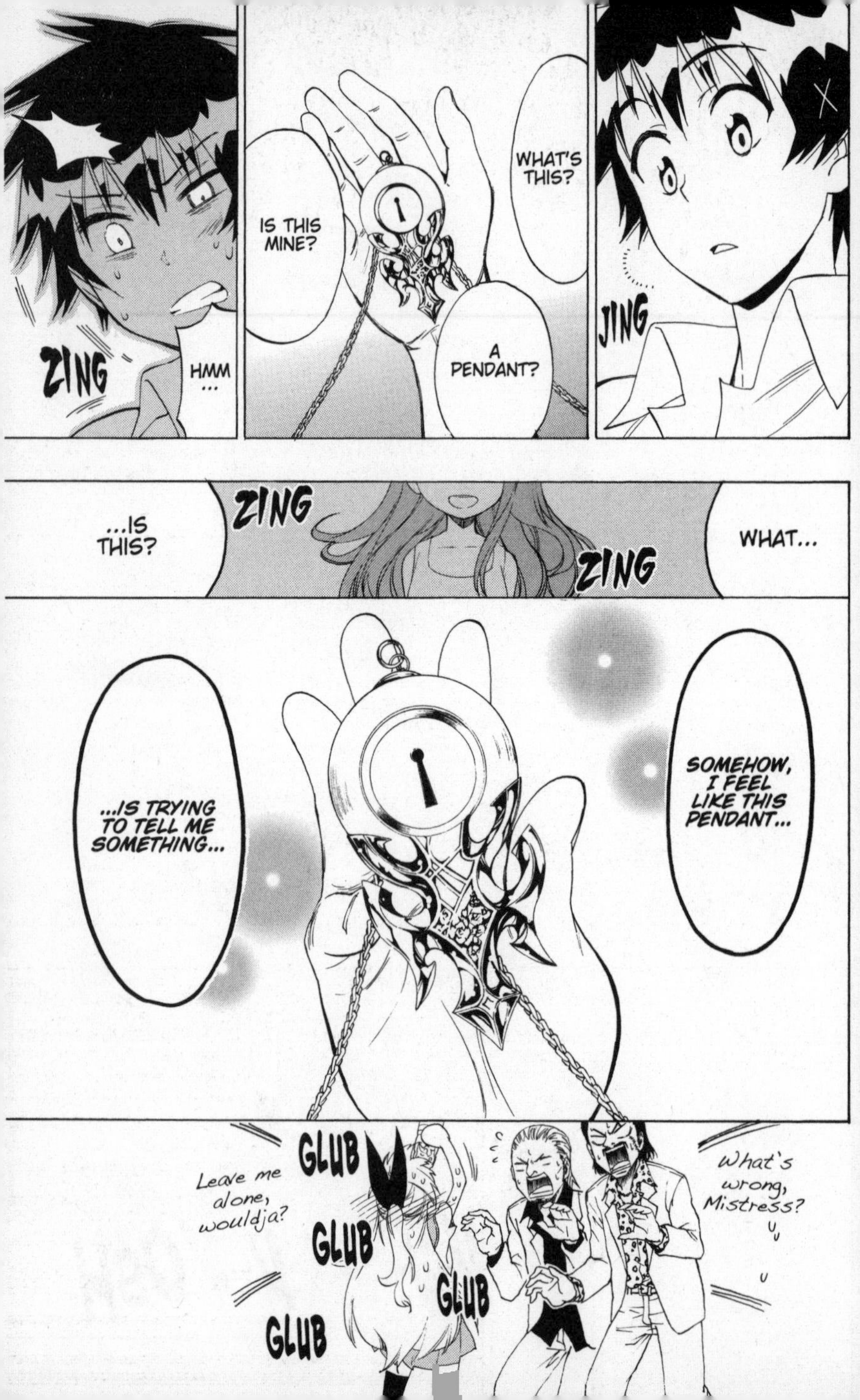
JING
WHAT'S THIS?
IS THIS MINE?
A PENDANT?
HMM...
ZING
WHAT...
ZING
ZING
...IS THIS?
SOMEHOW, I FEEL LIKE THIS PENDANT...
...IS TRYING TO TELL ME SOMETHING...
What's wrong, Mistress?
GLUB
GLUB
GLUB
GLUB
Leave me alone, wouldja?

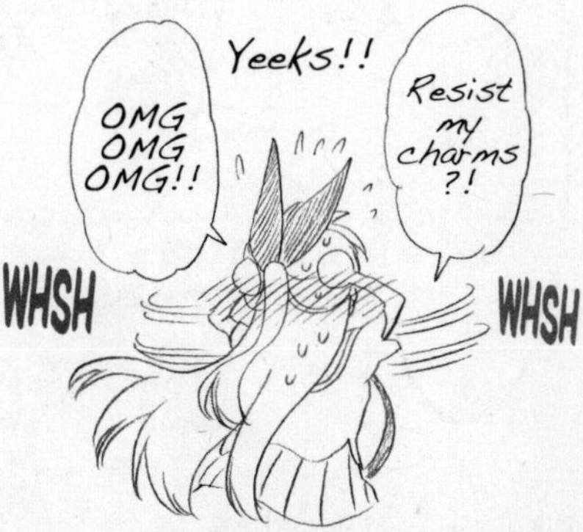
Resist my charms?!
Yeeks!!
OMG OMG OMG!!
WHSH
WHSH

Chapter 89: Recreation

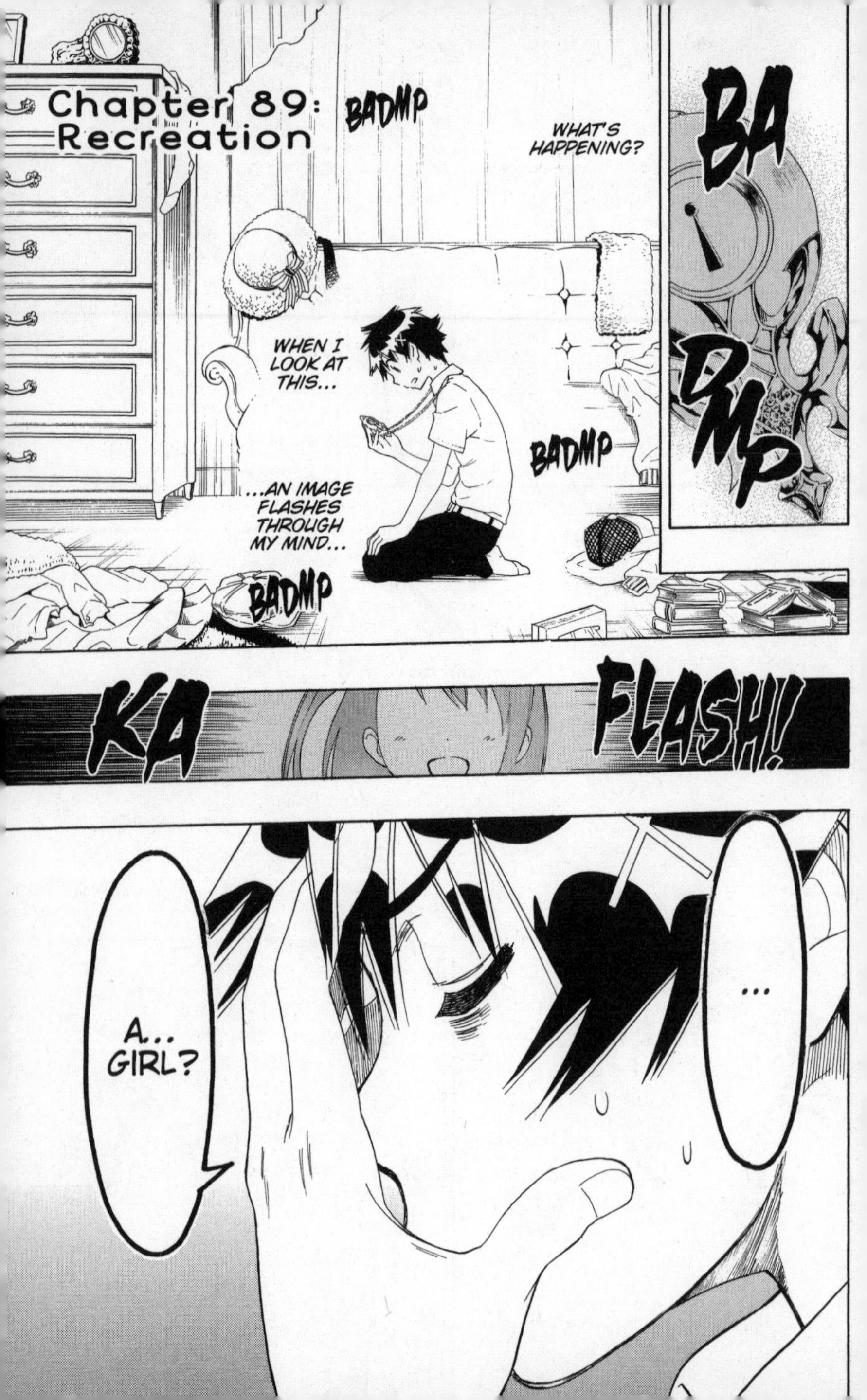
BA DMP
BADMP
WHAT'S HAPPENING?
WHEN I LOOK AT THIS...
BADMP
...AN IMAGE FLASHES THROUGH MY MIND...
BADMP
KA FLASH!
...
A... GIRL?

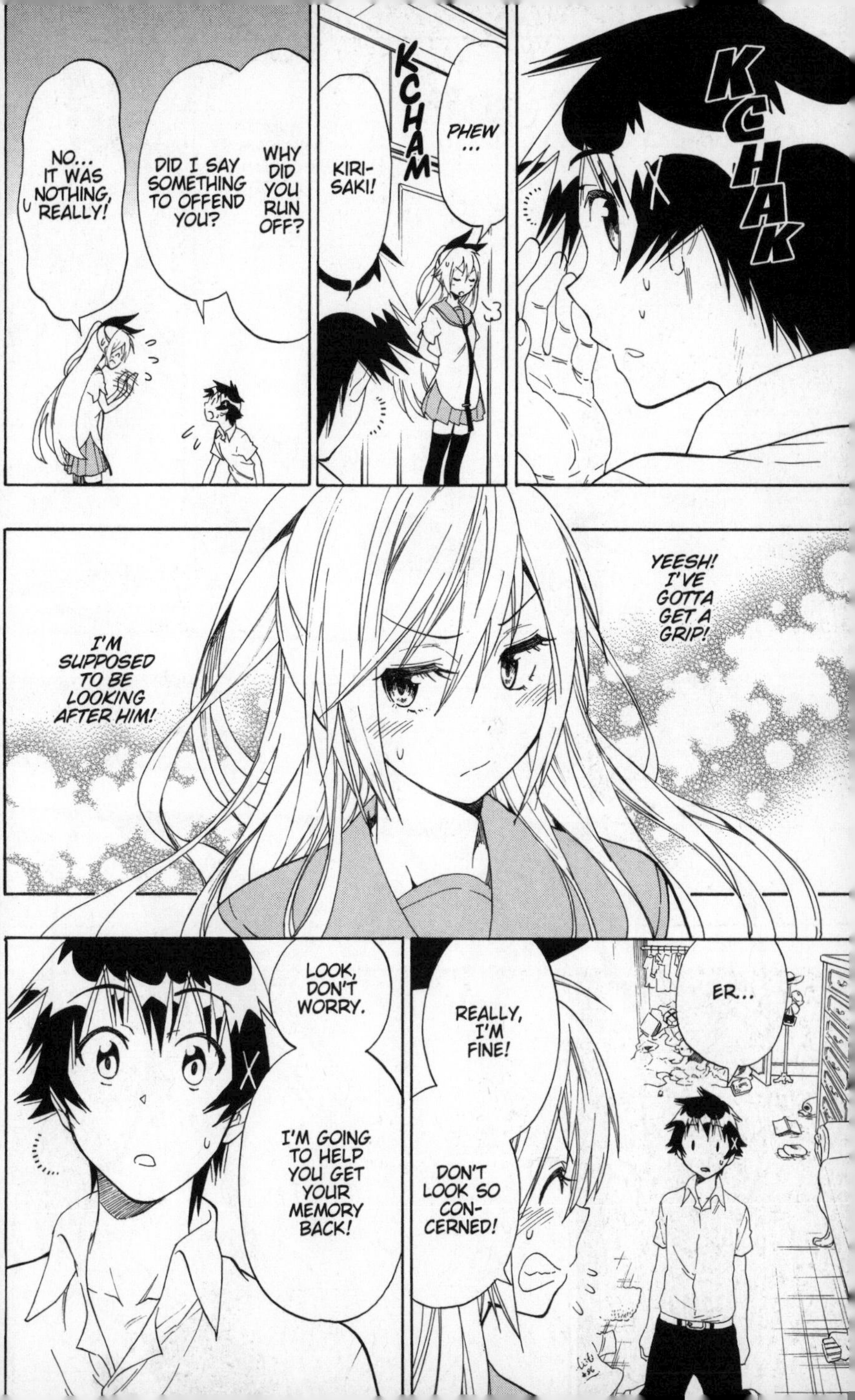
KCHAK
PHEW...
KCHAM
KIRI-SAKI!
WHY DID YOU RUN OFF?
DID I SAY SOMETHING TO OFFEND YOU?
NO... IT WAS NOTHING, REALLY!
YEESH! I'VE GOTTA GET A GRIP!
I'M SUPPOSED TO BE LOOKING AFTER HIM!
ER...
REALLY, I'M FINE!
DON'T LOOK SO CON-CERNED!
LOOK, DON'T WORRY.
I'M GOING TO HELP YOU GET YOUR MEMORY BACK!

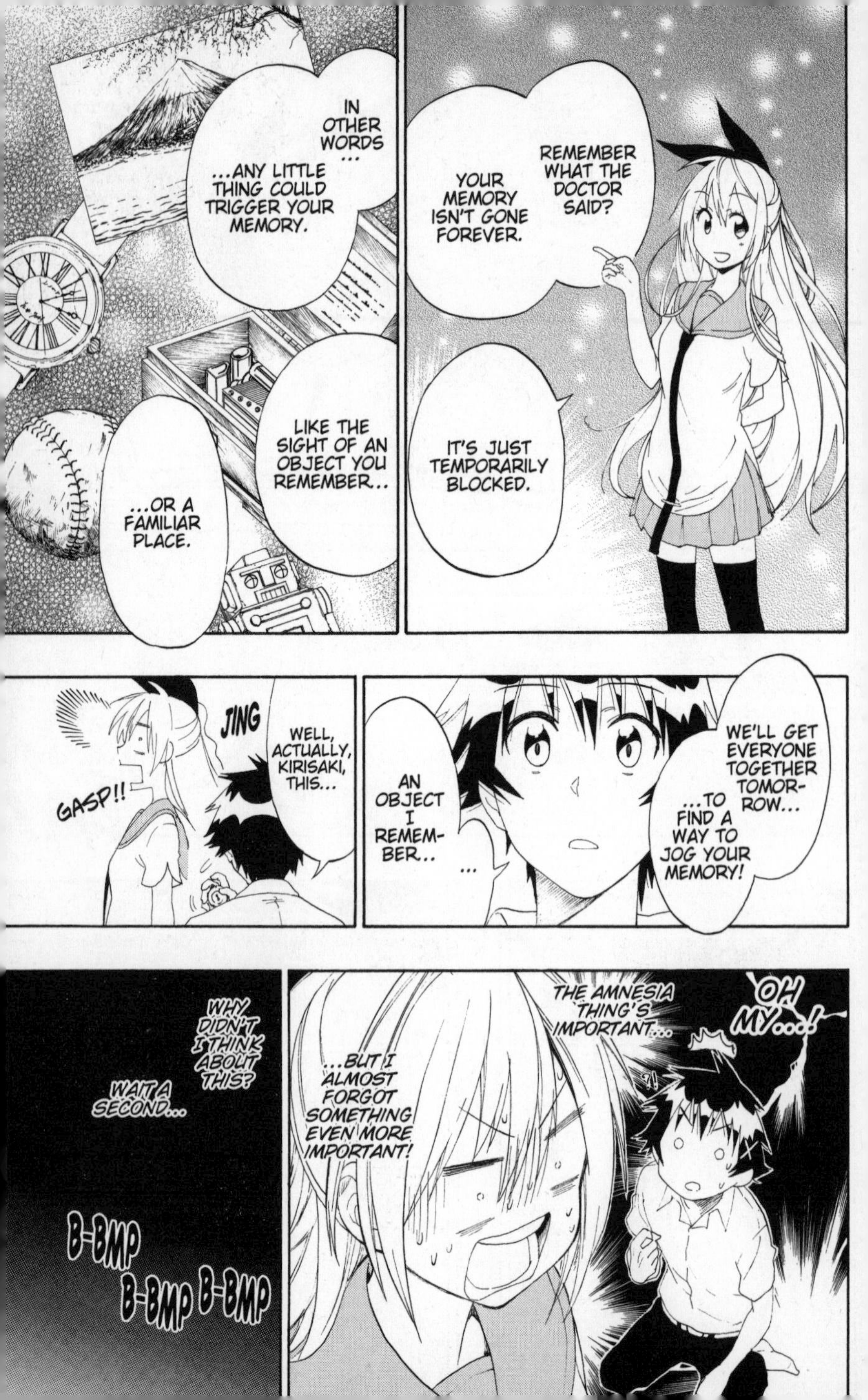
REMEMBER WHAT THE DOCTOR SAID?
YOUR MEMORY ISN'T GONE FOREVER.
IT'S JUST TEMPORARILY BLOCKED.
IN OTHER WORDS...
...ANY LITTLE THING COULD TRIGGER YOUR MEMORY.
LIKE THE SIGHT OF AN OBJECT YOU REMEMBER...
...OR A FAMILIAR PLACE.
WE'LL GET EVERYONE TOGETHER TOMORROW...
...TO FIND A WAY TO JOG YOUR MEMORY!
AN OBJECT I REMEMBER...
...
WELL, ACTUALLY, KIRISAKI, THIS...
JING
GASP!!
OH MY...!
THE AMNESIA THING'S IMPORTANT...
?!
...BUT I ALMOST FORGOT SOMETHING EVEN MORE IMPORTANT!
WHY DIDN'T I THINK ABOUT THIS?
WAIT A SECOND...
B-BMP
B-BMP B-BMP

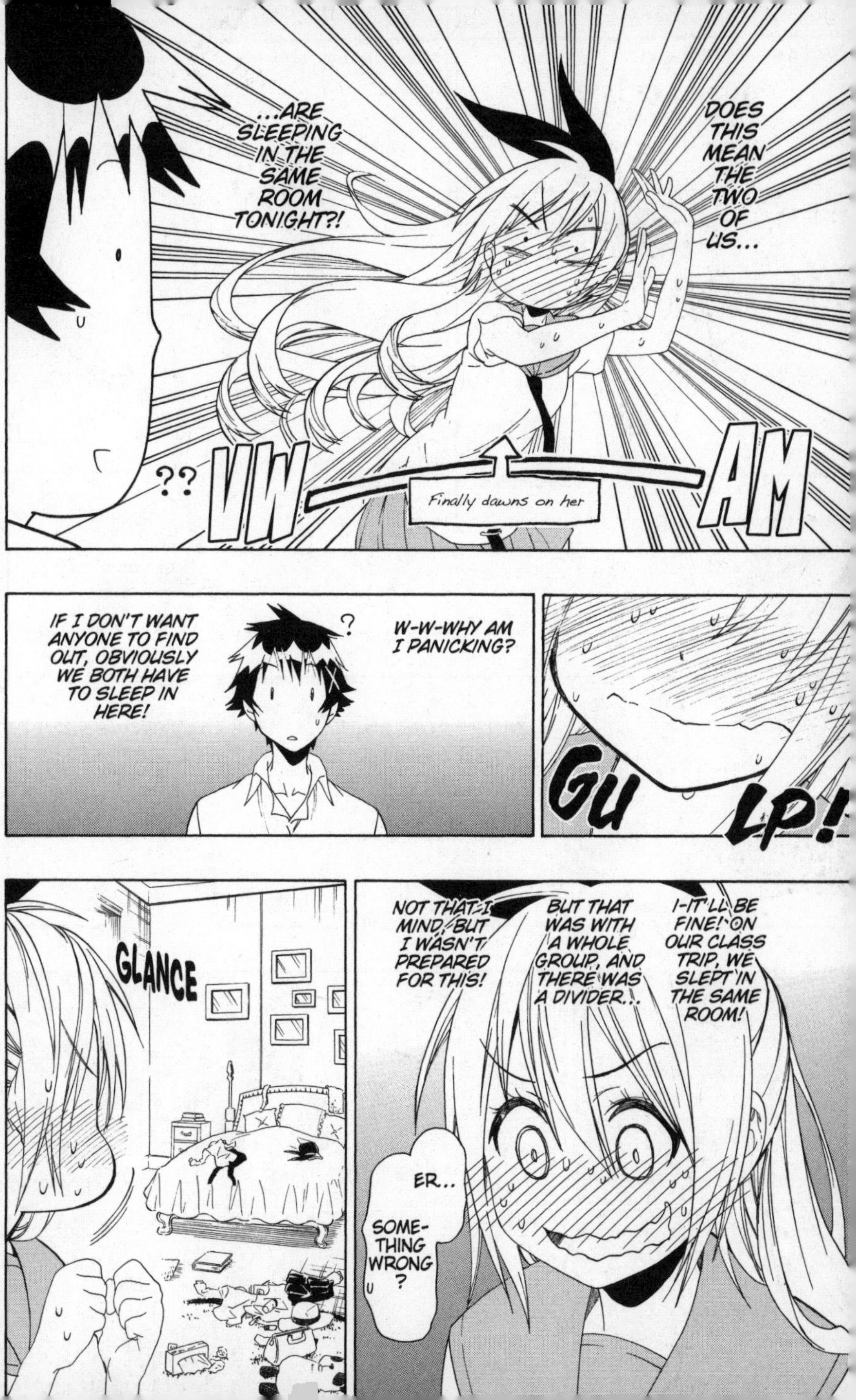
DOES THIS MEAN THE TWO OF US...
...ARE SLEEPING IN THE SAME ROOM TONIGHT?!
VWAM
Finally dawns on her
??
GULP!
W-W-WHY AM I PANICKING?
IF I DON'T WANT ANYONE TO FIND OUT, OBVIOUSLY WE BOTH HAVE TO SLEEP IN HERE!
?
I-IT'LL BE FINE! ON OUR CLASS TRIP, WE SLEPT IN THE SAME ROOM!
BUT THAT WAS WITH A WHOLE GROUP, AND THERE WAS A DIVIDER...
NOT THAT I MIND, BUT I WASN'T PREPARED FOR THIS!
ER...
SOME-THING WRONG?
GLANCE

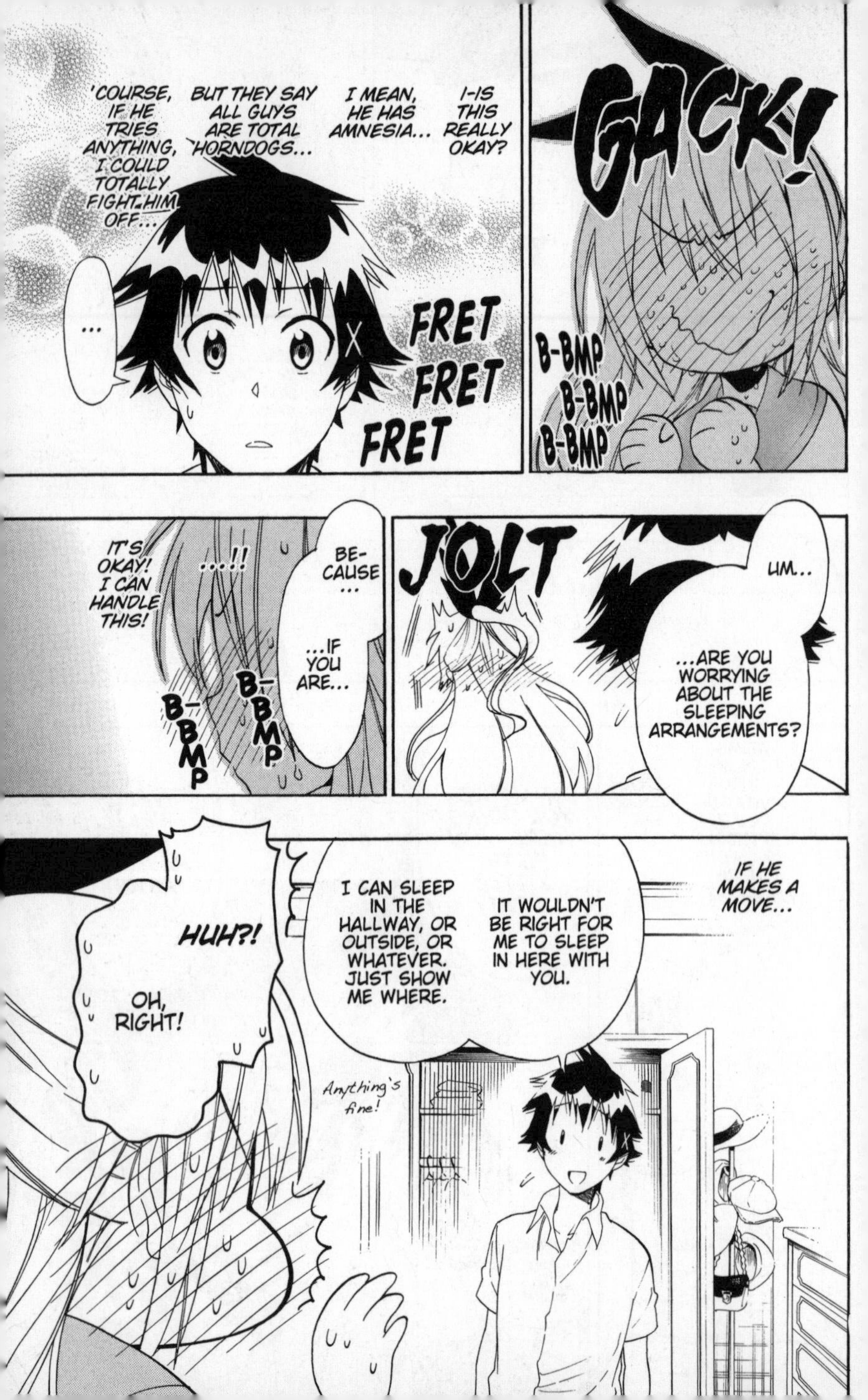
GACK!
B-BMP B-BMP B-BMP
I-IS THIS REALLY OKAY?
I MEAN, HE HAS AMNESIA...
BUT THEY SAY ALL GUYS ARE TOTAL HORNDOGS...
'COURSE, IF HE TRIES ANYTHING, I COULD TOTALLY FIGHT HIM OFF...
FRET FRET FRET
...
UM...
JOLT
...ARE YOU WORRYING ABOUT THE SLEEPING ARRANGEMENTS?
BE-CAUSE...
...IF YOU ARE...
...!!
IT'S OKAY! I CAN HANDLE THIS!
B-BMP B-BMP
IF HE MAKES A MOVE...
IT WOULDN'T BE RIGHT FOR ME TO SLEEP IN HERE WITH YOU.
I CAN SLEEP IN THE HALLWAY, OR OUTSIDE, OR WHATEVER. JUST SHOW ME WHERE.
Anything's fine!
HUH?!
OH, RIGHT!

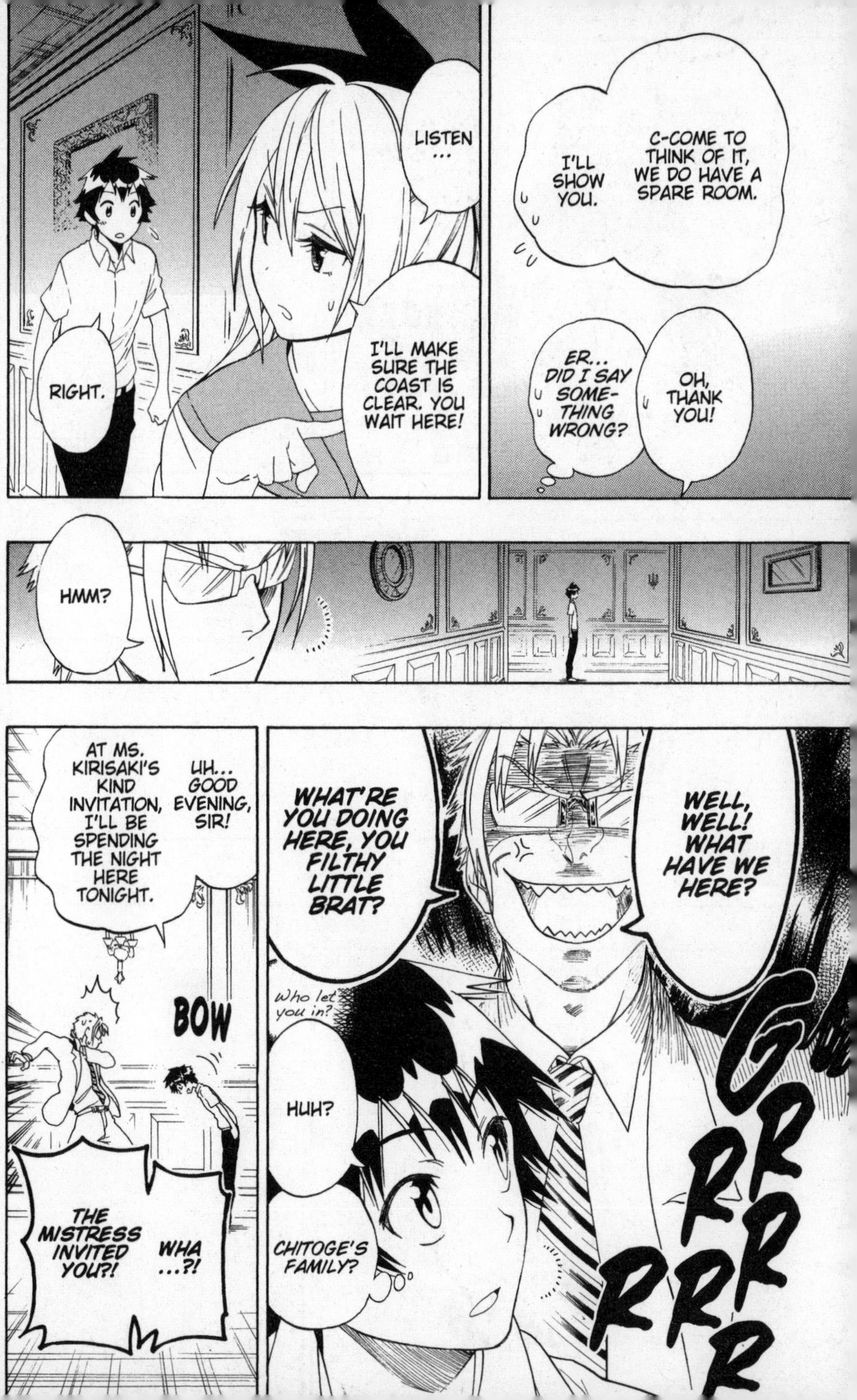
C-COME TO THINK OF IT, WE DO HAVE A SPARE ROOM.
I'LL SHOW YOU.
OH, THANK YOU!
ER... DID I SAY SOMETHING WRONG?
LISTEN...
I'LL MAKE SURE THE COAST IS CLEAR. YOU WAIT HERE!
RIGHT.
HMM?
WELL, WELL! WHAT HAVE WE HERE?
WHAT'RE YOU DOING HERE, YOU FILTHY LITTLE BRAT?
GRRRRRR
Who let you in?
HUH?
CHITOGE'S FAMILY?
UH... GOOD EVENING, SIR!
AT MS. KIRISAKI'S KIND INVITATION, I'LL BE SPENDING THE NIGHT HERE TONIGHT.
BOW
WHA...?!
THE MISTRESS INVITED YOU?!

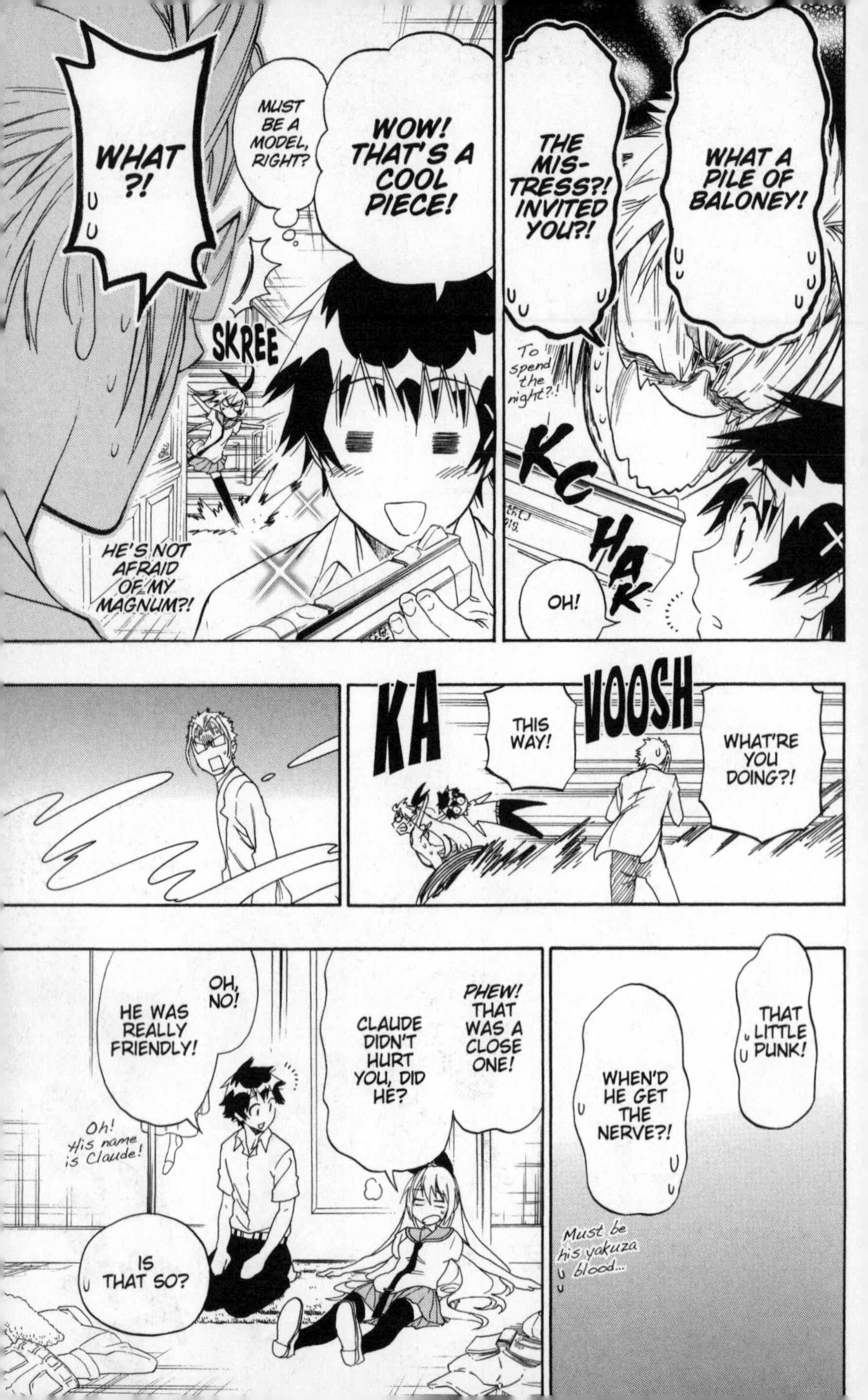
WHAT A PILE OF BALONEY!
THE MIS-TRESS?! INVITED YOU?!
To spend the night?!
KCHAK
OH!
WOW! THAT'S A COOL PIECE!
MUST BE A MODEL, RIGHT?
WHAT?!
SKREE
HE'S NOT AFRAID OF MY MAGNUM?!
KA VOOSH
WHAT'RE YOU DOING?!
THIS WAY!
THAT LITTLE PUNK!
WHEN'D HE GET THE NERVE?!
Must be his yakuza blood...
PHEW! THAT WAS A CLOSE ONE!
CLAUDE DIDN'T HURT YOU, DID HE?
OH, NO!
HE WAS REALLY FRIENDLY!
Oh! His name is Claude!
IS THAT SO?

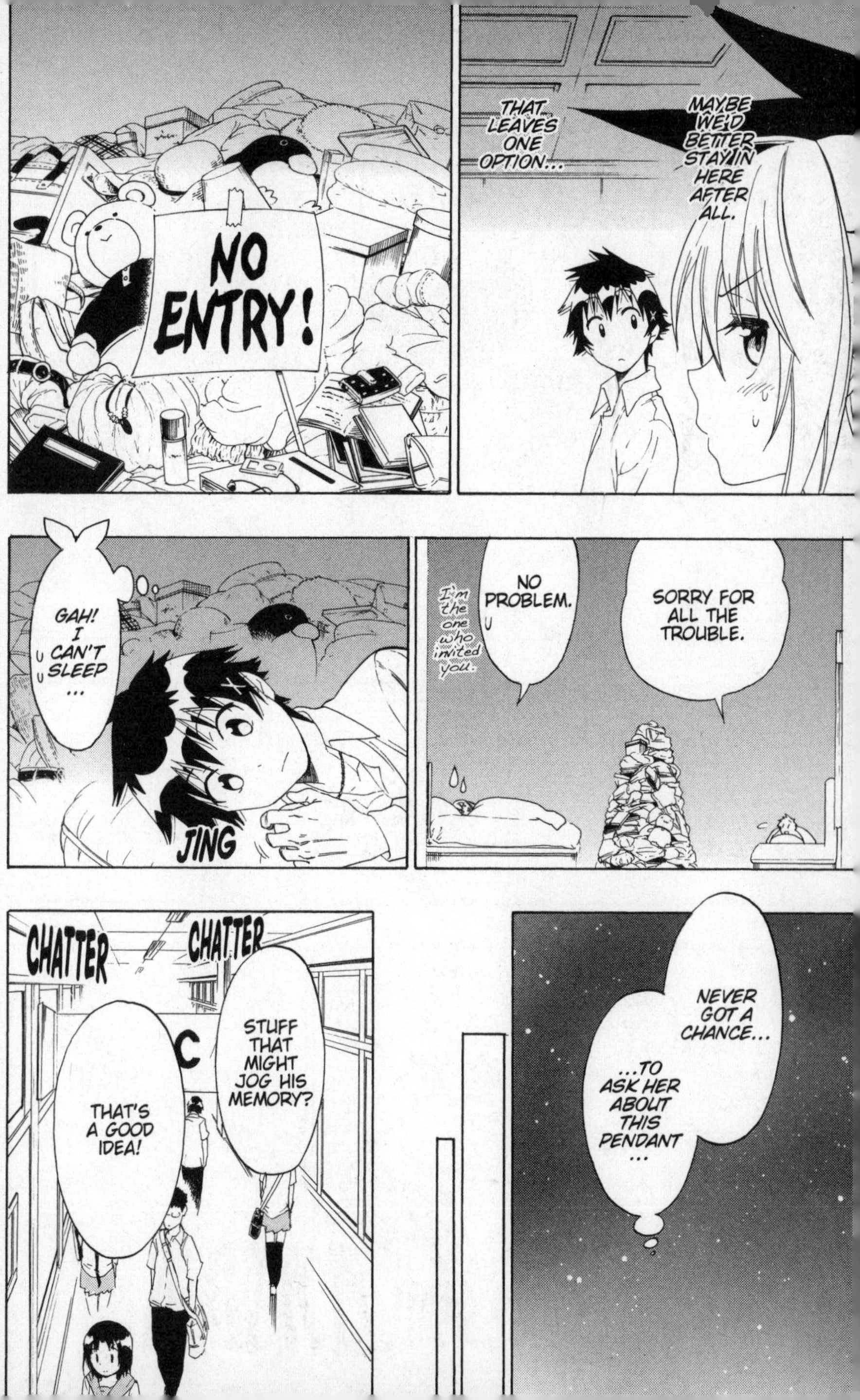
MAYBE WE'D BETTER STAY IN HERE AFTER ALL.
THAT LEAVES ONE OPTION...
NO ENTRY!
SORRY FOR ALL THE TROUBLE.
NO PROBLEM.
I'm the one who invited you.
GAH! I CAN'T SLEEP...
JING
NEVER GOT A CHANCE...
...TO ASK HER ABOUT THIS PENDANT...
CHATTER
CHATTER
STUFF THAT MIGHT JOG HIS MEMORY?
THAT'S A GOOD IDEA!
C

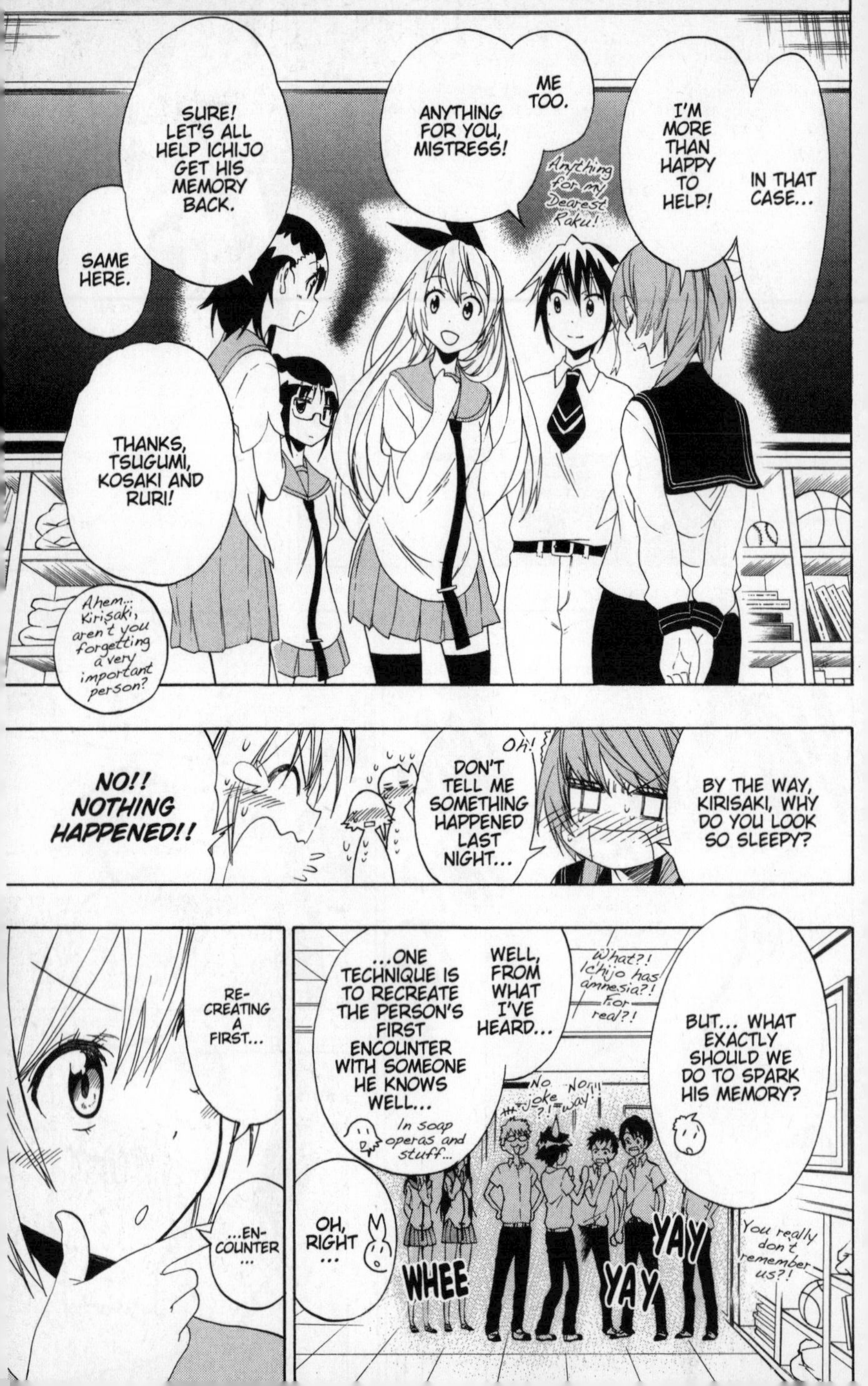
IN THAT CASE...
I'M MORE THAN HAPPY TO HELP!
Anything for my Dearest Raku!
ME TOO.
ANYTHING FOR YOU, MISTRESS!
SURE! LET'S ALL HELP ICHIJO GET HIS MEMORY BACK.
SAME HERE.
THANKS, TSUGUMI, KOSAKI AND RURI!
Ahem... Kirisaki, aren't you forgetting a very important person?
BY THE WAY, KIRISAKI, WHY DO YOU LOOK SO SLEEPY?
Oh!
DON'T TELL ME SOMETHING HAPPENED LAST NIGHT...
NO!! NOTHING HAPPENED!!
BUT... WHAT EXACTLY SHOULD WE DO TO SPARK HIS MEMORY?
What?! Ichijo has amnesia?! For real?!
WELL, FROM WHAT I'VE HEARD...
...ONE TECHNIQUE IS TO RECREATE THE PERSON'S FIRST ENCOUNTER WITH SOMEONE HE KNOWS WELL...
In soap operas and stuff...
No joke?!
No way!!
You really don't remember us?!
YAY
YAY
WHEE
OH, RIGHT...
RE-CREATING A FIRST...
...EN-COUNTER...

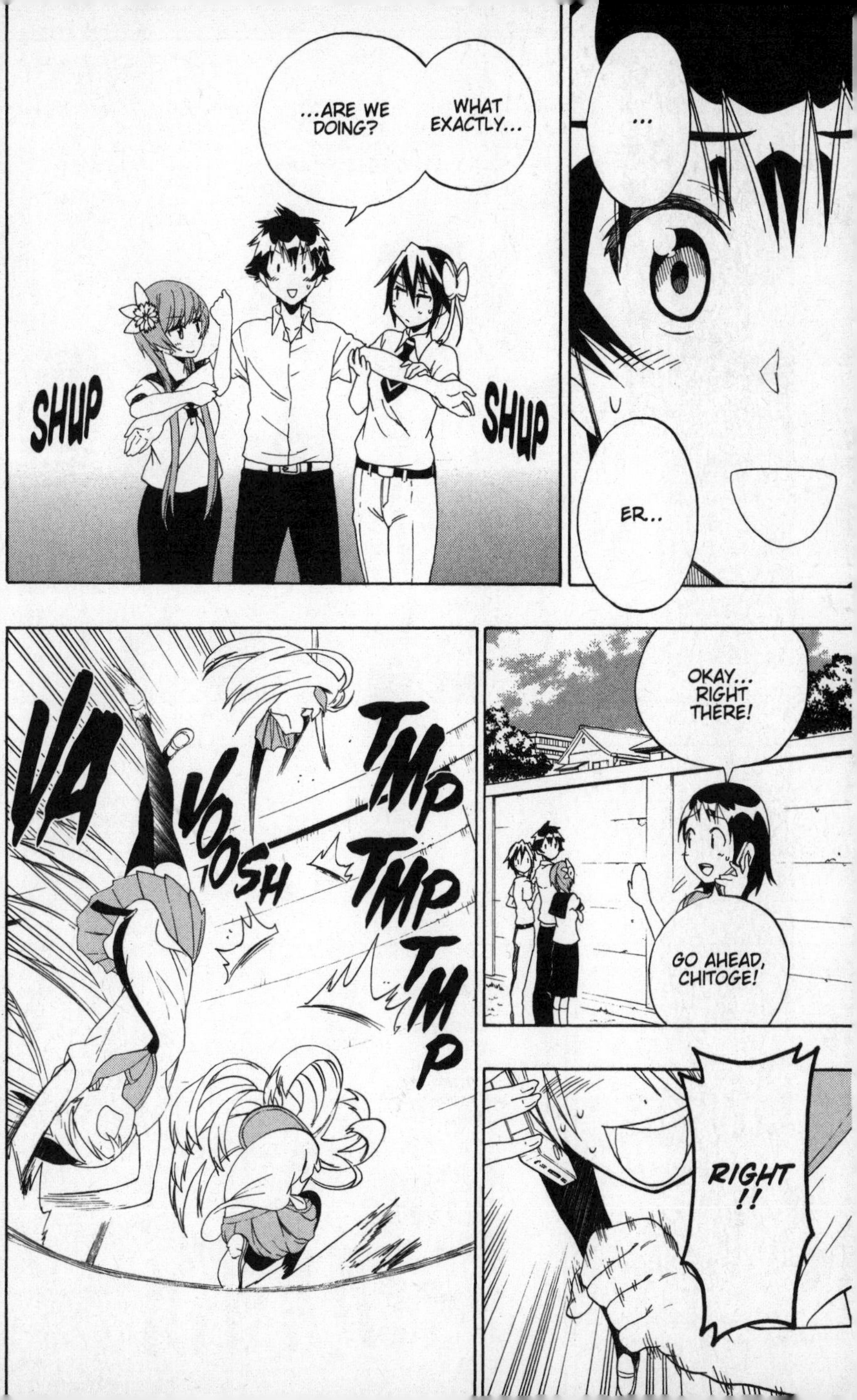
...
ER...
WHAT EXACTLY... ...ARE WE DOING?
SHUP
SHUP
OKAY... RIGHT THERE!
GO AHEAD, CHITOGE!
RIGHT!!
VA
VOOSH
TMP TMP TMP TMP

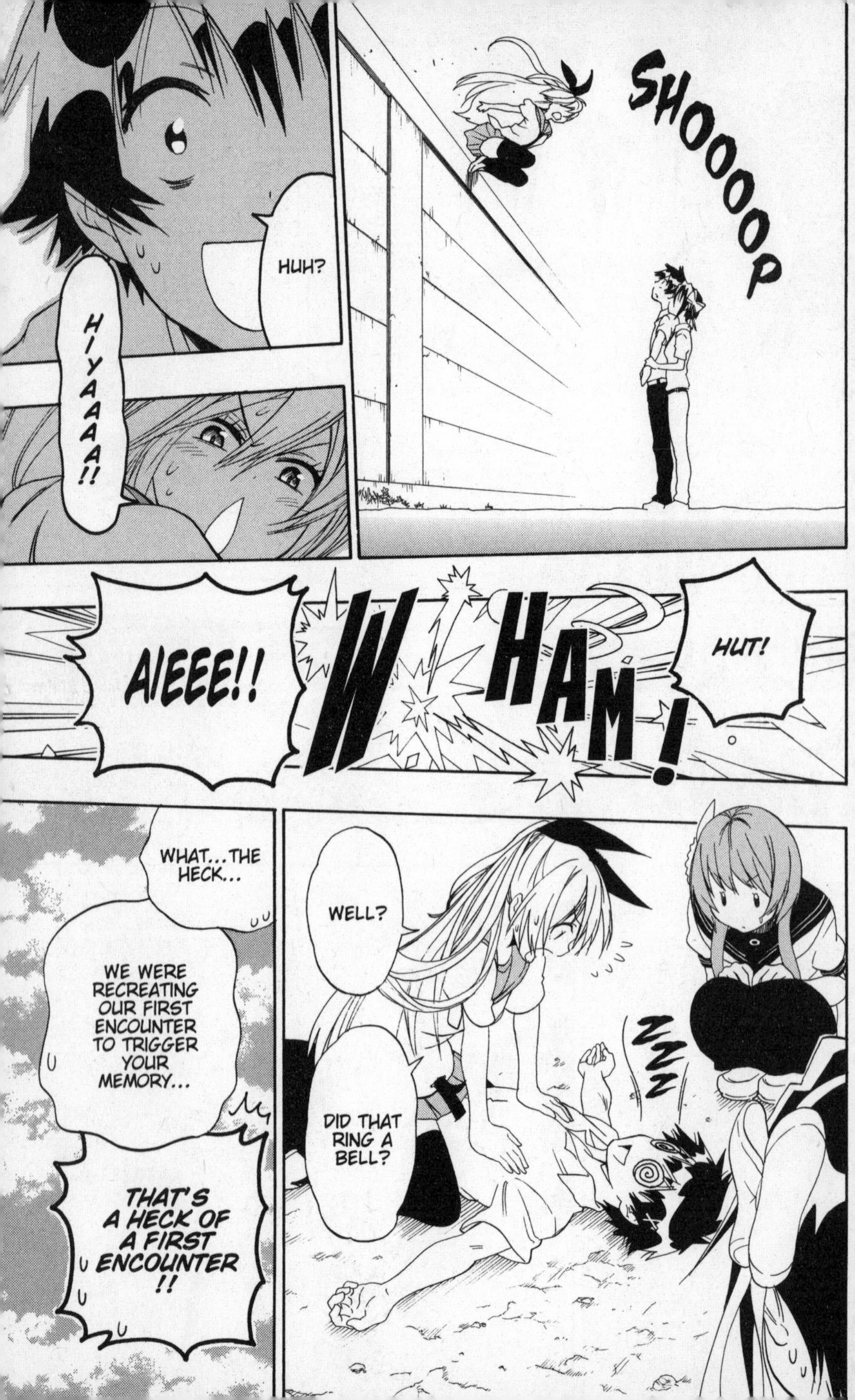
SHOOOOP
HUH?
HIYAAAA!!
HUT!
WHAM!
AIEEE!!
WELL?
DID THAT RING A BELL?
WHAT... THE HECK...
WE WERE RECREATING OUR FIRST ENCOUNTER TO TRIGGER YOUR MEMORY...
THAT'S A HECK OF A FIRST ENCOUNTER!!

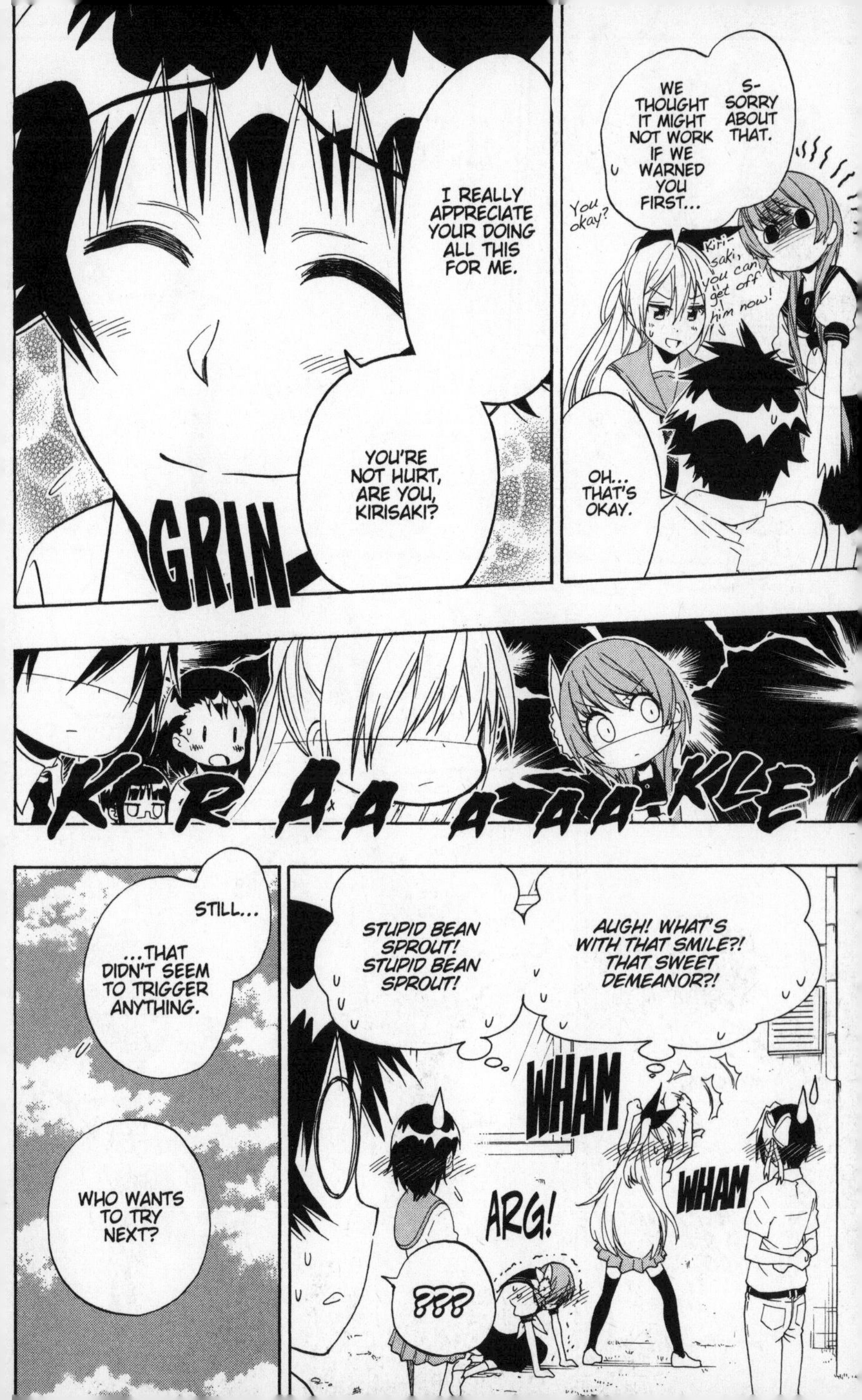
S- SORRY ABOUT THAT.
WE THOUGHT IT MIGHT NOT WORK IF WE WARNED YOU FIRST...
You okay?
Kiri-saki, you can get off him now!
OH... THAT'S OKAY.
I REALLY APPRECIATE YOUR DOING ALL THIS FOR ME.
YOU'RE NOT HURT, ARE YOU, KIRISAKI?
GRIN
KRAAAAAKLE
AUGH! WHAT'S WITH THAT SMILE?! THAT SWEET DEMEANOR?!
STUPID BEAN SPROUT! STUPID BEAN SPROUT!
WHAM
WHAM
ARG!
???
STILL...
...THAT DIDN'T SEEM TO TRIGGER ANYTHING.
WHO WANTS TO TRY NEXT?

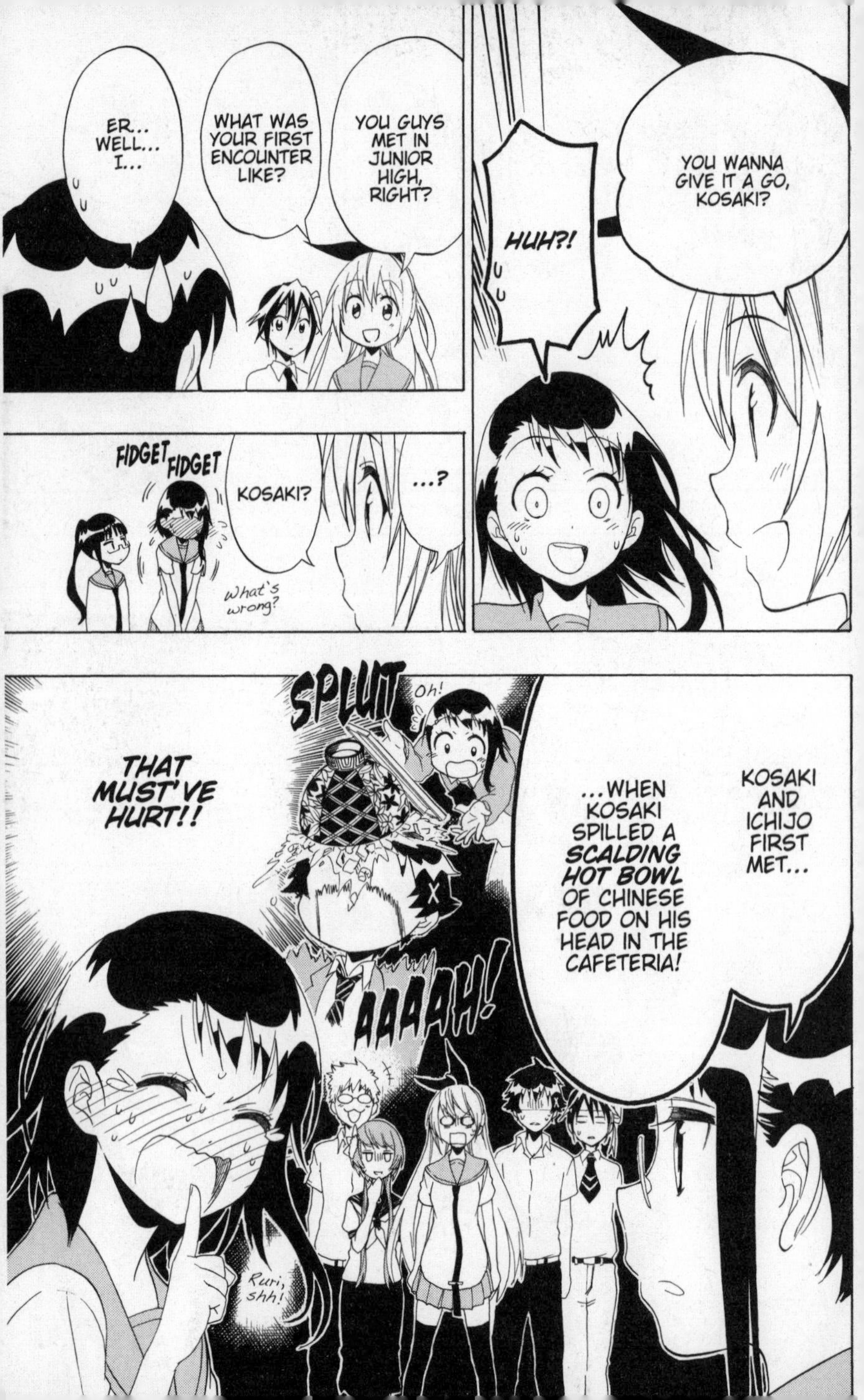
YOU WANNA GIVE IT A GO, KOSAKI?
HUH?!
YOU GUYS MET IN JUNIOR HIGH, RIGHT?
WHAT WAS YOUR FIRST ENCOUNTER LIKE?
ER... WELL... I...
...?
KOSAKI?
What's wrong?
FIDGET FIDGET
KOSAKI AND ICHIJO FIRST MET...
...WHEN KOSAKI SPILLED A SCALDING HOT BOWL OF CHINESE FOOD ON HIS HEAD IN THE CAFETERIA!
Oh!
SPLUT
AAAAH!
THAT MUST'VE HURT!!
Ruri, shh!

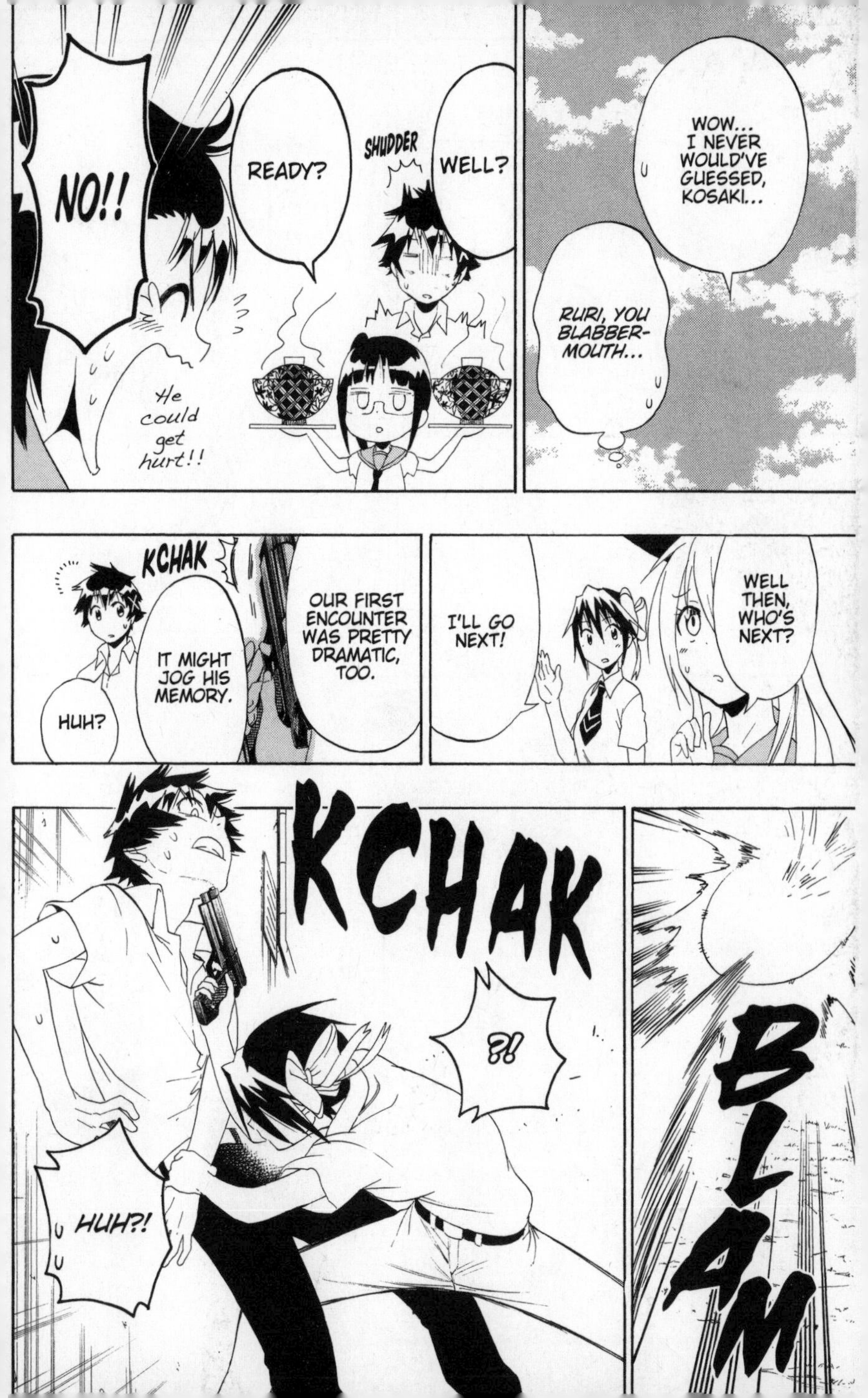
WOW... I NEVER WOULD'VE GUESSED, KOSAKI...
RURI, YOU BLABBER-MOUTH...
WELL?
SHUDDER
READY?
NO!!
He could get hurt!!
WELL THEN, WHO'S NEXT?
I'LL GO NEXT!
OUR FIRST ENCOUNTER WAS PRETTY DRAMATIC, TOO.
KCHAK
IT MIGHT JOG HIS MEMORY.
HUH?
BLAM
KCHAK
?!
HUH?!

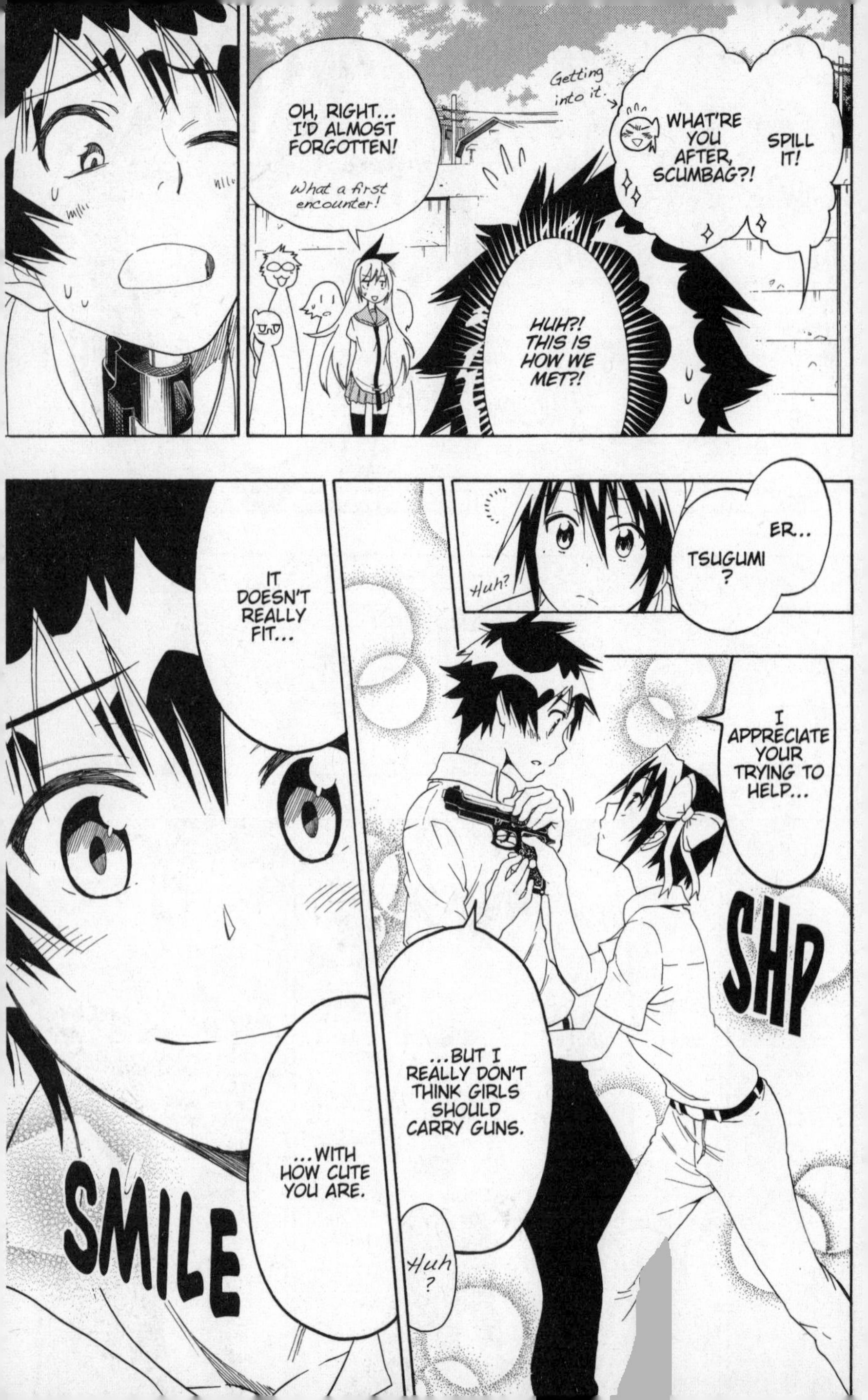
SPILL IT!
WHAT'RE YOU AFTER, SCUMBAG?!
Getting into it.
OH, RIGHT... I'D ALMOST FORGOTTEN!
What a first encounter!
HUH?! THIS IS HOW WE MET?!
ER... TSUGUMI?
Huh?
I APPRECIATE YOUR TRYING TO HELP...
SHP
...BUT I REALLY DON'T THINK GIRLS SHOULD CARRY GUNS.
Huh?
IT DOESN'T REALLY FIT...
...WITH HOW CUTE YOU ARE.
SMILE

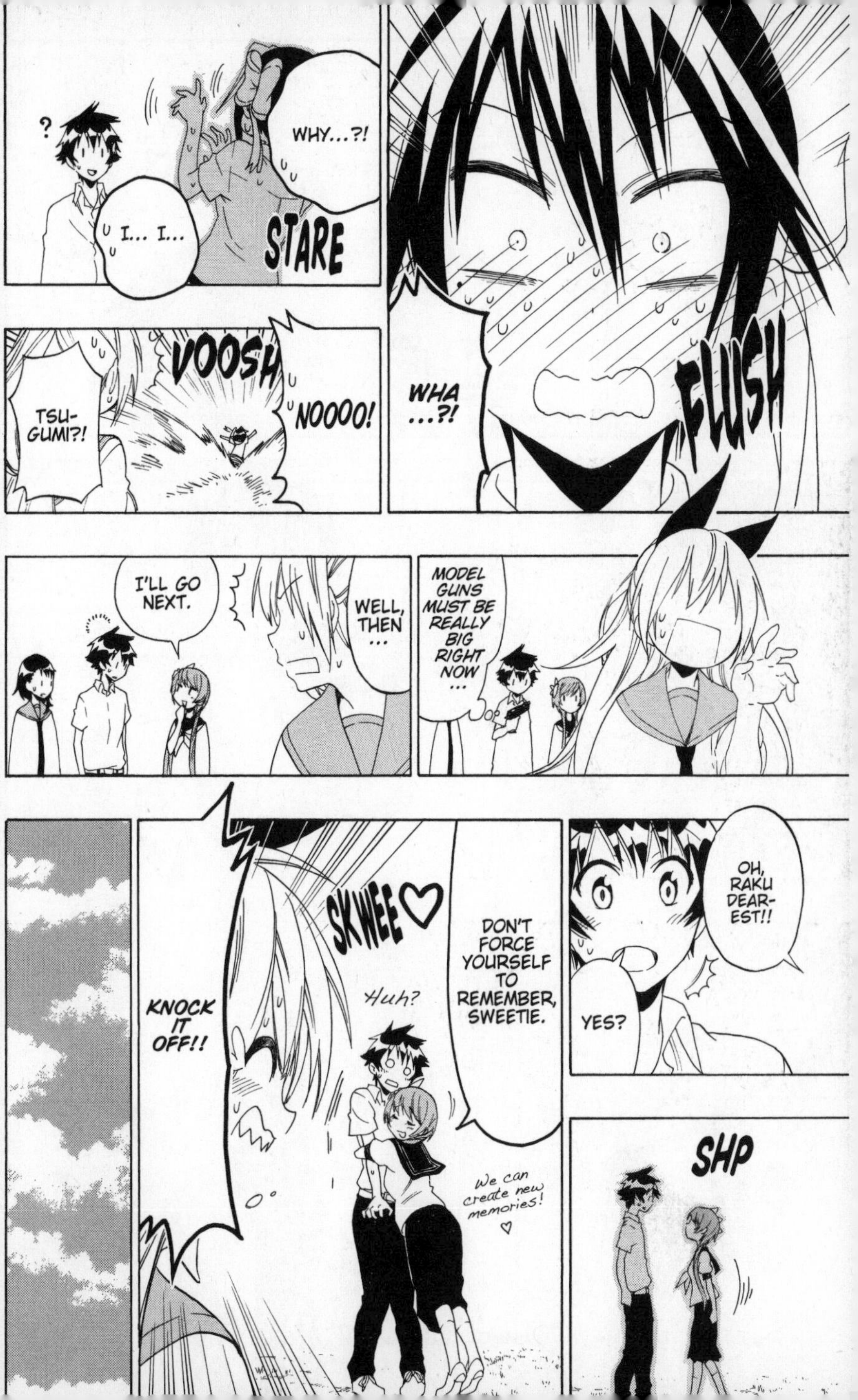
WHA ...?!
FLUSH
WHY...?!
STARE
I... I...
VOOSH
NOOOO!
TSU-GUMI?!
MODEL GUNS MUST BE REALLY BIG RIGHT NOW ...
WELL, THEN ...
I'LL GO NEXT.
OH, RAKU DEAR-EST!!
YES?
SHP
DON'T FORCE YOURSELF TO REMEMBER, SWEETIE.
SKWEE♡
Huh?
We can create new memories! ♡
KNOCK IT OFF!!

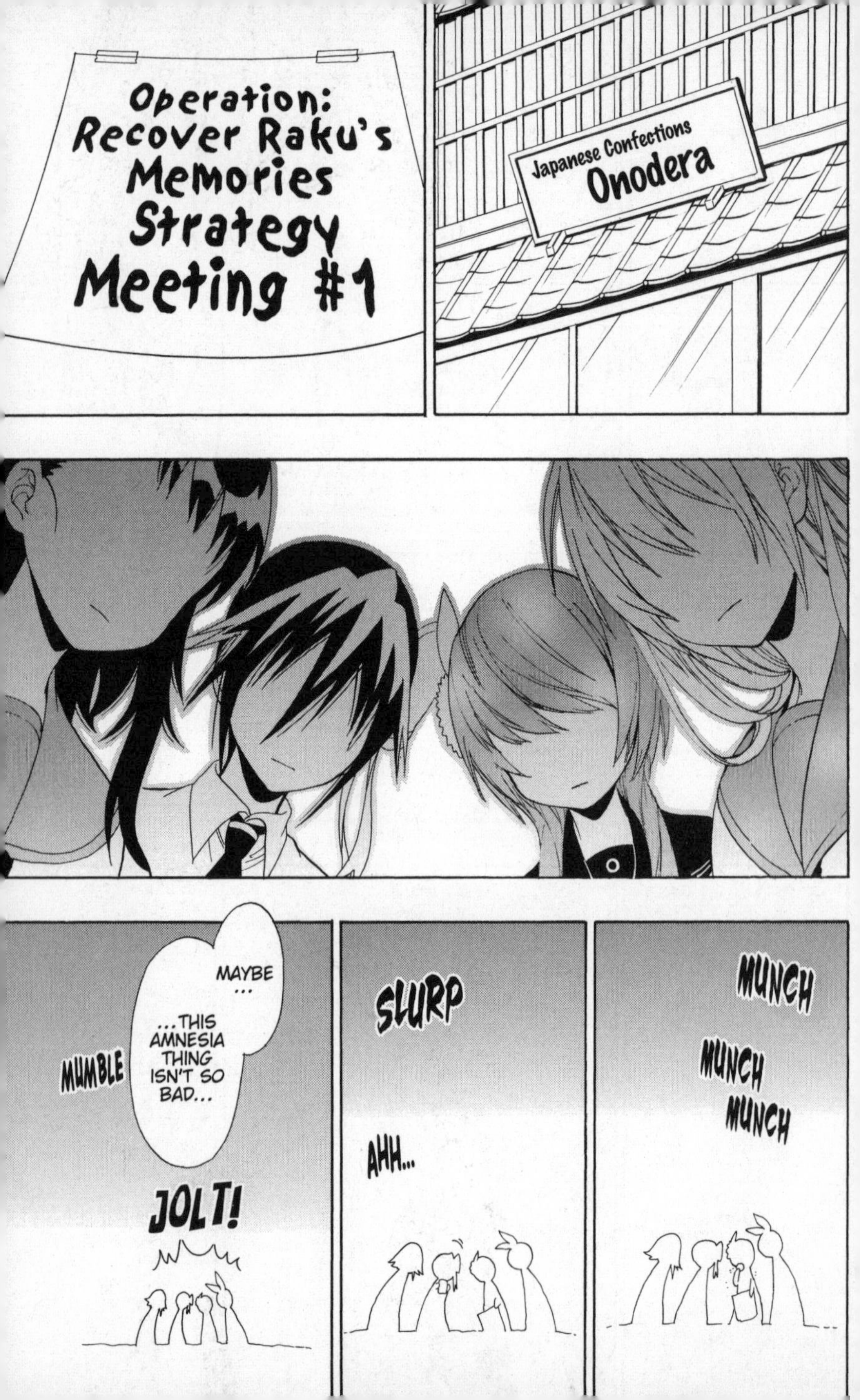
Japanese Confections
Onodera
Operation: Recover Raku's Memories Strategy Meeting #1
MUNCH
MUNCH MUNCH
SLURP
AHH...
MAYBE ...
...THIS AMNESIA THING ISN'T SO BAD...
MUMBLE
JOLT!

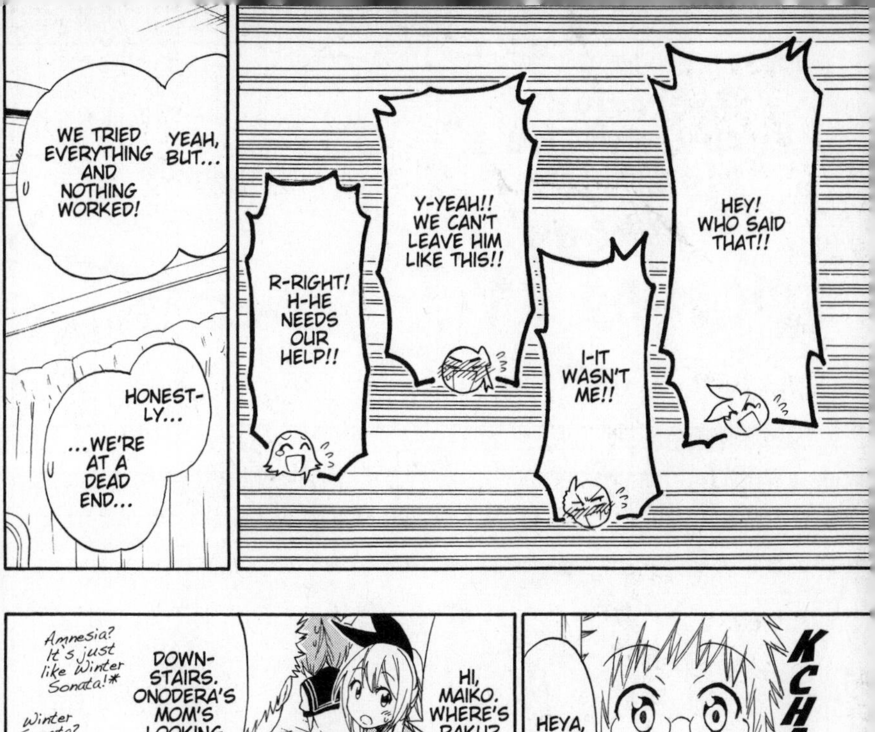
HEY! WHO SAID THAT!!
I-IT WASN'T ME!!
Y-YEAH!! WE CAN'T LEAVE HIM LIKE THIS!!
R-RIGHT! H-HE NEEDS OUR HELP!!
YEAH, BUT...
WE TRIED EVERYTHING AND NOTHING WORKED!
HONESTLY...
...WE'RE AT A DEAD END...
KCHAK
HEYA, LADIES!
HI, MAIKO. WHERE'S RAKU?
DOWNSTAIRS. ONODERA'S MOM'S LOOKING AFTER HIM.
Amnesia? It's just like Winter Sonata!*
Winter Sonata?

*NOTE: WINTER SONATA IS A POPULAR KOREAN TV DRAMA.

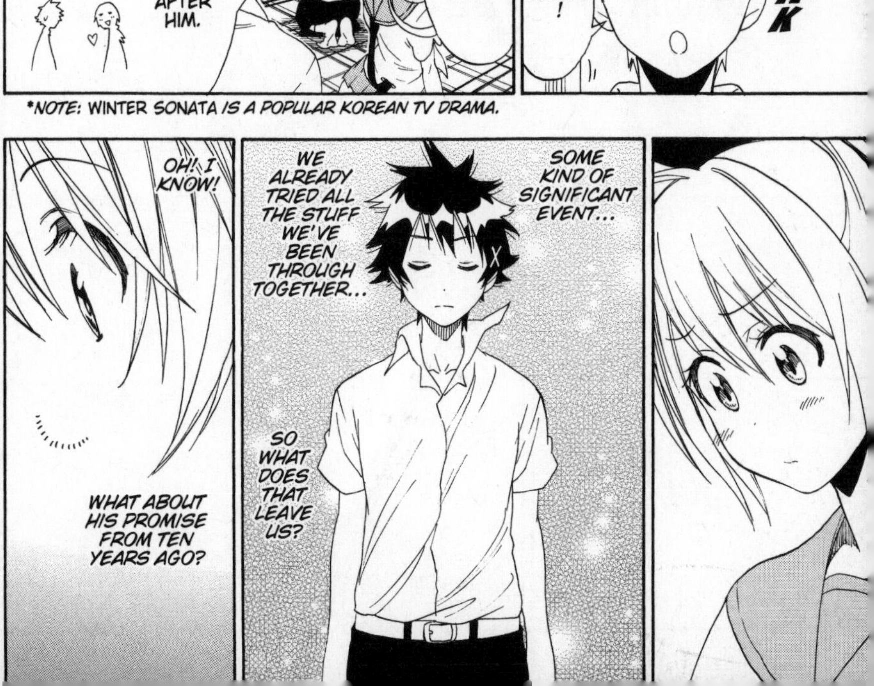
SOME KIND OF SIGNIFICANT EVENT...
WE ALREADY TRIED ALL THE STUFF WE'VE BEEN THROUGH TOGETHER...
SO WHAT DOES THAT LEAVE US?
OH! I KNOW!
WHAT ABOUT HIS PROMISE FROM TEN YEARS AGO?

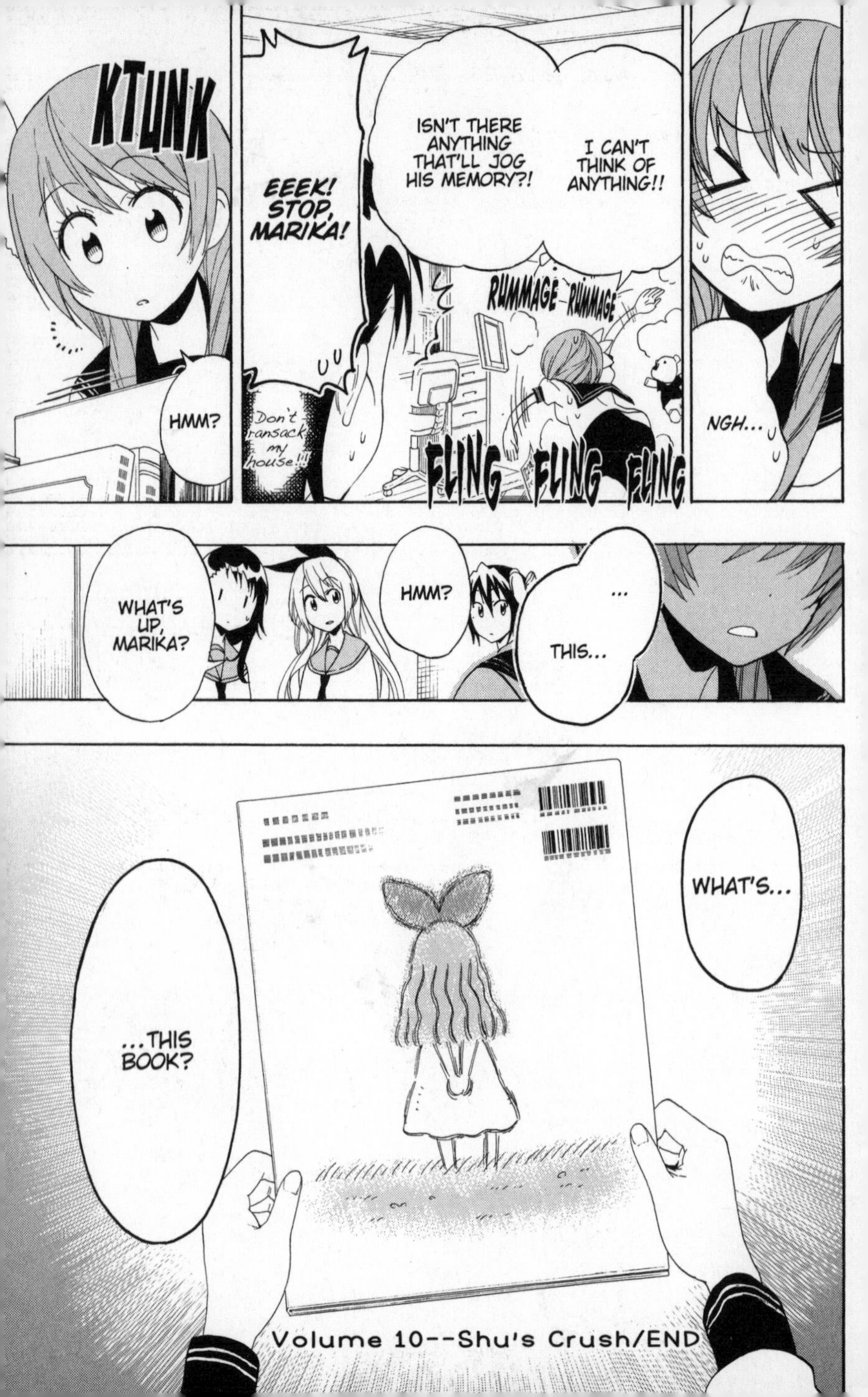
NGH...
I CAN'T THINK OF ANYTHING!!
ISN'T THERE ANYTHING THAT'LL JOG HIS MEMORY?!
RUMMAGE RUMMAGE
EEEK! STOP, MARIKA!
Don't ransack my house!!!
FLING FLING FLING
KTUNK
HMM?
...
THIS...
HMM?
WHAT'S UP, MARIKA?
WHAT'S...
...THIS BOOK?

Volume 10--Shu's Crush/END

☆ BONUS COMIC!! ☆

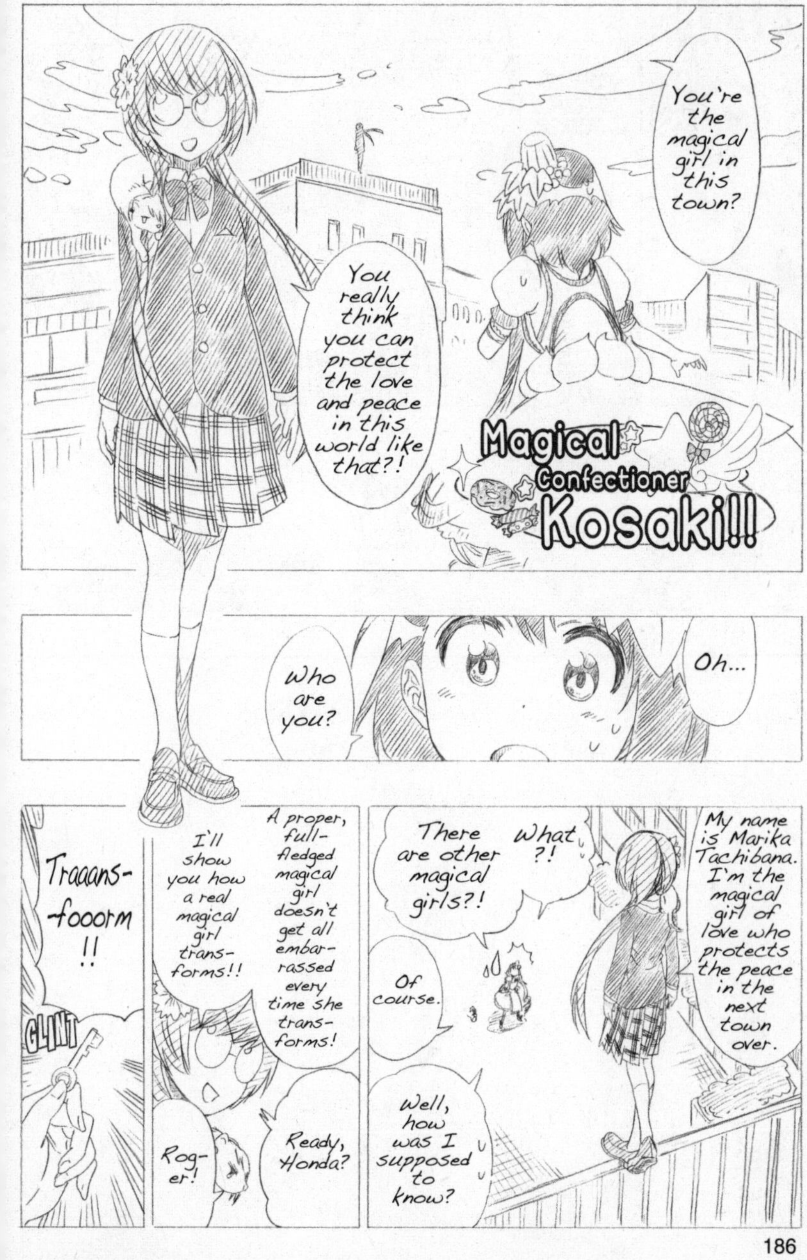
You're the magical girl in this town?
You really think you can protect the love and peace in this world like that?!
Magical Confectioner Kosaki!!
Oh...
Who are you?
My name is Marika Tachibana. I'm the magical girl of love who protects the peace in the next town over.
What?!
There are other magical girls?!
Of course.
Well, how was I supposed to know?
A proper, full-fledged magical girl doesn't get all embarrassed every time she transforms!
I'll show you how a real magical girl transforms!!
Ready, Honda?
Rog-er!
Traaans-fooorm!!
GLINT

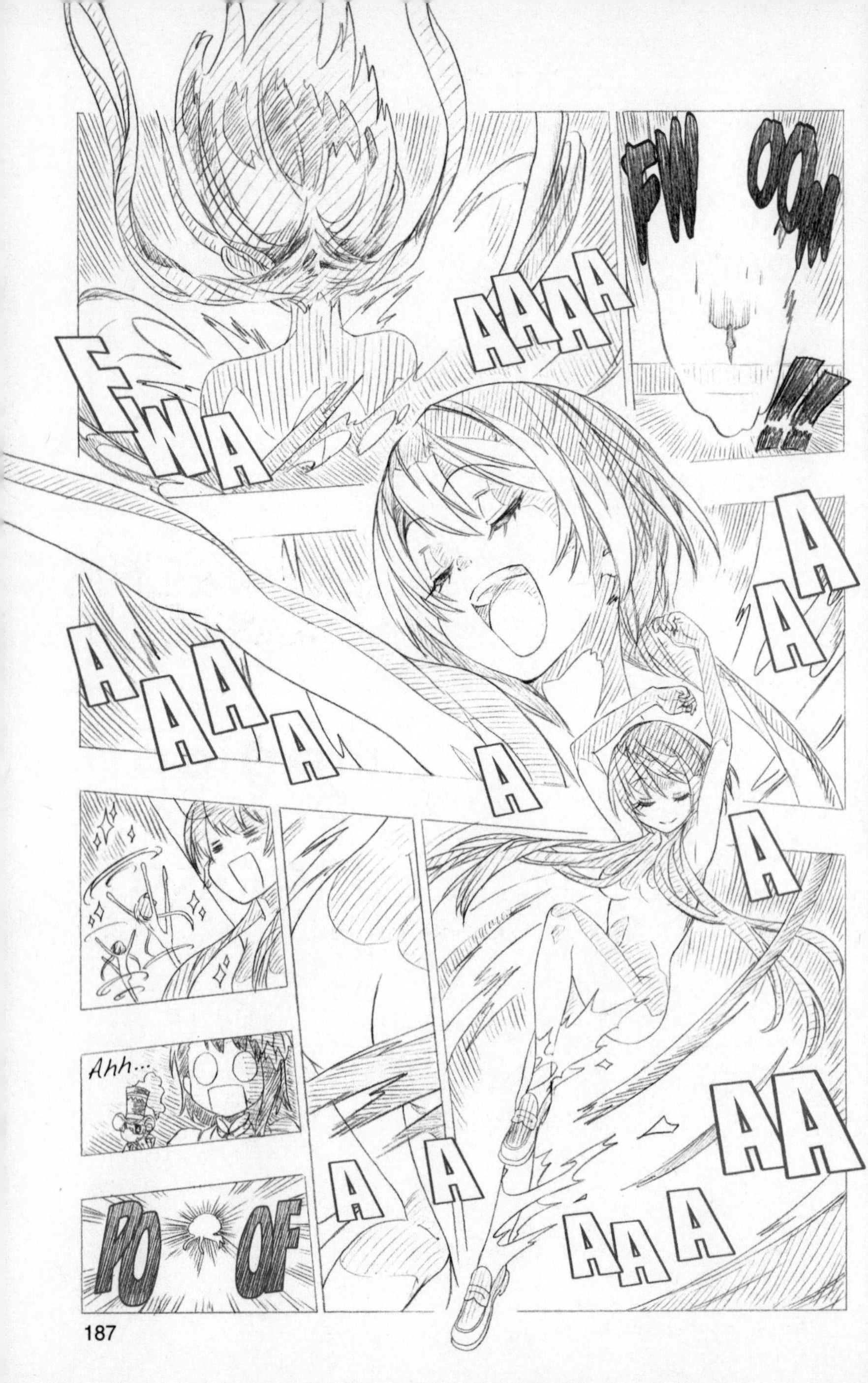
FW OOM
FWA
AAAA
AAA
AAAAA
A
AA
AAA
A A
Ahh...
PO OF

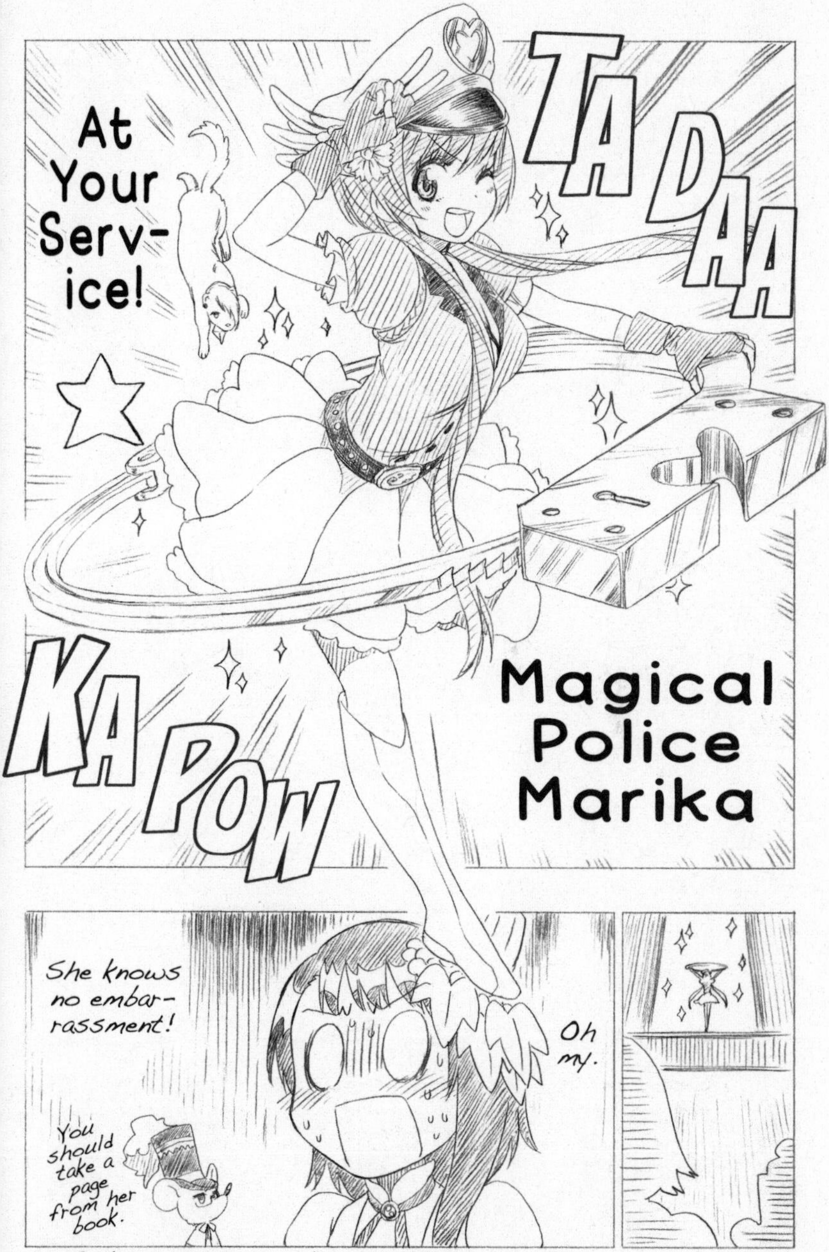
TADAA
At Your Serv-ice!
Magical Police Marika
KAPOW
Oh my.
She knows no embar-rassment!
You should take a page from her book.

To be continued...maybe!

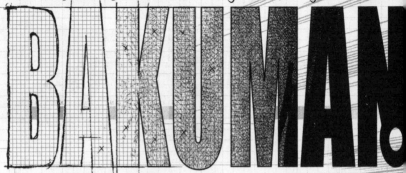

You're Reading the
WRONG WAY!

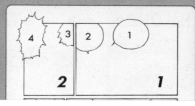

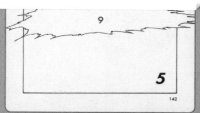

NISEKOI reads from right to left, starting in the upper-right corner. Japanese is read from right to left, meaning that action, sound effects, and word-balloon order are completely reversed from English order.

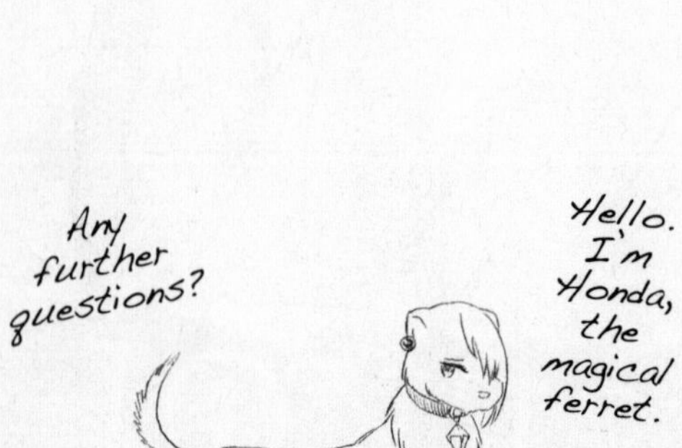
Hello. I'm Honda, the magical ferret.
Any further questions?

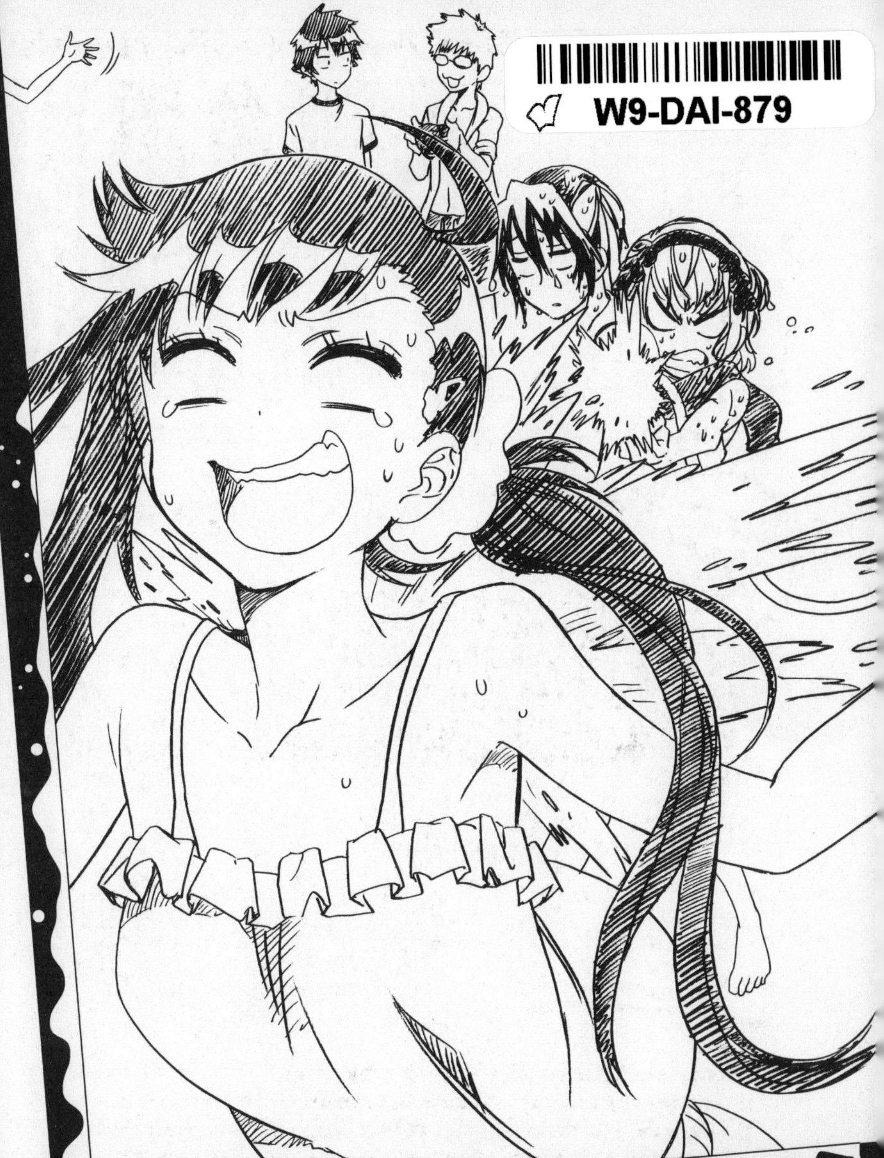

NISEKOI

False Love